BLAZING STAR

The Life and Times of
JOHN WILMOT
Earl of Rochester

*

ALEXANDER
LARMAN

HEAD
of
ZEUS

First published in 2014 by Head of Zeus Ltd
This paperback edition first published in 2015 by Head of Zeus Ltd

1 3 5 7 9 10 8 6 4 2

A CIP catalogue record for this book
is available from the British Library.

ISBN (PB) 9781781859247
ISBN (E) 9781781852644

Designed and typeset by
Ken Wilson | point918

Printed by Clays Ltd, St Ives PLC

HEAD OF ZEUS LTD
Clerkenwell House
45–47 Clerkenwell Green
London EC1R 0HT
www.headofzeus.com

For my father, who loved books

No glorious thing was ever made to stay
My Blazing-Star but visits, and away

LORD ROCHESTER,
'A Very Heroical Epistle
in Answer to Ephelia'

Contents

✻

Introduction

❧

WHEN THE ILL-FATED film of Lord Rochester's life, *The Libertine*, first screened at the Toronto Film Festival in 2004, early word was not good. While there was no screaming on the non-existent social media by disappointed Johnny Depp fans desperate to vent their spleen—something along the lines, perhaps, of 'WHAT IS THIS CR8P WHO CARES ABOUT SUM DEAD POET LOL WHERE IS CAPN JACK'—wild rumours began to circulate that the powerful distributor, Harvey Weinstein, was shocked at the film's apparently lurid and provocative content, which was said to include everything from necrophilia and graphically depicted orgies to a scene in which Rochester advances on a young page boy and declaims, in a poetic style unfortunately akin to that of Pam Ayres briefly possessed by the spirit of Jean Genet, 'You've cut me down, I must confess/But in my mouth your balls must rest.'

As usual, the rumours proved to be false. I discuss later on why *The Libertine* is both a disappointingly muddled account of Rochester's life and times and an artistic mishap on its own terms, but it is some-what regrettable from an entertainment perspective that the film didn't go further in its sensationalistic and lurid mythologizing. An on-form Ken Russell in his 1970s heyday might have worked won-ders with the short but spectacular life of John Wilmot, 2nd Earl of Rochester.

Indeed, Russell's trademark bombast and flamboyance might—for once—have seemed almost sedate in comparison with what really happened in Rochester's thirty-three-year span on the planet between 1647 and 1680. John Wilmot's adventures embraced tem-pestuous feuds with the great and good of the age (including the Poet Laureate, John Dryden); annual banishment from Charles II's court for his outrageous behaviour; the abduction of his future wife and subsequent imprisonment in the Tower of London; posing as an Italian doctor (and his wife) for the purpose of defrauding the gullible; and—of course—a very great deal of sex. When he wrote in a late poem that he had 'swived more whores more ways than Sodom's walls', it seemed less like a boast than a mere statement of fact. It was little wonder that he died, agonizingly, of syphilis.

As for his poetry, it was synonymous with the man, full of obscene humour, four-letter words and outrageous sexual detail, but displaying little obvious literary worth. Samuel Johnson huffed in a posthumous account of Rochester's life that he had 'blazed out his youth and his health in lavish voluptuousness' and accepted wisdom for centuries has been that the wicked Wilmot was one of the most notorious and dastardly men who ever set foot upon the earth. His name has become a byword for licentiousness; when Russell Brand was first building his reputation as a louche bon vivant, comparisons with his Restoration predecessor were often made.

But there is also another Rochester, who has not received his due. This man was a heroic naval officer, who served his country with much credit in the Anglo-Dutch War. He was an Oxford graduate of enormous intellectual and artistic curiosity who spent his formative years on the continent where he encountered many of the leading thinkers of the day, before returning to the social upheaval of the Restoration court where, unusually for one of the period's fops on the make, he never lost the common touch, even as he walked with the king. He was a fond (if capricious) husband and lover, a loving father and a faithful and loyal friend to many. Many of the more violent and cruel antics ascribed to him were either falsely attributed, or simply never occurred. His poetry explored the preoccupations of the age with a mixture of witty sophistication and original thought, and some of his love lyrics are amongst the most beautiful of the time. Hazlitt called his writing 'the poetry of wit combined with the love of pleasure', praised his 'passionate enthusiasm' and called his epigrams 'the truest that were ever written'. Dying cruelly young, he deprived England, and English literature, of one of its brightest lights, but even as he lingered on his deathbed, a lifelong interest in religion came to his consciousness once more.

So there are two sides of Rochester, neatly encapsulated in his fictional representation as Dorimant in his friend George Etherege's *The Man Of Mode*, of whom it is said 'I know he is a devil, but he has something of the angel yet undefaced in him.' It would be a misreading of his character to attempt either to dismiss Rochester as merely a diabolic rake, or to rehabilitate him as a decent and kindly man who has had a remarkably unfair posthumous reputation. What makes him such a fascinating figure, as both a man and a writer, is that the two sides of him were in constant opposition throughout his life, and remained so until his death. While this frustrates easy attempts at analysis, it makes for a fascinating and complex story.

Yet this book is more than just the story of John Wilmot. He stood at the centre of an era of social mobility the like of which England had never seen before. He was born at a time when every accepted idea, from hereditary monarchy to the role of Parliament, was being challenged, and where the resulting vacuum allowed first Cromwell and the Commonwealth and then Charles II to mould the country in their own image. As Rochester's fortunes and reputation rose, he found himself, a soldier's son, in a position where he became one of the leading men at court. It was an era where casual street violence was as likely to end your life as any plague or war, and where if you sold your body, you could prosper and rise to the top of court, just as easily as you might find yourself dead from disease before you reached adulthood. Everything was literally up for grabs.

The thirty-three years that Rochester lived were some of the most remarkable in the history of England. The age was rich in hard living and strong wine, but also in architectural innovation, literary achievement, philosophical investigation and scientific advance. It was a time of plague, and of fire. It was a time of uncertainty, as few knew whether this new age of libertine royalty would last, or whether it would be as short-lived as Cromwell's rule had been. It was a time of *carpe diem*, and of rebirth. Rochester, and those around him, turned the accepted orthodoxies that had lasted for centuries before on their heads in a brief, bawdy, brilliant historical moment. With their thoughts, words and actions, the 'merry gang' redefined society, for good or for ill, as the old certainties were swept away and a new world was explored, full of dangerous but thrilling contradictions—between piety and debauchery, obedience and free-thinking.

In this, as in many ways, he is a man who speaks to our own time as much as he did to his. Writing this while listening to the stultifying drone of Prime Minister's Questions in the background, I am reminded that we still need a man, or woman, who can stand up, expose the bland and cynical hypocrisies of politicians and self-appointed opinion-formers for what they are and refuse to place themselves on a pedestal of virtue, and instead argue that it is by embracing our flaws, contradictions and baser desires that we are set free from the dull and oppressive orthodoxies of everyday life. If Rochester epitomizes anything, it is free thought, free speech and free love—freedom, in fact, in all its forms.

Yet it is not for me to influence your reaction to Rochester, a polarizing figure if ever there was one. The opening lines of *The Libertine* promise, or threaten, 'You will not like me now, and you will like me a good deal less as we go on,' before announcing that he is 'up for it, all the time'. Whether you find yourself seduced or repelled by the Earl, boredom is never an option with him as your guide to Restoration England, in all its opulence and licence, baseness and cruelty.

And with that, as Rochester writes, 'Come on sir, I'm prepared…'

A note on sources

✿

IN COLIN DEXTER's Inspector Morse novel, *Death Is Now My Neighbour*, Morse and Lewis at one point find a piece of evidence that purports to be a poem by John Wilmot. Supposedly dated 1672, it reads at first glance as being nothing like Rochester's work:

> Ten Times I beg, dear Heart, let's Wed!
> (Thereafter long may Cupid reigne)
> Let's tread the Aisle, where thou hast led
> The fifteen Bridesmaides in thy Traine.
> Then spend our honeyed Moon a-bed,
> With Springs that creake againe—againe!

The poem is a forgery,* something easily deduced by the ever capable Morse, who instead realizes that it contains a code that leads to the murder's subsequent solution. However, whether intentionally or not, Dexter makes the point that the authenticity of Rochester's writing, more so than most other writers of his era, presents a problematic challenge for anyone reading his works, whether a scholar, biographer or casual enthusiast. Therefore, it is worth outlining the assumptions, decisions and speculations that I have made in the course of this book, and seeking to justify why they needed to be made at all.

The normal means of 'publication' for an aristocratic or courtier writer, such as Rochester, was for a fair copy of a poem to be made and then circulated in manuscript form. There was even some precise etiquette in how it was circulated, with most existing manuscripts showing where the poem would have been folded when it was passed between its readers. The outside bore either the work's title

---

* In fact, of course, it is an original work by Dexter, who faced the dilemma of how to write a Rochester pastiche that could be easily identified as not being his work.

or its contents, and often the name and address of its recipient. The work was not made public in any published form during the writer's life unless he (or she, in the case of Aphra Behn) wished it to be, so printed publication should be viewed as an accident rather than a deliberate intention on the part of the poet. This was, of course, different in the case of a professional writer such as Dryden, who explicitly wrote for publication and to earn a living by his pen.

During his lifetime, only three poems of Rochester's were published, namely his juvenile university works, and none of the others acquired a wider readership beyond the court. Instead, his reputation was entirely based on his actions, whether those he actually performed or those with which he was associated. The first time that any of his poems appeared, in 1680, they were explicitly derived from a variety of manuscripts, some of which were poems by him and others of which were merely attributed to him. His public reputation was such that certain, generally obscene, things were expected from him. Without an editor, or anyone with first-hand knowledge of his canon, there was no internal discipline or any definitive collection of his work, and so a confusion began that has persisted ever since. As the literary critic Keith Walker says in his 1984 edition of his work, 'the case of the texts of Rochester's poems is, I think, unique.'

As a result of his mother's destruction of his own manuscript verses posthumously, prompted by her horror and disgust at their contents, remarkably few poems in Rochester's own hand (a fairly identifiable hand, at that) still survive in so-called 'holograph manuscripts'. Rochester is not known to have made any explicit public statements linking himself to specific poems, whether in letters or by proclamation, although there are passages in some of his letters where the language directly echoes his poetry, especially in his epistles to Henry Savile, which implies that his readers, and friends, would have been familiar with them. Certainly, his enemies were, as can be seen by Mulgrave and Dryden's 1679 poetic attack, 'An Essay upon Satire'. Nonetheless, making a case that a given work purportedly by Rochester is actually his on the basis of internal evidence alone is tricky.

The major early editions that most editors have chosen (reluctantly) to use are the pirated and unreliable 1680 'Antwerp' edition, which has around thirty-four (of sixty-one) poems which are now believed to be by Rochester himself; a 1691 version edited and published by the bookseller Jacob Tonson, who adds another eight works while omitting many of the bawdier satires and editing stanzas from others (he writes that he has 'taken exceeding care that every block of offence should be removed'); and the so-called 'Portland Manuscript', currently residing in Nottingham University, which gathers together another twenty-eight poems, ten of which are in Rochester's hand. This makeshift canon of around seventy or so poems was to be the basis on which Rochester scholarship proceeded for the next two-and-a-half centuries.

Probably the foremost Rochester editor of the twentieth century, David Vieth, has also proved the most controversial. Assessing the Rochester canon at seventy-six poems in his edition of 1968, along with seven dubious ones which he includes in an appendix, Vieth made several decisions that have rankled with other scholars since, not least his dating of the poetry in chronological categories that include 'Prentice Work', 'Tragic Maturity' and 'Disillusionment and Death'. While I have broadly agreed with the attribution of the Rochester canon Vieth proposes, dating has proved to be a trickier subject. There is the occasional instance when a poem of Rochester's can be both authenticated and dated, as is the case with the February 1680 letter from Charles Blount responding to Rochester's translation of Seneca's *Troades*. These instances, unfortunately, are fewer than might be desired.

Instead, Vieth has based many of his dates on those found within or upon manuscript copies. If these do contain a date, this does not necessarily corroborate the year that a particular poem was written—it is possible that it might be wrong by at least a year in either direction, although probably not more than two. In the case of many poets this would be an irritation, but in Rochester's case such a question of dating is central. If, for instance, 'The Disabled Debauchee' first appeared in 1673, it reads as a light-hearted account of an imagined series of routs, somewhat akin to a dramatic monologue. If it is dated 1675 (and it is probably more likely to have appeared then), when Rochester's life had altered drastically, the temptation to see a greater autobiographical focus in the work is stronger.

The biographer, therefore, is forced to attribute and date the majority of the poems according to a mixture of internal information, reasonable circumstantial and historical evidence, and some literary detective work. I have tried to indicate, wherever appropriate, where definite fact ends and informed supposition begins, but it is a central question in assessing Rochester's life to determine which of the poems that he 'wrote' were really by him, and which have been falsely ascribed to him. It is a task that is simultaneously frustrating and fascinating.

The letters, meanwhile, are less problematic. First, Rochester's distinctive (and blessedly legible) handwriting means that questions of attribution only become an issue later in his life, when the letters written by amanuenses while he lay on his deathbed might or might not represent his genuine beliefs at the time (although most bear his signature). And secondly, although Rochester seldom dated his letters, many of the replies from such correspondents as Henry Savile, his wife and Buckingham are dated, often making it possible to determine Rochester's location as well as his actions at a specific time between 1665 and 1680. Occasionally, however, it has been necessary to speculate on the time of undated letters as well. On the whole, I have agreed with the conclusions of the critic Jeremy Treglown, whose excellent 1980 edition of Rochester's letters offers an impressive range of biographical and allusive material that makes a fascinating counterpoint to the contents of the correspondence. I have also included some previously unpublished letters found in the course of my research, most notably a collection in the National Archives of Scotland, which further our understanding of his relationship both with his mistress Elizabeth Barry and with his protégé the Earl of Arran.

It will remain a source of grievous disappointment for anyone interested in Rochester that his mother posthumously destroyed a huge hoard of his correspondence and other writings. The consequence is that, where we could have had a substantial body of authenticated work to enjoy and discuss, we have instead a more questionable, at times seemingly unreliable canon to deal with. Nonetheless, to quote Tom Stoppard's *Arcadia*, 'We shed as we pick up, like travellers who must carry everything in their arms, and what we let fall will be picked up by those behind.'

I regret that, for reasons of space, some notable poems by Rochester (most obviously 'A Letter from Artemisia in the Town to Chloe in the Country') have not been covered. I can only plead that this is a biography, not an exhaustive work of literary criticism. For the sake of ease and clarity, I have reproduced all text in modern English, without attempting any further editorial interference in matters of syntax or punctuation.

I

'A DISPUTE
'TWIXT
HEAVEN
and earth'

❖

[1647–1658]

ON 4 SEPTEMBER 1651, the flamboyant nobleman Henry Wilmot was the second most wanted man in England. The only person more eagerly hunted by Cromwell's Commonwealth army was Charles Stuart, the 21-year-old heir apparent to the English throne. As the two fled, a bounty of £1,000 (around £80,000 today) was placed upon Charles's head, nearly a hundred times more than the average labourer could have expected to earn in a good year. Only the most committed Royalist would not have been seduced by such a sum, and very few of them remained. Wilmot was one of the last.

The previous day had been a disastrous one for both men and their rag-tag army. Despite their best efforts, they had suffered a final, irrevocable defeat to Cromwell at Worcester. Charles's troops, mainly consisting of Scots, had been outnumbered, ill-prepared and lacking in morale. There had been a fleeting point where victory had seemed possible, thanks to Charles's courageous attack on the Commonwealth force attacking the south-east of the city, but the odds had been hideously against them, with the Royalist forces outnumbered two to one. Charles's rallying cry—'I had rather you would shoot me, than let me live to see the consequences of the day!'—proved to be a hollow one.

Wilmot was one of the few surviving lords who fled the field with Charles, as the gutters of Worcester ran red with Royalist and Commonwealth gore. He was a less high-profile figure than the aristocratic courtiers, such as the Earl of Derby and the Duke of Buckingham, who surrounded Charles, and so it was to him that Charles confided his immediate plan to flee to London, rather than to take the expected decision to make for Scotland and his supporters there.

In the frantic improvisations of the day, it proved a stroke of genius on Charles's part to have taken only Wilmot into his confidence; he was aware that the other lords, should they be captured, could only withstand so much torture before they were bound to blurt out details of his whereabouts. His concern, as it transpired, was justified; the Commonwealth soldiers proved adept at hunting down all of Charles's remaining supporters, with the exception of Buckingham, who fled to France. Their fate was, at best, imprisonment, but more often summary execution for the dual offence of having supported Charles and for daring to have allied themselves with the unspeakable Scots.

Charles and Wilmot adopted entirely different methods of travel as they criss-crossed England. The only thing that they had in common was the danger they faced. Had they been captured, it would have represented the final glory of Cromwell's victory. The past five years had seen Charles I's defeat, and then his execution, followed by a brutal quashing of resistance in Ireland. Cromwell's dictatorial power was at its height, and the public trial and almost inevitable execution of the heir to the throne would seal his reputation forever, as well as making further threats to the Commonwealth extremely unlikely. With this in mind, his soldiers were ordered to make finding Charles a priority. Posters sought 'Charles Stuart, son of the late tyrant', and over the next few weeks he adopted the disguise of a working man, using the pseudonym William Jackson. Charles, who had never touched manual labour before, proved a fast learner, dressing in tattered rags and uncomfortable shoes and smothering his distinctive dark looks (so much so that he was nicknamed a 'black man') with soot and grime.

Wilmot, by way of contrast, retained the habits of a privileged dandy. Refusing to take the sensible course of travelling around the country on foot, he instead moved from place to place on an expensive, if exhausted, horse, and took every opportunity to indulge in the fine food and living to which his status as a nobleman would have entitled him. He briefly adopted the pseudonym of Barlow, but found himself unable to remember it in times of danger and constantly changed his false names, much to his companions' irritation.

Many years later, when Charles dictated the rather subjective story of his adventures to the diarist Samuel Pepys, he reserved a fond recollection for his old travelling companion, whose courage and loyalty were matched only by his obstinacy even in the face of danger. Charles commented that Wilmot was a figure 'whom I still took care not to keep with me, but sent him a little before, or left to come after me'. This, given the flamboyance with which the older man conducted himself, was probably a wise move. Indeed, Charles said of Wilmot's sartorial vanity: 'I could never get my Lord Wilmot to put on any disguise, he saying that he should look frightfully in it, and therefore did never put on any.' The sole compromise to which Wilmot agreed, which he quickly began to regret, was that he would carry a hawk on his hand.

For six weeks, Charles and Wilmot dragged themselves over England. Legends soon arose, the most famous being of the oak tree in Boscobel House that Charles was obliged to scramble up while Commonwealth soldiers searched the grounds below, thus giving countless subsequent pubs the name 'The Royal Oak'. Dissemination of false rumours was rife; two of the favoured stories reported in the contemporary press were that Charles had fallen in with a notorious highwayman, Captain Hinde—presumably because he was the son of the executed monarch, association with brigands could not be too far away—and that he had adopted women's clothing as a disguise. Given that Charles was well over six foot tall,* with a swarthy complexion, this would seem fanciful, but it was nevertheless taken up by Cromwell's council of state as accurate fact.

It was a difficult, often tedious time. Charles was frequently reduced to boring holes through his small supply of gold coins for distraction, which were then handed out to those who had given him assistance. Danger was constantly near, and there were many close calls, such as when Charles had to be smuggled into a priest's hole because a gang of Commonwealth soldiers had heard a (correct) rumour that he was being concealed in Moseley Hall, which belonged to the Catholic and Royalist sympathizer Thomas Whitgreave. Thanks to Whitgreave's presence of mind in leaving the doors to the house conspicuously open and his pleading of ill health, Charles's

---

* This was in stark contrast to his father Charles I, who was a mere five foot four inches tall, possibly as a result of rickets contracted as a child.

luck held and his hiding place remained undiscovered. There was also a frustrating near miss when a promised escape from Charmouth in Dorset was foiled. This was said to have been because the sailor tasked with carrying the king and Wilmot to safety was locked in his house by his wife, who had guessed his intentions and was determined not to be left a widow should the result of the expedition prove fatal. Certainly, any boat carrying Charles would have been attacked on sight.

Eventually, thanks to the support and help of Royalist supporters, sympathetic Catholics and other well-wishers, Wilmot and Charles were carried across the Channel, landing in Normandy on 16 October. Even on their crossing luck had been on their side; a Commonwealth boat was searching for 'a tall black man, six feet two inches high', but the journey was a swift and uneventful one, and they were undetected. They entered Paris late on the 20th, where they were escorted triumphantly to the Louvre by Charles's brother James, Duke of York, his mother Henrietta Maria and other Royalist aristocrats. The news of Charles's escape was soon common knowledge throughout Europe. The leaders of the Commonwealth, who only days before had been speculating that Charles was at large somewhere in Worcester, were taken by surprise, but the propaganda machine soon recovered sufficiently to produce a mocking poster of Charles as 'a fool on horseback, riding backwards, turning his face every which way in fears'.

The consequences of Charles's death-defying escape, and Henry Wilmot's part in it, are crucial to understanding both Charles's psychology and his later relationship with Henry's son John Wilmot, 2nd Earl of Rochester. Although Charles undoubtedly suffered a good deal of physical discomfort and fear, as well as boredom, in the weeks between his defeat at Worcester and his arrival in France, his adventures were a source of excitement to him as well. He was still reminiscing about those weeks towards the end of his life, when he dictated a lengthy account of his travails to Pepys after a session at the Newmarket races; it was a story Pepys had heard the king tell before, some years earlier, when the royal yacht was approaching the shores of England on the eve of the Restoration.

Regardless of the many unfair, unkind or cruel things Charles did when he was king—and there were a good number that fell into all three categories—the period when he was on the run showed him at his best, possessed of a quick wit, sharp intelligence and boundless courage. Numerous eyewitness accounts testify to his ease at dealing with his future subjects in circumstances that no member of royalty would ever have conceived hitherto, and this sense of familiarity was something he never lost when he became monarch. His gratitude towards those who had helped him became legendary, with anyone who had given him shelter and aid awarded pensions and annuities, in some cases for time immemorial.

His greatest debt was to Wilmot. Foolish and vain though his friend had sometimes been, his boldness and constancy had proved vital in desperate circumstances. He was created Earl of Rochester in France in 1652, with the aim of lending more weight to Wilmot's status as a petitioner around the European courts, asking for support for Charles in exile. It might have seemed a mostly meaningless title, a bauble handed out by one exile to another, but, in due course, it would become a vital part of Wilmot's son's existence. As the two men received a heroic welcome in France, it was noted that Charles was both 'sad and sombre'. He was a king, but in name only, and he was destined to live on the charity of others until the Commonwealth came to an end. His comrade-in-arms might well have felt the same, had he considered what a quieter and less swashbuckling life might have been like with his wife and young son in Oxfordshire. As it was, he would never know.

Wilmot had already led an eventful existence by the time of the escape. Charles's mentor and adviser Edward Hyde, 1st Earl of Clarendon, made some grudgingly admiring comments that perhaps sum him up best:

> He was a man proud and ambitious, and incapable of being contented; an orderly officer in marches and governing his troops. He drank hard, and had a great power over all who did so, which was a great people.

Born on 26 October 1612, he had inherited the title of viscount after his father Charles and his two brothers had all died. He was a vehement anti-Parliamentarian, and equally vigorous Royalist. For services to Charles I, he was created Baron Wilmot of Adderbury, where he had a large and impressive manor house. He had also behaved with notable valour at the battles of Edgehill and Cropredy Bridge, where he had taken over Prince Rupert's position as commander of the Royalist cavalry. However, he had fallen out of favour with Charles for making unauthorized contact with the Parliamentarian commander-in-chief, Robert Devereux, the Earl of Essex, to try and broker a peace. As a result, Wilmot was briefly incarcerated in Exeter. After his release he headed to France in 1644, where he rightly believed he would be received as a welcome guest of the queen, Henrietta Maria, who admired his chutzpah and commitment to the Royalist cause. Upon his return to England, his conspicuous loyalty did not go unnoticed by Charles the younger, who made him one of his Gentlemen of the Bedchamber, and he facilitated the young prince's first serious love affair with the 'brown, bold, beautiful but insipid' aristocrat Lucy Walter, which led to the birth of the first of Charles's many bastard children: James. It was Wilmot who would later be responsible for the deal hatched with the Scottish armies, and he who stuck by Charles's side throughout.

In the course of a vigorous, hard-living and brief existence, Henry Wilmot first married Frances Morton in 1633, and after her death, Anne Lee in 1644. Anne's father, Sir John St John, was also a very prominent Royalist, and she, like Wilmot, was marrying for the second time; her first husband, Sir Francis Henry Lee, had died of smallpox in 1639. Her first child with Lee, also called Francis, was born the same year, and she soon had a second, Henry. Wilmot was not a man to be denied the pleasures of the conjugal bed, and his son with Anne—John—was born at Ditchley Park in Oxfordshire on 1 April 1647, All Fool's Day. The irony would not escape Wilmot's heir in later years.

The astrologer John Gadbury later wrote of John Wilmot's birth, no doubt with the considerable benefit of hindsight, that the stars upon his arrival in the world 'bestowed a large stock of generous and active spirits, which constantly attended on this native's mind, insomuch that no subject came amiss to him'. There were doubts over Henry Wilmot's paternity; in an age where bastardy was both common and the first tool of disinheritance, John's legitimacy was crucial. The antiquary Anthony à Wood wrote, 'I have been credibly informed by knowing men that this John, Earl of Rochester, was begotten by Sir Allen Apsley', a familiar of Charles, and goes on to describe Anne Wilmot as 'one notorious for her salaciousness'. However, Anne's overt piety and Apsley's military distractions after the fall of Barnstaple in April 1646 render this piece of tittle-tattle highly unlikely, on top of which the gossip circulated decades after the fact, by which time John himself had established a notorious reputation for salaciousness.

Likewise, although Wilmot was sporadically on the continent from his marriage in 1644, it was not until the fall of Oxford in June 1646 that his presence in England would have been potentially fatal. John's conception took place before Wilmot left England for France; it is conceivable that Anne accompanied him for a few weeks before returning, although the necessities of looking after her two elder sons make this an unlikely course of action. According to the usually reliable papers of the Earl of Clarendon, Wilmot—who, like his son John, took a delight in play-acting and subterfuge—was in July 1646 a secret visitor to Ditchley Park, the family home of Anne Wilmot's first husband, which she had then inherited, and this is a likely date for the conception.

Other compelling reasons for stating categorically that Henry Wilmot was John Wilmot's father include the strong, near-uncanny physical and social similarities between the two men. Both had the same heavy-lidded eyes and lazy half-smile, which offered seductive grace to women and convivial charm to men. Wilmot's drinking was well known to his contemporaries, although it did not blind him to his duties. Clarendon, who would later become an important figure in John's life, wrote: 'Wilmot loved debauchery, but shut it out from his business; never neglected that, and rarely miscarried in it.' Although this might seem at odds with some of his more colourful antics after the Battle of Worcester, the father and the son were as one in being men who were fiercely loyal to their true friends. As Clarendon said of Wilmot *père*, he 'violated [friendships]... less willingly, and never but for some great benefit or convenience to himself'.

Regardless of Wilmot's bravery and integrity, and that of those around him, there was little hope for the Royalist cause in early 1647. Cromwell's victory the previous year had been absolute, crushing the forces and spirits alike of his enemies. After fleeing from Oxford, Charles I had been sent around the country like an unwanted but crucial parcel. First, he was handed over to the English Parliament by the Scots and imprisoned in Holdenby House in Northamptonshire in January 1647. Here he stayed in uneasy spirits until June that year, when he became a political pawn in the tensions between the New Model Army, led by the moderate Thomas Fairfax, and Cromwell's Parliament. Fairfax's associate George Joyce seized Charles in June, transporting him to their headquarters at Thirplow Heath outside Cambridge, a move that strengthened their position even as it simultaneously undermined Cromwell's. The king was, after all, the most impressive hostage that anyone could hope to possess and, at this stage, was seen as a crucial part of whatever order arose from the ashes of the first civil war. A country without a king still seemed an impossibility.

As Wilmot cooled his heels in France at the court of the exiled queen Henrietta Maria in Saint-Germain-en-Laye, his wife was in the difficult position of raising her children single-handedly and attempting to cope with a national climate that was hostile towards her and all she stood for. Already a widow, she had to toe the delicate line between Parliamentary might and the Royalist sympathy that informed her character. Her first husband had been an ardent Parliamentarian, and given the puritan (with a small 'p') side to her nature, it was likely that she felt at least some sympathy towards this new era of austerity and godliness. (It should be noted, however, that Wilmot, like most of his peers, was far from being an unbeliever; Clarendon wrote that he 'had more scruples from religion to startle him, and would not have attained his end by any gross or foul act of wickedness'.)

Yet at the same time the suspicion that Anne's family connections might have informed her outlook made her a potentially dangerous figure for the new regime, and so her first duty, upon the birth of John, was to safeguard her family estate of Ditchley Park. Given the Parliamentarian rapaciousness for repossessing property that belonged to its enemies, it was a task that required a mixture of guile, political intelligence and immense personal strength. Anne Wilmot had all three. Contemporary portraits of her, including one by Peter Lely, show a woman not without a certain stately glamour, with an aristocratic mien that her son inherited; but they also reveal a set expression that implied dissatisfaction with the laborious business of portraiture, and possibly even with the inevitable extravagance of such an ornamental process.

If the king's situation was delicate around the time of John's birth, it worsened later in the year. Cromwell initially appeared not to have had any intention of executing Charles I, nor even of permanently imprisoning him. Instead, it was more likely that Cromwell hoped for political and religious reforms that would have given Parliament autonomy and turned Charles into little more than a puppet ruler. A more humble or even pragmatic king might have accepted Cromwell's terms and bided his time for a resurgence in royal fortunes when Cromwell, always a divisive figure, either died or fell out of favour. Yet Charles, with all the hereditary arrogance conferred upon him by the divine right of kings, was impatient, and in November 1647 he fled his guards and began plotting a further series of alliances and intrigues with the aim of his restoration to the English throne and a final defeat of the Parliamentary forces. Cynically, he offered the Scots Presbyterianism in England in exchange for their support, which he believed would swing the balance of power to his side.

He had miscalculated, and the results would prove fatal.

For the average man or woman in 1647, more concerned for their and their families' livelihoods than with the ideological, spiritual or political concerns of the day, the jostling for power going on at this time seemed impossibly remote, but its repercussions affected everyone. The first civil war was a bloody and prolonged conflict, turning families against each other and resulting in well over 100,000 deaths—a vast number in a country with around six million inhabitants.

The sides were unevenly matched, to say the least. The Royalists were a muddled, disorganized band who dealt in privilege rather than harsh realities, whereas the efficient New Model Army of the Parliamentarians—the 'Ironsides'—was made up of a coalition of Puritans and radicals and dissenters. Their success was down to the revolutionary idea that it should be skill at arms, rather than social background, that determined rank and leadership. Against their superior numbers and equipment, the gentlemen amateurs of the Cavaliers were doomed.

While battles had raged across the country, a vacuum had been created in which strange and unlikely people could flourish in the new ethos that was developing. Chief among these was Matthew Hopkins, the self-described 'Witchfinder General', who, in the period between 1645 and 1647, put hundreds of women on trial for suspected witchcraft, of whom at least 300 were hanged. (It is estimated that, of all the executions of this sort that took place between the early fifteenth and late eighteenth centuries, he was responsible for nearly half.) They were tortured in various enterprising ways, including searching for 'the devil's mark', which could be something as ordinary as a birthmark or mole, and throwing them into streams tied to chairs to see if they floated. The results were typically fatal either way.

It is highly likely that Hopkins was both sexually deviant and financially corrupt, pursuing his career more out of a desire to enrich himself than to save the country from an onslaught in supernatural visitation. His actions were tolerated by Parliament, albeit with some unease at his methods, in part because Hopkins was operating within the area of the strongest Parliamentary and Puritan influence, East Anglia. As Hopkins presented himself as a

God-fearing man who was accomplishing the Lord's work, an over-stretched Parliament was not inclined to look too closely into his barbaric actions.

Contrary to subsequent rumours that he was executed as a witch himself, Hopkins died peacefully at home in August 1647. Looked at in retrospect, it seems absurd and bizarre that, in the year John Wilmot was born, Hopkins would have been practising such an archaic and barbaric rite. Yet England was a divided place. Simultaneously, it was home to such thinkers and philosophers as Thomas Hobbes, whose *Leviathan* would soon become a key work, but it still clung to superstition and fear. The unknown could be exploited by anyone who saw that the world was changing and that the old order was about to be overthrown forever.

The most obvious representative of the old order was, of course, Charles I. After the doomed second civil war of 1648, in which a series of Royalist-oriented rebellions failed to come together as a unified force, it became clear to the Parliamentarians that the continued presence of a scheming and untrustworthy Charles as king could only lead to further trouble. The increasingly zealous Cromwell, tiring of his inability to impose his will on the country, was said to have remarked in a fit of rage: 'I will tell you, we will cut off the king's head with the crown on it.' This proved prophetic, carrying echoes of Henry II's similar comments about the similarly troublesome Becket, centuries before. After Colonel Pride's purge of the Rump Parliament, what had been unthinkable just a couple of years before —the trial of the king of England for treason—now became a reality.

For Wilmot, the news of the king's imminent trial, and inevitable execution beyond it, were ghastly tidings indeed. Had an arrangement been reached with Cromwell that would have allowed Charles to continue as king, even in the most limited circumstances, then there is little doubt that Wilmot could have returned to England, albeit under close watch and the inevitable suspicion that all of the Royalists faced. As it was, he had little to do in France but await the horrible news. It is impossible to know whether he had any grand but foolhardy scheme to return to England in an attempt to save the king. Even if he did, wiser heads or practical considerations prevailed, and Wilmot remained at the French court.

Charles's trial proceeded much as his enemies wished. Cromwell ensured that the 'traitorous' king would be found guilty by a carefully selected kangaroo court of 135 amenable judges, with fifty-nine of them happy to sign the king's death warrant. This was exactly what Cromwell had wanted; convinced that his victories meant that he had divine right on his side and that Charles was a man 'against whom the Lord had witnessed', he was content to ignore more mundane considerations in pursuit of his single-minded desire to seize absolute power.

The only surprise came in Charles's behaviour while on trial at Westminster Hall in January 1649. After his earlier arrogance and fecklessness, he proved his regal nature at the end. Accused of being 'guilty of the blood that hath been shed in this war' and a 'tyrant, traitor and murderer', he calmly refused to accept the court's jurisdiction, saying that his right of kingship was divinely ordained 'by old and lawful descent' and that all his accusers represented was 'a new unlawful unauthority'. Refusing to plead, he made a mockery of the court convened to try him, to the fury of his accusers.

Found guilty essentially of being king, he was beheaded with a single stroke of the axe on the freezing morning of Tuesday 30 January 1649. The cheering and jubilation traditional at public executions were absent. Instead, one spectator described how 'there was such a groan by the thousands present as I never heard before, and desire I may never hear again'. Perhaps it only then dawned on those assembled—Royalist, Parliamentarian, Presbyterian or of no party—what uncertain and troubled times awaited them.

For the exiled Charles II, as the Scottish Parliament proclaimed him on 6 February, and his circle, his father's death was a bitter shock. Having escaped England at the height of the Civil War in 1646, he had roamed Europe, heading first to his mother in France and then, in 1648, to The Hague, where his sister Mary and brother-in-law William were living, in a vain attempt to elicit military support from them. He had the poisoned chalice of kingship to contend with, which seemed to be little more than a thankless bauble. The price for his return to Britain with Scottish support was to accept Presbyterianism as the national religion, something that the new 'King' Charles, who was leaning towards Catholicism, was reluctant to countenance. The alternatives were either to waste his time at various European courts, or to return to England in arms and attempt to oust Cromwell and the Commonwealth and regain his crown and country. The immediate attractions of the latter were stymied by his lack of an army, while allying himself with any of the great powers of Europe, pro-monarchist though most of them undoubtedly were, raised the terrible spectre of England being invaded by a foreign army—and of Charles, if he was to be restored to power, having to pay them off. Principles and the divine right of kings alone were not enough.

Eventually Charles, wearying of his long confinement, took action to regain his throne by entering into a Faustian pact, signing a treaty with the Scottish Covenanters—a Presbyterian movement that was implacably opposed to Cromwell—at Breda on 1 May 1650. This treaty compelled him to recognize the Solemn League and Covenant, which promoted Presbyterianism as the national religion, and to acknowledge the Kirk of Scotland in England as well, which might have led to a struggle between his own instincts and the necessity of maintaining his crown. However, after the Battle of Dunbar in September 1650 saw the Scottish lieutenant-general David Leslie's ill-trained and fractious coalition of Royalists and Covenanters annihilated, there was little hope left. Charles, who had arrived in Scotland on 23 June, took personal command of the army, but to little effect. The Battle of Worcester the following year was the final roll of the dice, and despite Charles's bravery and quick-wittedness in his eventual escape, it proved to be a last hurrah. The Commonwealth was now the established order in England, and anyone who took sides against it did so at their peril.

As the country tore itself apart, Anne Wilmot was faced with great personal difficulty. Keeping Ditchley Park out of the clutches of the Commonwealth, which was keen to reward its supporters with the redistributed property of the former regime, would have been a difficult task for any woman living on her own, and it proved a constant struggle for Anne and her agent John Cary to retain her estates, which also included property in Buckinghamshire from her earlier marriage. There had been a 1650 ruling by the Committee for Compounding (which had been established in 1643 by Parliament in order to confiscate the property of Royalist supporters) that all of her husband's property was forfeit to the government; this she fought on the grounds that her estates had belonged to her previous husband rather than to Wilmot. She might have stated that she had 'many fears' as to her lack of experience at managing land, but her pragmatism and toughness, as well as her contacts with still influential figures such as Clarendon and the former MP for Aylesbury and John's guardian, Sir Ralph Verney, ensured that she managed to retain her properties, despite her and Wilmot's Royalist connections. Anne had found herself in a changed world, and it was one in which her family had to tread carefully.

There were many remarkable things about Cromwell's Commonwealth, even before he wielded absolute power and founded the Protectorate. Chief among these was the way in which religious freedom, the bedrock of this new English identity, was tolerated only if it was the *right sort* of religion. Catholics were persecuted, but this was nothing new. Where Cromwell distinguished himself was in all but obliterating the Anglican Church, first, by forbidding ministers to practise, and second, by the heavy-handed way in which churches throughout the country were robbed and desecrated. This had begun in the Civil War and continued throughout the Commonwealth and Protectorate. Clergymen would be prosecuted for blasphemy and ejected from office for a variety of offences, ranging from the reasonable (fornication, drunkenness and fighting) to the absurd (Morris dancing or public reading of the Book of Common Prayer). Things were so bad by 1656 that the diarist John Evelyn wrote of a collection organized by the Presbyterian minister Thomas Manton 'for persecuted and sequestered ministers of the Church of England, whereof divers are in prison'.

It was not just the clergy who faced a dictatorial regime. Press censorship had begun in 1647 and sought to abolish any potential sedition in pamphlets or other documents. Personal morality was also central to the work of the Commonwealth, and the Adultery and Fornication Act of 1650 made 'the abominable and crying sins of adultery, incest and fornication' punishable by death, with any unfortunate children resulting from these couplings automatically disinherited. Clearly this sort of bastardy was widespread enough at the time to warrant legislation. Offences of fornication or brothel-keeping attracted stiff prison sentences, whipping and branding (tellingly, there was only one successful prosecution for adultery recorded, indicating that there was a public distaste for conviction in these cases). Activities such as bear-baiting and cockfighting and all vaguely pagan rituals were suppressed, theatres were closed and their trappings disposed of, and Christmas, itself associated with 'carnal and sensual delights', was officially cancelled. Punishments for stepping out of line were severe: whipping was common for such minor infractions as playing football, a fine was imposed for going for a walk on Sunday and not observing the Sabbath, and imprisonment for swearing was normal.

This stood in stark contrast to some of Cromwell's more lenient and liberal-minded actions. Tolerance for Jews was reintroduced for the first time since the mid-thirteenth century, allowing them to live and work freely. It is equally likely that the cynical Lord Protector saw the potential for using them as 'able and general intelligencers', useful in providing information about enemies both foreign and domestic in exchange for their new sanctuary. Although Cromwell— a man who infamously demanded that he be painted 'warts and everything' in an apocryphal but pleasing story—had no interest in literature, theatre or art, believing them to be tantamount to graven images, he did have a surprisingly strong interest in music, which was believed by the Commonwealth Parliament to convey a sense of moral purpose. He allowed the first English opera to be produced in 1656—William Davenant's *The Siege Of Rhodes*—although it was described as 'recitative music' (music being permitted) rather than allowing that it had any taint of the theatrical.

Likewise, although the immorality and drunkenness that would be found in taverns was anathema to the Puritans, who described them as 'the great nurseries of mischief and impiety in this Commonwealth', the difficulty in regulating them in any serious manner meant that, although hundreds were closed down, the vast majority continued to flourish untroubled by the government. The English love of a good pint of beer was evidently not to be disturbed by the transitory arrangements of a new political system.

As there was now no chance of a military defeat of the Commonwealth, the rebellion had to be intellectual. The political philosopher Thomas Hobbes's 1651 work *Leviathan* had been written over the previous decade and proved to be hugely controversial. Hobbes's central argument was a complex and multifaceted one, a world away from the more simplistic views of God and man that the Commonwealth espoused. His point was that a social contract had to exist between government and its people, and that the best way of maintaining order and avoiding the chaos that would ensue via civil war or society's breakdown would be to have the rule of an absolute sovereign, not necessarily the king but someone with the level of power that the monarch had traditionally wielded. Hobbes was a well-known associate of the Royalist court in Paris, where he had headed in 1640 when his treatise *The Elements of Law* had angered Parliament and made his continued presence in England untenable. There, he encountered Henry Wilmot and others, but the secularist and quasi-atheist sentiments that he described managed to enrage both Royalists and Commonwealth supporters alike. In that, at least, he managed to unite popular opinion. He returned to England in 1651, submitted himself to Cromwell's council of state, and was allowed to live quietly in London without fear of prosecution on the understanding that he accepted Commonwealth authority. Nonetheless he, like many other perceived dissidents, was kept under close watch.

While all this occurred, Henry Wilmot remained far away in Paris. Eventually, Anne Wilmot tired of coping on her own and, in 1653, sent her elder children over to De Veau's Academy in the city. She herself followed early the next year, intending to see Wilmot and press him on his paternal and spousal obligations. Whether Wilmot and Anne and their family were reunited remains unclear—some chronicles attest to a meeting in Brussels in that year, others talk of a fruitless search for an errant husband—but it is likely that Wilmot, newly created Earl of Rochester and enjoying the dilettante life of the French court as best he could, did not want the encumbrance of a wife or children and made himself scarce. He had recently had some success with diplomatic efforts in Europe: he persuaded the German court to give Charles nearly £70,000, which was paid sporadically but nonetheless managed to keep the exiled court together for a few years.

John, meanwhile, remained at home in Ditchley, living apart from both his parents and his brothers. He was occasionally visited by his mother's extended families, including the St John and Lee clan, and by Verney, but the appeal of conversing with a small boy was limited. His early life was a fairly typical one for a privileged child, with wet nurses, tutors and various other parties ministering to his welfare. An early teacher of his was a Cambridge-educated clergyman, Francis Giffard, who was responsible for indoctrinating him in the ways of God and man, teaching him the Bible. It is too glib to say that the seeds of John's lifelong engagement with religion began here, but a later letter that he wrote to his son Charles, in which he expressed his belief that the early days of the boy's education would make him 'happy or unhappy forever', at least indicates an interest in spiritual and personal development that might have been inspired by his own experiences.

John was educated to the typical standards of a young gentleman of the time. He studied Latin from the age of seven or so, as he was introduced to the major writers and philosophers whose work was an integral part of a classical education. The seeds that were sown here would come to fruition later in his life, when his dazzling satires would nod, either explicitly or implicitly, to classical authors such as Catullus and Pliny the Younger. It is likely that an innocent seven-year-old boy was not exposed to the bawdier side of the ancients' more scatological sallies, and the chances of the God-fearing Mr Giffard having taught John Catullus' sixteenth poem in particular (which begins *pedicabo ego vos et irrumabo*—loosely trans-lated 'I'll bugger you and skull-fuck you'—before heading into even wilder areas) seem unlikely. It was not until much later in life that John encountered the more licentious side of the ancients, whether at court or at university, but their lewd insinuations would, in time, be as strong a literary influence as Mr Giffard's more seemly instructions.

While John learnt of great heroes and epic battles of bygone times, his father was planning his final attempt to return to England and regain the throne for his king. After Charles's defeat in 1651, there had been little concerted effort by English Royalists to rise up against the Commonwealth, but when Cromwell dissolved Parliament in 1653 and appointed himself the quasi-monarchical 'Lord Protector of England'—an office that carried with it as much pomp and grandios-ity as the king's had ever done—it became clear that some attempt had to be made to check his increasingly hubristic ambitions of absolutist rule.

Cromwell began to turn the country into a virtual police state with the introduction of so-called 'major generals'—soldiers who were responsible for keeping order and discipline; in practice, this meant that a network of spies spread throughout the country, and families were encouraged to inform on apparently dissident mem-bers. Their reward, they were loftily informed, would be salvation in the next life. Perhaps unsurprisingly, most declined to do so. In the few cases that did come to court the accused were inevitably found guilty, because of the difficulty of finding lawyers willing to defend them. A particularly perverse touch of the Protectorate was that not just the guilty, but the associates of the guilty, were liable to be imprisoned, and these associates would include anyone bold enough to stand in court on behalf of their clients and claim that their obvi-ous guilt was not so. Cromwell's combination of religious fervour and brutality influenced dictators for centuries to come; but he was not acting merely out of paranoia, rather from justified experience. Royalist plots to topple the Commonwealth and restore Charles II to the throne were an ongoing feature of at least the first half of the Protectorate.

In February 1655, Wilmot prepared to return to England and try to rid the country of the troublesome Protector. The plan he had hatched, which owed more to optimism than to experience, was to corral remaining Royalist support and to attempt to coordinate a successful military rising against Cromwell: a bold but deeply unlikely plan. The remaining Royalists consisted of the loyalist and secretive Sealed Knot group, which was led by the aristocrats Sir Edward Villiers (Clarendon's 'honest Ned') and John Belasyse, both of whom had maintained a low profile since the death of Charles (in the case of Villiers, hiding in France until 1652); and the more vivacious 'Action party', whose membership was an eclectic mix of country gentlemen such as Edward Grey and John Weston, who had Presbyterian contacts and had been under Commonwealth observation since the execution of Charles I. The only thing uniting these disparate men was a loathing of Cromwell, but the uneasy relationship of these groups to each other—the Sealed Knot favouring careful subterfuge and the Action party preferring open conflict—should have alerted Wilmot to the implausibility of forcing a military alliance between them.

Nonetheless, he and his comrade-in-arms Joseph Wagstaffe attempted to divide the responsibility for leading the rebellion between them. The intention was that it should spread across the country, encompassing everywhere from former Royalist strongholds in Oxford and Winchester to strategically useful places such as Newcastle and Chester. Initially, Wilmot would lead an uprising in Yorkshire, and Wagstaffe—a man who Clarendon described as fitter 'for execution than counsel', and one who loved to spend his time 'in jollity and mirth', probably a euphemism for heavy drinking—would take command of the West Country Royalists. The locations were chosen more in the spirit of optimism than because there was deep-rooted support in either area, but initially there seemed the ghost of a chance that the enterprise might work. Cromwell's spies, led by John Thurloe, secretary to his council of state, were all-powerful in England, but they had failed to stretch their tentacles into Europe, and Wilmot and Wagstaffe believed that various disenfranchised exiles were preparing to return from Europe to the country to raise arms against the Protectorate. There were even rumours that the New Model Army's commander, Fairfax, disillusioned with Cromwell, might have given his tacit support to a rising.

Were they to be successful, no doubt many Royalists had pleasing images of Cromwell being beheaded on the same spot where, six years before, Charles I had met his end, and their being rewarded with titles, land and the undying gratitude of Charles II. Unfortunately, this vision proved to be a bold but unfounded fantasy. When Wilmot assembled a force of a couple of hundred Royalists at the strategic point of Marston Moor outside the city of York on 8 March 1655, in the hope that the gates would be opened up and the city's support immediately bestowed upon them, it soon became hideously clear that he was mistaken. Just as the 1644 Civil War battle at the same location had seen a horrendous Royalist defeat, chaos reigned, as no assistance was forthcoming. Chivalry soon turned to farce, as Wilmot's assembled soldiers fled in all directions, pursued by the forces of the governor of York, Sir Robert Lilburne.

As at the Battle of Worcester, Wilmot showed as much alacrity in escape as he had done in planning the attack. This time deigning to adopt a disguise, he was nevertheless arrested at Aylesbury by a magistrate and placed under watch at an inn, to await the arrival of a military escort the next day. Continuing his giddy run of luck, Wilmot bribed the innkeeper with an extremely expensive gold chain and fled into the night with all his 'rich apparel'. He made it to London, where he lay low amidst Royalist sympathizers and the anonymous throng of inhabitants until he took safe passage to Antwerp later in the year. His hapless servants were less fortunate, being left behind at the inn and at the mercy of the furious military escort, which was expected to arrive at any moment. Bizarrely, Wilmot's good fortune was mirrored by that of several other high-profile Royalists such as Richard Mauleverer and Thomas Hunt, who had similarly hair's-breadth escapes from seemingly inevitable and humiliating public executions.

The only semi-successful part of the March campaign was the Penruddock Rising in Hampshire, led by Wilmot's co-commander Wagstaffe and Sir John Penruddock. Ignorant of the various failures of 8 March, they occupied Salisbury on 11 March, proclaimed Charles the rightful king, released prisoners from the local jail, and arrested the high sheriff of Wiltshire and held him hostage. Had they attracted any substantial support on their journey through Somerset and Devon, they might have offered a significant threat. However, as at Marston Moor, few joined them, perhaps all too mindful of the consequences of defeat by Cromwell's highly efficient forces. After a failed last stand in Exeter, Penruddock was arrested, condemned to death and executed on 16 May. Wagstaffe, however, managed to pull off another daring escape, leaping over a church wall on his horse and returning to Amsterdam by July that year.

Wilmot, Wagstaffe and the others might have left with their lives—and, in the case of Wilmot, he somehow managed to acquire replacement servants in London despite being one of the most wanted men in the country: an impressive feat under the circumstances. Nevertheless, it was clear, once they were reunited with Charles, that another uprising of this nature was impossible. Their embarrassing failure pointed to a lack of support in the country at large, indicating that many ordinary people would rather remain with the Cromwellian devil they knew than take a risk on an uncertain new king.

The nascent rebellion had been crushed with ease, partly because of over-optimistic incompetence, but the royal court, by now based in Cologne in an attempt to obtain more funding, also came to believe that there was a traitor in their midst. For someone without any obvious support in the European courts, Cromwell's spymaster Thurloe was unusually well informed about the actions and plots of the Royalists in exile; he was also able to round up Royalist sympathizers in England with suspicious ease. So a mole hunt began. The eventual malefactor was revealed to be Henry Manning, an occasional drinking companion of Wilmot, who had kept Thurloe updated with a flow of information that was probably equal parts fact and self-inflating fiction. Manning was not a significant figure in Cologne, but it was clear that he had to be disposed of, so he was brutally killed in a wood in December 1655. History does not record how Thurloe dealt with the removal of his diligent informant, but perhaps it is no coincidence that the following year he took charge of the post office, enabling him to intercept mail on a grand scale.

As his father continued to traipse around Europe soliciting donations and increasingly vain assistance for the court, John Wilmot began the next stage of his education. While it might have been traditional for the son of a nobleman to have attended one of the great English public schools such as Eton or Winchester, or studied under the leading headmaster of the day, Richard Busby, at Westminster, it was more expedient to Anne and her family to have her son educated locally—both for reasons of convenience and because of his father's notoriety—so he was enrolled at Burford Grammar School at the age of nine. It is possible that he was accompanied by Francis Giffard, but equally likely that he would have lodged with the headmaster or in another local notable's house.

The curriculum that he followed was a traditional one. We can glean what contemporary education then consisted of from Charles Hoole's 1660 book *A New Discovery of the Old Art of Teaching School*. Hoole, who had taught at Rotherham School, indicates that a classical education was the norm, with boys being taught a mixture of Latin grammar and literature. A grammar school education was designed to broaden and deepen the student's learning, leaving him with a wide knowledge of the likes of Ovid and Horace (Greek tuition was the preserve of the more famous public schools). There were daily prayers, psalm singing and Bible readings. It is also likely that there was a fearsome amount of corporal punishment; Hoole might have advocated sparing the rod, but his less enlightened contemporaries believed that this would merely spoil the child.

John Wilmot advanced unspectacularly through his modest grammar school education, building up his slender store of knowledge. Nevertheless, there were some unpleasant basic facts about this formative stage of his life: he had been abandoned by a father he barely knew, and his distant mother was more concerned with politicking than attending to her youngest son. A young boy's typical early education was laden with casual brutality and violence. If he endured this, it would have been against the background of a country where his family was treated with suspicion. The cumulative effect on a frightened, uncertain John Wilmot can only be imagined.

But in truth we know little of his schooldays, other than tiny, tantalizing hints. When Rochester writes of education in his poems, the results tend to be unedifying. Two of the more notable cases are a reference to schoolboy masturbation in 'A Ramble in St James's Park' and his wish, in 'An Allusion to Horace', that the playwright Nathaniel Lee, described as a 'hot-brained fustian fool', should be 'well lashed' at the legendary Richard Busby's hands in order to re-educate him about Hannibal and Scipio. Likewise, his letters contain no nostalgic reminiscences of his days at Burford. No records survive of whether he was a good or a weak student; after his death, Rochester's biographer and final confessor Gilbert Burnet reported that he had 'perfect mastery of Latin and the masterworks found within it', but Burnet has to be treated extremely carefully as a witness. However, there is one telling detail that Burnet notes. Upon being asked why the good felt no fear at the prospect of death, and the bad felt terror, Rochester was said to have replied that it was from 'the impressions that they had received from their education'. If this was the case, then Rochester, by no means fearless himself on his deathbed, dwelt far more upon his experiences at school than he let on.

As Anne Wilmot struggled to keep her estates together, her husband remained on the continent, involving himself in ever more Byzantine plots to aid the return of Charles II to the English throne.

In 1656 he was instrumental in an alliance between the Spanish and the Royalists to back an invasion of England, which was planned to take place in early 1658. However, having learnt from their mistakes, others in the exiled court did not share this appetite for Charles's restoration, and the foolhardiness of having an English king's return sponsored by a foreign power was again narrowly averted.

Henry Wilmot, who at the start of 1658 was based in Flanders, was still a relatively young man of forty-five. Charles had placed him in charge of the newly formed Grenadier Guards, and he was expected to be a leading figure in any military endeavour. However, it was not to be. Exhausted and worn down by nearly fifteen years of unsuccessful plotting, fighting and escaping, Wilmot's health, resistance and good fortune were finally depleted. When sickness spread through the ranks of the army in Ghent, he was in no state to resist it. He died of fever at Sluys on 19 February 1658 and was buried in Bruges by his Royalist cousin Lord Hopton. Many years later, his heart was exhumed and buried in the family vault at Spelsbury in Oxfordshire.

Wilmot's death had several immediate effects. One was to deprive Charles of one of his most stalwart and loyal lieutenants—a loss that for him was personal as well as military. There was to be no further major attempt to return Charles to the throne until after the death of Cromwell, indicating that the *carpe diem* spirit of Wilmot was now absent. Another consequence was that Anne was now a widow and in an even more awkward position, given that her late husband was both a notorious Royalist and a debtor, and his mortgaged estates were liable to be forfeited. And finally, while still a schoolboy of ten, John Wilmot inherited the grand-sounding titles of 2nd Earl of Rochester, Baron Wilmot of Adderbury and Viscount Wilmot of Athlone. With Cromwell's Protectorate at the peak of its powers, this new title seemed to mean little to Rochester, as he was now known. But fate, not for the first time in his life, was about to engineer a spectacular reversal.

[2]

'I all the
FLATTERING
YOUTH
DEFY'

✳

[1658–1664]

AFTER his father's death, Rochester continued his education at Burford, concluding it by around the age of twelve. Had he remained under Francis Giffard's careful tutelage, it is extremely unlikely that he would have done anything debauched or decadent. Indeed, his delicate constitution was such that Giffard had even slept in his room on occasion 'to prevent any ill accidents'. This mild-mannered childhood seems an unlikely contrast to the swash-buckling persona that Rochester later adopted, or rather had foisted upon him, yet stranger journeys have taken place during many senti-mental, or unsentimental, educations.

As Rochester prepared to head to university, it could scarcely have escaped his notice that England was in a state of flux. After Henry Wilmot's death, the country had gone through many rever-sals and changes. The all-powerful Cromwell and his Protectorate were at their most pompous and grandiose in 1657, when Cromwell had had himself declared Lord Protector in June in a ceremony at Westminster Hall. It was deliberately designed to have overtones of coronations, even if the old hypocrite made a great show of refus-ing a crown, presumably on the grounds that the robes of state and a gilded sceptre made the point more than adequately. Cromwell, middle-aged but not elderly at fifty-seven, appeared secure in his power, while Charles and the royal court overseas were in despair, with what little money they had running out and many of their keenest supporters, such as Wilmot, dying off.

However, the wheel of fortune soon turned, and in early 1658 Cromwell was struck down with malarial fever. His personal doctors were unable to reconcile the fact that such a godly and God-fearing man could be placed in these torments and failed to diagnose a serious but treatable kidney infection, with the result that Cromwell died, probably of septicaemia, in September 1658. There were few reports of spontaneous outbreaks of grief in the streets, save perhaps from those who had obtained preferment under Cromwell and now wondered whether his son Richard would continue the Protectorate in the same fashion.

They were very soon disabused of any notion that Cromwell *fils* would be continuing the family tradition. Richard entirely lacked his father's moral convictions and military experience, being instead possessed of a craven pragmatism that led him to various compromises and horse-trading with the New Model Army, who—suspicious of a man they saw as weak—ensured that the Protectorate-approved Parliament was dissolved in early 1659, to be replaced by their chosen Rump Parliament of army loyalists and Protectorate sceptics. In exchange for his personal debts being written off, Richard agreed in May 1659 to resign as Lord Protector, thereby effectively ending the last decade of Puritan government, and retired into obscurity. Royalists rejoiced, surprised but delighted at the change in their circumstances, and christened Richard with the gloriously abusive nickname 'Tumbledown Dick'. His father's dream of a non-monarchical England was at an end.

College records indicate that Rochester was entered by his mother's agent John Cary as a 'fellow commoner' at Wadham College, Oxford on 1 March 1659, but he did not take up his place there until 18 January 1660. This hiatus was not uncommon for young gentlemen of quality and meant that he arrived less a small frightened boy and more an adult in training, even at the age of twelve. It is likely that he spent the year or so between Burford and Oxford continuing his studies, probably in a less regimented fashion, reading the Bible and classical literature in the way that was expected of any young man.

When Rochester finally arrived at Oxford, the pendulum was swinging firmly back to Royalist sympathy. It was still several months before Charles II would be actually restored to the throne, with the former Parliamentarian George Monck playing a clever game to negotiate the bloodless return of the king across the water. Oxford had been strongly Royalist in the early years of the Civil War, with Charles I making his court there, and this had led to both the city and the university being regarded with much suspicion by Cromwell. He realized that the hub of intellectual discord that intelligent minds together bred could well lead to dissent, especially when set against his own straightforwardly brutish strain of thought (his own university, Cambridge, was where the Parliamentary movement made its eastern headquarters, and it produced most of the pro-Commonwealth writers of the day, such as Marvell and Milton). Cromwell made various attempts to control the university; Hobbes wrote of undesirable figures—'all who were not of their faction [and] divers scandalous ministers and scholars'—being purged. Cynically, Cromwell had himself made Chancellor of the university in 1650, presumably to keep an eye on any outbreaks of potential sedition.

The result of this was that Oxford began to head into a moral and intellectual decline that did not abate fully until centuries later. By Cromwell's death in 1658, many of the university's leading academics had been removed, and the emphasis was firmly on more Puritan interests. One toadying student, George Trosse, wrote that he was delighted that 'there were so many sermons preached, and so many excellent orthodox and practical divines to preach them'. As with the rest of England, discipline was strict; gambling and fornication were punished extremely severely by the university proctors, an elected group of senior men responsible for discipline, and malefactors could expect expulsion, a heavy fine or even imprisonment. Drinking, whether alcohol or coffee, was forbidden on Sundays, and sermons and overt displays of religiosity were the norm. College tutors were expected to be men of God who prayed daily with their pupils, and it was stated that 'no person may live idly in this University'. Had Rochester been a student a decade earlier, things might have been very different.

The contrast between the old and new orders was epitomized by Rochester's choice of institution. Wadham, Oxford's newest college, had been founded in 1613 by the wealthy landowner Nicholas Wadham's widow Dorothy. It was the former Warden of the college, John Wilkins, who had been largely responsible for its rise to eminence. Wilkins supported religious and social tolerance and founded the 'experimental philosophical club', which later became the Royal Society, during his tenure.

Unlike his predecessor Warden Pitts, who was expelled in 1648 for refusing to submit to the authority of Parliament, Wilkins took a broadly non-partisan approach to politics, with the result that even during the Protectorate Wadham continued to attract Royalist students, provided that they were able to keep their views to themselves. One especially notable student was Christopher Wren, who entered the college in 1650 and was closely associated with Wilkins throughout his time. Wilkins's successor as Warden, Walter Blandford, was a similarly skilful politician, eventually serving on the commission that restored Royalists to their previous places in society. He was approved of by the new royal court, as can be seen by his remaining in post until 1665.

By the time of Rochester's arrival, the college was self-governing and tolerant to all. The idea of Wadham having an unorthodox spirit at its heart persisted and has lasted to this day. This spirit, however, was set against the rigours of academic life. As an MA (Master of Arts) scholar, Rochester, who wore a more distinguished gown to mark him out from non-aristocratic undergraduates, had to attend theological discussions for two hours every other week. He was expected to attend chapel regularly, albeit one now with a restored Anglican, rather than Puritan, ethos, and sometimes the services began as early as 5 a.m. He then had a short break for breakfast before spending the time until lunch at lectures, or preparing for these lectures with his college tutor. Lunch itself—a plain meal of bread and cheese, washed down with weak beer—was a strict affair in which only Latin and Greek were allowed to be spoken; then the afternoon was spent at a mixture of lectures and university events, before the evening saw the presumably exhausted Rochester attend chapel and then see his tutor for private prayers and to discuss the activities of the day. It was a hard, demanding existence, and those responsible for enforcing it prided themselves on creating young men who were ready for whatever the world would throw at them.

At least, this was the theory. In reality, the wealthier students, who regarded Oxford as a sort of exotic finishing school and had little interest in the rigours of work, rebelled in style, aided by the new air of freedom that the Restoration brought with it. The 'strange effeminate age', as Anthony à Wood later called it, saw men, from aristocrats to poor students, dress in affected style, and the women who fraternized with the undergraduates don breeches. Unsurprisingly, in this place of cross-dressing lewdness, bisexuality and sodomy were rumoured to be rife,* as was drunkenness.

Colleges vied with one another to see which was the most debauched. The students of St John's made it their mission to attend chapel drunk, while Balliol men were made 'perfect sots' by their 'perpetual bubbling'. It was said that three MA students of All Souls, an especially notorious college, were so drunk at the Mitre tavern that they frightened the hostess to death. It was far from uncommon for students to die of alcohol poisoning; one bishop's son was found dead with a brandy bottle held tight within his grasp. Students welcomed the new spirit of freedom with relish; when, shortly after Rochester began his studies, it was announced on 13 February 1660 that a free Parliament had been declared, the news was celebrated with bonfires all over the city into which animals' rumps were thrown, symbolizing the contempt and hatred with which the Rump Parliament had been regarded.

The fellows were no better. Magdalen and New College were notorious for their buying and selling of places, and at least one university ceremony had to be postponed because the Vice-Chancellor was too hungover to officiate. Proctors, allegedly responsible for discipline, made it their business to be 'known boon blades' of the town, famous for their sexual and alcoholic prowess. Syphilis and disease were rife. Cromwell's carefully nurtured home of Puritanism and religious observation had become the perfect cradle for a young Rochester—as the antiquarian and scholar Thomas Hearne later

---

* This was confirmed in spectacularly public fashion in the eighteenth century when Robert Thistlethwayte, then-warden of Wadham, fled to France in 1737 after being accused of making homosexual advances to his student William France.

put it—to 'become debauched'. Like other students, Rochester was free for the first time to drink, whore and gamble with abandon, for which he needed a seasoned Virgil to guide his fresh-faced Dante. This came in the red-faced, corpulent form of a don named Robert Whitehall: scholar, poet and drunkard.

Initially, Rochester had no mentor at university. Although his perennial tutor Francis Giffard had accompanied him to Oxford, he had soon reluctantly left him in the hands of a new tutor, Phineas Berry; Giffard later said to Hearne, with more than a hint of sour grapes, that he had been 'supplanted'. Gilbert Burnet described Berry as 'a very learned and good-natured man', whom Rochester 'ever used with much respect, and rewarded him as became a great man.' The truth was that Berry was a ridiculous and ineffectual figure, more interested in drinking coffee in the newly founded coffee shops than he was in ministering to his students or keeping discipline. It was noted a few years later that Berry, by then a senior proctor, flattered a group of undergraduates by describing them as 'men that are examples rather than to be made examples of', and was then mocked and baited by these 'examples' as they kicked a barrel up the street and disrupted an academic procession.

Such a figure was hardly likely to inspire Rochester. Indeed, when he later wrote in 'A Satire against Reason and Mankind' about 'frantic crowds of thinking fools', it is tempting to think that he had Berry in mind, flapping about ineffectually as he tried to keep order. Although the young boy would presumably have proceeded in his studies for the first few months with some semblance of decorum, it is likely that he and his contemporaries were swept up in the excitements of what Burnet cattily terms 'the general joy that overran the whole nation upon his Majesty's Restoration', and that the study of Latin and Greek would have been less compelling than the opportunity to run amok for the first time in his life. The man who transformed Rochester, for better or for worse, from an innocent, rather nervous boy into a self-assured young adult was Whitehall. Although this man has hitherto existed as a shadowy footnote in Rochester's life, he should be given far greater credit—or blame—for the emergence of Rochester's spectacular character.

Whitehall, the son of a clergyman, was born in 1624 and had a glittering academic career at first, being a King's Scholar under Richard Busby at Westminster and then studying at Christ Church at Oxford. An avowed Royalist, he fell foul of the Parliamentary regime in 1647 for refusing to submit to Cromwell, saying 'I can acknowledge no visitation but King Charles' and, to add insult to injury, putting his thoughts into a glib little couplet:

> My name's Whitehall, God bless the Poet,
> If I submit, the King shall know it.

He was duly expelled in July 1648, for his arrogant defiance (to say nothing of his terrible versifying), and his life at Oxford looked like it was over before it had started. However, it was a time when even the most apparently committed Royalist had friends in unlikely places, and Whitehall, who was always entertaining company, was a familiar of the MP and regicide Richard Ingoldsby, a cousin of Cromwell. After a good deal of nodding and winking, Whitehall returned to Oxford in 1650 and was elected to a fellowship at Merton, then as now one of the university's most academically prestigious colleges.

Whitehall's movements over the next decade are mainly shadowy. He was awarded his MA in 1652, wrote sycophantic verse addresses to both Oliver and Richard Cromwell, when the latter was installed as Chancellor of Oxford in 1657, and was apparently given a licence to teach at the University of Dublin, although there is little evidence that, in a climate where Anglo-Irish relations reached their nadir as a result of Cromwell's violent incursions, he ever took himself away from his familiar haunts. Whitehall was moderately far-sighted as an academic, preferring the study of geography and mathematics to scholasticism, and in one of his poems he rails against 'the common foe, church discipline'. Anthony à Wood dismissed him as 'a pot poet', and, had it not been for the arrival of Rochester at the university in 1660, Whitehall would have been lost to history, another shambling red-faced disappointment of a man. However, his presence in the younger man's spiritual and physical upbringing proved to be a decisive one.

Although there is no record of when Rochester and Whitehall met for the first time, it was around Rochester's thirteenth birthday—although Wood, in his definitive 1691 history of Oxford University and the writers it produced, *Athenae Oxonienses*, mentions the two of them meeting when Rochester was still twelve. Rochester, as an aristocrat, was allowed to mix with the dons in their common room, and it was here, almost certainly, that he and Whitehall came across one another and their unorthodox friendship began. It was an auspicious and formative occasion in both of their lives. Whitehall, by then 'loined with sack and faced with claret', was a rambunctious, Falstaffian figure, not especially witty in himself but certainly the cause of wit in others. For Rochester, who had only ever known virtuous, worthy men such as Giffard and Ralph Verney, Whitehall was a revelatory figure. The concept of a young boy learning from another, older man had its roots in Greece and antiquity, and few would have found anything strange in the idea of Rochester being taken up in this fashion by Whitehall, even if some of their subsequent actions were unusual, even by the standards of the time.

What he learnt from Whitehall can be conjectured. Although Wood sneers that Whitehall 'pretended to instruct [Rochester] in the art of poetry', it is likely that the older man introduced him to the previously Puritan-forbidden delights of Elizabethan drama, such as the works of Shakespeare and Marlowe, which were considered a decadent relic of debauched times in the Protectorate. Philip Massinger's comedy *The Guardian* was performed in Oxford in July 1660, the first time that a play was publicly staged since the Civil War, and it is perfectly possible that Rochester and Whitehall saw it together. The latter would perhaps have especially enjoyed the titular character of Durazzo, who is described in the play both as 'jovial and good', possibly ironically, and 'an angry old ruffian'.

That Whitehall and Rochester had a close relationship is clear. Wood notes that Whitehall 'absolutely doted' on the boy. Although no portraits of Rochester at university exist, there is little doubt that he was a good-looking, even beautiful young man, and one who attracted the attention of all those around him. Whitehall, himself no beauty, cheerfully wrote of himself that he lived in 'Bachelor's Row', and added, meaningfully, 'maybe he is overwhelmed in love that he dares not reveal and was minded… to remove all suspicion by palliating it with a contrary guise'. This is not so far from 'the love that dare not speak its name' of Wilde's day, and it is possible to see his friendship with Rochester in Platonic terms, with Whitehall the older, experienced man and Rochester the eager boy.

It was certainly under Whitehall's influence that Rochester 'grew debauched' and took to drinking heavily. Taverns such as The Three Tuns and The Mermaid catered to the 'good fellows' of the university, and with the Puritan edicts against drinking and drunkenness lifted, many took full licence of the opportunities presented to them. Whitehall, thoughtful as ever when it came to debauchery, lent Rochester his academic gown for 'night rambles' of this sort, enabling the boy to make his way through the streets after an evening's libation unmolested by proctors. Had they all been as inefficient as the hapless Phineas Berry or one of the 'known boon blades', the subterfuge would probably have been unnecessary. This was the young Rochester's first taste of disguise and dissimulation, something that his father had been familiar with but then still an alien concept to the boy.

Yet intoxication on its own lacks the sense of subversion that the term 'debauched' implies, so the idea of Rochester as a catamite, willing or coerced, has to be considered. Sodomy was widespread but illegal in the seventeenth century in all walks of society, punishable by a sentence of hanging. Although this was seldom carried out, the lesser charge of attempted buggery still carried the penalty of imprisonment and time on the pillory, where the convict would be both verbally and physically abused. For someone in a position of authority such as Whitehall, it would have been catastrophic, the more so because his former sponsor Ingoldsby, although not out of royal favour, lacked the influence that he had previously possessed.

However, institutional pederasty was rife at this time. Wood wrote that the fellows of All Souls elected a good-looking boy with the intent of 'kissing and slobbering' on him, and a poem by John Marston refers to the possibility of a 'pedant tutor' using a child like 'Phrygian Ganymede'. Wadham later became notorious for homosexual activity, revelling in its nickname of 'Sodom', and had Whitehall wished to have a sexual relationship with Rochester, he could have done so unbothered in the prevailing moral culture of the college.

What Rochester made of this can only be guessed at. Interestingly, there is no reference to Whitehall made in Burnet's *Life*, which might indicate that, twenty years later, Rochester felt ashamed or regretful of his involvement with the older man. However, Burnet's heavy editorializing of anything that did not fit in with his grand plan might have led him to omit any fond recollection of Rochester's former mentor. Certainly, Rochester retained enough affection for Whitehall to correspond with him for the rest of their lives. Whitehall sent him his portrait and a 'Hudibrastic verse epistle' in 1667, stating, in a reference to his flushed face in the picture, that 'that red letter in each cheek / Speaks Holyday, not Ember Week / So incorporeal, so airy / This Christmas 'twill be ta'en for fairy', and Rochester was given one of only a dozen copies of Whitehall's 1677 work *Hexastichon hieron*. Wood suggests that this work, a collection of biblical verses, was 'chiefly composed' for Rochester, indicating that Whitehall still felt great affection for his protégé nearly two decades after he had left his charge. Had it been a relationship merely based on carnal gratification and exploitation, it is unlikely to have endured, although it is possible to see Whitehall as ever the Falstaffian schemer, keen to maintain influence within court. Another recipient of the book was Charles II, implying that Whitehall was reluctant to give up his jockeying for position.

Something that Whitehall was highly likely to have been involved with, however, was Rochester's poetic development. The first poem attributed to Rochester is a piece of laudatory verse addressed to Charles II upon his return to England, dated around May 1660 and signed 'Rochester, Wadham College'. As Rochester's first work, it bears reprinting in full:

> Virtue's triumphant shrine! who dost engage
> At once three Kingdoms in a Pilgrimage;
> Which in ecstatic duty strive to come
> Out of themselves as well as from their home:
> Whilst England grows one Camp, and London is
> Itself the Nation, not Metropolis;
> And loyal Kent renews her Arts again,
> Fencing her ways with moving Groves of Men,
> Forgive this distant homage, which does meet
> Your blest approach on sedentary feet:
> And though my youth, not patient yet to bear
> The weight of Arms, denies me to appear
> In Steel before you; yet great SIR, approve
> My manly wishes, and more vigorous Love;
> In whom a cold Respect were Treason to
> A Father's Ashes, greater than to you;
> Whose one Ambition 'tis for to be known,
> By daring Loyalty, your Wilmot's son.

For a thirteen-year-old, this is impressively accomplished writing, taking the traditional poetic trope of a paean of praise to a new ruler and offering a heartfelt, personal perspective on his accession. The most interesting passage is the last third, which, in its references to 'the weight of Arms' and 'your Wilmot's son', would have served to remind Charles—hardly by then a shrine of virtue—both of his friend's loyalty and of Rochester's willingness to emulate his father's military prowess, had the occasion called for it.

The other poems ascribed to Rochester from his Wadham days are a Latin elegy on the death of Mary, the Princess Royal, 'Impia blasphemi', and a longer poem, 'To Her Sacred Majesty, the Queen Mother', commiserating with her on her loss. As Mary died on Christmas Eve 1660, the poems can be confidently dated as early 1661. There is less of interest in these ambitious but rather strained poems, save an early touch of satire (possibly dictated by Whitehall) when he attacks the incompetent physicians who failed to save Mary's life:

And the forlorn Physicians imprecate,
Say they to death new poisons add and fire;
Murder securely for reward and hire;
Art's Basilicks, that kill whom ere they see,
And truly write bills of Mortality;
Who least the bleeding Corps should them betray,
First drain those vital speaking streams away.

If the intention behind the poems was to curry royal favour, it succeeded. Charles, whose gratitude towards all those who had helped him in his travels was at its peak, ordered in February 1661 that Rochester be granted a pension, paid retrospectively since his arrival at Oxford, of £500 a year, the equivalent of around £40,000 today and a fortune to a thirteen-year-old undergraduate. Given that Charles and Rochester had not yet met, unless their paths had crossed on a fleeting royal visit to Oxford in late 1660, this was an act of impetuous generosity rather than a carefully considered reward. However, in what would be a constant factor in Rochester and Charles's relationship, the generous promise was seldom backed up with the arrival of the funds themselves.

On 9 September 1661, Rochester's career at Oxford, which had lasted just over a year and a half, came to an end. At the formal ceremony of Convocation, he was awarded the degree of Master of Arts. Tellingly, the Chancellor of the university was now Edward Hyde, the Earl of Clarendon, whose appointment symbolized the way in which a role that had once been synonymous with Cromwell had now returned to Royalist hands. Clarendon's association with Rochester, a cousin by marriage to his mother's first husband, had been lifelong, and there was clear and obvious symbolism in the way that Rochester had the degree conferred upon him 'very affectionately... by a kiss on the left cheek'. Although few present would have known of the bond between the two, Rochester was being welcomed into the Royalist establishment even at his young age. His final act as a student was to endow Wadham College with four splendid silver pint pots. Like many a careless young undergraduate, he left several of his bills unpaid, much to his mother's later chagrin.

The importance of Rochester's Oxford career has been much discussed. As he attended the university for a relatively short time (though normal by the standards of the day), his close association with Whitehall coloured his impressions of the university. No reference is ever made to his having acquired any other friends or companions there, or having been influenced by any of the leading figures there (there is no evidence, for instance, that he ever met Wren, who was at Oxford throughout 1661). Yet what his studies undoubtedly did was to place him on the road of experience. The 'debauched' nature of his time at university, which Burnet put down to 'the humour of the time [that had] wrought so much upon him', was one of sexual deviance and alcoholic overindulgence. It is also possible that the syphilis which would plague him throughout his life was first contracted from a prostitute in one of the city's many whorehouses or alehouses, which were frequented by the students and workers of the town alike. (Their presence was so notorious that one street by Merton was known as 'Grope Cunt Lane', later commuted to 'Grope Lane'.) With tertiary syphilis not appearing for over a decade after first contact, the seeds of Rochester's later illness may have been sown here, if he lost his virginity at this young age. However, the university was also a source of intellectual excitement, and even the early poems that we have of Rochester's hint at an emerging, questioning intelligence that would develop more fully over time.

When Rochester left Oxford, he was fourteen years old. Not quite old enough to be presented at court, he instead was able to complete his education by undertaking the traditional adventure of a young nobleman, the European grand tour. The displaced Francis Giffard was presumably not thought to be worldly enough to accompany Rochester across Europe, and, much as he might have enjoyed it, there was never any question of Whitehall leading his protégé across the taverns and brothels of the continent. It was the prerogative of Charles II to suggest a potential tutor for the grand tour for any young nobleman, and he nominated a man named Andrew Balfour. Charles had been introduced to Balfour by his own physician, Sir John Wedderburn, when he arrived at court, and was impressed by his erudition and charm.

Balfour occupies an interesting position in Rochester's life as he was one of the very few mentors and substitute father-figures he acquired who was clearly a moral and decent person. Burnet refers to him as a 'learned and worthy man', and also notes, towards the end of Rochester's life, 'how much he was obliged to love and honour this his governor', valuing him second only to his parents as a loved one. Even allowing for exaggeration, their relationship was a close one. Balfour came from a wealthy Scottish family, and studied philosophy and arithmetic at St Andrews, later completing his studies at Oxford and in Italy and France, where he had recently graduated from the University of Caen in 1661. Knowing something of Europe, and being, at thirty, young enough to remain energetic but old enough to act as a responsible mentor to Rochester, he accepted Charles's request and the two men set off together in November 1661, along with Rochester's 'servants and trunks'. Like his father, he was unwilling to attempt the trip in anything other than luxury.

For the next three years, Rochester and Balfour travelled across Europe together. Rochester is not known to have produced any poetry during this period, and although he must have written to his mother and possibly to Verney and Clarendon, none of his letters exist. The only definite proof of his whereabouts at this time is that he was briefly enrolled as a visiting student at the University of Padua in 1664, where he signed the visitors' book, and that earlier that year he was received by Balfour's friend Walter Pope in Venice. For anyone interested in Rochester, this period might be frustratingly opaque, were it not for the indefatigable Balfour, who later wrote an account of his travels. Published posthumously as *Letters to a Friend*, the book offers what the subtitle terms 'excellent directions and advices for travelling through France and Italy'. Given that Balfour was far from a professional grand tourer, it seems appropriate to take this account and retrospectively apply it to his journey with Rochester, even if the latter is not mentioned by name once in the story.

If one expects stories of how Rochester 'swived more whores, more ways than Sodom's walls', then the reader is likely to be disappointed. Instead, Balfour offers a minutely detailed piece of social history that gives a fascinating insight into what the privileged, gilded youth of the day experienced. Certainly, the tour appears to have been designed with Balfour's own interests and enthusiasms in mind, rather than trying to cater for Rochester's emergent desires. Yet, despite the debaucheries of Oxford, Rochester remained an intellectually curious, self-assured young man, and the pleasure that he took from his journeys was that of a sophisticated young nobleman who was completing his education in style. Had he not had these three years travelling, then it is highly unlikely that he would have acquired the poise and élan that were to be such features of his later appearance at court.

Assuming for the sake of argument that Balfour's account in his book relates to his travels with Rochester, their adventure can be reconstructed in precise detail. They left London for France in late November 1661, staying at Dieppe when they arrived. The early accounts of their travels offer some amusing details of the social world of wealthy seventeenth-century France, such as visiting the enormous bell at Rouen Cathedral and tasting the much-renowned cream at Sotteville. Their lodgings were humble but comfortable, and the young Rochester probably enjoyed his first experience of European life.

However, his arrival in Paris in early 1662 is vastly more significant. Balfour and Rochester spent most of the year together there, and the experience of *la vie Parisienne* was an immensely formative one for the younger man. Louis XIV, the so-called 'Sun King', had been ruling since 1654 and had gradually been increasing his influence to create an absolutist monarchy. After the death of his long-serving and hugely capable first minister Cardinal Mazarin in 1661, Louis decided that he was able to govern alone and set about reforming France on a scale that was barely conceived of by his predecessors. He revolutionized the tax system, saving the country from bankruptcy, introduced a countrywide series of courts, massively reduced the independence of the nobility, and improved the military, even as he brokered complex peace treaties.

For energy backed up by achievement, there was nobody like him in Europe; certainly, Charles (who had raised a much-needed five million francs, or around £250,000, by selling him Dunkirk in 1662) looks like an amateur in comparison. The greatest demonstration of his opulence was his palace at Versailles. Balfour and Rochester visited the unfinished building during their visit, and even in its embryonic state Balfour was moved to call it 'a most delicate fine place'. Perhaps his Scottish sensibilities might have been more tested had he seen it a couple of decades later, in all its glitzy, gaudy glory.

Another aspect of Louis' reign that might well have appealed to Rochester was his status as a patron of the arts. Molière was granted the title of Troupe de Monsieur, effectively licensing him as court playwright. His witty, socially pointed satires were influential on the licentious Restoration comedies that were about to become popular in England, and there is a good chance that Rochester and Balfour both saw his play *L'École des femmes* when it was first performed at the Palais Royal in December 1662. Although the play's wry account of sexual and romantic shenanigans seemed impossibly daring when it was produced, and unthinkable to have been staged without royal approval, the cynicism that it expressed about male and female relations was an influence on Rochester, a man who would later begin a poem with the words 'Love a woman? You're an ass!'

It is impossible to say whether Rochester was sexually active during his travels with Balfour, but it is unlikely that his mentor was as eager to drive him towards the taverns and whorehouses of France as Whitehall would have been. It is probable, however, that Rochester encountered some of the more notorious figures at court. He visited Charles's sister Henrietta, who was nicknamed 'Minette', and carried a letter of introduction from the king. As was typical for a royal sister at the time, she had been used for political marriage and had been married to her cousin, the flamboyant Philippe, Duke of

Orléans, to strengthen military bonds between France and England.

Philippe was a remarkable figure by the standards of that, or any other, time. Rampantly and prodigiously homosexual, with occasional grudging forays into the marital bed, he also had a penchant for donning female attire and adopting the personae of shepherdesses and milkmaids. His inclination for buggery—what Mazarin described as 'the Italian vice'—was tolerated as it was felt that this would distract him from taking any interest in the royal throne. However, the dissatisfied Henrietta purportedly began an affair with the uncompromisingly heterosexual King Louis, leading to an outraged Philippe becoming even more blatant in his actions. Whether the child that was eventually born to Henrietta was the result of Philippe's sporadic carnal incursions or Louis' bastard daughter can never be known, but either way it reinforced the idea of the French court as a licentious and potentially dangerous place, and it was to this that Rochester was exposed.

At the time, however, Rochester found himself at a court that was deeply in thrall to libertine ideas. These were espoused in comedy by Molière, but had been expressed as serious philosophy by Montaigne in the sixteenth century, who posited the idea that people should not live according to strictures laid down by society or religion, but instead should be free to follow their own inclinations. This admirably far-sighted view was quickly taken up by the wits of the court, and Rochester may have encountered the poet Nicolas Boileau (whose lengthy, topical satires would later directly influence 'A Satire against Reason and Mankind') and the aristocratic wit and memoirist François de la Rochefoucauld, as well as Molière. It is unlikely that, if they did meet him, they would have taken a great deal of notice of a fifteen-year-old boy, so any personal acquaintance would have probably been slight. It was still a fecund time, though, and an impressionable young man could have drunk deeply from the well of learned experience.

Not so Balfour, who cheerily decried France as a place in which 'out of Paris there is little... to be seen or learned'. He gives a litany of his favourite bookshops, eulogizes Graves—the 'best wine about

Bordeaux'—and treats the various unlikely sounding holy relics at Saint-Denis with the raised eyebrow that they deserve, remarking drily upon 'one of the nails that fixed our saviour's body to the cross' and 'the lantern that was carried before Judas when he betrayed our saviour'. Eventually, by the beginning of 1663, Balfour and Rochester had seen enough of France and took a boat from Cannes to Italy, which would prove a rather different experience for them.

If France was licentious enough, with the king's homosexual brother rampant and daring philosophical ideas being muttered around court, then Italy—the country that had produced Machiavelli, Caravaggio and the Borgias—was steeped in sin and style, in roughly equal measure. If Rochester's sexual escapades in France consisted of avoiding (or allowing) the advances of bored noblemen, then Italy was a different and more productive experience for him. Not for nothing was Signior Dildo said to be a 'noble Italian' in the titular poem.

Even the honest Balfour was driven to subterfuge upon arrival, with the Italian authorities conducting a thorough search of all visitors for 'prohibited books' and 'secret weapons', but he noted, with the confidence of a worldly man, that 'there are ways enough to convey books, or any other thing of whatsoever nature'. Whether this was a reference to bribes or the placing of forbidden items in intimate places around the body is unclear, but either way Rochester might, albeit briefly, have seen a more grubbily practical side of his governor than the idealized philosopher. It probably also pleased him that Balfour, suspicious of the quality of Italian water, forbade its consumption, indicating that they should instead refresh themselves with wine.

The two men travelled at a leisurely pace through the sites and glories of Renaissance Italy. The country was at relative peace at this time, although a heavy plague three decades earlier in Milan had caused chaos and the Counter-Reformation had increased papal power immensely. Artistically, Italy was in the midst of the *seicento* and was entering the Baroque era, which was beginning to dominate art and architecture, and which offered Rochester a chance to see how the tastes of the wealthy were becoming far more opulent and grandiose. If Balfour had nothing but praise for the 'beautiful' city of Florence and its 'glorious' Medici Chapel, he was sceptical about the comforts that were on offer, describing Italian bed linen as 'very nasty' and standards of accommodation as 'unclean'.

Eventually, they arrived at Rome, and temptation was again thrust upon Rochester. This was partly the usual carnal attractions of a large and cosmopolitan city, especially if he diligently followed his mentor's instructions and only drank wine, but there was also the possibility of his being wooed into the Catholic faith. No evidence exists to suggest that Rochester ever had any personal interest in popery, unlike Charles II, but for an impressionable young man the temptation of a religion where sins could simply be washed off the slate after confession was considerable. Balfour arranged various audiences and receptions with friends of his, almost certainly innocently, and the two were received at the Vatican. It is likely that the young aristocrat was both flattered and beguiled by the trappings of Catholicism, a world away from the drabness of Cromwell and Puritanism. The beautiful young man was considered enough of a notable figure to have a portrait painted by the contemporary draughtsman Lorenzo Magalotti—at least the likeness is said to be of Rochester, although it bears little resemblance to other images of him. Yet the religious orthodoxy he had encountered during his time at Burford and in Francis Giffard's instruction was also hardwired within him, and was to remain so for the rest of his life. In a sense, Rome epitomized the two sides of him in constant conflict: the sensual pleasure-seeker and the intellectually curious orthodox. This time, it seems as if orthodoxy triumphed.

Balfour and Rochester continued to travel around the classical sites of Italy after they left Rome, visiting Mount Vesuvius and the Doge's Palace in Venice in late 1664. The latter city, famed for its architecture and art, had also become synonymous with homosexuality, which Balfour tactfully describes as 'people of many nations with different habits', but also boasted many of Europe's finest courtesans. Quite possibly Rochester, like many a cosmopolitan young man, sampled all the pleasures that the city offered.

After their incursion there, the two headed to Padua and its university, where Balfour was somewhat alarmed by the poor reputation of the students and their 'beastly custom of carrying arms in the night'. Here, where he studied briefly, Rochester was an *ultramontane*, or foreign student. He was not alone; the city thronged with foreigners of all kinds, who naturally divided into subsets based on national background, and it was far from uncommon to see students fighting those from the countries of their enemies. The university had an excellent reputation for the study of law and philosophy, and Elizabeth I's spymaster Francis Walsingham had been a student the previous century. Lectures were lengthy, deeply formal and, thanks to the thick Venetian dialect in which they were delivered, near-incomprehensible to many.

Padua was also famous for its scientific excellence. Galileo had been chair of mathematics, and the anatomical theatre and public dissections were legendary. Here, Rochester might well have developed his lifelong interest not only in the sexual aspects of the body but also in its corporeal, transitory nature. For a man who took pleasure in exposing the skull beneath the skin, it seems unthinkable that he was not inspired, and perhaps terrified, by what he saw.

Eventually, Balfour and Rochester prepared to leave behind Italy's penetrating academia, excellent wine and filthy inns and returned to Paris in late 1664. Here, Rochester had another reception with Henrietta, where he was entrusted with a letter for Charles II. This simultaneously served as a formal means of introduction to the court at Whitehall and furthered diplomatic relations between France and England, thereby enveloping Rochester in the world of politics. By now seventeen, he was an assured and confident young man, for whom the successes of the grand tour had been a necessary step in his maturity and social and sexual development. His gratitude to Balfour was sincere and generous, to the point that he insisted that Balfour remain for a while as his guest after their return to England.

When he finally arrived at court for the first time on Christmas Eve 1664 to deliver Henrietta's letter, a comet blazed through the

sky. Visible since 14 December and simultaneously a source of wonder and fear, it was believed to be a portent, although whether for
good or ill nobody knew. In a later letter Charles described it as 'no
ordinary star', perhaps with the intention of flattering his friend
Wilmot's young son by association. Rochester, newly arrived at court
and ready to make a name for himself, may have enjoyed the symbolism of a brief, brilliant light making an indelible impression on all
who saw it.

[3]

'The easiest

KING

A N D

BEST-BRED MAN

alive'

✳

[*1660–1664*]

ON 23 MAY 1660, with Rochester in the first months of his university career, his sovereign Charles II departed from the Dutch port of Scheveningen, bound for England. On his arrival, he would be acclaimed by Parliament as the lawful and rightful king. The ship that he sailed on had previously been known as the *Naseby*. Perhaps mindful of the fact that this had been the battle where Charles I's army had been annihilated, thus effectively ending the Civil War, Charles ordered that its name be changed to the *Royal Charles* before he sailed. As many as 100,000 people cheered him as he departed, accompanied on board by courtiers, Royalists and the remains of his exiled family. It was undeniably a triumphant occasion, and one that the king, on the cusp of turning thirty, no doubt enjoyed. Yet Charles's thoughts were not solely of pageantry and pomp. Instead, they turned to vengeance.

Even after Cromwell had died and his hapless son Tumbledown Dick had taken his place, there was still uncertainty whether a restoration of the monarchy could take place. The various uprisings that the Royalists had coordinated had all failed miserably, in no small part because there was little public appetite for the return of the monarchy. The Commonwealth and Protectorate regimes had been repressive, small-minded and often brutal, but they had become a way of life. 'Better the devil you know' was the shrugged response of many to the topsy-turvy complications of government.

Throughout 1659 and during the early part of 1660, the exiled royal court was a very sorry affair. Fantastical rumours came from England, relating that many cities were on the verge of rising. The closest that these had come to fact was when Sir George Booth, a former Parliamentarian, attempted to coordinate a Royalist uprising in August that year. He was defeated by the Parliamentarian general John Lambert at Winnington Bridge and was reduced to fleeing from the battle disguised as a woman—but was soon discovered. One observer, a Dr Moore, wrote that Booth's 'glorious pretext of a free Parliament and the subjects' liberty, is all ended under a wench's petticoat; which makes many conclude him to be rather a fool, knave or coward'. Lambert was subsequently made major-general of all the armed forces in England. It looked as if neo-Cromwellian military rule would become the norm.

Charles, whose movements over those months took him from one country to another in vain search of money and backing for an attempted coup, could have been forgiven for resigning himself to a peripatetic lifestyle of drifting around Europe, stateless, throneless and powerless. He fell into a deep depression, with the same feelings of impotence and misery that he had experienced after his escape from Worcester in 1651. His only hope of regaining the throne was to enter into an agreement with a military power such as Spain, again offering the undesirable prospect of invading his own country with the backing of foreign money. As 1659 drew to an end, the earlier hope and euphoria brought about by Cromwell's death ebbed away. However, Charles's life was typified by sudden reversals of fortune, and 1660 was to be no different. This time, he owed everything to the unlikely figure of General George Monck.

Monck was initially a supporter of Charles I, but then transferred his allegiance and became an arch-Parliamentarian. While still a Royalist, he was imprisoned in 1644 by Fairfax, changed allegiance, and was then released, in part due to his previous experience fighting in the Irish War, and redeployed to Ireland, where he negotiated an armistice. This, typically, his Parliamentary superiors refused to honour. He was then sent to Scotland, where he was made commander-in-chief of the army, and then governor, a safe role for an avowed loyalist. His friendship with Cromwell was deep and sincere, and his transferred loyalty to the Protectorate absolute. Tellingly, when Charles II wrote him a letter in 1655 which appeared to suggest that he might be persuaded to change sides once more, Monck had no hesitation in sending Cromwell a copy, who then encouraged him to apprehend Charles should he ever appear in Scotland. There is no reason to doubt that Monck would have done so.

However, on 1 January 1660, prompted by General John Lambert declaring against the Rump Parliament and in favour of an interim government, a Committee of Safety that he belonged to, Monck's army left Scotland and began to progress towards London. For what purpose it was initially hard to judge. Charles's supporter John Mordaunt wrote of Monck's motives that month that 'it will be like the last scene of some excellent play, which the most judicious cannot positively say how it will end'. Virtually any option appeared open to him, equipped as he was with a large, powerful and well-trained army. Some speculated that he would ally himself with Lambert and create a military power that would put either of the men in the role of Protector, while others, more optimistically, suggested that he would return to his Royalist origins and declare for Charles II.

Monck may have been unsure himself what he hoped to achieve by his return to London. Perhaps he would even have sided with Tumbledown Dick, reviving his fortunes with the aid of a loyal army behind him. However, it was not to be. When he encountered Lambert's forces on his march, there was no grand alliance, nor even a pitched battle. Instead, Monck subsumed Lambert's confused and chaotic men, who had not been expecting to encounter such a well-armed and trained adversary, into his own ranks and arrived in London on 3 February. Here, he bided his time for a week before playing his hand and asking for the election of a new Parliament. Those in power were hardly in a position to refuse a strong military force, so a new Convention Parliament, mainly Royalist in its construction, was created in March.

By this point, the recall of Charles seemed an inevitability. Lambert, the most implacable enemy of the crown, was captured (by Robert Whitehall's old friend Richard Ingoldsby) and sent to the Tower, accused of having plotted to stir up a mutiny, and Booth, divested of his wench's petticoat, was released. Monck, by now committed to the restoration of Charles as the country's best means of unifying itself, contacted him secretly and negotiated the basis on which he might return to England as king. Monck knew that Charles's first instinct might be to attempt to tear England apart with mass persecution of Puritans and Parliamentarians alike, and so the Declaration of Breda was agreed in early April 1660. The conditions of this were that Charles would issue a general pardon to those who had opposed him in the Civil War and Interregnum, that all who had bought property confiscated from the Royalists would be allowed to retain it, that religious toleration would be observed, and that the army would become the servant of the crown and be paid monies owed to it in full. Nonetheless, the same Act declared that no public Acts passed by Parliament since 1641 were binding, as they took place without the king's consent.

To some extent, Charles's hands were tied. Had he refused any of the conditions that Monck suggested, his sole chance of a Parliament-approved restoration would have disappeared, and his remaining supporters with it. He lacked money, support, a home or status; even his clothes were threadbare. To be offered them all, even with strings attached, was an opportunity that he could not refuse. However, even with his back against the wall, Charles would not join fully in the 'free and general pardon' that Monck asked for, instead specifically exempting 'such persons as shall hereafter be excepted by parliament'. This set the scene for the revenge that Charles, with Clarendon's aid, visited upon those who he saw as responsible for his father's murder, his long exile, and the deaths of many of his friends and supporters.

Monck, knowing that those who Charles wanted removed from the scene were no friends to him, assented. The Declaration of Breda was made public on 1 May, by which time the ever-fickle Parliament had unanimously approved the king's restoration. This was helped by a tactful letter that Charles had written to the Commons' Speaker, in which he claimed that the monarchy and Parliament had a symbiotic relationship and that the powers of each institution 'were best preserved by preserving the other'. Flattering the 'wise and dispassionate men and good patriots', he ended his letter by alluding to his eventful experiences abroad, saying 'we, and we hope our subjects, shall be the better for what we have seen and suffered'.

A little humility and tact went a long way. When Charles heard that Parliament had proclaimed him king, he gratefully began making a stately progress from Breda in a grand entourage of over seventy coaches, receiving the Parliamentary commissioners who came armed with enormous sums of money, rumoured to have been at least £50,000 in bills and gold sovereigns. Such were the perks of kingship. Charles, who had been living hand to mouth for years, was overwhelmed at the way in which his fortunes had suddenly changed. He received well-wishers, sycophants and offers of sex by the score. He thanked the first, ignored the second, and was discerning with the third.

Eventually, he departed on the *Royal Charles*, accompanied by the commissioners, his family and Clarendon, who had as much of a vested interest in the success of the restoration as Charles did, given the two men's long history together. The commander of the fleet charged with supervising the king's return was Edward Montagu, and he had a young assistant, a naval clerk called Samuel Pepys. Pepys had already begun keeping his famous diary, and his entry for 23 May is telling. He writes of 'infinite shooting off of the guns, and that in a disorder on purpose, which was better than if it had been otherwise'. Still, Charles had been away for nearly a decade. A little pageantry could be tolerated.

It was on this journey back, Pepys reports, that Charles began to tell the story of his adventures while escaping from Worcester. Pepys notes that he was 'ready to weep' as Charles recounted the story of the privations that he had undergone—'four nights and three days on foot, every step up to the knees in dirt, with nothing but a green coat and a pair of country breeches on'. Even when he reached France, 'he looked so poorly that people went into the rooms before he went away, to see whether he had not stolen something or other'. Charles was not sharing these anecdotes in a spirit of light-hearted ribaldry, a happy man excited about resuming his rightful throne. Instead, Charles, described as 'very active and stirring' by Pepys, prepared for his future actions by impressing upon his various supporters the torments and sufferings that he had undergone. His father's fate was notorious, but few knew what had happened to the prince. Now, he was determined to let the world understand, before taking swift and brutal action against his enemies.

Charles landed in Dover on Friday 25 May 1660, eschewing the ornate boat sent for him to make the final journey to shore by barge. Pepys noted that one of the king's favoured dogs—presumably a spaniel—'shit the boat, which made us laugh, and me think that a King and all that belong to him are just as others are'. Charles's ability to connect with his subjects and be 'just as others are' proved crucial throughout the early days of his return to England, when the celebrating and joy masked a deeper uncertainty as to whether he would be a wise, kind ruler, or a despot.

Greeted with, as Pepys put it, 'all imaginable love and respect' by Monck, Charles began his journey, greeted with near-hysteria along the way. It was a remarkable volte-face from even a few months before, when it had seemed that the only way for him to present his kingship was through armed insurgency. Now, all was smiles and rejoicing. Aware of the symbolism that his return carried, he first headed to Canterbury, where he inducted Monck, Montagu and two others into the Order of the Garter, pointedly rewarding the former Parliamentarians and loyal Royalists alike, before he entered London on 29 May, his thirtieth birthday.

Tens of thousands thronged the streets, desperate to see this near-mythical figure. Some were the sons of those who had tried to capture or kill Charles a decade earlier; others were his would-be captors themselves. Yet, as John Evelyn wrote in his diaries:

> all this without one drop of blood, and by that very army, which rebelled against him… such a Restoration was never seen in the mention of any history, ancient or modern… nor so joyful a day, and so bright, ever seen in this nation.

He could be forgiven his hyperbole, because he was sharing in an event that was the polar opposite of Charles I's execution a decade before. That had been characterized by judicial violence and met with a chilled, appalled silence. Now, everyone wanted to forget the horror of the past decade and look for something optimistic and fresh. Tellingly, one of the first places that Charles visited was the Banqueting Hall at Whitehall, outside which his father had been executed. With the handsome, charismatic young king eager to mend fences, claiming in a speech that he was 'set to endeavour by all means for the restoring of this nation to freedom and happiness', the days of persecution and misery appeared over.

Of course, they were not. Charles sought to present a calm, jocular exterior, but inside he was hell-bent on revenge against those who had wronged him. The Act of Oblivion and Indemnity that Parliament passed in August 1660 offered a pardon to all who had served against the king, with the sting that it also meant severe punishment for anyone who had been responsible for the regicide of Charles I. The great figures of Cromwell's government often owed their fortunes and favour to their willingness to be complicit in Charles I's execution. Initially, seven men were exempted from the general pardon, then more were added as it became convenient for the new regime.

While Charles took great pains to present himself as rising above petty vindictiveness, allowing Clarendon to deal with much of the politicking and horse-trading between the Commons and the Lords, his true wishes could be discerned in a speech given by Orlando Bridgeman, Chief Justice of the Common Peace, who declared that the blood of Charles I 'cries for vengeance, and it will never be appeased without a bloody sacrifice'. The accused men represented the crème de la crème of Cromwellian influence, and the result of their trials was a foregone conclusion, with the judges and jury as carefully vetted to ensure the right verdicts as they had been for Charles I's execution. The fate of Major-General Thomas Harrison, the first to be executed, was typical. The seventeenth of the fifty-nine commissioners to sign Charles I's death warrant and leader of the anti-Royalist Fifth Monarchist group, he was hanged, drawn and quartered in spectacularly bloody fashion at Charing Cross on 13 October 1660.

On and on it went. The regicides made speeches from the gallows in which they defended their actions as arising from principle and called upon God to be their witness. Evelyn called upon the 'miraculous providence' of the same God as he saw their bloodied remains prominently displayed in public. Residents of Charing Cross, where many of the executions took place, complained that the smell of gore was making the air putrid.

Charles made sure that he mixed mercy with harshness. The poet John Milton, who had published pamphlets urging republicanism, such as *The Ready and Easy Way to Establishing a Free Commonwealth*, had his books burnt and his arrest ordered, but interventions from powerful friends, including the MP and poet Andrew Marvell and the Secretary of State William Morice, saw that he was eventually released from prison, albeit with a steep fine of £150.

Others were less fortunate. Clarendon saw to it that many of the surviving regicides at home and abroad were killed, whether judicially in England or simply by being assassinated in Europe, as in the case of the Swiss exile John Lisle, murdered in a Lausanne churchyard in 1664. Those who were not thus disposed of were either showily pardoned or, more commonly, imprisoned indefinitely. Charles ensured that he was never associated with any of the extrajudicial executions; possibly he was unaware of them, as Clarendon once noted that it was beneath the dignity of the new king to be seen to engage with his father's murderers on their level. The hand of vengeance stretched all over the British Isles, and the Scottish turncoats, as they were seen, were not forgotten, especially those who had once been familiars of Charles. One such man executed in Edinburgh was a Scottish nobleman, Sir Archibald Johnston, Lord Warriston. Captured in France after many travels and driven mad by psychological and probably physical torture, his eventual death was a relief of sorts. His young nephew Gilbert Burnet, who observed his execution, would later write biographies of both Rochester and Charles II.

As the round of killings and deaths went on, attitudes began to change. What was initially enacted as the righteous and just application of vengeance spread to encompass reprisal against anyone who was seen as a threat to the new regime. Those who were suspected of plotting against Charles and the monarchy were summarily executed, as was any dissident element. The most ghoulish moment of all came on the anniversary of Charles I's death, 30 January 1661. The corpses of Oliver Cromwell and others who had been responsible for Charles's execution were exhumed, taken to the Old Bailey, posthumously given the death sentence, and then hanged and decapitated, before their heads were stuck up on poles. Cromwell had already been hanged in effigy the previous year, but Charles had ordered the likeness to be taken down. The real thing would prove to be far more gorily compelling. For all his charm and social ease, Charles was implacable when it came to dealing with his enemies, and after the bloodbath that followed his accession to the throne, it was made clear that mercy would be tempered with a dedication to settling old scores that would put an Old Testament deity to shame. Rochester would still see the heads and other parts of the regicides' bodies at the city gates seven years later.

It was not all bloodshed. Charles was equally keen to ensure that those who had supported him in the years of exile were well rewarded. Monck was the most notable recipient of royal favour, being created Gentleman of the Bedchamber and Duke of Albemarle as well as having the Order of the Garter bestowed upon him, symbolizing his crucial place in Charles's esteem. The king ran the risk of controversy by rewarding those who had accompanied him in exile over those who had remained in England; the dispossessed joked bleakly that 'the king had passed an act of oblivion for his friends and of indemnity for his enemies'. Charles had no desire to reward those who had been passive in their loyalty to the crown, and most of those who were raised to office and given pensions were those who had been of vital use to him over the previous decade without any definite expectation of personal gain.

Charles was both canny and just in those he chose to reward. The likes of Monck and Clarendon (who was given his earldom in 1661 after being created Baron Hyde in 1660) were obvious figures to whom he owed a debt of gratitude, but just as important were people such as Thomas Killigrew, a former playwright who had been at the king's side during the years of exile. Regarded by Charles as a licensed fool of sorts, he was created Groom of the Bedchamber, as well as being given the unofficial role of court jester. Pepys later noted of him that 'he may with privilege revile or jeer anybody, the greatest person, without offence, by the privilege of his place'.

Others were not forgotten either. Rochester, as noted earlier, was awarded a substantial pension in belated gratitude for his father's service, and many of those involved in the Worcester flight were also well recompensed. This generosity came about because Charles was, temporarily at least, in the best financial situation he had enjoyed since his childhood, thanks to the annual grant of £1.2 million that Parliament voted him to run the government. (In practice, he never received anything like this amount, so he had to introduce taxes to compensate.) He had his father's estates and property restored to him, most conspicuously the royal residence of the Palace of Whitehall, and also his goods, jewels and pictures, which a House of Lords committee voted should be returned to him immediately, on pain of seizure from their new owners by the armed forces.

In the official list of gifts and handouts, porters, barbers and pages were rewarded as often as great lords and ministers of state, and these payments were often associated with statements that they were made 'in consideration of the faithful service he has done us during this time of our being in foreign parts'. Many of those who had been exiled with Charles were still young enough to take an active part in England's government. Pepys reports, with some irritation, that the naval offices were overrun with Cavaliers such as James, Duke of York and Prince Rupert, whose associate Sir Robert Holmes's presence was particularly unwelcome to Pepys 'because of the old business he attempted upon my wife'.

Charles's attitude towards handing out titles and favours at the start of his reign mirrored the profligacy with which he scattered them in exile. There, they were little more than toys with which to buoy his followers' spirits, but now they were concrete signs of royal favour. At times, his naïvety showed. Charles scattered Irish titles and gifts as if they were confetti, ignoring the delicate political balance that had existed ever since Cromwell's violent incursions. He seemed to believe that Ireland was a more convenient alternative to America as a means of dispensing land. One trusty follower, a Henry Legge, was awarded the impressive but impractical gift of '3,000 acres of profitable land in Connaught'; the fact that one was hard pressed to find three acres of profitable land in 1660 Connaught had escaped his notice. However, the purpose behind Charles's actions was clear, and welcome: being seen to recognize those who had backed him for the past decade was a sure way of maintaining loyalty at a time when the future of his throne was by no means secure.

Another difficulty Charles had to face within days of becoming king was the foreign situation. His personal relations with the Dutch were very strong (when he left that country, he had been given gifts including gold plate and art), but the memory of the First Anglo-Dutch War of 1652–4 was still fresh, and the vexed question of trade routes lingered. It was clear that Charles's diplomatic skills were to be tested if he was to maintain England's sovereignty. His relationship with his cousin Louis XIV of France was close, but Spain remained a troublesome question. When Charles traipsed around Europe, he had hoped that Philip IV might come to his aid and potentially help him invade England, but now that he was king, the balance was more delicate. France and Spain were traditional enemies, and whichever one he chose to support would turn the other against him immediately. However, his family connection with Louis tipped the balance, and so, emboldened by his decision, Charles decided to act decisively by strengthening his country's long-standing alliance with Spain's long-standing nemesis, Portugal. He did this by contracting an extraordinary marriage.

The 23-year-old Catherine of Braganza of Portugal was a highly sought-after royal bride for the monarchs of Europe, who knew that she offered a fantastic sum of money as her dowry (rumoured to be around £360,000), international influence and trading privileges, as well as a necessary military partner. Charles married her on 21 May 1662, in some haste; he had probably only met her for the first time the day before. She spoke neither French nor English, so they communicated awkwardly in what little Spanish Charles had gleaned on his travels.

Catherine was an unlikely wife for the worldly king, having led a sequestered and cloistered life. Contemporary portraits, such as that by Jacob Huysmans, show a shy-looking, rather plain young woman, attired in expensive clothes and jewellery as befitted a queen, but without any sense of regality. Their marriage was not to result in children; she suffered three miscarriages, thereby depriving Charles of a legitimate heir. She was regarded with suspicion and distrust by many because of her Catholicism—although Charles I had also been married to a Catholic—and her lack of English. She was miserable, bored and homesick, all the more so because Charles, if a neglectful husband to her, was certainly a great lover of other female company.

If Rochester's famous description of Charles as 'a merry monarch, scandalous and poor' has often had the first part taken as praise and the second part discarded, then it is equally true that his preceding scornful comment—how 'restless, he rolls about from whore to whore'—was less a libel on the king and more an accurate reflection of his torrid sex life ('sex' rather than 'love' is the fitting description). The roots of this clearly stem from his European exile. A period of boredom, depression and poverty coincided with a rich period of sexual dalliance.

In addition to scores of casual liaisons with various anonymous women, Charles fathered at least four acknowledged bastard children before he became king. The first, James, by Lucy Walter, was eventually created Duke of Monmouth, while the others—Charlotte FitzRoy, Charles FitzCharles and Charlotte FitzCharles—became, respectively, a society lady, a leading figure at court and a nun. (Notably, Charlotte's mother was Elizabeth Killigrew, sister of Charles's jester Thomas; this bond brought the two men even closer.) While this was held up by contemporary Puritans as an instance of his moral turpitude, by the time Charles came to the throne, his open-minded and open-breeched attitude towards sex was approved of by most people, who felt relief that their own indiscretions would no longer be punished by whipping or imprisonment.

When Charles returned to England in 1660, there were few women in London who would not have succumbed to his advances, and he was besieged by ladies at court. Most had an agenda. Some were put forward by their parents as potential marriage material, while other, more pragmatic families attempted to use their beautiful daughters to curry their own favour with the king. Some husbands were equally happy to pimp out their own wives if it advanced their careers. The rewards, after all, were almost limitless: patronage, gifts and money flowed towards those who were fortunate enough to share the king's bed. Being in his esteem was rather like having the full glare of the sun directed towards you—a blinding, brilliant experience that only ever lasted a short time, but was mesmerizing while it did. However, even the great seducer could meet his match, and that came in the beauteous, scheming form of Barbara Villiers.

Although Nell Gwyn is traditionally the most famous of Charles's mistresses, she was essentially an unsophisticated and pretty actress who happened to capture the king's eye at an opportune moment. Barbara was an entirely different proposition. The daughter of Viscount Grandison, an ardent Royalist killed in the Civil War, she, like Charles, grew up penniless. She was also a first cousin of Rochester's mother Anne, although the two women could scarcely have been more dissimilar. Her response to the days of Protectorate rule was to embrace a hedonistic and sexually eager outlook for which she would have been imprisoned and whipped, had it been made public: a fate that would have befallen any man or woman in a similar situation.

Perhaps tired of pining for the exiled prince, Barbara married the staid and steady lawyer Roger Palmer, who soon found himself defeated. In the Restoration era women found themselves liberated in London society for the first time, but what Barbara epitomized was less liberation than full-blown sexual renegade status. She had set her cap at Charles while he was still at The Hague, when she and her husband joined the throng of those attempting to receive royal favour. Palmer was armed with a gift of £1,000 and his undying support; his wife's charms were sufficient recompense in themselves. Charles was enraptured. The difference between her and many of the other would-be royal mistresses was that she was working entirely on her own terms, rather than being cajoled into pimping herself by a husband or family. Portraits of her, often painted by the adoring Peter Lely, show a remarkably attractive woman with a full, sensuous mouth, magnetically captivating eyes and luscious dark hair. She was an impressive match for anyone, and it was only fitting to many that she should become the king's acknowledged mistress. Pepys acknowledged as much himself when he wrote in July 1660 that Charles intended 'to make her husband a cuckold'. So it proved, and she was pregnant with her first child, Anne, almost immediately. Her reputation at court was assured.

Barbara Villiers was a woman of such unremitting personal vileness and greed that she became immediately notorious. Burnet described her as 'most enormously vicious and ravenous', and her supposed friend and companion Mary Manley said of her that she was 'querulous, fierce, loquacious, excessively fond or infamously rude'. The author of the poem 'Signior Dildo' later referred to her sardonically as 'that pattern of virtue', and as soon as she was allowed to dominate court society, she wasted little time in trying to ingratiate herself with anyone perceived as her inferior. Pepys was torn when describing her, simultaneously saying 'I can never enough admire her beauty' and undercutting this with 'I know well enough she is a whore'. Her dreadful temper, spurious sense of entitlement and extravagance were legendary. Charles lavished her with an annual pension of £5,000 (around £400,000 today), and considerably more in gifts and jewellery. She spent equally enormous sums in an evening's unsuccessful gambling. Palmer was created Earl of Castlemaine in 1661, possibly as a reward for accepting the situation with good grace, and Barbara was referred to as 'Lady Castlemaine' thereafter.

The quiet, rather timid Catherine did not stand a chance against

this highly sexed Delilah and proceeded to undergo a series of humili-
ations, watching as bastard after bastard was born to Barbara in
the first half of the 1660s. The cruellest touch came in 1662, when,
against Catherine and Clarendon's wishes, Barbara was created
Lady of the Bedchamber, thereby allowing Charles constant access
to his *maîtresse-en-titre* and allowing her to flaunt her position as the
king's consort. Catherine attempted to veto this appointment, was
overruled by Charles, and had to suffer her presence at court. The
first time the two women were introduced by Charles led to a near-
hysterical meltdown on the part of Catherine, but thereafter he
compelled her to acknowledge Barbara both socially and privately.
Barbara celebrated her victory by having her portrait painted by
Lely in several guises, including Minerva, the goddess of wisdom,
and, most notoriously, as the Virgin Mary flaunting one of her bastard sons by the king, Charles FitzRoy.

Charles's treatment of his wife, while appalling on a personal
level, should be viewed in the context of the time. Flaunting one's
mistress in public was something done by gentlemen of quality,
and Charles was the exemplum of quality. We can only speculate on
which particular sexual charms of Barbara proved the most compelling—Pepys alludes to her possessing 'the skills of Aretino', a
notorious Italian sixteenth-century erotic poet. Yet the far greater
consequence that this relationship had was to alienate Charles from
Clarendon, long his most consistent counsellor and guide. While
Clarendon accepted that it would be absurd for Charles to be 'ignorant of the opposite sex', he saw that the unrestrained Barbara was
an embarrassment to the court and begged Charles to give her up.
He thereby drew an uncharacteristically stinging letter from the
normally amicable monarch: 'if you desire to have the continuance
of my friendship, meddle no more with this business... whosoever I
find to be my Lady Castlemaine's enemy in this matter, I do promise
upon my word to be his enemy as long as I live.'

While Charles was accessible and charming, there was a determined, even bloody-minded side to him too. Like his father,
he believed that kingship allowed him to do as he pleased, and

consequences and the feelings of others could be damned. He had other affairs, as did the ever-lascivious Barbara, but he found himself in an ideal position. He had his wealthy and tame 'little queen', his sexually voracious mistress, a mixture of wise heads to counsel him and younger ones to entertain him, and drink, lavish banquets and entertainments by the score. Although some thought his unfettered dedication to pleasure was distasteful and ostentatious, many more considered the new, unrestrained age to be an exciting and fruitful one, and Charles the suave and all-welcoming figurehead of the time.

During the Commonwealth, to be fashionable and elegant was considered anathema to the Puritan regime. The diarist Sir John Reresby noted that 'the common salutation to a man well dressed was "French dog" or the like'. However, Charles's own French family connections, to say nothing of the time that he had spent in exile there, ensured that he would soon bring about what Evelyn described as a 'politer way of living'. For men, this could be a tricky balancing act. Go too far in ostentation and one ran the risk of being seen as an effeminate and ridiculous fop, but dress in too drab a manner and the result was to be called puritanical and behind the times.

To appear successful at court, lavish clothing for men was a necessary expense. 'I must go handsomely whatever it costs me,' wrote Pepys, 'and the charge will be made up in the fruits it brings.' His diary records how his long black cloak was discarded in favour of a short one, 'long cloaks being now quite out', but then this was superseded by a coat and sword 'as the manner now among gentlemen is'. Eventually, this fashion developed even further into more elaborate outfits that might encompass a knee-length waistcoat, gorgeously decorated with gold and silver threads and tassels, a lace cravat, breeches, a fine linen shirt and a dress sword. The latter item was more a fashion accessory than an expected accoutrement to gallantry. All of this was worn under an elaborate and expensive wig. It is little wonder that Charles needed a Gentleman of the Bedchamber, a Master of Robes and a barber to attend to his everyday attire. He was no wilting violet when it came to spending serious money on his clothes. When he first came to England, he ordered five suits and cloaks from his Parisian tailor Claude Sorceau at a staggering cost of £2,000, or about £160,000 in today's money. He was somewhat inconsistent in his views, complaining to a no doubt astonished Parliament in 1662 that 'the whole nation seemed... a little corrupted in their excess of living... all men spend much more in their clothes... than they had used to do'.

For women, the process was an even more demanding and expensive one. The wife of a figure at court, or a great lady, dressed in her finery at all times in public, advertising her wealth and status by donning the most lavish attire that money could buy. This normally consisted of a gown made of silk or velvet, with a lengthy train and a petticoat underneath. The effect was then set off by braids and different linings, all of which made women look like beautiful, strutting peacocks. These various accoutrements could cost an obscene amount of money, sometimes running to hundreds of pounds for costumes for special occasions. Hair was generally an elaborate construction of frills, curls and extensions, and could take a couple of hours of preparation to give it the curled and bunched effect that is often seen in portraits.

Fashion accessories such as fans, purses and gloves were obligatory for ladies of quality, and often had symbolic connotations. A fan rapidly opened and closed, for instance, denoted sexual availability, while dropping one's glove was often intended as a hint to one's gallant that picking it up would be a precursor to later bedroom favours. Jewellery was hugely desirable and could cost the earth; Charles was said to have spent nearly £10,000, or £800,000 today, on a pair of diamond earrings, presumably for the rapacious Barbara. At a time when the average gentleman of quality was lucky to earn £500 a year, this was a staggeringly excessive sum.

To be beautiful was everything, and great pains were taken—and great expense expended—to look one's best. Both sexes ladled on vast amounts of cosmetics and make-up, which consisted of a variety of bizarre substances that included everything from urine and extract of snail to white lead and rosewater. These were slathered all over faces, hands and any other exposed part, and then beauty spots made of velvet or leather were placed over any marks or blemishes. In this way, even those who had unsightly pox scars or boils could hold their own at court. Even as the plays of the time mocked fops and courtesans who spent huge sums and effort on beauty products, which could frequently melt under the heat of candlelight or sun, there was an ever-growing appetite for more expensive and elaborate ways of concealing one's true identity. This could even lead to dying for one's art. At least one great lady of the time perished of mercury poisoning, having used so much of the stuff that it killed her. Others suffered the misfortune of having their teeth turn black, resulting in another round of treatments and palliatives.

People took such time and pains to advertise themselves because they were, essentially, all actors on an elaborately created set, with the king as producer, director and leading man—with the occasional touch of diva thrown in. Charles's easy-going nature did not conceal the fact that his court was a showy place where etiquette and a certain standard of manners prevailed at all times. Nobody was allowed to sit down in the king's presence unless they were asked to, or to turn their back on him while leaving the room.* Conversation was intended to be light, witty, clever and suggestive, preferably all at once. Men and women were entirely conscious of their rank and standing in the social order, and in the perilous game of snakes and ladders that they played, it was as easy to lose royal favour as it was to gain it. Charles was like a bright but easily bored child, wanting to be entertained at all times and taking very badly to indolence or those who would get in the way of his fun.

The court was a place where everyone knew the part they had to play, and those who succeeded did so because they had learnt their script to perfection. Royal mistresses had to be beautiful, sexually adventurous, discreet and entirely lacking in jealousy or personal whims.† In return, they were lavishly rewarded, often making advantageous marriages to wealthy lords and retiring from court,

---

* A tradition that holds true to this day in royal circles.

† Although Barbara Castlemaine, by my count, fulfils the first two and no more.

rich and sated, in their mid-twenties. Courtiers and wits had to be funny, gallant and capable of drinking their body weight in alcohol, should they wish to keep up with the king's desires. Charles's carnal and culinary requirements soon became legendary; contemporary accounts of royal banquets make breathless reference to dozens of dishes ranging from larks and veal to macaroons and cheesecakes, all washed down with brandy, beer and even—a recent import— champagne (first found at court in the early 1660s, it is referred to as 'brisk', on account of the steady rise of the bubbles in a glass). Charles's ironic nickname 'Old Rowley' probably alluded as much to his appetite for food and drink as it did to his sexual prowess. The actual Old Rowley was, fittingly, a racehorse. There is an enjoyable story that this nickname spawned a popular song of the day, revolving around Old Rowley's lecherousness and bed-hopping. When Charles heard a maid at court singing the song, he was said to have smilingly advanced towards her, saying joyfully: '''Tis Old Rowley himself, madam.'

Even if the fleshy excess and gluttony seems off-putting, even revolting, to those who were not in the midst of the court, there can be little doubt that, after the drabness and bleakness of the Commonwealth, Charles brought fun and glamour back into people's lives. The playhouses reopened, operating with a mixed repertoire of new, sexually charged comedies and revivals of Shakespeare and Jacobean plays, often in new versions by the fashionable writers of the age. The theatres could hold anything up to 800 predominantly male attendees, from nobles to servants, in such places as the Lincoln's Inn Theatre, home to William Davenant's Duke's Company. They were illuminated by wax candles, and the scenery tended to be portable, to allow for rapid set changes. Tickets cost anything from one shilling for the ordinary visitors perched in the gallery or sitting on benches in the pit to four shillings for the gentlemen and ladies of fashion in their boxes, who were more interested in holding assignations and mocking their enemies than they were in watching the entertainment on stage. (Pepys was appalled at the 'ordinary prentices and mean people' who made up much of the audience.) Visual arts flourished, with painters such as Lely and Huysmans finding themselves wealthy men, swamped by commissions from those of means who wanted to be immortalized, often in classical or heroic guise. Corpulence, gout and blemishes were tactfully omitted.

It is possible, with some imaginative licence, to reconstruct the typical day of a man or woman at court in the early 1660s. Rising early at home, either with one's husband or wife or, more daringly, with one's lover, the first part of the morning was taken up with dressing, aided by maids and servants. Breakfast was hearty, consisting perhaps of mackerel, or a slice or two of cold beef, probably with the first glass of wine of the day. After this, it was time to begin social obligations at court. Either a sedan chair or a four- or eight-horse coach (depending on ostentation and means) was the appropriate way of arriving at Whitehall, where the first priority was to head for the newly convened 'drawing rooms', an innovation imported by Queen Catherine, where another new import, tea, was consumed, gossip swapped about shenanigans and royal favour, and Charles flattered, were he present. Lunch, if taken, was similar to breakfast, and heavy on meat and fish.

In the afternoon, once make-up had been reapplied and a short walk taken in one of the nearby pleasure gardens or one of the great parks, Hyde or St James's, there was some gaming with dice, often for excessive stakes of money. Barbara Castlemaine, for instance, once lost £25,000 (around £2 million today) in one sitting. Yet to lose a great deal of cash and do so with humour and fortitude would have been graceful and gained you royal favour and a measure of respect from the other hangers-on.

Eventually, as the evening drew in, there was either an event at court such as a great ball, or a grand feast—the king dined publicly at the Banqueting House on Sundays, Wednesdays and Fridays, watched* by a carefully vetted selection of nobles and commoners, and the spectacle, as elsewhere in Europe, was regarded as a grand

* Although Charles, tiring of being gazed at by the great unwashed, all but abandoned the practice as early as 1663.

entertainment for the onlookers. This might have been preceded by a trip to the playhouse to plot scandal, or to don a mask and flirt outrageously with other men and women of quality or, even more excitingly, with those who were mere prostitutes, actresses or coachmen, which gave a sense of danger and unpredictability to the outcome. The night ended with drunkenness, often relieved by sex, whether in a grandly comfortable bed or in the grubbier surroundings of the same park in which a turn might have been taken earlier. Then, mercifully, sleep beckoned and a few hours were caught before the whole performance began afresh the following day.

To many, this might seem wearyingly mechanical and repetitive, rather than fun. Certainly, the amount of effort involved in seeking such pleasure was monumental. However, the stakes were high, and those who managed to serve with glory found themselves with titles, property and an endless variety of sexual partners from among the highest in the land. Those who disappointed or showed a lack of willing were either embarrassingly cast out from court or, still worse, had their land and property taken from them and given to those who were apparently more deserving. It was not a constant or consistent time, but playing the game with style could see vast success bestowed upon the best players.

A poem that has often been ascribed to Rochester but which feels too sketchy and obvious to be taken seriously as a work of his, is a near-contemporary satiric account of the everyday goings-on of a rake and libertine. Entitled 'Regime de Vivre', it has an appealingly licentious energy to it:

> I rise at eleven, I dine about two,
> I get drunk before seven, and the next thing I do,
> I send for my whore, when for fear of a clap,
> I spend in her hand, and I spew in her lap;
> Then we quarrel and scold, till I fall fast asleep,
> When the bitch growing bold, to my pocket does creep.
> Then slyly she leaves me, and to revenge the affront,

At once she bereaves me of money and cunt.
If by chance then I wake, hot-headed and drunk,
What a coil do I make for the loss of my punk!
I storm and I roar, and I fall in a rage.
And missing my whore, I bugger my page.
Then crop-sick all morning I rail at my men,
And in bed I lie yawning till eleven again.

The poem was passed in manuscript form from courtier to courtier, accompanied by whispered gossip about who the writer was, with especial interest in its depiction of sodomy. Allusion to it was both scandalous and intended to amuse; casual bisexuality was rife at Whitehall, as it had been at Oxford, although its open propagation was still frowned on. The poem itself shows the reverse side of the lavish play-acting and scheming that dominated the court. The anonymous narrator is more interested in sex and alcohol than pretending to be a grand man of fashion, mindful of the prevalent venereal disease that most prostitutes carried, but easily roused to temper by alcohol and the casual opportunism of theft. Rochester's oft-debated bisexuality has often been ascribed to fleeting references such as the one in 'The Disabled Debauchee': 'And the best kiss was the deciding lot/ Whether the boy fucked you, or I the boy.' Whether or not Rochester was the writer or subject of 'Regime de Vivre', the poor defenceless page is all too representative a victim of many an alcohol-fuelled debauch.

It is more tempting to see the hilariously amoral day described as a common experience in the lives of many young, bored men on the fringes of court and society life, who were not expected to put in daily appearances at the tea salons and gaming tables. They were more likely to spend their evenings drinking cheap, strong red wine at such popular taverns as The Cock—fittingly named—in Covent Garden, where they would sup on meat and pea soup before drunkenly disporting themselves, either with one of the fifteen hundred or so whores who thronged the streets of Restoration London, or in even more spectacularly public fashion.

Shortly before Rochester returned to court, there had been some very bad business involving the young playwright Charles Sedley. Sedley had been in company with some others at The Cock on 16 June 1663 and had taken a glass or six, all of which had compelled him to strip naked, defecate in the street and, in the no doubt shocked words of Pepys:

> [act] all the postures of lust and buggery that could be imagined, and abusing of scripture… preaching a Mountebank sermon from that pulpit… that being done, he took a glass of wine and washed his prick in it and then drank it off; and then took another and drank the King's health.

Even by the standards of the time, this was appalling. There was a public riot, with the onlookers throwing missiles and rocks at Sedley and his friends, who responded in kind by chucking urine-filled wine bottles back at them. Eventually, they were summoned to Westminster and indicted for causing a riot, and Sedley was fined an eye-watering £500—a year's income for many. Unabashed, he cheerily asked: 'Am I the first man ever to have been charged so much for shitting?' Most ordinary people would have been bankrupted by such a fine, but Sedley was in favour with Charles, who, amused by the goings-on, authorized that the fine be paid out of the royal purse. Sedley, undaunted by such an unpleasant scrape, continued in this vein, with Pepys noting in October 1668 that he and his friend Charles Sackville, Lord Buckhurst, had been found 'running up and down all the night with their arses bare, through the streets; and at last fighting, and being beat by the watch and clapped up all night'. Again, royal indulgence led to their salvation; Pepys tells 'how the King takes their parts; and the Lord Chief Justice hath laid the constable by the heels to answer it next Sessions'.

Charles, then, set great store by correct behaviour at court, but he also delighted in bawdiness and unrestrained wickedness, as long as it was entertainingly done. The 'merry monarch', enjoying himself immensely in this new world that he was in no small part responsible for creating, was content to allow virtually anything to take place, but even he would be challenged by the reappearance at court of a truly extraordinary figure, whose presence would threaten to upturn the basis on which the Restoration had occurred. Rochester might have been a surrogate son to Charles, but his intellectual curiosity and single-minded determination to question the whole basis of contemporary life through his poetry and actions alike would prove stimulating and challenging and would, eventually, be instrumental in bringing down the whole façade of court. The prodigal would return, and bring a new order with him.

[4]

'HIS BOASTED

HONOUR

AND

dear-born

fame'

*

[1665–1667]

THE TOWER of London in 1665 was still a forbidding place. While torture, prevalent around the time of Elizabeth I, had been outlawed, it was still offered, informally, to prisoners who were especially high-profile malefactors. While the Tower was less barbaric than the cesspit-like common jails of Newgate and the Fleet, with conditions comparatively clean and decent, it was still a place where the walls seemed to echo with the screams of the long-deceased, and where only the hardiest and most self-assured man—or the wealthiest—might manage to make himself comfortable.

Rochester, who became a guest of the Tower on 27 May 1665, was certainly self-assured, but hardy or wealthy he was not. Barely eighteen years old, he had ample time to reflect, as he took what meagre exercise and sustenance he was allowed, on the folly of what he had done. Less than six months after he had formally arrived at court, with the expectation of a glittering career as one of Charles's most beloved and trusted courtiers, he was now in a position where he was, at best, out of royal favour, and at worst in possible danger of a capital charge against his life. As would become usual, the trouble stemmed from a woman.

When Rochester entered Whitehall in 1664, his first thought had been to establish himself as a great man. To do this required royal patronage, which he had, and a wife, which he did not. Although he had no money other than his royal pension, he had a title and influential friends such as the Duke of Buckingham and Henry Savile, the licentious 22-year-old son of the arch-Royalist Sir William Savile, who was newly arrived at court and similarly eager to glut himself with the pleasures of town with like-minded company. Rochester was also friendly with Savile's elder brother George, who was made Marquess of Halifax in 1668. A more serious and politically engaged man than his brother, George was nonetheless a close friend of Buckingham and an intimate of the circle close to the king. Likewise,

Rochester's good standing with the king endeared him to many aristocratic and wealthy families keen to marry off their daughter in a socially advantageous fashion. The young man was handsome, tall and witty, all characteristics that made him infinitely preferable as a husband to some of the pox-ridden sybarites who were other candidates for marriage.

There were many young women of quality who were attached to the court, and one of the most notable both in looks and breeding was Elizabeth Malet. Fifteen years old in 1665, she was the granddaughter of Sir Francis Hawley, a wealthy Royalist and supporter of both Charles I and Charles II. She was sought after by many of the leading young men at court, including the MP and naval officer Edward Montagu and William Herbert, 6th Earl of Pembroke, who no doubt had their eye as much on the rumoured £2,500 a year that she was set to inherit as on her physical charms.

Fortunately, a match between Elizabeth and Rochester was thought probable, thanks in no small part to his mother's scheming with her cousin Barbara Castlemaine to facilitate the marriage upon his return from his grand tour. As Barbara had a tight grasp on the king's ear, as well as his other organs, Charles's approval was soon granted for the match, and Rochester was encouraged to press his suit. Barbara's own relationship with Rochester was a complex one; later on he would mock her in his poetry, but then he was content merely to try to kiss her when he saw her alighting from her carriage in Whitehall, for which he was knocked to the ground. Unabashed, he was said to have murmured an impromptu verse from his recumbent position: 'By heavens, 'twas bravely done / First to attempt the chariot of the sun / And then to fall like Phaeton.' Perhaps the grand harlot was keen to see him married off so as to distract him in future from such sallies.

Rebuffed kisses aside, all this was meat and drink to the young man. To be offered an intelligent, attractive and moneyed wife was joyous enough, but to do so with the blessing of Charles confirmed that the stars had aligned in Rochester's favour. He had his first chance to woo Elizabeth in the early months of 1665. What Elizabeth initially made of the witty, debonair Rochester is unknown, as none of their early letters survive, but given her own reputation for sharp wit it is probable that she warmed to the charming young man. An independent woman even at her young age, she was intent on making her own choice, rather than being bullied into it. However, theirs was still an unequal match, given his lack of fortune and darkly whispered rumours about his father's reputation for inconstancy and drunkenness. Sir Francis did not look particularly kindly on him, and while the king's support counted for a great deal, his suit showed little immediate sign of being accepted.

As Rochester's dissatisfaction grew throughout the early months of 1665, the impulsive young man decided that there was a better option than waiting around for the various machinations to align in his favour: namely, abducting Elizabeth and marrying her by force.

Although this sounds an unusually harsh means of entering into matrimonial bliss, abduction was at least a semi-accepted means of allowing younger sons or the otherwise unmoneyed to have a chance of attaining their beloveds. Although it was traditionally the case that marriage was a formal and much-planned union between two families, each of whom could obtain something from the other, rather than a romantic match, there were still those who sought to run away with their would-be wives. A couple could be married by the local parson as swiftly as possible, and while such an act was technically illegal and liable to see the participants fined, the chance of a young man being able to marry an heiress would more than cover any financial penalties.

However, to dissuade people from taking this risk, there was a legal deterrent to the effect that 'all ravishments and wilful taking away or marrying of any maid, widow or damsel against her will or without the assent or agreement of her parents' were extremely serious crimes that could result in imprisonment or, at worst, execution. Of course, few parents approved of their daughters being abducted, although some of the more financially minded took the unorthodox circumstances of their scion's betrothal as a crafty means of reducing or even forfeiting the dowry that they would have been required to give in a conventional match. Rochester's decision to abduct Elizabeth Malet stemmed more from impatience and a headstrong attitude than from necessity. It is likely that Charles's willingness to help him with his suit would have been enough eventually to help him win his wife, had he been patient. This is also the first significant account of the emergence of Rochester as a public figure, earning a reputation as a devil-may-care libertine in the true sense of the word—as a free-thinker who ignored conventional codes of behaviour and morality. Rochester, a young man in a hurry to make a name for himself, knew that his actions would result in public infamy. But he may have blithely believed that he would remain in Charles's favour even after such an action, knowing the king's fondness for chutzpah and daring.

On 26 May 1665 Elizabeth Malet was heading home after dining at Whitehall with her grandfather Sir Francis Hawley and her friend Frances Stuart. Pepys, who provides a contemporary account of the abduction, describes it with relish. Elizabeth 'was at Charing Cross seized on by both horse and footmen and forcibly taken from [Hawley] and put in a coach with six horses and two women provided to receive her, and carried away'. As abductions go, this was clearly a considered and ostentatiously public display—designed to arouse the excited chatter of the likes of Pepys—as well as a practical-minded one; a six-horse carriage would be a speedy and efficient means of making a rapid getaway. Rochester himself travelled separately in another, less showy vehicle. It is probable that he was headed for Oxfordshire, either to Ditchley Park or to Adderbury Manor, his father's house nearby on which his mother had renewed the lease in 1661.

Unfortunately, Rochester had reckoned without the indefatigable Hawley, who set out in immediate pursuit of his grand-daughter's captor and, after a frantic chase lasting several miles, managed to apprehend the earl at Uxbridge. Whatever passed between Rochester and Hawley that evening is not noted by Pepys. Perhaps some colourful epithets were exchanged by both men, especially as there was no sign of Elizabeth, who had been spirited away. Nevertheless,

Rochester was not so foolish as to attempt a quarrel with Hawley and so returned to London, tail firmly between his legs.

He might have guessed that his behaviour would not go unpunished, and so it proved. The next day, Charles, furious at his protégé's insolence and embarrassed at the disrespect shown to Hawley, had him committed to the Tower for his 'high misdemeanours' and ordered that Elizabeth be found and restored to her family. She was soon discovered, unharmed and possibly rather exhilarated by the whole adventure, and returned home, once again to be subjected to the romantic suits of several eligible men. Crucially, Rochester's 'rape' had only been one of physical, rather than sexual, possession, meaning that her highly prized virginity was believed still to be intact—unless, of course, she had had a previous liaison with one of her would-be suitors (although that would have been social suicide).

As for Rochester, it dawned on the young man that he had gone too far, misreading Charles's tacit support for the match as approval for a rash and bold action. Once the adrenaline of his exploits had worn off, he found himself in an unpleasant predicament, facing severe consequences for his actions. Frightened, he wrote a 'Humble Petition' to the king from the Tower, begging forgiveness for his 'first error', saying that 'he would have rather chosen death ten thousand times' than incur Charles's displeasure, and claiming that 'inadvertency, ignorance in the law, and passion' were the causes of his offence. Charles, ever mercurial, may have been amused or irritated, but external events were about to change Rochester's fortunes irrevocably.

Britain in the seventeenth century was a place used to plague. There had been outbreaks in 1603, 1625 and 1636, when tens of thousands of people had died. Bubonic plague had originally been spread by the bite of an infected flea; those who had both literary knowledge and a wry sense of humour recalled John Donne's poem 'The Flea' and its statement 'Wherein could this flea guilty be / Except in that drop which it sucked from thee?' 'Guilty of the death of thousands' might have been the rejoinder. Bubonic plague was an especially hideous means of death: essentially, the body rotted while the unfortunate subject was still alive, a decay manifesting itself in vomiting of blood and agonizing pain and seizures.

Those who knew their history still talked in hushed tones of the infamous Black Death of the fourteenth century, which had killed tens of millions all over the world, reducing the global population by nearly a quarter. While the latest plague was on nothing like the same scale, its arrival in London in early June 1665 led to panic among the gentry and aristocracy. This led to the king and his followers leaving the city at the end of the month, bound for Oxford. In an irony that Charles surely appreciated, he mirrored the actions of his father two decades earlier in the Civil War by setting up a new court there, away from London and the ever-present risk of fatal infection.

Before he left, the Rochester business momentarily distracted him. It was both an endearing habit and a sign of inconsistency that Charles was seldom angry with his favourites for very long. While Rochester's behaviour had been embarrassing and presumptuous, it also amused the king, whose own inclinations had often tended towards the swashbucklingly licentious, and the 'Humble Petition' did not fall on deaf ears. So it was that, on 19 June, Rochester was released from the Tower, but he was conspicuously not invited to join the court at Oxford.

Rochester was relieved to be free from captivity, but all else seemed lost. He was out of favour with Charles and his best hope of a financially advantageous marriage was dashed. Pepys noted in his diary that 'my Lord Rochester is now decidedly out of hopes' of Elizabeth, and the more socially acceptable and far better-mannered Edward Montagu was the logical choice for the union. However, almost unbelievably, Charles still refused to give his assent to a match between Montagu and Elizabeth; perhaps this was the result of his residual loyalty towards Henry Wilmot's son and a feeling of faint distaste for a man who, although the model of a gentleman, was nonetheless the son of a former Parliamentarian. Alternatively, it may simply be that the matter did not interest him enough. Plague ravaged London and his first major international conflict was at hand, so squabbles over arranged marriages for courtiers must have appeared very small beer.

Nonetheless, Rochester, unwilling to give up on Charles's favour so quickly, hit upon a bold solution that would simultaneously improve his standing at court and have the effect of wooing Elizabeth back. He would go to war.

The First Anglo-Dutch War, fought by Cromwell and the Commonwealth, ended supposedly with an English victory. However, the auspices under which it had ended were dubious, and the central issue that had led to its commencement—namely, a dispute over trade rights—was not resolved, so a second engagement was inevitable. This, in the unlovely shape of the Second Anglo-Dutch War, duly arrived in March 1665. It had been hoped that the Restoration would lead to a détente, and for a time Charles's good personal relations with the Dutch (whose lavish hospitality he had enjoyed while in exile) smoothed matters over.

However, for reasons of realpolitik, war soon followed. Charles, still a relatively new and untested monarch, felt the need both to engage in some sabre-rattling and to ensure a steady source of income via overseas trade. Despite some attempts on the Dutch side to bring about peace, such as ceding New Amsterdam (or New York, as it was subsequently called) to the British in 1664, the appetite in England was clearly for a quick and lucrative war. Therefore, with Charles's consent and approval, a situation was engineered whereby, after various guerrilla attacks on both sides, England could declare war on the Dutch with impunity. Charles's hope was that he would win as impressive a victory as Cromwell had. An early battle off the coast of Lowestoft on 13 June 1665 was a clear win for the English and appeared to augur well for further success.

It was under these circumstances that Rochester, perhaps rashly, offered to follow in his father's footsteps. Probably expecting an easy campaign and a chance to regain his battered reputation, he joined his romantic rival Edward Montagu's father, Lord Sandwich, with his fleet. Soon, in early July, he was placed on board the flagship

Revenge, under the command of Sir Thomas Tiddiman. His head full of thoughts of rich prizes and derring-do, he hoped that this was a sinecure of sorts. At first, all went well. Under Tiddiman, the ship was bound for Norway with the intention of capturing the Dutch East India Fleet, wealthy and apparently an easy target.

The arrogance that the English demonstrated would soon be to their cost. They had numerous close calls and near-shipwrecks; on one occasion the entire fleet arrived at a harbour that was about a third of the size that they needed. As Rochester wrote in a letter to his mother, 'It was God's great mercy we got clear and only that we had no human probability of safety.' When he reached the port of Bergen on 1 August 1665, 'full of hopes and expectation', his happy thoughts of rich pluckings of 'shirts and gold, which I had most need of' were soon dispelled. The Dutch ships had already arrived, and after a short delay, a desperate fire-fight began the following day. As Rochester notes in his letter, 'in three hours time, we lost some 200 men and six captains, our cables were cut and we were driven out by the wind.' Although he puts a brave face on the action, saying 'we came off having beat the town all to pieces without losing one ship', it had not been a successful engagement and had failed to produce any of the hoped-for booty.

The fight itself, a comparatively minor battle, is made more interesting by a fascinating metaphysical story that Gilbert Burnet recounts. Rochester (who Burnet says showed 'as brave and as reso-lute a courage as was possible', an opinion also held by Sir Thomas Clifford, a leading naval commander and member of the Privy Council) was on board the *Revenge* with two other young men of breeding, Sandwich's nephew Ned Montagu and George Windham. All three were terrified at the apparent prospect of imminent death, and Rochester entered into a formal pact with Windham that, should either of them die, 'he should appear, and give the other notice of the future state, if there was any'. Montagu, perhaps less supersti-tious than the others, refused to have any part in this arrangement, despite an equally strong foreboding of his approaching death.

During the fighting, all three fought bravely, despite their nerves and inexperience, until late in the day, when Windham finally panicked and began to tremble violently. Montagu ran to his assistance, but then a cannon-ball killed Windham and ripped out Montagu's stomach, killing him within the hour. Rochester, who escaped unscathed, watched the death of his friends with horror. Having led a relatively sheltered life, the sight of bloody and painful death was a great shock to him, even in an age when casual violence was rife. Yet, when the battle was over, he waited with a mixture of excitement and anxiety to see if a spectral Windham would come from beyond the grave to give him details of 'the future state'.

However, no ghost ever came, much to Rochester's disappointment. According to Burnet, Rochester claimed that Windham's non-appearance 'was a great snare to him during the rest of his life', although 'he could not but acknowledge it was an unreasonable thing for him to think that beings in another state were not under such laws and limits that they could not command their own motions but as the Supreme Power should order them' and that 'one who had so corrupted the natural principles of truth, as he had, had no reason to expect that such an extraordinary thing should be done for his conviction'.

In this, we see the early signs of what would become a lifelong duality in Rochester's intellectual outlook, a man torn between a calmly considered and dispassionate observation of the world as it stood and an almost child-like and desperately expressed desire to believe in the possibility of another, more rapturous existence beyond. In this, he was not unusual. To believe in the existence of a religious afterlife was orthodox, even obligatory. What makes the story so compelling (unlike some of Burnet's other tales) is the ring of truth that it has for Rochester. If the Elizabeth Malet saga had shown him as a swaggering, devil-may-care libertine, this reveals the *penseur* who sought desperately for a cosmic reassurance that there was more to life than mere fleshy engagement, whether in sex, eating and drinking or fighting. Had a ghostly Windham appeared to him, Rochester might well have been a happier and more contented man—assuming, of course, that he did not die of shock at the sight.

Nevertheless, Rochester was not purely traumatized by the experience, whatever Burnet might say. The jaunty tone of the letter to his mother that he wrote the following day (in which, self-deprecatingly, he apologizes for being 'tedious') is capped off by a splendidly wheedling postscript in which he says, 'I have been as good a husband as I could,* but in spite of my teeth have been fain to borrow money.' The letter's gossipy but factual tone reads as if he has at least one eye on having it reach a wider, possibly royal, audience and regaining the king's favour. Rochester was never someone purely sentimental in his dealings with his mother, or with anyone else for that matter.

He continued to serve in the navy after this, with some distinction. He was involved in another battle on 9 September 1665, when the English fought against eighteen Dutch vessels. The result of the conflict was an English victory, with a thousand Dutch prisoners taken, two of their ships destroyed and many of the others captured. Rochester was sent to Charles and the displaced court in Oxford on 12 September, complete with a dispatch from Sandwich concerning the battle. In it, Sandwich was keen to praise the actions of the young sailor, describing him as 'brave, industrious and of parts fit to be very useful in your majesty's service'.

When he arrived at court, the reconciliation with Charles was a happy and long-desired one. Rochester had not seen Charles since the failed abduction attempt of May, and the last three months had placed a strain on what was previously a close relationship between the two men. It is wrong to over-sentimentalize what passed between them when Rochester returned; Charles was a king attempting to rule a country from a satellite court while plague ravaged the capital city, while Rochester was an errant and rash young man who had done some brave service in the country's name. Charles did not respond to the young prodigal's arrival with tears, outstretched arms and the killing of the fatted calf.

Nonetheless, his return to royal favour ensured that the debacle of the abduction was forgiven completely, and on 31 October Rochester

---

* 'Husband' meaning 'a thrifty, careful man', in this context, rather than a married one.

was granted a one-off payment of £750 by the Privy Seal as a gift, a thank-you present for services rendered. As he roamed around Oxford, his former tutor Robert Whitehall, as drunken and dissipated as ever, continued to prop up the taverns, although the circles that Rochester moved in had widened as exponentially as Whitehall's breeches. Their paths may nonetheless have crossed, although Rochester was now able to mix with the finest examples of quality in the land, whether they were courtiers or courtesans, rather than skulking around taverns in his erstwhile mentor's borrowed gown.

The weeks passed pleasantly enough for Rochester, who indulged all his desires, social, alcoholic or sexual. Gilbert Burnet wrote, fancifully, that upon his return from war 'he had so entirely laid down the intemperance that was growing on him before his travels that at his return he hated nothing more', but also notes, more believably, that 'falling into company that loved these excesses, he was, though not without difficulty and by many steps, brought back to it again'.

Burnet exaggerates the difficulty. As a young bachelor, and a handsome one to boot, Rochester was a familiar face around women of quality, although he had the good sense and tact to avoid embroiling himself with any of the king's mistresses, otherwise a second casting-out from Eden for this chastened Adam would have been inevitable. Barbara Castlemaine, herself no guileless Eve, was, at this stage in her pomp, openly flaunting herself as the royal concubine. She had a rival in the comely form of Frances Stuart, who had been present on the night of Elizabeth's abduction and who was rumoured to have previously had a brief dalliance with Barbara herself, before she was seen as a threat to the latter's complete hold over the king. Although Charles's relationship with Frances had probably only been platonic, despite the Pepysian gossip that she too was a 'common mistress' to the king, it was enough to send the famously foul-tempered Barbara into paroxysms of jealous rage.

A more important figure in Charles's life who was in Oxford at this time was a young actress, Eleanor 'Nell' Gwyn, who had had some success in a play by John Dryden, *The Indian Emperor*, earlier that year. She was the mistress and acting partner of the well-known star actor of the day Charles Hart, and the two specialized in playing a pair of ill-matched but witty lovers, an act with some foundation in fact. She and some of the other actresses who were at court were there to provide entertainment to the exiled king, being granted the right to wear the king's livery and proclaimed 'women comedians in His Majesty's Theatre'. While her affair with the king did not begin until 1667, her good looks and pleasant character caught his eye long before.

For all the distractions offered by 'pretty, witty Nell', Charles's thoughts lay on other matters than simple fornication and indulgence. After a strong start, the Anglo-Dutch war was beginning to drift, not least because France was on the verge of entering into a treaty with Holland, which would have been militarily and socially disastrous. Clarendon, never a supporter of what he described as 'this foolish war', was ordered to make peace with Holland before any treaty with France could be struck, but it seemed as likely that the Dutch would ally with the powerful Habsburgs as with the French. Charles's hopes for a quick, complete military victory looked likely to be dashed.

There were other matters at home that were beginning to concern him, too. After the initial excitement of his return had worn off, there were murmurs that the licentious atmosphere at court was morally poisonous, and dark rumours persisted about the extraordinary behaviour exhibited by some of the more notorious members of Charles's circle. It was said of Barbara Castlemaine that she had done everything from seducing her servants to practising witchcraft (the former, at least, she probably was guilty of). She was far from popular, and a libellous notice was put up at Merton College, where she had given birth to her fifth child, George, during the court's stay at Oxford in December 1665, saying: 'The reason why she is not ducked? Because by Caesar she is fucked.' As it was Oxford, the note was written in both Latin and English. Charles, furious when he heard of this, offered a reward of £1,000 for intelligence about who was responsible, but none was forthcoming. Had Charles had both courage and conviction and a less priapic temperament, he could have dropped the increasingly embarrassing Barbara. His refusal to do so, and continuing instead to father children by her, meant that much of the shine was taken off his initial popularity.

To address the religiously tinged campaign of castigation of his behaviour, Charles saw to it that the Five Mile or Nonconformists Act was passed in 1665. Despite his own sympathies leaning to the suspect faith of Catholicism, he attempted to introduce a new religious orthodoxy shortly after the Restoration which, in its own way, was as forbidding as Cromwell's. The Church of England was re-established and it was made compulsory to attend church every week, under pain of being fined a shilling. It proved to be a popular activity, although mainly for swapping news and gossip rather than for religious observance. The text used for services was the Book of Common Prayer, which was introduced in 1662 and which was deliberately designed to drive a wedge between Nonconformists and Anglicans.

Nonconformists were further stigmatized by the Five Mile Act, which forbade dissenting clergymen from living within five miles of a parish from which they had been banned, unless they swore an oath of allegiance to the king and promised never to disobey his laws again. To do otherwise meant losing their influence, as well as their living. Nearly a thousand ministers were prepared to suffer this fate, with the result that Charles now had a substantial number of resentful, disenfranchised clergymen who were only too happy to rail against the sin and iniquity of the royal court.

Rochester watched these developments wryly. He still retained some vestige of Francis Giffard's religious instruction, as he would do all his life, but his enquiring and cynical mind was also open to other possibilities. A typical example of this came in an extempore poem that dates from about this time, when Rochester returned to Adderbury, only to find the sexton singing the psalms of a notoriously awful pair of sixteenth-century writers, Thomas Sternhold and John Hopkins, in a church at nearby Bodicote. Hearing the caterwauling noise that this unfortunate man produced, Rochester was said to remark:

Sternhold and Hopkins had great qualms
When they translated David's psalms
To make the heart full glad;
But had it been poor David's fate
To hear thee sing, and them translate,
By God! 'Twould have made him mad.

It is not reported what the tuneless sexton said in response. However, Rochester did not have the monopoly on wit in his encounters with clergymen. On a visit to Whitehall, he was greeted by the royal chaplain and theologian Isaac Barrow, a shambolic, slovenly and pale figure who Rochester, like most of the wits at court, regarded as a joke. Bowing in an ironic way, Rochester parodied the conventional excessive greetings of the day by saying, ironically, 'Doctor, I am yours to the shoe-tie.' Barrow, responding smartly, bowed even lower and replied, 'My lord, I am yours to the ground.' Rochester, vexed by this impertinent response, countered with 'Doctor, I am yours to the centre [of the earth].' Barrow, not to be outdone, answered, 'My lord, I am yours to the Antipodes.' Rochester, losing his temper and feeling angered that he was to be outdone by a man he referred to as 'a musty old piece of divinity', executed an even more ridiculous bow and shouted, 'Doctor, I am yours to the lowest pit of hell!' At this point, Barrow, showing a sharp wit that put many of the courtiers to shame, departed, saying, 'There, my lord, I leave you.' Rochester, for once, was outmatched.

Charles's court, including Rochester, returned permanently to London on 1 February 1666. The plague, which at its peak the previous September had been claiming 7,000 lives a week, had now died down and was more of a threat to France than England, having travelled across the Channel via trading vessels. London was a diminished place, with the theatres and parks having been shut during the plague, and many people welcomed Charles's return as a means of injecting some much-needed life and vitality into a city that had recently come close to feeling the hopelessness that it had experienced throughout much of the Commonwealth era. Once again, optimism and excitement coursed through London, and Rochester's rising fortunes seemed to mirror those of the city.

On 21 March, to symbolize the closeness of the bond between him and Charles and his renewed standing in royal favour, Rochester was created Gentleman of the Bedchamber. This was a position that carried a substantial annual salary of £1,000 a year and provided lodgings in the Stone Gallery at Whitehall, a prestigious area of the palace overlooking the Privy Garden, where his neighbours included the likes of Charles's first cousin Rupert and, while she was in favour, Barbara Castlemaine. The lodgings enabled the king's familiars to be in close contact, as well as making them available to fulfil his desires. The role was an exacting one, rather than a mere sinecure; tasks that Rochester performed in rotation with the eleven other Gentlemen included serving private meals, helping dress and undress Charles, sleeping on a mattress next to his bed, and, unofficially, acting as a pander and facilitator of his sexual liaisons. He was expected to perform these tasks for a total of a month each year, or more often if his fellow Gentlemen were absent on an approved purpose. The tasks were not only demanding and time-consuming but faintly squalid at times. Some might have considered acting as a glorified nursemaid to anyone—even the king—as beneath them.

Rochester did not. Part of this was because he was still a bachelor, enjoying untrammelled access to the various women of 'quality' who were traipsing through Charles's quarters. The king might have had *jus primae noctis*—'right of the first night'—allowing him the richest sexual spoils, but Rochester and the other members of the 'merry gang', who were also Gentlemen of the Bedchamber, most notably Buckingham and Buckhurst, also benefited. The other reason was that, still mindful of his transgressions with Elizabeth Malet the previous year, Rochester wanted to press his suit once again and required Charles's renewed assistance. The intimacy that the monarch and the Gentlemen of the Bedchamber enjoyed led to an opportunity to talk in a far more candid fashion than was otherwise possible at court. Elizabeth was being pursued vigorously by Edward

Montagu but had no interest in his advances; she shocked him at one point by jokingly suggesting that the only sort of proposal that she would accept was an elopement. Rochester, and his dashingly wrong-headed attempt at abduction, remained in her thoughts.

The year 1666 was a good one for Rochester. In June he received a commission in Prince Rupert's regiment of horse guards, a prestigious appointment that only those who were at the peak of royal favour were given. In the same month his military prowess was also called upon once again when he was given royal leave from his bedchamber duties to rejoin the now losing English side in the Anglo-Dutch war. Fighting earlier that month had gone disastrously. The Four Days' Battle off Ostend, which had lasted from 1 to 5 June, had resulted in a heavy defeat, despite the English being under the capable command of George Monck, Charles's sponsor at the Restoration. It was estimated that 1,800 men were killed, nine ships destroyed or captured, and as many as ten captains dead. By any standards, this was an embarrassingly bad defeat, so much so that Rochester's old ally, Sir Thomas Clifford, wrote to Charles to say that 'some of the English captains deserve hanging'. In this vacuum of competence, Rochester had ample opportunity to distinguish himself.

Rochester had joined the flagship that Clifford was on, the *Royal Charles*, by 20 June, when the commander Sir Edward Spragge notified the king that the young earl was on board. He arrived in the midst of a confused and frightened group of people, all frantically attempting to blame one another for the debacle that was now unfolding. Rochester, a veteran of the bloody and horrific fighting of the year before, was able to put his previous experience to good use. On 25 July he behaved in a conspicuously gallant manner, volunteering to carry a message from Spragge to another ship while under heavy fire. As Burnet said, this behaviour 'was much commended by all that saw it'. Given that most of the other young men who were on board died, lacking Rochester's experience (and luck), his actions were a rare moment of heroism in what was an increasingly dismal series of bloody and unsuccessful engagements. They were not unnoticed at court, and it is likely that Charles would have recalled Rochester for another round of prizes, titles and honours, had something even more seismic not occurred.

London in 1666 was still essentially a medieval city. The streets were tightly packed together, with the poorer areas crowded and filthy. One of the reasons for the plague's rapid spread the previous year was that basic hygiene was non-existent, so that anyone at risk of illness—children and the elderly and infirm, among others—saw their chances of death vastly increased. Houses and shops jostled for space brick by brick, and they were also placed near countless sources of fire and heat, ranging from bakers to foundries. There were even tons of gunpowder, left over from the Civil War, stored in private houses.

It was perhaps inevitable that a fire should break out. It did so on Sunday 2 September at Thomas Farriner's bakery in the appropriately named Pudding Lane, just after midnight. What was not inevitable was the way in which a fire that could have been locally suppressed spread through the streets like the apocalypse. In a few hours, dozens of important buildings and as many as 300 houses were destroyed, and as the wind helped spread the fire, the inferno seemed uncontrollable. London, it appeared, would be turned to ash.

For another three nights, the city burnt. The devastation stretched from the Tower of London in the east to Fleet Street and Ludgate in the west, going as far north as Moorgate. Tuesday saw the destruction of St Paul's; in one of the hideous moments of irony that marked the devastation, the cathedral had been covered in wooden scaffolding and lit up like a tinderbox. When the fires eventually died down on Wednesday evening, it was estimated that as many as 200,000 people were homeless and £10 million worth of damage had been caused; countless houses and churches had burnt to the ground, as well as such important public buildings as the Custom House and the Royal Exchange. Traditional estimates of the death toll have been low, but given how few accurate censuses must have existed at the time, it is likely that many more died than the ten or so people who have been accounted for.

The belief that many held was that the fire was a divine judgement on the decadence of Charles's court. While the previous six years had been an enjoyably free-spirited time for some, others had found it a combination of the restrictive and the hypocritical, with the newly licentious and permissive atmosphere of the time and rumours of unrestrained libidinousness at Whitehall sitting uneasily with the ongoing news of military defeat in the Anglo-Dutch war and the uncertain implementation of the Book of Common Prayer. The Great Fire of London did not spell the end of the Restoration, but it certainly heralded the end of the beginning. Despite rumours of his efforts at assistance, whether genuine or propaganda, the fire closed the first chapter in the story of Charles as an entirely accessible, everyman monarch, and instead launched a more cynical age, where those newly in positions of power and influence would come to the fore, and where older and wiser heads would despair or, on occasion, roll.

Rochester returned from naval service shortly after the end of the fire, unscathed in body but with a mind full of the horrors and deaths that he had witnessed. He came home to a city half erased, but his base of Whitehall and the grounds around lay undamaged. Perhaps he felt a sense of kinship with those who had suffered in the weeks before, but he also—reasonably—believed that after several months of death, devastation and hopelessness, his thoughts should rest on pleasure, rather than further horrors. One of the sources of this pleasure was a renewed attempt to woo Elizabeth Malet, this time by words rather than frantic carriage rides. He continued various other romantic intrigues, including one with the young actress Sarah Cooke, but it was the witty, sophisticated Elizabeth who was his best match.

With the potential marriage between Edward Montagu and Elizabeth having foundered by August 1666 (Montagu was said by Pepys to dislike 'the vanity and liberty of her carriage', a remark that smacks of a rejected lover's hurt feelings), Elizabeth was still a virginal prospect. While he made no official approach, perhaps knowing it was unlikely to meet with approval from her grandfather Sir Francis Hawley, Rochester secretly began a correspondence with Elizabeth, attempting to seduce her this time by wit and charm. Like many a young man of the time, he chose to use poetry as his tool.

Poetry—or at least verse—in the Restoration era was a normal part of everyday life for everyone, whether they were aristocrats or commoners. It was a public rather than private art, designed to be read aloud, or even sung. Lyric songs were sung in the taverns and at the theatres, and it was considered a refined and ladylike art to be able to sing a lyric with a mellifluous voice. Booksellers, meanwhile, did a roaring trade with collected editions of these verses, with titles such as *The Academies of Compliments*. It seemed to many of the new breed of courtiers that they could do a good deal worse for themselves than get involved in this new style of entertainment. Not that they needed the money—at least, most of them did not—but it was an unrivalled source of fun.

By the time Rochester arrived at court in 1664, the courtier poets Sackville and Sedley were already notorious for their public escapades, most outrageously Sedley's indecent exposure and pranks at The Cock tavern. Their closest antecedents were not the metaphysicals such as Donne or Marvell, but the 'Cavalier poets' such as Richard Lovelace, John Suckling and Robert Herrick, who flourished between the reigns of James I and Charles I. Beginning with probably the best known of their number, Ben Jonson, they produced exuberant, witty poetry that gloried in the *carpe diem* spirit, celebrating sex, life and love. There was also a strong pro-monarchical bent in their work that, for obvious reasons, fell away after the execution of Charles I in 1649.

By the time of the Restoration, the only surviving figure of these Cavalier poets was Herrick. Aged seventy-five in 1666, and far from young and glamorous, he had retired to his restored living at the vicarage in Dean Prior in Devonshire. The Restoration courtier poets shared the Cavaliers' closeness to the king, but this closeness did not translate into po-faced solemnity or a desire to live quietly. Instead, they joined their king in what Clarendon described as 'drollery and railery', claiming that they 'preserved no reverence towards God or man, but laughed at all sober men'. Their chosen means of entertainment and mockery, both of society and of each other—including Charles—was verse.

Any Restoration courtier worthy of the name wrote poetry,* albeit to wildly varying degrees of competence. Some of their writing was little more than rhyming bawdy squibs or parodies and 'answer poems'—replies to the works of others; these were designed to be used as part of an ostentatious display of public wit, with the intention of furthering the author's name and reputation at court. Some took pains to celebrate Charles, his mistresses and the newly restored monarchy, while others, such as the future Poet Laureate John Dryden, used it as a public art and called themselves 'poets'. If poetry was written down, it was seldom for publication, which the well-to-do regarded as beneath them, or for financial gain, but was intended to be passed around in manuscript, either in the original hand of the writer or, more likely, in a fair copy dictated to a scribe. Some of these scribes, most notably 'Captain' Robert Julian, self-styled 'secretary to the muses', made a good living out of producing forgeries in leading writers' styles and distributing them as if they were genuine. This had the effect of allowing scurrilous satire and obscene suggestion to circulate in a clandestine and underhand fashion, delighting the elite with speculation on which of their number was responsible. They were not answerable to patrons or publishers, but to themselves and each other.

At this stage, Rochester used poetry both to entertain and flatter others (as his university verses had done), to jockey for position at court, and to woo Elizabeth with his wit and intelligence. That it also offers an insight into his—or his avatar's—love-struck condition is a by-product of his art. In one poem, probably dating from around this time or slightly earlier, ''Twas a dispute 'twixt heaven and earth', we see one of the many deliberately idealized women who

---

* Little if any work survives from royal ministers, indicating either that they were unable to write poetry or, more likely, that it was considered below their station. Likewise, one looks in vain for any poetry from Charles.

appear throughout Rochester's work. The mock-heroic first verse certainly gives the sense of a young man anxious to prove himself a lover both in words and in action:

> 'Twas a dispute 'twixt heaven and earth
> Which had produced the nobler birth.
> For heaven, appeared Cynthia with all her train,
> Till you came forth,
> More glorious and more worth,
> Than she with all those trembling imps of light
> With which this envious queen of night
> Had proudly decked her conquered self in vain.

It is certainly a charming enough account of idealized love, but what it lacks is a sense that it is addressed to a sentient human being rather than a figure as idealized and distant as the 'envious queen of night'.

Another couple of poems, 'Give me leave to rail at you' and 'The Discovery', seem of a piece with ''Twas a dispute' and can probably be dated to the same period. They convey the idea of a man frustrated by his supposed lover's refusal to commit to him, as Elizabeth delayed her acceptance of Rochester, mindful of other, more deserving suits. In 'Give me leave', the narrator initially asks much-merited permission to insult and chide his would-be lover for her lack of commitment to him ('I ask nothing but my due,' he sniffily remarks); but then, resignedly, he moans 'I must be your captive still' and ends the verse by saying 'Ah! Be kinder, then, for I/ Cannot change, and would not die.' The second verse, which much later appeared in his adaptation of Fletcher's play *Valentinian*, takes on a more resigned tone. The narrator, apparently now despairing of obtaining his lover's affections, starts to rail against the world rather than just her:

> Kindness has resistless charms;
> All besides but weakly move,
> Fiercest anger it disarms,

And clips the wings of flying love,
Beauty does the heart invade,
Kindness only can persuade;
It guilds the lover's servile chain
And makes the slave grow pleased and vain.

Rochester may have felt 'the wings of flying love', but the 'servile chain' was not his accustomed stance. In 'The Discovery', an authentic note of disdain and anger is soon struck:

Since so much scorn does in your breast reside,
Be more indulgent to its mother, pride;
Kill all you strike, and trample on their graves,
But own the fates of your neglected slaves:
When in the crowd yours undistinguished lies,
You give away the triumph of your eyes.

While it seems impossible to consider Rochester signing himself 'Yours undistinguished', there is more than a hint of the wild, whirling accusations and rhetorical fluency of his later social satires here, especially in the near-hysterical invocation to 'Kill all you strike, and trample on their graves'. At last the poet calms down and ends on a more restrained note, murmuring bitterly that 'Love has carefully contrived for me / The last perfection of misery', and claiming that 'my worst of fates attends me in my grave / Since, dying, I must be no more your slave.'

While there is clearly a tongue-in-cheek element of exaggeration here, giving an edge of charm to what would otherwise be so much blustering and absurdity, the underlying point is clear: he is frustrated and surprised by the unwillingness of his would-be lover to commit to him. The parallel between Rochester and Elizabeth is irresistible.

It is probably around this time that Elizabeth wrote one of her own poems in a letter to Rochester, which feels like a response to 'Give me leave to rail at you'. Her riposte, if such it was, is witty and clear-sighted; it begins 'Nothing adds to love's fond fire / More than scorn and cold disdain' and goes on to strike a far less angry note than Rochester's fiery lyric:

> I, to cherish your desire,
> Kindness used, but 'twas in vain.
> You insulted on your slave;
> To be mine you soon refused;
> Hope not then the power to have
> Which ingloriously you used.
>
> Think not, Thyrsis, I will e'er
> By my love my empire lose.
> You grow constant through despair:
> Kindness you soon would abuse.
> Though you still possess my heart,
> Scorn and rigour I must feign;
> There remains no other art
> Your love, fond fugitive, to gain.

What the 'fond fugitive' made of this bold and witty response is unrecorded, but it is likely that Rochester was delighted to have found a match both in intellect and in wit. Yet the two were publicly estranged. Pepys reports a conversation between himself and John Ashburnham, another Groom of the Bedchamber, in late November 1666 in which Ashburnham claimed that Elizabeth had said of her would-be suitors 'that my Lord Herbert would have had her—my Lord Hinchingbrooke was indifferent to have had her—my Lord John Butler might not have her—my Lord of Rochester would have forced her; and Sir Francis Popham (who nevertheless is likely to have her) would kiss her breach to have her'. Assuming that the touch of witty earthiness that ends the account came from Elizabeth Malet, rather than Pepys, Rochester's ardour by this point came as much from her simpatico qualities as her inheritance.

Two of his early poems, probably dating from around this time, give a fascinating insight into Rochester's treatment of love. In the first, he might be wryly commenting on the various machinations that he has had to undergo in order to win Elizabeth's hand. It begins amiably enough:

> My dear mistress has a heart
> Soft as those kind looks she gave me
> When, with love's resistless art
> And her eyes, she did enslave me.

So far, so generic. However, the poem soon takes a more surprising, and vitriolic, turn:

> But her constancy's so weak –
> She's so wild, and apt to wander* –
> That my jealous heart would break
> Should we live one day asunder.

Another love song, 'While on those lovely looks I gaze', has a similarly unusual tension between the idealized object of desire and the wooer. The unnamed woman referred to is being pursued by a 'wretch', who looks forward to 'his pleasing, happy ruin' as a direct result of being accepted by his would-be lover. The end of the first verse has a particularly magnificent moment of self-abuse, when the poet, thinking on a time when he might end up in the happiest *petite mort* of all, declares:

> 'Tis not for pity that I move:
> His fate is too aspiring
> Whose heart, broke with a load of love,
> Dies wishing and admiring.

---

* The Rochester scholar Nick Fisher makes the helpful suggestion that 'She's' and 'her' might be editorial additions, implying that it is indeed Rochester who is 'wild and apt to wander'.

Whether this was Rochester writing autobiographically or simply showing off his amorous intentions by proxy, it amuses as much as it charms. The second verse continues this strain of conflating love and death, with the now rampant narrator all but drooling over his fate in orgasmic rapture, looking forward to how 'the victor lives with empty pride / The vanquished die with pleasure'.

By the end of 1666, Rochester was far from 'vanquished' when it came to his pursuit of Elizabeth. His dogged persistence was finally successful, and the two of them were married on 29 January 1667 at the Knightsbridge chapel of Westminster Abbey. On 4 February they astonished all society when they appeared together for the first time in public at the Duke's Theatre for a performance of the play *Heraclius*. The match was less controversial in 1667 than it might have been two years earlier, partly because Elizabeth's apparent disdain for her other suitors had caused the admirers of this modern-day Penelope to drift to other, less demanding prospects, and partly because the previously reluctant Sir Francis Hawley looked differently on the idea of his grand-daughter marrying a man who was now an acclaimed military hero—even if, as Pepys notes, their marriage 'was a great act of charity, for he hath no estate'. Pepys ignores Rochester's various royal grants, but there was nothing settled on either Adderbury or Ditchley, so there were mutterings at court that he had married purely for money. The less cynical might have suggested that charity was superseded by her love for a charming, witty and handsome man whose high standing at court was mirrored by his private devotion to his fifteen-year-old bride.

Even Anne Wilmot was, initially at least, pleased. In a letter that she wrote to her friend and counsellor Ralph Verney on 15 February, she anticipated that he had heard of her son's 'sudden' marriage and noted that, despite the match taking place 'contrary to all her friends' expectation... the King I thank God is very well satisfied with it, and they had his consent when they did it'. However, sentiment took second place to practical necessity for Anne, as she asked Verney for advice on how 'to get [Elizabeth's] estate... [It is] a great concern of a young man and a high concern to me.' Anne, far from a wealthy woman, was more interested in her daughter-in-law's fortune than her person.

Rochester, then, prepared to turn twenty with an adoring, wealthy wife, royal favour, a glittering reputation for heroism and bravery, and what was becoming a well-known name. Had he embraced a less tumultuous life simply as an MP or a high-profile courtier, this would now be the end of his story. However, Rochester was a man drawn to conflict like a moth to a flame, and his actions over the following years would result in his name becoming a notorious byword for immorality, wickedness and debauchery. In another world, that name might have been equally associated with wit, intellectual daring and—that rarest of rare things—integrity.

Throughout his life, this integrity would be the only thing that he could cling to.

[5]

'A new
SCENE OF
FOPPERY
began'

*

[1667–1671]

WHILE ENGLAND suffered from the combined effects of the Great Fire of London, the growing likelihood of defeat in the Anglo-Dutch war, and mutterings that Charles's court was unworthy and morally bankrupt, Rochester, at least, was enjoying himself. He spent the early months of his marriage with Elizabeth both in London and at Adderbury, where the meetings between the witty young heiress and Rochester's stern, puritanical mother, who soon disapproved of her daughter-in-law, can only be imagined. When he was called away to minister to the king, whether at the Newmarket races (where Charles's equine namesake Old Rowley was put through his paces and where the court drank and wenched to excess) or at Whitehall, he wrote his wife impressively passionate love letters.

Those that survive give an insight into a character whose reputation as a man about town went before him, but who was nevertheless aware that it would be politically expedient to convey an impression, at least at first, that he had changed his ways. This alleviated the doubts of Elizabeth's family, not least Sir Francis Hawley. In one letter, Rochester wrote to her: ''Tis not through vanity that I affect the title of your servant, but that I feel a truth within my heart... [there is] no pleasure but in your smiles, no life but in your favour, [and] no heaven but in your love.'

This is poetic and affecting, but it has the faint sense of Rochester adopting yet another persona to add to those of student, traveller, sailor and courtier—this time that of devoted and faithful husband. As he had already begun to do, Rochester offered a dazzling kaleidoscope of versions of himself to whoever he happened to be in contact with. Court wits saw a heavy-drinking, hard-living young man who matched them riposte for riposte and glass for glass, just as Charles saw in this surrogate son both the echo of his friend Henry Wilmot and an idealized version of his own youth. Only later would his enemies paint Rochester as the devil incarnate.

As he advanced himself at court, Rochester became something of a celebrity, smoothly building on his reputation for bravery and derring-do and combining it with charm and good looks. A contemporary letter by the essayist and dilettante Charles de Saint-Évremond said of him that he was 'graceful, tho' tall and slender, his mien and shape having something extremely engaging'. It went on to praise his intellectual abilities, saying that 'his wit was strong, subtle, sublime and sprightly' and that he was both 'perfectly well-bred and adorned with a natural modesty'. Perhaps most endearingly of all, he was a brilliant conversationalist. Saint-Évremond praised his talk as being 'so engaging, that none could enjoy without admiration and delight, and few without love'.

When it is asked what a young, handsome Rochester looked like, the answer can be supplied by referring to the most famous picture of him, found today in the National Portrait Gallery in London. It nestles snugly next to a particularly unflattering portrait of an aged, ravaged Charles II, probably by Thom as Hawker, and within spitting distance of Pepys, Nell Gwyn and Dryden. It has been rumoured to be by the leading portrait painter Jacob Huysmans and painted at some time between 1665 and 1670. While the Huysmans attribution is doubtful—he generally painted far grander figures than the youthful Rochester—the portrait can be dated to around 1667 or 1668, given that the man portrayed looks as if he is still in his early twenties. The painting has usually been attributed to the Dutch artist William Wissing, a protégé of Peter Lely, but given that Wissing was a decade younger than Rochester, it seems unlikely that he would have painted him while still an infant prodigy.

The picture shows Rochester, lavishly attired in a classically styled tunic, depicted in gorgeous hues of red and gold. The initial impression is of someone simultaneously relaxed and important, with the elaborate wig that he wears as the crowning touch. The subject looks out at the audience with a calm, serene and rather haughty expression that mirrors that of some of the great royal mistresses, implying in a sense that Rochester's fortune lay as much in patronage as theirs did. The authentic touch of Rochesterian wit comes in the presentation of the monkey on the left, a jabbering little animal that is offering Rochester a torn leaf from a book, perhaps of its own poetry. The monkey became a key motif in his later work, especially in 'A Satire against Reason and Mankind' (Graham Greene's early biography *Lord Rochester's Monkey* made famous Rochester's association with the creature). Monkeys were not uncommon in Restoration England. Pepys kept one as a pet, but was often angered by its unreliability and inability to behave respectably: the parallel with Rochester is unmistakable.

Faced with the diminutive animal, Rochester responds by placing a laurel on its head, all the while holding a sheaf of unreadable papers—love letters? poems? affairs of state?—in his left hand. A briefly sketched, almost token pastoral scene behind him to the right offers an ironic counterpoint to the drollery depicted. No doubt the portrait was stage-managed by Rochester himself to offer his own commentary on the literary and social affairs of the day, albeit in an apparently inoffensive manner. The wider implication, that his pet monkey could write as well as most of the overpraised hacks of the day, would have been noted, and chafed at. The first-appointed Poet Laureate, John Dryden, might have seen this as the first sally in an uneasy and eventually combative relationship between the two men.

This portrait, more than any other, shows Rochester as a man in full control of how he represented himself to the world at large. Intelligent and witty, it was a magnificently ambiguous and challenging calling card and alerted everyone who saw it to the presence of a new and hugely significant figure at court. By contrast, the artist John Michael Wright's 1668 portrait of Dryden, newly created Laureate and crowned with a laurel wreath, shows a man lacking both good looks and obvious charisma. If Rochester saw the picture, he probably enjoyed the disparity between the two.

While Rochester relaxed in the early days of his marriage, the Anglo-Dutch war cast a shadow over the country. The fighting went embarrassingly badly for England, especially when a Dutch fleet managed to sail into the English Channel on 12 June 1667, destroying three ships and capturing the flagship, the *Royal Charles*—an ignominious end for the ship that had heralded the Restoration by bringing Charles home from exile. This was a catastrophic blow to national pride, and on 21 July a hastily arranged peace treaty ended the war (ironically enough, this took place at Breda, where less than a decade earlier Charles's return to England had been ratified by Parliament). The results were dire, both for the country and for the king, who was rumoured to have engaged in amorous activity even as his flagship was towed away. An anonymous lampoon soon circulated:

> As Nero once with harp in hand surveyed,
> His flaming Rome, and as it burnt he played:
> So our great Prince when the Dutch fleet arrived,
> Saw his ships burnt, and as they burnt, he swived.

Charles, embarrassed and furious at the outcome, sought desperately for a high-profile scapegoat and soon alighted on Clarendon. The unfortunate earl had managed to alienate virtually everyone at court over the previous years, whether it was for his contempt for 'royal whore' Barbara Castlemaine or for his involvement in the unpopular Act of Indemnity. Never mind that Clarendon had sought to limit England's involvement in the war from the outset, or that he had desperately sought peace with France: it was now declared that he was responsible for the war's failure and had connived with the enemy, selling Dunkirk to the French for his own purposes. Various other accusations were flung around, from his being accused of having used the stones of the destroyed St Paul's to build his palatial new home, Clarendon House, to being a papist, polygamist and sodomite. Most of the charges lacked veracity, but the overall impression was a furiously negative one, and Charles dismissed Clarendon from office on 30 August 1667.

His fate was soon sealed once he had irreparably lost royal support. An immensely energetic and potent figure, he had made many enemies and many of them were happy to connive in his downfall. He fled to France, fearing the worst. When Parliament convened on

10 October, Clarendon was sentenced to exile and stripped of his office in absentia. Eventually, he was informed that if he returned to England again, he would be impeached for high treason and executed. It was a truly ignoble end to one of the great political careers of the time. Eventually, in 1674, he died in France, still an exile—a diminished figure who had suffered from ill health in the last years of his life.

Rochester's involvement in his mentor's downfall was small but crucial. As he did not attain his majority until early 1668, he was not yet in a position to vote in the House of Lords, but he nevertheless appeared at the opening of Parliament, as well as signing the petition in November 1667 that decreed that Clarendon should be arrested if he returned to England. His decision was a coldly calculated moment of realpolitik; his loyalty was to Charles and the court, rather than to one of his mother's closest advisers and the man who had affectionately kissed him on the cheek as he handed him his Oxford degree. By throwing in his lot so explicitly with the king, he proved himself a very willing subject, just as Clarendon's influence came to an end. In a later impromptu verse, Rochester declared 'the Devil take Hyde', indicating a final severance of all relations between the two men. His decision to turn against Clarendon proved to have wider repercussions than he might have guessed, not least because it angered his mother, who remained grateful to her former benefactor.

The co-signatories of the petition included George Villiers, the Duke of Buckingham, and George Monck, the Duke of Albemarle. Although Albemarle was irreparably associated with the military failure of the recent war, Charles was still grateful to him for his actions that led to the Restoration, and so he continued to be a figure at court, albeit no longer young at nearly sixty and inevitably diminished in influence. Buckingham, however, was an entirely different case, and it is fair to describe him as Rochester's most significant mentor from this point onwards.

Although later portraits show him as a bloated, debauched figure, his face lined with the effects of wine and sexual excess, he was a beautiful youth, first painted as an angelic blond-haired boy by Van Dyck. Like Rochester and many other aristocratic young men of the time, Buckingham had grown up without a father. Buckingham *père* was a hugely influential figure in the early Stuart court, probably James I's lover and a close supporter of Charles I until his untimely assassination in 1628. His son was a surrogate elder brother to Charles II, brought up in the royal household practically from birth. He was taught for a while by Thomas Hobbes, but was a wayward student; it was said that he masturbated in his lessons, hinting at an early reputation for salaciousness. After graduating from Cambridge, he served with distinction on the Royalist side in the Civil War and followed Charles into exile on the continent, before returning in 1657. While his machinations were entirely self-interested, he nevertheless regained royal favour when Charles returned, being created Gentleman of the Bedchamber and Lord Lieutenant of the West Riding of Yorkshire.

His great nemesis was Clarendon. The two men loathed each other—Clarendon believing that Buckingham was venal and unworthy of holding high office, Buckingham seeing Clarendon as a poisonous voice in Charles's ear and accusing him of treachery and papist sympathies. Clarendon hated Buckingham so much that he bribed spies to follow him and report on his movements, which were said to be as licentious as those of any man alive. Buckingham had also done himself few favours with his behaviour at the outset of the Anglo-Dutch war, demanding a seat on the naval council of war and generally making a nuisance of himself. Lesser men might have found themselves in trouble, but Charles, amused by his arrogance, sent him to Yorkshire, frustrating Clarendon.

Buckingham was helped immensely by the contempt that many at court felt for Clarendon, which allowed him to get away with actions such as his attack on Clarendon's ally the Marquess of Dorchester, whose periwig he pulled off in an argument—an act of enormous symbolic insolence. While he was briefly imprisoned in the Tower of London in June 1667—perhaps in the quarters that Rochester had occupied a couple of years before—he was pardoned and released in

July, thereby allowing him to spearhead Clarendon's downfall, which he did with gusto.

Clarendon and Buckingham were studies in contrast. The older man was principled to the point of pig-headedness, to such an extent that he was unable to understand the new age that he found himself in. Disapproving of the Restoration era that he, as much as anyone, had engineered, he found himself an anachronism amongst the younger and more decadent figures of the time. Buckingham, by contrast, lived up to Burnet's censorious comments: 'He had no principles, either of religion, virtue or friendship... pleasure, frolic and extravagant diversions was all that he laid to heart... he was true to nothing, for he was not true to himself.' Like Rochester, he thrived in this new era, where everything was up for grabs, because he was a pragmatist who had no existing set of beliefs to bind him. By the end of 1667, Buckingham had been created minister of state and was the most powerful man in the country. He was so influential that Pepys felt driven to say, 'The King is now become... a slave to the Duke of Buckingham.'

If Rochester wished to take any figure at court as his mentor, then Buckingham was the obvious choice. In addition to his wealth and good standing with Charles, he had a Mephistophelean charm that impressed and seduced the younger man. It is a mark of how close their relationship became that a letter exists from Buckingham to Rochester, asking his protégé to cover his duties as Gentleman of the Bedchamber because of an appointment to go hunting; in it he notes: 'I am very particular in this matter that your Lordship may see I am a man of business, and take the liberty of troubling you upon this occasion because I had rather be obliged to you than anybody else.' The combination of flattery with the implicit claim to superior status—he is 'a man of business'—was a typically brilliant ruse, and probably achieved its desired end.

A man described as 'both the father and mother of scandal', Buckingham had a great facility for making himself indispensably entertaining, so much so that Burnet commented on his 'great liveliness of wit', in addition to 'his peculiar faculty of turning all things into ridicule'. Both of these would prove substantial influences on Rochester, as would his undoubted talent for extricating himself from difficult situations. He was by no means unpopular; the diarist Sir John Reresby called him 'the first gentleman of person and wit I think I ever saw', and he associated with a set at court that included Edmund Waller, Abraham Cowley and Samuel Butler, as well as Thomas Sprat, historian of the Royal Society. As interested in the arts and sciences as he was in drinking and sex, he conducted experiments at his home laboratory and played the violin with some skill.

Buckingham was also a poet and playwright. While his work lacks the intellectual brilliance of Rochester's later poems, it is suavely executed nonetheless, offering an insight into the concerns of those in the inner sanctum of court. An early libertine poem of his, sometimes called 'The Honest Lover', probably dating from around this time and dedicated to the Countess of Shrewsbury, neatly captures the energy and joie de vivre that many at court brought to the priapic excitements of the time:

> Since you will needs my heart possess,
> 'Tis just to you I first confess
> The faults to which 'tis given:
> It is to change much more inclined
> Than women, or the sea, or wind
> Or aught that's under heaven.
>
> Nor will I hide from you the truth
> It has been, from its very youth,
> A most egregious ranger
> And since from me it has often fled
> With whom it was both born and bred
> 'Twill scarce stay with a stranger.

The black, the fair, the gay, the sad
(Which often made me fear 'twas mad)
With one kind look could win it:
So naturally it loves to range,
That it has left success for change;
And, what's worse, glories in it.

Oft, when I have been laid to rest
'Twould make me act like one possessed,
For still 'twill keep a pother;
And though you only I esteem,
Yet it will make me, in a dream,
Court and enjoy another.

And now if you are not afraid,
After these truths that I have said
To take this arrant rover
Be not displeased, if I protest
I think the heart within your breast
Will prove just such another.

The message is headily appealing, a giddy *carpe diem* exhortation to go forth and take pleasure in loving 'the black, the fair, the gay, the sad' in turn. Although the narrator appears to pay lip service to constancy by saying 'I only you esteem', the 'arrant rover' will not be quietly enjoying the pleasures of hearth and home at any point soon. Buckingham presents a seductively captivating view of interpersonal relations that his young protégé Rochester would have taken to heart.

Rochester's attitude towards constancy changed while under Buckingham's patronage. While it is anachronistic (and naïve) to think of him as ever a purely faithful husband, it is also cynical to think that a man who could write to his wife 'I would fain make you the author and foundation of my happiness' was doing so merely out of habit—although, of course, Rochester's high-flown rhetoric could be seen as verbal brilliance rather than sincere emotion. A similar tension between showing apparently heartfelt sentiment and adopting the arch persona of the removed lover dominates one of his greatest love lyrics:

> Absent from thee I languish still:
> Then ask me not, when I return
> The straying fool 'twill plainly kill,
> To wish all day, all night to mourn.
>
> Dear: from thine arms then let me fly,
> That my fantastic mind may prove
> The torments it deserves to try,
> That tears my fixed heart from my love.
>
> When wearied with a world of woe
> To thy safe bosom I retire,
> Where love, and peace, and truth does flow,
> May I contented there expire.
>
> Lest once more wandering from that Heaven,
> I fall on some base heart unblessed;
> Faithless to thee, false, unforgiven,
> And lose my everlasting rest.

In contrast with the jauntily swaggering tone of Buckingham's lyric, in which constancy is looked upon with an amused man-of-the-world disdain, there is a combination of wit and spiritual anguish in Rochester's poem that recalls Donne. The narrator acknowledges his heart 'once more wandering', as Buckingham does, but the idea of how he might 'fall on some base heart unblessed' has the biblical echo of Satan and Adam alike being expelled from the Eden of his wife's affections. This religious interest is strengthened by Rochester's final invocation of how he might be 'unforgiven' and 'lose my everlasting rest' in his beloved's 'safe bosom', where, in happier circumstances, he might 'contented there expire'.

It is a pleasing coincidence that in 1667 Milton published a work entirely concerned with the effects of a similar fall, *Paradise Lost*; Rochester probably did not read it then, given the old blind poet's status as a renegade and republican, but there might well have been mutterings at court about this strange, epic work, itself the product of no less a 'fantastic mind'. Rochester probably read *Paradise Lost* in the early 1670s, possibly when the book's 'revised and augmented' edition appeared in 1674. Although no evidence exists that Rochester and Milton ever met, each must have been aware of the other's interests and concerns via their mutual friend Andrew Marvell, and Rochester's later poem 'The Fall' feels heavily indebted to Milton's eroticized passages between Adam and Eve, even if Rochester's sexual explicitness would have been alien to the older writer.

Like Milton, Rochester was given to introspective self-awareness that verged on melancholy. This might partly be a poetic affectation, but was also an inevitable result of the brief moments of respite from a hard-living, heavy-drinking lifestyle that would have stunned even the hardiest of constitutions. As a result of this, he set great store by alternating between licentiousness and near-despair, as he questioned the entire basis of the world in which he found himself. In one letter to Elizabeth, he wrote, ''Tis not an easy thing to be entirely happy, but to be kind is very easy, and that is the greatest measure of happiness.' He acknowledged his own faults in a self-deprecating fashion while writing to her—'I must not be too wise about my own follies, or else this letter had been a book dedicated to you and published to the world'—but was also able to say of himself, 'I am not in pain to satisfy many, [so] it will content me if you believe me and love me.'

As he busied himself at court, few doubted that Rochester was fully adept at surrounding himself with pleasure. On 2 October 1667 he had another annual pension of £1,000—around £80,000 in today's money—authorized by Charles, for vaguely defined 'services to the King', and the following week he took his seat in the House of Lords, where he proved a largely disengaged participant, save at the great formal occasions, where failure to attend incurred royal displeasure. The next few months proved a comparatively frugal period in terms of literary composition, and there were few occurrences of note, with the only major public event taking place on 28 February 1668, when Rochester was appointed Ranger of Wychwood Forest and Gamekeeper of Oxfordshire.

If Rochester was not openly engaged in either heroic or disreputable acts, however, it was still a hugely eventful time. The so-called 'merry gang' of Rochester, Buckingham, Sedley, Buckhurst and Savile, as well as various good-time members, charged around the taverns and brothels of London, brawling, drinking and whoring until their bodies wilted with exhaustion and disease. In Rochester's case, this torrid activity came about as he founded a secret club known as the 'Ballers', the purpose of which was to enjoy orgies of sex and exuberant consumption of imported French wine. The nickname literally meant 'those who attended balls', but the innuendo was obvious. It was commonly enough known for Pepys to be familiar with it, and in one diary entry he referred to their 'dancing naked, and all the roguish things of the world' and called them a 'loose, cursed company', although he did allow that they were 'full of wit', and he took delight at having been present at their gathering of 'mad bawdy talk' in late May. This club even imported leather dildoes to use in their shenanigans; a later letter from Savile to Rochester bemoans the confiscation of 'those leather instruments' by the overzealous agents of the custom house.

Prostitutes in 1668 London were well-frequented members of society, even if the fire of two years before had been disastrous for many of the brothels that had permeated the city. With their destruction, savvy independent operators could flourish. The so-called 'Crafty Bawd' Damaris Page was London's most infamous madam, whose habit of supplying press-ganged young men to serve as sailors endeared her to some of the highest in the land, such as the naval commander Sir Edward Spragge, who once said to Pepys, 'As long as Damaris Page lives, I shall not lack men.' Gentlemen of quality visited her whores, who were believed to be 'clean'; they were armed only with primitive condoms fashioned from sheep's guts, leather or linen.

While the Ballers took care, on the whole, to visit Page's whores and to restrict their nocturnal visitations to 'women of quality' who attached themselves to Whitehall, Rochester had no such scruples. Profligate and egalitarian in his sexual tastes, he slept with everyone from ladies at court to the whores of the cheapest brothels in the city. His sexual appetites, aided by the consumption of copious quantities of wine, were at their peak, and even by the standards of the time, his near-mania for putting flesh into flesh was remarkable.

It was a far cry from his wife's far more sedate life in Adderbury. Elizabeth became pregnant in around summer 1668, but Rochester, balling away, was a peripatetic visitor home. A letter that he wrote in May 1668 castigates her, hypocritically, for being an infrequent correspondent, saying, 'You know not how much I am pleased when I hear from you, if you did you would be so obliging to write oftener to me, I do seriously with all my heart wish myself with you.' Interestingly, he strikes contradictory notes about his relationship to the court, both loathing and thriving on his time there. In one breath he bemoans that '[I] am endeavouring every day to get away from this place which I am so weary of, that I might be said rather to languish than live in it', and then, as if unable to help himself, resorts to sharing court gossip with her: he describes great women's ailments and makes a sneering allusion to Elizabeth's maternal grandfather Sir Francis—'he drinks puppydog water to make himself handsome, but [his intended wife] having heard he had a clap, has refused to enter into conjugal bonds til she be better assured of his soundness.'

What Elizabeth made of all this can only be imagined, as few of her letters to Rochester survive. Probably lonely and frustrated, she would have felt disheartened and miserable. A subsequent letter of Rochester's makes excuses for his infrequent correspondence—'if two letters from me came not to your hands this last week and that before, they have miscarried'—but the demands of Whitehall and the Ballers proved more compelling than writing to her. One poem that he wrote, discovered in the surviving manuscripts of Rochester's letters and apparently an extempore response to her servant's request for an answer,* strikes an intriguing balance between sincerity and disinterested wit, with the odd outright lie merrily thrown in:

> I am, by fate, slave to your will
> And shall be most obedient still.
> To show my love, I will compose ye,
> For your fair finger's ring, a posy,
> In which shall be expressed my duty,
> And how I'll forever be true t'ye.
> With low-made legs and sugared speeches,
> Yielding to your fair bum the breeches,
> I'll show myself in all I can,
> Your faithful, humble servant, John.

It was a demanding time for everyone. Charles had begun his notorious relationship with Nell Gwyn, having 'inherited' her from Charles Buckhurst, and jokingly referred to himself as her 'Charles the Third', alluding to her previous relationships with Buckhurst and the actor Charles Hart. The fiery Barbara Castlemaine found herself marginalized, although her relationship with Charles had been in decline since the birth of her fifth child by him, George, in 1665. She still took other lovers, ranging from an acrobat, John Hall, to her second cousin John Churchill, and enjoyed gifts and patronage, but, at twenty-eight, her appeal was coming to an end and she was all too aware that Charles, never a constant figure, was seeking to supplant her. Her outbursts of temper remained impressive, but her days of enormous influence at court were over.

With the moral authority of Clarendon revoked, a new air of liberty settled on Whitehall. Burnet wrote, scathingly, that 'the court fell into much extravagance in masquerading; both king and queen, and all the court, went about masked, and came into houses unknown,

---

* This was credited to Rochester in 1758 by the eighteenth-century publication *The Literary Magazine*, which noted that Elizabeth 'sent a servant on purpose desiring to hear from him being very uneasy at his long silence'.

and danced. People were so disguised, that without being on the secret none could distinguish them.' Of course, Rochester enjoyed the opportunity to disguise himself, even if the disguise that others took such delight in was for him a further means of projecting another identity. Others dressed up for an evening as entertainment, but Rochester took it more seriously. Burnet supposes that his masquerades (in the form of such personae as porters and beggars) are a means of following 'mean amours', and sometimes for 'diversion', but this misses the point. Like a method actor, he threw himself so fully into his roles that Burnet's puzzled comments in his later book *Some Passages in the Life and Death of John Earl of Rochester*—that 'even those who were in the secret, and saw him in these shapes, could perceive nothing'—were quite accurate. These subterfuges were not restricted to Whitehall; even in Adderbury he was rumoured to don disguise to elicit unfavourable comments about 'the rakehell, Lord Rochester', and then to take whatever action he deemed appropriate, which more often than not was a fight, followed by the taking of a glass. As Charles had found before, disguise had the happy effect of eliciting truth.

Commenting on other such dissimulation outside Whitehall, Pepys noted on 2 December 1668 that he 'heard the silly discourse [of Charles]... telling a story of my Lord Rochester's having his clothes stole, while he was with a wench; and his gold all gone, but his clothes found afterwards stuffed into a feather bed by the wench that stole them'. This is perfectly possible, indeed even probable. What Pepys neglects to mention is that this could well refer to another semi-apocryphal story of Charles and Rochester's intimate involvement at the Newmarket races at this time. Charles, always making an effort to be discreet in sexual matters, disguised himself while visiting one of the 'women of quality' who were on hand to service the royal court in temporary exile, but while he was engaged in burying the royal sceptre, Rochester saw to it that his clothes and money were hidden. When Charles had finished his labours, he found himself embarrassed for money, and, in desperation, offered his royal ring to the brothel-keeper as surety. Taking it to a nearby goldsmith, the jeweller realized that it was the king's and the madam returned to the brothel, grovelling in fear. Charles, surrounded by his terrified and panicking subjects, summoned up something of the amused suavity of his cross-England flight from nearly two decades before, and was said to ask, 'Will this ring stand a second bottle of wine?'

Relations between Rochester and Charles were not always so amicable. On 16 February 1669 a dinner was given at the Dutch ambassador's to commemorate the uneasy peace between the two countries. A good deal of drink was had, and in the half-exuberant, half-paranoid atmosphere, Thomas Killigrew, the so-called king's jester, managed to upset Rochester sufficiently with his 'mirth and raillery' that Rochester was driven to box him on the ear. What he mocked him about was not recorded, but the normally even-tempered Rochester was unlikely to have responded so violently to anything other than an extremely fool-born jest, possibly about his then childless marriage, or some half-witted jibe about his comparatively lowly standing.

Had most others committed such an act of disrespect, they would have been arrested and sent to the Tower. However, Rochester was sufficiently in favour with Charles not only not to be punished, but to be seen publicly with him the next day. This attracted a good deal of surprised and disgusted reaction—Pepys wrote that the king had made himself look 'cheap' by having 'passed by' Rochester's actions and that it was to his 'everlasting shame' that he had taken for himself 'so idle a rogue' as his companion. Pepys was never a particular admirer of Rochester's, and this description of him summed up what many felt about the young debauchee. Charles's apparent amusement at Rochester's actions only served to frustrate many, who felt that the moral bankruptcy of the court was epitomized by this laissez-faire attitude.

Charles might have let the matter slip, were it not for the Secretary of State, Henry Bennet, whose idea the dinner had been. Angry and humiliated, Bennet made it clear to Charles that Rochester's behaviour had gone beyond the pale and could even result in a major diplomatic incident. He demanded Rochester's expulsion from court, but the king proposed a compromise. After a visit to the Newmarket races, Rochester was dispatched to Paris on 12 March 1669 in company with the newly appointed diplomat Ralph Montagu, ostensibly to deliver a letter to Charles's sister Henrietta, but in reality to pay lip service to the idea that this notorious man should be disciplined for his actions. It was a reasonable solution, and Rochester accepted. In the letter Charles praises his errant protégé: 'Pray use him as one I have a very good opinion of. You will not find him to want wit, and did behave himself in all the Dutch war as well as anybody, as a volunteer.' En route to Paris, Rochester wrote to his heavily pregnant wife: 'I hold you six to four I love you with all my heart, [and] if I would bet with other people I'm sure I could get two to one... it will content me if you believe me and love me.' He hoped for an uneventful couple of months, perhaps retracing his steps to some of the haunts visited on his grand tour, but, as ever, he was incapable of restraint.

The first problem that Rochester faced was that his reputation had preceded him, but not in the best of ways. The incident of his striking Killigrew was well known in the French court, but rather than treating it with the relaxed humour with which Charles had regarded it, Louis XIV refused Rochester a reception, stating that 'those that struck in Kings' presences should have no countenance from him'; he also implicitly criticized Charles's tolerance of his favourite's actions by saying that he would be equally opposed to 'those that the King his good brother of England frowned on'. As a result, Rochester's later poetic references to French royalty are utterly uncomplimentary: his notorious satire on Charles II alludes to 'a French fool wandering up and down', and he writes, 'All monarchs I hate, and the thrones they sit on / From the hector of France, to the cully [dupe] of Britain.' It was also subsequently rumoured, in the 1745 publication *The Agreeable Companion*, that Rochester had defaced a marble pillar at Versailles in honour of Louis' military triumphs with this simple but hugely insulting couplet:

Lorrain he stole, by fraud he got Burgundy,
Flanders he bought, 'ods you shall pay for it one day.

Had this been proven to be the work of Rochester, a hugely embarrassing diplomatic crisis would have followed, but if it was him, he
remained undetected. However, there were many other difficulties
that arose during his French sojourn. On 19 April he was assaulted
and robbed by a gang of six masked bandits on the Pont Rouge,
who made off with his favourite periwig, and on 21 June he was
involved in an unseemly scuffle at the theatre along with his fellow
libertine William Cavendish, as they were attacked by a retinue of
Louis' guards acting on anti-English sentiment. Rochester escaped
unharmed, but Cavendish was badly wounded and would have been
killed had others not intervened.

Rochester's thoughts lay as much on the birth of his first child
as they did on the excitements and intrigues of the French court. In
a letter that he wrote to Elizabeth from Paris, he expresses a desire
to be assured of her well-being: 'I should be infinitely pleased with
the news of your health, hitherto have not been so fortunate to hear
any of you but assure yourself my wishes are of your side as much
as is possible.' The tone of the letter is anxious and seeks reassurance, and it was a relief when he was allowed to return home in July
and head to Adderbury, to find his daughter alive and well. She was
named Anne after his mother. A letter from Ralph Montagu to Henry
Bennet describes Rochester as having lived 'discreetly' in Paris, something of a euphemism, but also says that 'he has other good qualities
enough to deserve… your Lordship's favour and countenance'. Once
again, Rochester managed to charm and impress those around him
and emerge triumphant from a potentially compromising situation.

The next few months were a time of peace and relaxation in his
life, as he had little to distract him other than his new child and marital occupations. His health was still relatively good, with the effects
of his whoring and drinking more an occasional inconvenience than
an ongoing agony. When he returned to Whitehall for the opening of
Parliament in late October 1669, he expected to spend the rest of the

year in the quieter manner to which he had become accustomed, but the demands of the merry gang and the Ballers meant that trouble was never far away. It was his bad luck at this time to make a lifelong and implacable enemy, in the unlovely shape of John Sheffield, the Earl of Mulgrave.

Mulgrave was the son of Edmund Sheffield, a Cromwellian councillor, but he had proved his worth to the Restoration court by volunteering in the navy, where he served without particular distinction in the Second Anglo-Dutch War. He was nearly the same age as Rochester, but could scarcely have had a more different life. Constipated, vain and bitter where Rochester was amicable, self-deprecating and generous, Mulgrave had spent his formative years in self-education, desperately trying to cast off the taint of association with a despised regime. Both men wrote poetry, but while Rochester's was frequently brilliant, Mulgrave's was unstintingly dreadful.* The differences extended back to their progenitors, too. While Henry Wilmot was swashbuckling, daring and reckless, Edmund Sheffield had been cautious, reliable and prudent. His most notable achievement was to be responsible for the preservation of game in the former royal forests of Lincolnshire. While no doubt useful, this hardly compares with Henry Wilmot's simultaneously hot-headed and noble attempts to bring about the Restoration without money, influence or arms.

Had personality and family been the only differences between the two men, their quarrels would have been insignificant. However, Mulgrave was notoriously thin-skinned and soon found himself convinced that he had been libelled by Rochester—or, as he put it in his groaningly flatulent memoirs: 'I was informed that the Earl of Rochester had said something of me which, according to his custom, was very malicious.' Ironically, this was one of the few occasions when Rochester *hadn't* ridiculed someone, as Mulgrave soon realized, but the pomposity of the man was so great that 'the mere report... obliged me... to go on with the quarrel'.

* A typical Mulgrave couplet: 'Defects of witty men deserve a cure / And those who are so, will the worst endure.'

Satisfaction having been demanded, the preparations for a duel were farcical. After a fight on horseback had been agreed, Mulgrave and his second headed to Knightsbridge the day before. There, they were taken for highwaymen and treated accordingly. The next day, Rochester turned up with 'an errant lifeguardsman' as his second and promptly excused himself from the encounter on the grounds that he was not in a fit state to fight. Mulgrave begged him to have a quick tussle at least, on the grounds that both men would be laughed at if they returned to court without such an encounter, but Rochester continued to refuse, citing his poor health and saying that he would inevitably lose such a duel. Mulgrave noted that, when this account was spread around court, Rochester 'entirely ruined his reputation as to courage', and sneeringly and insincerely remarked 'of which I was really sorry to be the occasion.'

In fact, Rochester was feigning ill health through prudence rather than cowardice. The Killigrew business was still fresh in the king's memory and to be involved in a very public fight with another high-profile member of court would be socially disastrous. For once, he emerged from the encounter without any culpability, saying, with an appealing air of faux-innocence when questioned about the matter: 'I have never been angry with the Earl of Mulgrave, and I have no reason to believe that he was so with me; for his lordship hath always carried himself so gently and civilly toward me.'

Perhaps because of this, Rochester continued to keep a low profile throughout much of 1670. He spent the first few months of the year at home in Adderbury, where Elizabeth conceived their second child—a boy, Charles, who was born at the end of the year and named after the king, its godfather. Sackville, who represented Charles at the baptism, wrote Rochester a drolly witty letter on 24 December 1670 in which he announces that he will be the infant Charles's 'lieutenant general against the world, the flesh and the devil', and—referring to his own licentious behaviour—that he is 'resolved to behave myself so discreetly that the Enemy, as vigilant as he is, shall have no suspicion of the quarrel'. 'The Enemy' is, of course, Satan, and Sackville goes on to claim: 'I must confess this with some unwillingness... I begin a war against a prince I have so long served under.' So much for the young Charles receiving godly advice from his surrogate godfather. Little poetry of any worth was produced during this time; instead, Rochester amused himself with free translations and *jeux d'esprit*. This is not to say that he was lacking things to do; Elizabeth's stepfather Sir John Warre died in early 1670, with the consequence that Rochester's doubtful expertise in financial affairs were called upon.

Meanwhile, Charles was consumed with larger state decisions, aided by Buckingham. Following Ralph Montagu's arrival in Paris in 1669, the relationship between England and France, enhanced by a diplomatic visit by Buckingham and Savile that summer, was warmer than it had been since the Restoration. Building on this good relationship, Charles proposed a new treaty that would supersede the existing Triple Alliance with Sweden and the Dutch Republic. A condition of this treaty (the Treaty of Dover) was that Charles would declare himself Catholic, a risky move at a time when anti-papal feeling was as high as ever in England, and would in return be granted the enormous sum of two million crowns, after which England and France would join forces against the Dutch Republic. The clause about Charles's Catholicism was kept secret, so the negotiations took place while his courtiers had no idea of the enormity of what they were attempting.

The treaty was signed on 27 May 1670, and it was completed amidst merry events that saw Charles's sister Henrietta briefly return to England for a month's revelry and celebrations. One of her attendants, Louise de Kérouaille, caught the king's eye and soon became a royal mistress, strengthening what would be a decidedly cordial *entente*. Henrietta's presence was scarcely a coincidence, given that she had been an informal go-between for the two courts for many years, but her fiercely jealous husband Philippe resented what he suspected was her rampant infidelity with everyone from Louis XIV downwards. While he was hardly a model of sexual probity, Philippe's intense pride was damaged by stories that his wife—even if she was married to him mainly in name only—was free with her favours.

When she returned to France in late June, she was sequestered by Philippe, and a mere matter of weeks later what Rochester called the 'saddest story in the world' was reported—namely, that she had died on 29 June after taking a strong opiate that her doctor had prescribed. Rochester, by now in London, wrote to his wife to recount the story of her death, adding that a distraught Charles, who had been informed of his sister's death by the ambassador Ralph Montagu, was in 'the highest affliction imaginable'; he strongly implied that Philippe's ill behaviour and threats were linked to the death, before remarking that their correspondence had become 'very tedious' and chiding her for not writing to him enough. As if conscious that this struck something of a downbeat note, he requests some ale and signs off with a blithe 'Tarara'. He gives his address as Arbor House in Portugal Road, Lincoln's Inn Fields, next to the playhouse there, rather than Whitehall—perhaps because his earlier lodging had only been temporary, or because this was the house that he used for his more outré assignments.

A year that had begun quietly and promisingly soon spiralled into debauchery. Rochester was enjoying his usual cornucopia of carnal entanglements, and it was around now that the first serious signs of syphilis manifested themselves, as he complained of severe pains that he put down to 'kidney stones'. It is possible that he did not know the truth about the potential seriousness of his condition, and equally possible that he did not care, viewing it as a form of payment for the pleasures he enjoyed.

Evelyn's contemptuous comment of 24 November 1670 that Rochester was 'a very profane wit' was typical of wider society's judgement on him. The Mulgrave affair might have been trivial, but it had damaged his reputation for being gallant and courageous, and now he was little more than another vapid man about town. Burnet later recounted that it was around this time that he was driven 'deeper and deeper into intemperance' and that 'he had broke the firm constitution of his health'. Burnet's famous saying that 'for five years together he was continually drunk' may refer to this point in time, and the 'violent love of pleasure and disposition to extravagant mirth' would become prominent in his imagination and life.

Up until late 1670, the poetry that he had sent to Elizabeth and passed around court in manuscript maintained a seemly decorum, influenced by Donne and the metaphysical; he constructed classical dialogues between Strephon and Daphne and wrote tender romantic lyrics. No wider audience yet had any inking of the emergence of Rochester as a writer. However, after this, his verse began to toughen and coarsen in its combination of witty exuberance and scatological bawdiness. The conflict between the world, the flesh and the devil both fascinated and overwhelmed Rochester, resulting in poetry that went beyond mere obscenity into sublime muck, where under every rutting body lay an already rotting corpse.

Two typical examples of this new style of poetry come in the shape of his Chloris songs, which date from around this time. In the first, a pastoral scene is soon interrupted by an 'amorous swain', with violence on his mind. The hallmarks that typified Rochester's later, more obviously bawdy work are found here in miniature. Even the choice of the name 'Chloris', the nymph of spring and flowers, is a knowing one; 'flowers' was Restoration slang for menstrual discharge. It comes as little surprise, then, that this apparently bucolic scene is soon undercut, with the amorous swain given to violent, possessive action. Worse is to come:

> She faintly spoke, and trembling lay,
> For fear he should comply,
> But virgins' eyes their hearts betray
> And give their tongues the lie.
>
> Thus she, who princes had denied
> With all their pompous train,
> Was in the lucky minute tried
> And yielded to the swain.

As an example of the *carpe diem* tradition, this is interesting in that the female carnal drive is given its due, with the 'comely shepherd' a passive figure who, unlike Chloris, is not allowed an interior voice.

Men in general are ridiculed, with the 'pompous train' of princes—perhaps Rochester had the frippery of Whitehall in mind—held up against the 'lucky minute' of Chloris's sexual awakening. The poem might begin with 'harmless thought', but it contains some unusually subversive ideas, a mile away from the more blatant libertine writing of such contemporary poets as Buckingham.

What the song is not is especially bawdy—something that was soon corrected by a closely related poem by Rochester, 'Fair Chloris in a pigsty lay'. The pastoral idea has now been ridiculed to such an extent that Chloris is found amongst a 'tender herd' of pigs, 'murmuring gruntlings' as they sleep. This is contrasted with her dreams, when one of her 'love-convicted swains' comes to her, with a truly tragic vision:

> Fly, nymph! Oh fly ere 'tis too late
> A dear, loved life to save;
> Rescue your bosom pig from fate
> Who now expires, hung in the gate
> That leads to Flora's cave.

As with much of his later social satire, the unexpected use of bathos skilfully undercuts the pastoral idyll. As with the other song, the swain has thoughts beyond animal husbandry on his mind:

> This plot, it seems, the lustful slave
> Had laid against her honour,
> Which not one god took care to save,
> For he pursues her to the cave,
> And throws himself upon her.
>
> Now pierced is her virgin zone;
> She feels the foe within it.
> She hears a broken amorous groan,
> The panting lover's fainting moan,
> Just in the happy minute.

The use of the ironic term 'the happy minute', implying a lack of success on the swain's part, adds to the weird half-horror, half-hilarity of the poem, and looks forward to Rochester's subsequent poem about premature ejaculation, 'The Imperfect Enjoyment'. There remains a final twist:

> Frighted she wakes, and waking frigs.
> Nature thus kindly eased
> In dreams raised by her murmuring pigs
> And her own thumb between her legs,
> She's innocent and pleased.

Taking away the shock value engendered by this being the first significant work of Rochester's that moves into an explicitly bawdy register, the closing verse again renders the male figure redundant. Chloris is able to take her satisfaction into her own hands, and rejects the world of artifice and mankind in favour of 'nature thus kindly eased'. The temptation with much of Rochester's poetry is to take his words as constantly ironic, but if the closing statement that Chloris is 'innocent and pleased' is taken at face value, then he makes the bold claim that male sexual prowess is a frightening yet ultimately irksome irrelevance.

This statement stands at odds with Rochester's public behaviour, not least his whoring and membership of the Ballers. However, as a letter of Savile's of 26 January 1671 attests, Rochester was making as much use of 'those leather instruments', his dildoes, as he was his own penis, perhaps indicating impotence or incapability, as Savile makes explicit reference to the dildoes 'your Lordship carried down [a box] of'. It is unclear where Rochester obtained these dildoes; they might have been a remnant of his French sojourn the previous year, or especially imported at his request. Even as Savile was promising, mock-heroically, that 'your Lordship is chosen general in this war between the Ballers and the farmers'—the custom officers who had confiscated the dildoes in a fit of righteous disgust—and claiming that he and Rochester's other cronies were 'perpetually drinking [his] health, no man oftener nor in greater glasses', a sense was creeping into Rochester's world that the time for carefree jokes and jests of previous years had passed. From this point onwards, his wit grew bleaker and more pointed and his antics more obscene, even as his health declined irreversibly. The brilliant young man had given way to a prematurely aged and suffering cynic. Yet, though down, he was far from out.

'The loving
DRUNKARD
OR THE
drunken
LOVER'

❖

[1671–1673]

ROCHESTER had many unlikely acquaintances at court, but one of the unlikeliest was the Poet Laureate John Dryden. If any word sums up Dryden, it is 'stolid'. His writing was stolid; his appearance, flabby, self-assured and soft, was stolid; even his sexual intrigues were stolid. He was said to have remained faithful to his wife Anne, possibly out of incompetence at philandering rather than on principle, with his only mistress being rhyme itself. Dryden was hugely influential on his contemporaries, and upon such later writers as Alexander Pope and Samuel Johnson, but his overarching stolidity, especially in comparison with writers such as Rochester, Marvell and Milton, has proved to be his undoing for some modern readers. Dryden's verbosity seldom disguised an intellectual poverty that was expressed both in verse and, more unfortunately, in drama.

His *magnum opus* was *The Conquest of Granada*, which was staged in two parts, each of five acts, in 1670 and 1671. A tragic-heroic drama revolving around a tormented love affair taking place at the height of the Battle of Granada in 1492, it featured a protagonist, Almanzor, who was much given to speeches of turgid, hilariously self-regarding bombast. Dryden professed himself delighted with his hero, claiming that he was responsible for 'a perfect pattern of heroic virtue'. He was also pleased that he had created the antithesis of the standard philandering rake-protagonist of Restoration comedy; Almanzor's love for Boabdelin, the virtuous fiancée of the Moorish king, remains pure and honourable throughout.

The play's pomposity and ridiculous length led the Restoration wits to guy it with glee. Buckingham and others came up with a straightforward parody, *The Rehearsal*, which was performed later in 1671 and then published in 1672. It saw a talentless, egotistical playwright Bayes—the Dryden figure—construct a hyper-heroic drama entirely drawn from other heroic dramas, with ridiculous and nonsensical plot developments and absurd characters, such as Prince

Pretty-man and Drawcansir, the latter an imbecilic figure who kills whoever he can, 'sparing neither friend nor foe'. The cutting depiction of Bayes shows one whose absurdly convoluted plotting cannot fail to convey a lack of imagination. Dryden, stung, later guyed Buckingham in his satire *Absalom and Achitopel*, but it was a mark of *The Rehearsal*'s success that Restoration theatre continued to be synonymous with bawdy satire and farcical comedy rather than overblown tragedy.

Rochester and Dryden themselves were on friendly enough terms in 1671, having met at court after Dryden was created Poet Laureate in 1668 and Historiographer Royal in 1670. Initially, Rochester acted as a supporter of the older man's play *Marriage-à-la-Mode* by bringing it to Charles's attention, and possibly rewriting some of the comic dialogue; a lengthy section of the comic subplot contains a disquisition on the perils of impotence and premature ejaculation, subjects closer to Rochester's interests than Dryden's. Dryden's 1672 dedication to Rochester claimed, in gushing tones, that 'you have not forgot either the ties of friendship or the practice of generosity'. Yet Dryden, despite his Laureateship, was not one of the Whitehall set. He was gauche and given to embarrassing faux pas, such as the incident in June 1671, reported in the poet Thomas Shadwell's 1682 anti-Dryden diatribe *The Medal Of John Bayes*, when—in front of Rochester, Charles and others who were debating how best to spend the afternoon—he blurted out, in an apparent attempt to keep up with the wittily lewd conversation he was privy to, 'Let's bugger one another now, by God.' Whether true or not, this summed up Dryden, a man who, as Shadwell sneers, 'boasts of vice / which he did ne'er commit'. It was little wonder that he referred to court as having 'much of interest but more of detraction'.

Though he might have had a hand in *The Rehearsal*, Rochester did not write his own direct parody of *The Conquest of Granada* at the time, but he was certainly aware of its failings, which stemmed as much from unseemly haste as literary incompetence (when informed that Dryden had written a new play in three weeks, he asked, 'Three weeks? How the devil could he have been so long about it?').

Instead, he was more preoccupied with following his wayward poetic muse, although he parodied a famous line from *The Conquest* in his poem 'The Imperfect Enjoyment'. The description of the heroine Boabdelin—'Her tears, her smiles, her very look's a net'—becomes, in Rochester's version, a reference to a comely whore: 'Her hand, her foot, her very look's a cunt.' If we assume that the poem's precise textual satire indicates that *The Rehearsal* was performed shortly before 'The Imperfect Enjoyment' was written, it offers a valuable insight into the mock heroic-tragic account of premature ejaculation and subsequent impotence that Rochester depicts. Whether or not it is a biographical account drawn from experience matters less than its evocation of masculine frailty and sexual frustration, which was becoming a central feature of his poetry.

The poem shares many interesting similarities with the Chloris works that pre-dated it. Taking the masculine rather than feminine perspective, it again ridicules the idea of male sexual prowess, referring mock-heroically in its first verse to the narrator's phallus as 'the all-dissolving thunderbolt' which then dissolves into 'liquid raptures'. Tellingly, the female is not named or identified other than as 'she' or 'her'; instead, her 'balmy brinks of bliss' or 'nimble tongue' act as her character—indeed, her 'very look' is sexually attractive, although the results are unsuccessful:

> But I, the most forlorn, lost man alive,
> To show my wished obedience vainly strive:
> I sigh, alas! and kiss, but cannot swive.
> Eager desires confound my first intent,
> Succeeding shame does more success prevent,
>
> And rage at last confirms me impotent.
> Ev'n her fair hand, which might bid heat return
> To frozen age, and make cold hermits burn,
> Applied to my dead cinder, warms no more
> Than fire to ashes could past flames restore.

The narrator describes himself as 'trembling, confused, despairing, limber, dry', the last word surely a self-regarding term about his poetic ability as much as it is about his sexual prowess:

> Thou treacherous, base deserter of my flame,
> False to my passion, fatal to my fame,
> Through what mistaken magic dost thou prove
> So true to lewdness, so untrue to love?
> What oyster-cinder-beggar-common whore
> Didst thou e'er fail in all thy life before?
> When vice, disease, and scandal lead the way,
> With what officious haste dost thou obey!

Although poetry had many purposes and functions in Restoration England, poems were not generally written by a syphilis-haunted young man who was moaning about his, or his avatar's, inability to maintain an erection. There had been earlier verse that discussed impotence, such as Ovid's *Amores* 3.7, although this had been censored before and since Rochester's time and was regarded as little more than filth prior to the Restoration, much as 'The Imperfect Enjoyment' would later be. Yet it is this incongruity that leads to the poem's wonderfully baroque language—it is hard not to pronounce the stuttering mini-aria of 'oyster-cinder-beggar-common-whore' without an imagined stress on the last word—with its knowingly fanciful comparisons of the imprecise organ to 'a rude, roaring hector' and 'a rakehell villain'.

Rochester's attention to detail is such that some of the smaller nuances could easily be missed. A patriotic allusion to 'king and country' is amusingly juxtaposed with the observation that 'vice, disease, and scandal lead the way', implying that 'king and country' are hardly worth bothering with. 'Brutal valour' might be a wry comment on his own much-garlanded activities in the Anglo-Dutch war, but it might also refer to the casual street violence in which the merry gang took such delight. Finally, the image of the penis as nothing but 'a common fucking-post' reduces it to something cheap

and insubstantial, likening it to a gate that hogs might relieve themselves on, grunting. An allusion to Chloris and her fantasy-inducing
pigsty is never too far away. Finally, Rochester adopts a profane
quasi-liturgical register to curse the unfortunate member:

> May'st thou to ravenous chancres be a prey,
> Or in consuming weepings waste away;
> May strangury and stone thy days attend;
> May'st thou ne'er piss, who did refuse to spend
> When all my joys did on false thee depend.
> And may ten thousand abler pricks agree
> To do the wronged Corinna right for thee.

A 'chancre' was an ulcerous sore on the penis occasioned by venereal
disease, probably something Rochester had first-hand experience of
by then, and 'strangury' and 'stone' were similarly vile complaints,
being slow and painful urination and kidney stone illnesses. Brilliant
and hilarious though 'The Imperfect Enjoyment' is, a work that was
enjoyed in manuscript copies by court wits such as Savile and Buckhurst who probably had their own experience of unfinished pleasure,
there is also something depressing about its unflinching look at the
skull beneath the skin, with Rochester's firework-like wit set against
the omnipresent background of decay and corporeal failure.

Illness was something that virtually everyone who led the licentious and decadent existence of court now experienced. Syphilis,
or 'the great pox' as it was known, was a problem for both sexes.
Probably originating in the New World and transmitted to Europe
by the crew of Columbus's ships, the disease reached England in the
sixteenth century. Its coming was first announced by the chancre
Rochester refers to, followed by heavy sweating, rashes and open
sores, for which treatments tended to be mercury-based. The results
were normally unpleasant, involving mental illness, rotting teeth and
noses, and loosened hair. This, however, was not fatal. It was the final,
tertiary stage that resulted in madness, paralysis and even death.

The unsavoury impact of syphilis stretched over every part of society, from the lowest street whore to the aristocracy and, it was rumoured, to Charles himself. Rochester was particularly badly afflicted. A letter from the courtier John Muddiman to him in September 1671, when he was resting at Adderbury, expresses regret that his 'eyes could endure neither wine nor water', and also makes reference to his 'sudden start', implying that his departure from London was triggered by a nasty bout of syphilitic illness.

It is, of course, equally possible that his indisposition was the result of heavy drinking; an earlier letter that Rochester wrote to Henry Savile from Bath in June 1671 muses on their alcohol intake, in remarkably candid and sincere fashion, without regret but with prematurely elegiac wistfulness. The friendship between Rochester and Savile had developed during their time in the Ballers, and while Rochester still looked to Buckingham as a mentor and inspiration, Savile was, at twenty-nine, closer to his own age and place at court. His letter claims that:

> that second bottle, Harry, is the sincerest, wisest and most impartial downright friend we have, tells us truth of ourselves, and forces us to speak truths of others, banishes flattery from our tongues and distrust from our hearts, sets us above the mean policy of court prudence, which makes us lie to one another all day, for fear of being betrayed by each other at night.

The eulogy continues in similarly mock-heroic vein:

> I believe the errantest villain breathing is honest as long as that bottle lives... I have seriously considered one thing, that, of the three businesses of this age, women, politics and drinking, the last is the only exercise at which you and I have not proved ourselves errant fumblers.

The letter reaches a climax when Rochester urges him to 'let us appeal to friends of both sexes and... live and die sheer drunkards, or entire lovers... it is hard to say which is the most tiresome creature, the loving drunkard or the drunken lover'.

Certainly, both categories were something that Savile and Rochester had had great experience of, particularly the former. Rochester might make jocular reference to Savile's 'fat buttocks' and his piles, but his friend was capable of athletic, if wildly inappropriate, behaviour. Muddiman's subsequent letter describes Savile's attempt to seduce the highly regarded widow Elizabeth Percy, Lady Northumberland. 'Tempted by his evil genius', Savile was visiting Althorp and decided, presumably drunkenly, to attempt to have his way with her. Frightened, she sounded the alarm, and Savile was forced to flee (here, Muddiman adds the charmingly Molesworthian comment that he 'retired overwhelmed with despair and so forth'). This episode was a source of enormous shame and embarrassment for Savile, who made himself scarce in Europe, given the certainty of punishment had he been found in England. Muddiman sardonically remarks that Northumberland's family 'breath nothing but battle murder and sudden death: so that either way we are like to lose a very honest fellow', but it was a timely reminder that, even in the gilded world of the court, certain actions were seen as beyond the pale. Drunkenness and lechery were tolerated, but insulting people of quality was not.

Although actions of this kind were frowned upon, to see them dramatized was hugely popular. One beneficiary of the public appetite for scandal and sexual skulduggery was the young playwright William Wycherley. An Oxford graduate and a secret Catholic convert, he found fame with his daringly sophisticated play *Love in a Wood, or, St James's Park*, which was produced in early 1671 at the Theatre Royal, Drury Lane, where it played to around 650 people for six performances. It was the norm for no new play to be staged for more than a week, as it was thought audiences were unlikely to come back more often unless a new production was being staged, and only the successful ones were allowed to last even as long as six days. Wycherley's play concerns the amours of three young gentlemen, Ranger, Valentine and Vincent, and features such caricatured figures as the lecherous usurer Alderman Gripe and the affected widow Lady Flippant; it was a huge success, with innuendo-laden humour and bawdy situations marking it as one of the first of the 'second breed' of Restoration comedy, where the humour was both satirical and accessible. Wycherley, nobody's fool, dedicated the published play to Barbara Castlemaine, his occasional lover. While she had been supplanted in the king's bed, she still held a good deal of sway at court and was a useful ally, or implacable enemy.

Rochester met Wycherley around this time, and the two men became friends. Both were witty, both enjoyed drinking and the company of loose women, and both looked at Whitehall with a clear-eyed cynicism. Later, Rochester would praise him in 'An Allusion to Horace' as 'slow Wycherley' and claim that he 'earns hard whate'er he gains… he frequently excels, and at the least / Makes fewer faults than any of the best.' The figure in the play that Rochester is closest to is the libertine character of Ranger. Introduced in 'a French house', a tavern of low reputation, Ranger declares that 'Women are poor credulous creatures, easily deceived' and announces his intention to take 'a ramble to St-James Park tonight, upon some probable hopes of some fresh game I have in chase'.

Ranger might end the play preparing for 'the bondage of matrimony' to his witty mistress Lydia, but Rochester took away a rather different view of female nature. It was soon after he saw *Love in a Wood* that Rochester, by now bored, alone and incapacitated in the country, began one of his most excoriating satires, 'A Ramble in St James's Park', the title of which was an explicit reference to the play he had recently seen and which parodied Edmund Waller's 1661 sycophantic poem of praise, 'St James's Park, as lately improved by his majesty'. The opening sees the narrator in full tavern-bothering social mode, exchanging trivial gossip with his familiars:

> Much wine had passed, with grave discourse
> Of who fucks who, and who does worse,
> Such as you usually do hear
> From those that diet at the Bear,
> While I, who still take care to see,
> Drunkenness relieved by lechery,
> Went out into St James's Park
> To cool my head and fire my heart.

Matters soon take a stranger and more vivid turn, as Rochester's poetic imagination soars in a hitherto untapped way. 'Strange woods spring from the teaming earth' and tell a fantastical tale of how 'ancient Pict', frustrated of his evening's assignation ('jilting, it seems, was then in fashion') 'would frig upon his mother's face', and this would result in 'rows of mandrakes tall' rising above, 'whose lewd tops fucked the very skies'.

This bizarre location, then, is now the setting for the lewdest of goings-on, where 'buggeries, rapes and incests [are] made'. All society comes 'unto this all-sin-sheltering grove', and Rochester treats the reader to a laundry list that ranges from 'great ladies' and 'fine fops' to 'prentices, poets, pimps and jailers'. With an air of triumph, Rochester concludes that 'here promiscuously they swive'. St James's Park is no longer just an ordinary place for nocturnal sexual assignations, but a Dantean purgatory where lust dominates all.

It is a mark of Rochester's philosophy that he saw not just the skull beneath the skin, but the soul under the skeleton. There was always some part of him, up until his death, that remained hopelessly attached to beauty and truth, and here it finds a fleeting, initially enraptured expression:

> Along these hallowed walks it was
> That I beheld Corinna pass.
> Whoever had been by to see
> The proud disdain she cast on me
> Through charming eyes, he would have swore
> She dropped from heaven that very hour,
> Forsaking the divine abode
> In scorn of some despairing god.
> But mark what creatures women are:
> How infinitely vile, when fair!

Again, another idealized woman appears, but the use of the name 'Corinna' rather than 'Chloris' or 'Daphne' is significant; Corinna was an ancient Greek poet rather than a deity, indicating that

Rochester's interests in personification here were earthly, rather than divine, even if she had 'dropped from heaven that very hour'. His point is that her beauty might appear to be that of a goddess, but her behaviour is animalistic, not even human. The model for her could well have been a maid and dresser known to him named Elizabeth Foster, the niece of a Knightsbridge tavern-keeper who had had sexual relations with a number of people throughout London in 1670–1 and infected all of them with the pox. Muddiman describes her in his letter as 'a damsel of low degree' and 'very fit for the latter part of your treatment'—presumably a good seeing-to by Rochester; the poem is at least in part inspired by his desire for revenge on Foster.

The next fifty or so lines see Rochester tearing into three representatives of contemporary society, first in the shape of a Whitehall man about town and toady to the king, who 'ventures to do like the best', but, 'wanting common sense', 'converts abortive imitation / To universal affectation', meaning that every one of his actions, whether it is loving, living or looking, is done 'by rote', while dressed in his royal livery.* This character is an attack on all of the courtiers, including, of course, Rochester himself. The second, a 'Gray's Inn wit', is a squinting and penurious law student, and the third a young man waiting to achieve his estate. The three 'confounded asses' speak 'in a strain 'twixt tune and nonsense' in clichéd amorous terms, and the ever-lusty Corinna, whose 'cunt cries "Yes!"', is all too ready to embrace their advances.

This is fairly straightforward social satire, witty and well observed but not much more remarkable than the work of another court poet, such as Buckingham, save for the obscenity of the language. Where 'A Ramble' becomes more interesting is in what occurs next. The poet, despairing of his own abilities, asks that:

> Some power more patient now relate
> The sense of this surprising fate.

---

* The model here might have been a 'Mr Butler', described by Muddiman in his letter as 'a gentleman of the cloak and gallow shoe'.

> Gods! That a thing admired by me
> Should fall to so much infamy.

As with 'The Imperfect Enjoyment', the tone has darkened, from mere observation to near-hysterical comment. Rochester bemoans Corinna's failing to satisfy her lusts with 'some stiff-pricked clown' or 'well-hung parson', which he claims he would have 'praised', on the grounds that 'natural freedoms are but just' and 'there's something generous in mere lust'. However, he soon takes a more misogynistic view, describing her as a 'damned abandoned jade' and 'a whore in understanding / A passive pot for fools to spend in', before climaxing with the condemnation 'The devil played booty, sure, with thee / To bring a blot on infamy.'

This is disturbingly cold, even with its wit and wordplay, but passion is soon added to the mix. The next thirty or so lines are directed as much towards the various women who have wronged Rochester, either by infecting him with syphilis or by trifling with his (self-confessedly mercurial) affections, as they are towards Corinna, railing at her for her treachery to 'humble, fond, believing me' and furiously pillorying her 'lewd cunt', which is said to be 'drenched with the seed of half the town'. These lines are undoubtedly disturbing to read but make a fascinating counterpoint to his letters to his wife, which, at this point, were still temperate and reasonable in their ideas and statements.

In 'A Ramble', however, women and 'cunt' are all-devouring and threatening. Of its seven uses in the poem, all but the first are directly sexualized and in relation to Corinna, and the two in this passage are particularly vicious, with the words 'lewd' and 'devouring' leaving the reader in no doubt about Rochester's opinion of his former inamorata. The details are visceral, perhaps even unpleasantly so—'the seed of half the town' and 'my dram of sperm' are an explicitly physical commentary on male–female relations.

For all this, it is important to remember that Rochester is writing not as John Wilmot, 2nd Earl of Rochester, but in a poetic persona as part of the satirical tradition. Therefore, when the narrator describes himself as 'humble, fond, believing me', there is a knowing element of self-deprecation here that helps to undercut some of the more scabrous and shocking statements. The narrator is consciously performing a self-penned monologue, the theme being 'female inconstancy', and is improvising wildly, throwing in ever more ridiculous and absurd metaphors and descriptions as he continues. Given Rochester's own ability to produce a witty extempore piece of verse, the poem may have had its roots in speech, perhaps as the written remnant of a particularly giddy night's drink-provoked harangue. Certainly, the final section contains a marvellously splenetic curse:

> May stinking vapours choke your womb
> Such as the men you dote upon!
> May your depraved appetite,
> That could in whiffling fools delight,
> Beget such frenzies in your mind
> You may go mad for the north wind,
> And fixing all your hopes upon't
> To have him bluster in your cunt,
> Turn up your longing arse to the air
> And perish in a wild despair!

Syphilis, probably the 'stinking vapours' that Rochester refers to, led to madness, and this curse was especially trenchant if it alluded to one of the women who had infected him with the illness. The narrator produces a list of impossible occurrences to show the implacable nature of his hatred of Corinna: 'cowards shall forget to rant... physicians shall believe in Jesus / And disobedience cease to please us' before he ceases 'to plague this woman and undo her'. The desire for eternal revenge could be an echo of Donne's poem 'The Apparition', where he announces that he will come to his faithless lover as a ghost, and 'since my love is spent', terrify her into 'a cold quicksilver sweat'. In both poems, the poet wishes to wreak revenge on his former inamorata while they have a new lover—in Rochester's case, in the 'most lamentable state' of marriage. However, Rochester has even more vicious intent, announcing his desire to have Corinna 'loathed and despised' and expelled from town—and court—and driven into 'some dirty hole alone'. He would have her 'chew the cud of misery / And know she owes it all to me'. He builds to a final half-magnificent, half-bathetic rhetorical flourish:

> And may no woman better thrive
> That dares profane the cunt I swive!

Rochester's satire is directed at virtually all of society, with a deliriously scatter-gun assault on the worthies of the day, but it is also aimed squarely at himself. If 'The Imperfect Enjoyment' tackles his physical impotence, then 'A Ramble' tackles something that courtiers of the day feared even more: removal from royal favour and subsequent redundancy. The narrator rants, and rails and curses, but ultimately his threats of vengeance and supremacy ring entirely hollow, as he remains a peripheral voyeur, ready to comment on the actions of others but, unmanned by betrayal and illness, unable to interfere. It was a self-aware reference to what Rochester saw as his waning influence at court. After a remarkable debut, the Killigrew and Mulgrave incidents had not helped his reputation, and his frequent bouts of ill health had frequently removed him from the action altogether.

He remained out of London until early 1672, sometimes at Adderbury but mainly at Ditchley and at Woodstock. He avoided his wife as far as he could while recovering from the various illnesses that were bedevilling him; a bemused and hurt note from Elizabeth from this time reads: 'Though I cannot flatter myself so much as to expect it, yet give me leave to wish that you would dine tomorrow at Cornbury, where necessity forces, your faithful humble wife, E. Rochester.' A touching postscript states: 'If you send to command me to Woodstock when I am so near as Cornbury, I shall not be a little rejoiced.' Their relations were suffering as a consequence of her absence at her family's estates in Enmore; the difficulty of remaining in close quarters with Anne Wilmot led to her departure, and she and Rochester did not see each other for months. Whether or not he saw her on that occasion, he clearly felt a sense of guilt at his neglect.

A letter that he sent her upon his return to court mixed remorse with wit. It begins with a self-effacing comment: '[To] run away like a rascal without taking leave, dear wife… is an unpolished way of proceeding, which a modest man ought to be ashamed of.' Rochester was anything but modest, but he was self-aware enough to realize that he had not only 'left [Elizabeth] a prey to [her] own imaginations' but also left her to the mercy of the dragon-like Anne Wilmot, whom he refers to as 'my relations, the worst of damnations', as he expresses the hope that, belatedly, 'my mother be merciful unto you'. He then moves into his familiar parody of scriptural language, this time setting his sights on the liturgy of the funeral service: 'I commit you to what shall ensue, woman to woman, wife to mother, in hopes of a future appearance in glory.' He ends with good wishes to his children, claiming penury wittily by saying 'excuse my ill paper and my ill manners to my mother, they are both the best the place and age will afford'.

Elizabeth, in charge of two young children, was both bored and frustrated. Like many witty and beautiful young heiresses of the age who had been much prized in town, she found herself out of sorts when removed from her urban milieu, sequestered either to her own family's estate or to a cold, decrepit house in the middle of the countryside, where she had to live with Rochester's domineering mother and his young nieces, Eleanor and Anne Lee, both of whom took exception to this arriviste. A more cheerful companion for her was Anne Wilmot's indefatigable agent John Cary, who remained a constant presence at Adderbury; a note of Rochester's refers to an order for firewood he had placed with Cary on Elizabeth's behalf. Rochester, who approved of the agent, described him as 'seldom failing in anything he undertakes'.

One of the few things that united Rochester and Elizabeth at this time was poetry, although their writing was entirely different. While Rochester's verses were designed mainly to be passed in manuscript around a select group of friends and acquaintances at court, with the intention of amusing and shocking, Elizabeth's writing, at least in the few poems of hers that survive in manuscript, was unlikely to have been intended for anyone's consumption, save possibly that of her husband. Her poem 'Chloris' misfortunes that can be expressed' can be read as her own despairing commentary on the situation that she finds herself in. When talking of her lover's absence, it is hard not to draw a parallel with her husband's long disappearances:

> Such conquering charms contribute to my chain
> And add fresh torments to my lingering pain
> That could blind love, judge of my faithful flame
> He would return the fugitive with shame
> For having been insensible to love
> That does by constancy its merit prove.

The distinction between Elizabeth's constancy and the 'lingering pain' of the fugitive is sufficiently pointed that we may imagine that this poem, at least, was intended for her husband. Nonetheless, a tone of testy and growing irritation can be detected in Rochester's replies to her letters. In one note, he responds: 'I have too much respect for you to come near you whilst I am in disgrace, but when I am a favourite again I will wait on you.' In another he claims: 'the difficulties of pleasing your ladyship do increase so fast upon me, and are grown so numerous that to a man less resolved than myself never to give it over, it would appear a madness ever to attempt it more.'

Rochester found ministering to his family a bind and irritation. He talks of 'my constant resolutions to satisfy you in all I can', but this is undercut by a sourer comment:

> Since you have thought it a wise thing to trust me less... it has
> been out of my power to make the best of my proceedings... at a
> distance, I am likeliest to learn your mind, for you have not a very
> obliging way of delivering it by word of mouth.

He ends this especially peremptory letter by saying: 'If therefore you will let me know the particulars in which I may be useful to you, I shall show my readiness as to my own part, and if I fail of the success I wish, it shall not be [my] fault.' How Elizabeth reacted to this can only be imagined, so perhaps the hastily scribbled postscript—'I intend to be at Adderbury some time next week'—was a last-minute sop to her hurt feelings.

When Rochester returned to London, things had changed once again. The Theatre Royal had burnt down in a fire on 25 January 1672, depriving the city of one of its major playhouses and forcing a hasty rearrangement of many of the leading players and playwrights of the day. The larger devastation that had been wreaked six years before was being partially ameliorated by the grand designs of Christopher Wren, who would be knighted the following year for his contribution to rebuilding the fabric of the city, including St Paul's and fifty-one city churches. However, the grander and more ornate ideas that he had submitted to Charles were never adopted, in no small part because the king was in a state of penury. An ill-advised third Dutch war, this time with French support, was expensive and limped on until 1674, when it resulted in stalemate and a hastily made peace. Rochester, in poor health, did not volunteer for battle on this occasion, or ever again.

More than ever, Charles was losing his grip on his kingdom. A Declaration of Indulgence was issued on 15 March 1672, allowing religious liberty to Catholics and Protestant Nonconformists, but it was an unpopular move that was rescinded by Parliament the following year. Distracted by the attentions of the aristocratic Louise de Kérouaille and the earthier charms of Nell Gwyn, both of whom were lavished with gifts and property (and the title of Duchess of Portsmouth for Louise, with whom he had even conducted a mock wedding the previous year), he was no longer the vigorous, popular ruler he had been, but a weak and lecherous presence who was open to the ridicule of his courtiers and former friends.

It was a result of this perceived weakness that open satires on Charles began to circulate at court. The most protracted and grotesque was a lengthy burlesque, often ascribed to Rochester, entitled

Sodom. Subtitled *The Quintessence of Debauchery*, it probably began its composition in 1672, with subsequent variations continuing long after Rochester's death, up to a printed version (attributed to the 'E of R'), which appeared in 1689, along with some of Rochester's poems, and was promptly destroyed for obscenity and its publisher, the bookseller Joseph Streater, fined. (Among subsequent additions that might have incurred displeasure was the introduction of a parody of Louis XIV as 'Tarsehole the King of Gomorrah'.) *Sodom*'s central character, Bolloximian, king of Sodom, is a none too subtle parody of Charles. The figure is introduced saying, 'Thus in the zenith of my lust I reign / I drink to swive, and swive to drink again'—another spoof of *The Conquest Of Granada*, this time its opening 'Thus in the triumphs of soft peace, I reign / And, from my walls, defy the powers of Spain'; he is the epitome of sexual and social corruption, his credo expressed in the lines: 'My laws shall act more pleasure than command / And with my prick I'll govern all the land.' The plot, such as it is, involves Bolloximian wearying of conventional sex—'I no longer cunt admire / The drudgery has worn out my desire'—and turning instead to sodomy, proclaiming that 'buggery may be used / O'er all the land, so cunt be not amused'. The women of the kingdom, in return, adopt lesbianism as their creed.

The authorship debate over *Sodom* has persisted since its creation. As with the poem 'Regime de Vivre', the temptation for both Rochester's contemporaries and later admirers or enemies has been to ascribe to him anything that was public and obscene composed between 1665 and 1680. It has been commonly attributed to Rochester since it became public knowledge that it existed, not least because of its early publishing history; in 1698 the publisher Henry Hill was the first man to be prosecuted by the Court of King's Bench for publishing an obscene book—namely, the collected poems of Rochester and *Sodom* in one volume. That Rochester knew of it is certain; that he contributed to it, likely; that he was the sole author, doubtful. The reasons for ascribing at least some of it to Rochester are that there is an unfettered wit and imagination in places that feels closely related to his satirical verse, such as a lengthy paean to female masturbation with a horse's tail, and such touches as the mockery of his enemy Mulgrave as the obsequious pimp Pockinello and the guying of Barbara Castlemaine as the sex-mad Fuckadilla. There are also sharp moments which combine wit with social observation that are reminiscent of Rochester at his most acute, such as when it is said of Cuntagratia, the Catherine of Braganza substitute: 'Her cunt no longer invites / Clad with the filth of her most nasty whites.' As an allusion to the queen's barren state, it combines wit and repulsive imagery as brilliantly as many of Rochester's satiric poems. There is even an occasional moment of tenderness; a moment between two lovers sees her vagina described as 'the workhouse of the world's great trade / On this soft anvil all mankind was made', which is as striking and memorable as anything in Rochester's verse.

All the same, the flashes of intelligence and brilliance present are outweighed by a frequent heaviness of language and characterization. The mock-heroic form, with its parodies of Dryden, is not developed in any interesting or exciting way, instead merely existing as a vehicle for a succession of increasingly vulgar and obscene epithets. The very crudeness of the rhymes and sentiments could conceivably be seen as an allusion to Dryden's own lack of expertise at writing drama, but is more likely to be a result of a group of court wits writing the play as a means of airing their discontent at Charles and their enemies. Tellingly, none of the merry gang make an appearance in the play, suggesting either that they were seen by the writer(s) as above criticism, or, more likely, that most of them were involved in its construction. The episodic feeling only adds to this suspicion.

Sodom is not an enjoyable piece of writing, unlike most of Rochester's poetry. Beneath all the sexual references and obscene words lies a genuine sense of misanthropy and despair, occasioned by the disease-ridden streets of London, the corrupt heart of the court, and all the scheming men and women on the make, whether they are prostitutes or aristocrats. Poorly written, vulgar and repetitive it might be, to say nothing of being mostly unamusing, but as a howl of anguish at the colossal disappointment that the moral vacuum of the Restoration had been, it is a vital historical document, perhaps indicating that Rochester's influence was as present in the serious business of its satire as it was in its humour.

As 1672 went on, Rochester faced an eclectic selection of problems. His financial situation, always precarious, was worsened by the court's inability to pay the annuity due for his position as Gentleman of the Bedchamber. A letter from Sir Robert Howard, Secretary to the Treasury and a family friend, states, in a somewhat embarrassed fashion, that 'I will wish as much speed as I can endeavour to serve in the particulars of your wages and pension', but this would not be done 'so directly', as the 'King's affairs are at the time very pressing'. Perhaps Rochester, receiving such a letter while sojourning in Somerset in August 1672, smiled wryly and wondered whether it was Charles's love or military affairs that distracted him so much. The incompetence of the court's accounts was such that a warrant issued for £500 on 9 September was cancelled immediately afterwards, probably owing to lack of funds to pay it.

Rochester, always embarrassed for money, was obliged to borrow from Elizabeth, and a wheedling letter describes him being denied money from the court until 'I am well enough to fetch it myself'; and he claims, perhaps disingenuously, 'if I had not pawned my plate, I believe I must have starved in my sickness.' Elizabeth was more concerned by the ill health of her son Charles. Rochester wrote that he was 'extremely troubled for the sickness of [our] son as well as in consideration of the affliction it gives you, as the dearness I have for him myself'. The child suffered from what appeared to be scrofula, which was widely known as the 'king's evil', as it was believed to be curable by the king's touch. Rochester, somewhat bizarrely given his low opinion of Charles, wrote to Elizabeth of his plans that his son 'comes up to London this week to be touched'. This unlikely practice was widespread throughout England and France, and had been for most of the seventeenth century. With the assumption that the king was somehow possessed of healing powers, he touched many afflicted people, many of whom were said to have been miraculously cured. It is more likely that royal physicians and surgeons put about the idea to bolster Charles's fraying reputation. Certainly, Charles could not be accused of shirking his duty, frequently touching hundreds of people at a time. It was estimated that over the course of his reign, he touched nearly 100,000 of these unfortunates.

In Charles Wilmot's case, as in so many others, it was in vain. It is more likely that the unfortunate infant had inherited syphilis from his father, as the symptoms were similar to those of scrofula. The child was sufficiently recovered to be at home later in the year, as a letter from Rochester indicates that he had sent a spaniel called Omrah, 'so much reverenced at Indostan [i.e Whitehall]... at the feet of the Great Mogul [i.e Charles]', along with a doll for his daughter. However, he remained a sickly boy for at least the next year.

Rochester's own health continued to suffer and was not helped by his continued proximity to the distractions and temptations of court. He was still only twenty-five, but the effects of syphilis were starting to ruin his health beyond repair. In a letter to Elizabeth in September, he bemoans that 'I recover so slowly, and relapse so continually, that I am almost weary of myself', claiming that his long absence from Adderbury is because 'in the condition I am, Kensington and back is a voyage I can hardly support'. If he was incapable of making such a comparatively short journey in London, then heading to Oxfordshire was even more impractical. When in town, he visited one of the king's surgeons, Florence Fourcade, where he had his 'gut griped', an unpleasantly intimate procedure that involved grabbing a suspected kidney stone between finger and thumb and squeezing it. The procedure incapacitated him, and he wrote in October 1672 that 'we are now in bed so that we are not in a condition of writing either to thy merit or our desert', before passing his good wishes to his daughter Anne.

Elizabeth, still at odds with her mother-in-law, was frustrated by her husband's continued absence, as the suspicious Anne Wilmot had an extremely low opinion of her abilities as both a wife and a householder. Rochester's gaily imparted advice to his wife—to 'be not too much amazed at the thoughts my mother has of you, since being mere imaginations they will as easily vanish as they were ground-lessly created'—was considerably easier to give than to follow.

At last, Rochester recovered sufficiently to head home. A letter that he wrote to Elizabeth in late 1672 makes an allusion to an epistle of hers being 'something scandalous', presumably with her patience of him exhausted, but expresses his desire to leave court, with all its attendant horrors and difficulties, and to be 'very shortly with you'. The letter strikes an atypically sentimental and romantic note, as Rochester, perhaps relieved to be feeling better and to be on good terms with his wife once more, playfully jokes that 'it was my design to have writ to my Lady Anne Wilmot [his daughter] to intercede for me' and looks forward to resuming 'my service to you'. An added boon was that he was appointed Deputy Lieutenant of Somerset on 31 October 1672, which shows his continued place in royal favour, something that he was careful to maintain despite his growing con-tempt for Charles.

He left London and played at being a happy husband and loyal son for a short time in Adderbury. It was an act that suited his purposes temporarily, just as the other acts he had engaged in had done. How-ever, his thespian interests were about to be tested further, when he encountered the woman who would be his great love, and greatest challenge.

'LEAVE
THIS
gaudy, gilded
stage'

✳

[1673–1674]

AT THE START of 1673, Rochester was suffering from a combination of lingering syphilis and debilitating drunkenness, rendering him less active than previously, but he was still aware of life beyond the court as he divided his time between Adderbury and London. In particular, the theatre played a considerable part in his life and interests. When he was not adopting costumed disguises to play out roles of his own creation in public, he took a great interest in both the writers and the performers of the time. An obsequious letter from Dryden in London to Rochester in Adderbury in April 1673, after Rochester had acted as a patron of sorts to him by offering him literary rather than financial assistance with the creation of *Marriage-à-la-Mode*, refers to 'the most handsome compliment, couched in the best language I have read' that he had previously been sent by Rochester. Dryden goes on to say, flatteringly but knowingly, that 'your Lordship can write better on the meanest subject than I can on the best'.

If Dryden was something of a buffoon to the court set, he could nonetheless sometimes illuminate their world with the insight of an outsider. He continues his half-praise, half-coded criticism of Rochester by going on to talk of how the earl's reputation had caused such 'unmannerly and ungrateful' writers as Dryden to regard him:

> You are above any incense I can give you, and have the happiness of
> an idle life, joined with the good nature of an active. Your friends
> in town are ready to envy the leisure that you have given yourself
> in the country; though they know, you are only their steward, and
> that you treasure up but so much health as you intend to spend on
> them in winter. In the meantime, you have withdrawn yourself from
> attendance, the curse of courts.

Dryden's letter is disparaging about Buckingham, who had planned to lead an invasion of Holland, saying that he 'will not be satisfied but with his own ruin, and with ours... 'tis a strange quality in a man to love idleness so well as to destroy his estate by it'; but the implicit criticism of Buckingham reflects on Rochester as well. Pepys had infamously described Rochester a few years earlier as 'so idle a rogue' and Dryden might have been offering him some veiled advice in the comparison. To the distant observer, Rochester's life seemed a pleasant and undemanding one. He had a loving wife, two young children and the run of two fine houses in Ditchley and Adderbury. He was also part of the elite set of wits and courtiers in London. He took his pleasure in town and performed his duty in Adderbury, and neither was especially onerous. In short, he appeared contented.

However, Rochester was anything but content. When he received Dryden's letter, he was lingering in tedium at Adderbury and in attendance on an ill Elizabeth, rather than enjoying 'the happiness of an idle life'. Lacking money and the company of the Ballers and feeling the growing effects of his illness, he concealed his fears beneath the usual round of drinking and brothel-creeping. By immersing himself in carnal or alcoholic pleasure, he blotted out his doubts and worries for a night or so, but they soon returned. He also acquired a reputation for rash actions, far from the gallant naval reputation he had once held. While at court in March 1673, he had ducked out of a duel with the short-tempered Robert Constable, Viscount Dunbar, and both men had narrowly avoided censure in the House of Lords on 22 March as a result of the intended combat. As with his dispute with Mulgrave, the cause of this was a trivial misunderstanding over a libel Rochester was believed to have written, but it was still considered politic that he absent himself to the country for a while. Away from the distractions of town, he frittered his time away.

In a witty pastiche of a letter begging for charity, he wrote to Savile asking that he assist 'in preserving your humble servant Rochester from the imminent peril of sobriety, which, for want of good wine more than company (for I drink like a hermit betwixt God and my own conscience) is very like to befall me'. A bored Rochester asks that his friend perform an act of 'sacred friendship' by pointing him towards 'the best wine in town'. Savile, who had been given the usual royal decree of forgiveness since the debacle with Lady Percy at Althorp the previous year and had become MP for Newark, was advised grandly that a gift of wine would ensure that he, Savile, was 'no longer hovering 'twixt the unequal choice of politics and lewdness'. The underlying implication is clear: while he remained frivolous and witty in his correspondence, Rochester felt frustrated at the apparently stagnant direction that his life was taking, as his sporadic outbreaks of ill health rendered a more engaging existence impossible. Nonetheless, help, of a sort, was at hand.

Elizabeth Barry, a young would-be actress, arrived in London in 1673. The fifteen-year-old daughter of the lawyer Robert Barry, she was no great beauty, with heavy features, dark hair and a slightly over-large nose. But those who met her were struck by her charisma, and these included the poet and playwright William Davenant's daughter Lady Davenant, who took her up when she arrived in town and attempted to indulge her wish of a theatrical career.

What then transpired involves both a romantic myth and a more prosaic reality. The myth put about by the eighteenth-century actor, playwright and Poet Laureate Colley Cibber in his memoirs—and one that has generally been believed since—is that Elizabeth Barry was initially a useless and untrained actress. Cibber describes her as having 'a very bad ear' and claims that it was 'impossible to make her fit for the meanest part'; it was considered that 'she never would be capable of any part of acting'. Her dreams of taking to the stage were nearly dashed before they had even begun, when she appeared in the actor Thomas Betterton's company, playing Draxilla in Thomas Otway's *Alcibiades*. Otway was a former actor who, beset by stage fright, had abandoned performing in favour of writing and saw his work staged by Betterton at the Dorset Garden Theatre. Unfortunately, Elizabeth Barry's performance was said to be disastrous.

Enter, like a character from an unlikely fairy tale, Lord Rochester. Cibber's anecdote continues that Rochester, returning to London and in need of a new distraction, found himself approached by various interested parties at the theatre and told about this unsuccessful

woman. Seeing himself in the role of Pygmalion to this unlikely subject, Rochester entered into a wager with the playwright George
Etherege that, within six months, he would turn Elizabeth Barry
into the finest actress of her generation, who would be so successful
that she would later be described by Dryden as 'always excellent'.
Rochester, a hard taskmaster, forced her to rehearse to the point that
she was no longer a bad actress playing a part on a stage in a contrived and artificial manner, but a real woman who entirely understood the underlying truth and complexity of what she was saying.
His unorthodox technique was a success. She was said to have made
her debut proper as a leading actress in a production of Roger Boyle's
tragic drama *Mustapha* at the Theatre Royal; she took the lead role
of Isabella and played in front of Rochester, Charles and others, and
'the whole theatre resounded with applause'.

It is a charming story, but not a credible one. For a start, the dates
are askew. Rochester probably first encountered Elizabeth Barry in
1673 and she appeared in *Mustapha* in 1675, so he would have lost his
bet at the very least. Likewise, given that *Alcibiades* was also first
performed in 1675, it is unlikely that she could have gone from ama-
teurishness to professional excellence so quickly. The sources for
this tale are Cibber's autobiography and the French nobleman and
English court habitué the Comte de Gramont's notoriously unreliable memoirs; both of these were published a considerable time after
the events that they describe, by which time Rochester's name gave
credence to any unlikely tale involving a young woman.

This is a shame, as the story perfectly encapsulates many of
Rochester's interests and abilities. Had he tutored Elizabeth Barry
in this fashion, it would have reflected a simultaneous interest in the
artifice of the theatre and performance, mirroring the duality that
he adopted throughout his life. What is certainly true is that the two
began a love affair that would become the most serious extra-marital
involvement of Rochester's life, and one that would affect both his
writing and his attitudes immeasurably.

A poem that he wrote around this time, almost certainly inspired
by his association with Elizabeth Barry in its allusions to the theatre

and stage, indicates a poetic ambivalence about the world of play-acting and disguise that both of them inhabited:

> Leave this gaudy, gilded stage,
> From custom more than use frequented,
> Where fools of either sex and age
> Crowd to see themselves presented.
> To Love's theatre, the bed,
> Youth and beauty fly together
> And act so well it may be said
> The laurel there was due to either.
> 'Twixt strife of Love and war the difference lies in this:
> When neither overcomes, Love's triumph greater is.

While Rochester divided his time between the idleness of Adderbury and the more frenetic excitements of London, change was afoot. An Anglo-French army besieged Maastricht in June 1673, resulting in an allied victory and great celebrations at court. Rochester's sardonic response to the success was to write a satirical poem, 'Upon his drinking a bowl', which carefully and explicitly repudiates his past military career ('With war I've nought to do/ I'm none of those that took Maastricht/ Nor Yarmouth leaguer knew'); continues his teasing allusions to sodomy with a mention of 'two lovely boys' whose 'limbs in amorous folds entwine'; and then ends with a final, carnally triumphant paragraph that fully expresses the debauched credo of the twenty-seven-year-old Rochester:

> Cupid and Bacchus my saints are:
> May drink and love still reign.
> With wine I wash away my cares,
> And then to cunt again.

The momentary triumph of Maastricht was soon forgotten, and jockeying for position and influence at court became the order of the day for the likes of Buckingham, who, always a political animal, had allied himself with the newly formed Country party, which eventually became the Whig party. Opposed to the anti-tolerationist policies of Charles and his ministers, who continued to support only the 'Established Religion and Laws', it set up a schism at the heart of Whitehall between Charles, who looked weak and out of touch, and the reformers. Rochester did not take either part, but looked on from the sidelines, amused but uninvolved.

Instead, perhaps revitalized by the start of his affair with Elizabeth Barry, he found his poetic muse revived. Between November 1673 and late January 1674, he contributed to the bawdy social satire 'Signior Dildo'. This poem exists in several different versions, all of which mock the marriage of Charles's brother James to Mary of Modena, who thereby became the Duchess of York. It must originate at some point between Mary's arrival in London on 26 November and the poem's being cited in a letter from the soldier Sir Nicholas Armourer to the politician Sir Joseph Williamson on 26 January, indicating a comparatively swift composition. Anti-Catholic feeling ensured that this marriage, conducted solely for political ends, was an unpopular one, and the discontent was soon translated into verse.

The reason why the poem cannot be ascribed solely to Rochester is that, as with *Sodom*, it has a cruder and less witty feel to it than his other contemporary work. The copy-text credits Rochester alone, but other versions credit Fleetwood Sheppard and Charles Sackville, so there was clearly confusion over who was responsible. The central thrust is undisciplined and scatter-gun, with dozens of verses consisting of a simple recurring idea—namely, that some great lady of court is sexually unsatisfied by the foppish and unmanly Englishmen and thus uses the 'noble Italian' Signior Dildo. Again, as with 'The Imperfect Enjoyment', Rochester and the other writers ridicule the idea of male sexual prowess and potency, but while that poem used escalating absurdity to hilarious effect, 'Signior Dildo' comes less to a shuddering climax than to a half-hearted whimper. It might be more amusing at shorter and more focused length, but as it continues in one version for two dozen verses, and in others for three dozen, it ends up being more tiring than effective.

All the same, there are some wonderfully Rochesterian moments in it. His notorious cousin Barbara Castlemaine is mocked in particularly virulent but witty style:

> That pattern of virtue, Her Grace of Cleveland,
> Has swallowed more pricks than the ocean has sand;
> But by rubbing and scrubbing so large it does grow,
> It is fit for just nothing but Signior Dildo.

The list of those ridiculed and pilloried is lengthy, ranging from the singer and royal mistress Mary Knight to Elizabeth Percy; the latter is referred to in a verse that was either written or inspired by Henry Savile, as it makes knowing allusion to his incursion into her bedroom at Althorp:

> By the help of this gallant the countess of Ralph
> Against the fierce Harrys preserved herself safe.
> She stifled him almost beneath her pillow,
> So closely she embraced Signior Dildo.

A poem such as 'Signior Dildo' was written for the amusement of those at court, passed from aristocratic hand to hand, and treated with a certain detached pleasure at the witty conceit that the verse contained. This was a common and accepted means of entertainment, taking place most days in some form, and could lead to a certain notoriety; such was the success of 'Signior Dildo' that dildoes became known as 'Signiors' after it appeared. Rochester, however, was not always content merely to amuse. Instead, his coruscating disdain for the shallow, hypocritical world of the court, typified by the king himself, led him to write one of his most trenchant satires on the subject, at around the same time as the composition of 'Signior Dildo'. While Rochester had little personal animosity against Charles (apart from his failure to pay him his various grants), the king's personal and regal failings were so glaring that it fell to a gifted writer to articulate them in verse. Entitled 'A Satire on Charles II', the poem refuses to pull any punches from the start. Charles is mocked as 'the easiest King and best-bred man alive', but one with 'no ambition' who is content to wander 'up and down / Starving his people, hazarding his crown'.

To an even greater degree than in his earlier satires, Rochester takes aim at the materialist and carnal values of the court with scrupulously moral disdain. Britain, synonymous only with 'the best cunts in Christendom', has become a place of starving and desperate people, where the earlier excitement and optimism of the Restoration has given way to nothing other than self-indulgence. Rochester spent a good deal of time outside London and saw a beaten, battered country, one simultaneously worn down by the after-effects of civil war and the Protectorate and Charles's ill-fated foreign adventures. The story of the king having sex ('for love he loves, for he loves fucking much') while the *Royal Charles* was stolen informs the contemptuous disgust with which Rochester presents his moral judgements on his monarch. Of course, there were others who were also responsible for this state of affairs:

> His sceptre and prick are of a length;
> And she may sway the one who plays with th'other,
> And make him little wiser than his brother.
> Poor prince! Thy prick, like thy buffoons at court,
> Will govern thee because it makes thee sport.
> 'Tis sure the sauciest prick that e'er did swive,
> The proudest, peremptoriest prick alive.
> Though safety, law, religion, life lay on't,
> 'Twould break through all to make its way to cunt.
> Restless he rolls about from whore to whore,
> A merry monarch, scandalous and poor.

The metaphor of the sceptre—a symbol of immutable authority—being interchangeable with the royal penis again reflects Rochester's fascination with emasculation and impotence, but here on a far grander scale than simple masculine vanity. As Rochester writes, 'safety, law, religion, life' must all give way to royal restlessness. And yet, despite all the sex, and the illegitimate children produced by royal mistresses, not a single royal heir was born.

Rochester's half-fond, half-dismissive attitude towards the various royal mistresses is then made explicit as he describes Louise de Kérouaille (here called 'Carwell', a corruption of the surname) as 'the best relief of his declining years'. Charles was forty-three at the time, but beset by ill health possibly caused by a form of syphilis. The royal body is mocked as having 'dull, graceless ballocks', and even the valiant efforts of Nell Gwyn, with 'hands, fingers, mouth and thighs', are painful and in vain. Rochester's contempt is not limited just to Charles, but instead to the whole business of kingship:

> All monarchs I hate, and the thrones they sit on,
> From the hector of France to the cully of Britain.

A bracingly honest satire against the king, it shows how far Rochester had progressed from the frightened young man eight years before who claimed that he would rather have chosen death ten thousand times than have upset his ruler. Now it was dangerous enough, in the atmosphere of paranoia and distrust that had infected the court, even to write such a virulent satire. After its creation, it would not have been gaily passed from hand to hand, owing to how scurrilous it was; instead, a few fair copies were made (a surviving one of which is dated 1673) and shown only to his most reliable and trusted friends. However, with all the desire to shock and subvert that lived within him, Rochester was about to make another significant step into infamy.

Charles was, by and large, open-minded when it came to personal comments made about him. He regarded it as sport, one that he was as complicit in as his favourites, and he took pride in coming back with a well-timed riposte. One night, at dinner, Rochester was asked to provide an extempore poem about Charles, and he replied, perhaps after a glass of wine, with the following:

God bless our good and gracious King,
Whose promise none relies on;
Who never said a foolish thing,
Nor ever did a wise one.

Charles, taking the sally in good spirit, answered: 'That's true; for my words are mine, while my actions are those of my ministers.' It was a neat answer, and a telling moment of self-deprecation, which he was skilled at coming up with to defuse tension. However, in December 1673, an unfortunate encounter took place that would colour our relations between Rochester and Charles forever afterwards.

At dinner at court, in the lead-up to Christmas, a rumour had reached the royal ears about a scurrilous poem that ridiculed many of the leading women of the day. Charles, who had had carnal knowledge of most of those featured, was intrigued and amused by the idea, and asked Rochester to hand him over the satire, which he believed to be 'Signior Dildo'. Rochester by accident—or design—instead handed Charles the explosive satire that he had written about him earlier that year. He might always have wished Charles to see it and had it on him for that very purpose.

The resulting scene can be imagined only as one of the Old Masters might have painted it. In the centre is Charles, with his habitual expression of amused levity gradually giving way to a combination of horror, surprise and anger. To his right stands Rochester, smirking at his impudence but beginning to realize the enormity of his actions. Around the central pair are the great men of court, such as Buckingham, Savile and Sackville, all simultaneously amused by, and fearful of, the hugely public nature of such an act; whether they had known the satire or not, there was no mistaking Charles's wrath. And scattered around the room are the uncomprehending royal servants, mistresses and hangers-on, all of whom witness the royal wrath in all its fury.

Traditional biographical accounts of this incident, such as that of Gramont's, have Rochester as a blundering drunken idiot, incapable of distinguishing the (comparatively) mild satire of 'Signior Dildo' from the altogether more scurrilous libel of the satire against Charles. This is possibly true. However, given the authenticity of the sentiments expressed within the poem and the weariness with which he writes about the false life of court in his letters, it is equally likely that Rochester, summoning up a moment of self-destructive bravado, decided deliberately to hand over the 'wrong' poem and be damned, taking masochistic pleasure both in his certain punishment and in the knowledge that Charles would have the smile wiped off his face when he saw the unsentimental reality of how he was regarded by his favourites.

Unsurprisingly, the 'merry monarch' was enraged by what he read. Fleeing upon seeing Charles's wrath, Rochester was straightaway formally banished from court, in what was the most serious breach of relations between him and Charles since his attempted abduction of Elizabeth nearly a decade before. That, for all its impropriety and arrogant dismissal of rules, could be put down to youthful high spirits of a kind. But this was an unforgivable breach of trust. As with Clarendon, formal banishment meant that to return uninvited would incur a potential death sentence, and all of Rochester's endowments, pensions and payments were suspended with immediate effect. He returned to Adderbury a penitent Adam, cast out of his surrogate father's affections, for what might have been forever.

It was said by the antiquary and biographer John Aubrey, as a result of this and other incidents, that Rochester had the devil enter into him whenever he passed Brentford on his way back to London, and that this satanic possession lasted until he left and returned to Adderbury or Woodstock. While Aubrey, who was no admirer of Rochester, was indulging in poetic licence, he hit upon a central aspect of his character and how he was perceived. Satan was commonly believed to encourage those who were otherwise temperate and sane to commit lewd acts and to behave disgracefully. Rochester, himself no stranger to 'the demon drink', was restrained, if bored, in the country, pouring his intellectual energies into his poetry. In town, it was another matter, and the incident with Charles soon became the year's most talked-about occurrence in fashionable circles, arousing shock and reluctant admiration in equal parts.

The diabolic had become a source of fascination for many in the Restoration world. Those who had read *Paradise Lost* babbled excitedly about the central character of Satan, a sympathetic and articulate figure rather than the one-dimensional Vice, tempter of morality plays, while those who were less well-read equated Satanism with the interest in Catholicism emanating from the court, now that both Charles and his brother James were married to Catholics. While Matthew Hopkins's witch-finding of three decades earlier seemed impossibly remote, the idea that one of the court's most charismatic and seductive figures might literally be possessed by the devil was both horrifying and exciting—and of course made Rochester even more of a man of intrigue and magnetism.

The intriguing and magnetic man, meanwhile, was at home in Adderbury with his family in a state of trepidation and weariness. He had plenty of time to reflect on the ungrateful way in which he had repaid Charles's generosity and patronage, and also to brood on his forced estrangement from Elizabeth Barry. A misanthropic poem, dating from around this time, might offer some insight into his miserable and bored state of mind, especially as far as issues of love and romance were concerned:

> Love a woman? You're an ass!
> 'Tis a most insipid passion
> To choose out for your happiness
> The silliest part of God's creation.

> Let the porter and the groom,
> Things designed for dirty slaves,
> Drudge in fair Aurelia's womb
> To get supplies for age and graves.

Rochester had many ways of artificially lifting himself from his low spirits. In town, this consisted of drinking, whoring and cavorting with the Ballers. In the country, where the opportunities were more limited, if they existed at all, lifting his spirits depended more on his remembrance of these events, which often took poetic form. With his wife and mother at hand, to say nothing of young children, he was unable to lead the free and easy life of London, whither he had no idea if he would be allowed to return. The second part of the poem indicates how Rochester considered these day-dreams:

> Farewell, woman! I intend
> Henceforth every night to sit
> With my lewd, well-natured friend,
> Drinking to engender wit.
>
> Then give me health, wealth, mirth and wine,
> And, if busy love entrenches,
> There's a sweet, soft page of mine
> Does the trick worth forty wenches.

Whether Rochester really was bisexual, itself an anachronistic concept, is hard to gauge from his poetry alone. There are numerous allusions to homosexual, as well as heterosexual, liaisons throughout his verse, but his letters are mostly devoid of any romantic or sexual passion towards men, with the major exception coming in some of his correspondence with Savile. Rochester once wrote, in French, that he was 'a tired bugger' and makes various allusions to some potential homosexual blackmail in which he was involved at the end of his life. That he had sex with both men and women, from his time at university onwards, is almost certain; few contemporary courtiers did not. As early as 1663, Pepys noted that homosexual liaisons at the court took place with impunity, saying 'buggery is now grown as common among our gallants as in Italy'.* That Rochester was primarily heterosexual is likely, but he loved to shock and to cross

---

* 'Buggery' was not simply a term for anal sex; it covered everything from bestiality to oral sex, as defined in the 1533 Buggery Act: 'an unnatural sexual act against the will of God and man'.

boundaries. 'The sweet, soft page' that he writes about becomes a symbol of his resistance to the status quo, as the court of Charles II, while undeniably licentious, drew a line at the open recognition of sodomy (perhaps unsurprisingly given that Charles himself was avowedly heterosexual). While prosecutions for buggery were rare, it was still officially regarded as a capital crime on a par with treason, and could be used as a pretext for imprisonment, exile or even execution, if it was politic to do so.

Rochester's 'lewd, well-natured' drinking companion referred to here was almost certainly Savile. In a letter that he wrote probably at the start of 1674, while stating that he is temporarily living alone at Adderbury (presumably his wife and children were at her house at Enmore), he continues to display his affection for his friend, claiming: ''Tis not the least of my happiness that I think you love me... if there be a real good upon earth, 'tis in the name of friend, without which all others are merely fantastical.' The tone of Rochester's letters to his main recipients are all subtly different. The swooning romance of his early correspondence with Elizabeth soon gives way to a mixture of jocular banter and irritated pedantry. His dealings with Elizabeth Barry are fond and apologetic and sometimes feel disingenuous, as if he is writing a love letter that is as much for public consumption as for private enjoyment. But it is with Savile that Rochester's voice feels most authentic, as he moves between mock-grandiose biblical parodies, gossip and apparently heartfelt displays of affection.

There was also always a tinge of what Rochester termed 'the melancholy experience' that underpinned the jokes and fondness. Rochester, always interested in philosophy, was becoming increasingly convinced that the world was, as Hamlet put it, 'weary, stale, flat and unprofitable', and when he was bored at home, he took to wondering what the meaning of it all was. Writing to Savile, he openly questions why friendship is so debased in 'the most difficult and rare accident of life', and takes a startlingly clear-headed view of life at court: 'you... think not at all, or at least as if you were shut up in a drum, you can think of nothing but the noise is made upon you.' Rochester claims to desire the 'competent riches' that would be attendant on this position, but the letter clearly comes from a bored, lonely man who laments 'the inconveniences of solitude' and finds himself caught between the Scylla of empty chatter at Whitehall and the Charybdis of tedium in the country. He may have loathed the drum-like noise and the endless whirligig of events, but at least they stimulated him, while the only company he could enjoy at Adderbury while his family were away was that of his increasingly querulous and disapproving mother.

In a simultaneous letter to Elizabeth, Rochester mentions that Anne Wilmot is 'now resolved against ever moving' from Adderbury and that this will necessitate a removal of their family. Anne, who had recently renewed the lease on the house, was a difficult presence, and her immutable desire to stay there led Rochester to write, perhaps with tongue in cheek, that 'fate shall direct, which is (I find) the true disposer of things whatever we attribute to wisdom or providence'.

In this instance, he was proved right, perhaps guessing that his fortunes would rise once more. While the offence that he had caused Charles was considerable and would be a lasting source of conflict and tension between the two men, the king was well aware that, with the rise of Buckingham and others who were less than well disposed towards him, he could not afford to ostracize a man who, at the very least, could be relied upon to support him in exchange for much-needed money and land. Thus, forgiven, Rochester's banishment was rescinded in January 1674 and his grants restored, and he officially returned to Whitehall on 16 February and put his name to a petition in which he dutifully criticized Catholicism and all its works. (Gramont tells a story that he returned anonymously in late 1673 and busied himself with the citizens of the city while keeping an ear to the ground for Whitehall gossip; however, like most of Gramont's tales, there is no proof of this.)

Perhaps in exchange for his renewed and conspicuous loyalty, Rochester was created Ranger of Woodstock Park on 27 February, a high-profile appointment that also carried with it the gift of the High Lodge there. This news was reflected in a jocular letter Rochester wrote his wife in which he claims that he will 'be with you shortly... [and] think myself a very happy man', and suggests that 'I will deliver you immediately'. He might also, for once, have been in funds, as is suggested by his statement that 'money you shall have as soon as ever I come to you'.

It was a happier time for Rochester. Restored to royal favour, he soon capitalized on this by being given the related and greater title of Keeper of Woodstock Park, which carried another pension (had Charles been reliable in paying the various annuities that Rochester was granted, he would have been a wealthy man by this point). The new Drury Lane theatre opened on 26 March 1674, allowing Elizabeth Barry an opportunity to be noticed on what was then the city's most prestigious stage, and the affair between herself and Rochester was proceeding in fecund fashion. Meanwhile, he became a father again, with his second daughter born in late June. In a simultaneously uxorious and knowingly provocative move, he christened her Elizabeth.

Yet even while Rochester, briefly riding a wave of personal and public happiness, appeared content with his lot, his rancorous poetic muse still compelled him to look at the world, the flesh and the devil and produce a characteristically biting response to it. Two satires that he was associated with at this time were 'Tunbridge Wells' and 'Timon', an adaptation of Boileau's third satire. 'Collaboration' is probably too strong a term to describe what occurred when poetry was written by more than one hand in the Restoration court. Instead, a poem might be added to by a jealous or unimpressed fellow courtier and then redistributed accordingly, or two separate poems might be conflated and turned into a manuscript copy. Thus, a poem could be 'by' two separate writers who had never exchanged any ideas about the work at all, or in some cases had never met.

'Tunbridge Wells', like 'Signior Dildo', is unlikely to have been the work of Rochester alone. The episodic accumulation of its structure lacks the discipline and ironic control that Rochester's greatest work is known for. It also feels like a more sedate reprise of the panoramic social satire of 'A Ramble In St James's Park', where all facets of society are held up for mockery and scorn. The difference is that 'Tunbridge Wells' feels more strained and consequently less witty. By way of comparison, take the bitingly laconic anger of 'A Ramble' when it describes an ardent young blade trying to woo a faithless woman:

> One, in a strain 'twixt tune and nonsense,
> Cries 'Madam, I have loved you long since.
> Permit me your fair hand to kiss',
> When at her mouth her cunt cries 'Yes!'

Compare this with the more mannered and less satisfying verbiage in 'Tunbridge Wells' on a similar theme:

> The would-be wit, whose business was to woo,
> With hat removed, and solemn scrape of shoe
> Advanceth bowing, then genteelly shrugs,
> And ruffled foretop into order tugs,
> And thus accosts her, 'Madam, methinks the weather
> Is grown much more serene since you came hither
> You influence the heavens; but should the sun
> Withdraw himself to see his rays outdone
> By your bright eyes, they would supply the morn,
> And make a day before the day be born.'
> With mouth screwed up, conceited winking eyes,
> And breasts thrust forward, 'Lord, sir!' she replies.
> 'It is your goodness, more than my deserts,
> Which makes you show this learning, wit and parts.'

It is likely that Rochester was at least involved in some amendments and additions to this poem, as the odd flash of wit is of a piece with his other verse of this time; the last ten lines or so act almost as a prologue to 'A Satire against Reason and Mankind'. There is also an interestingly approving reference to Marvell, the only one found anywhere in any writings attributed to Rochester. Nonetheless, the comparatively plodding nature of the work makes it more likely that a lesser court poet, such as Savile, was responsible for the bulk of its creation and that Rochester was credited as sole writer posthumously.

Another argument against its being a Rochesterian satire is that Rochester was engaged on 'Timon' at about the same time, and that work, in its brio, allusive complexity and wit, feels more in the spirit of his 'mature' poetry. It has been suggested that Sedley or Buckingham, rather than Rochester, is the author of 'Timon', but its wry intelligence, at least in its first half, feels much more like the work of the latter. Proving authorship definitively is difficult because no circumstantial contemporary evidence exists for one writer or another having written the work. Most readers, therefore, tend to judge the poems on the basis of internal evidence and subsequent attribution in early printed forms, which of course were often not authorized. Perhaps appropriately, 'Timon' is a rich and all-enveloping comment on the confused and confusing age in which it was written, taking the form of a dialogue where the main speaker, Timon, is an avatar for Rochester, or at least his public persona. The classical allusion could either be to Timon of Athens, the misanthrope, or to the satirical poet Timon of Phlius. Or, of course, to both: Rochester was seldom sparing when it came to displaying his intellectual prowess.

As with 'The Disabled Debauchee', the protagonist, Timon, is nearing the end of his life. An anonymous figure asks him whether 'thou droop'st under a night's debauch', in a reference both to sexual and physical infirmity, and goes on to mention his debts to 'needy rogues', to whom he owes money on credit, or 'on tick'. Rochester-as-Timon offers a wry insight into the everyday boredom that he faces at court. Buttonholed by a 'dull dining sot', he finds himself compelled to head to an inn with the god-awful bore, whose tedium is compounded by his belief that his fascination with poetry is sufficient to make him interesting. Reading various anonymous satires, the fop at last comes across one that was 'so sharp' that it had to be Timon's—though Timon himself expresses his scepticism that his work had proliferated so far as to reach this mediocre man. What follows is a fascinatingly self-aware comment on the attribution of anonymous court poems, in which context it is particularly amusing:

> He knew my style, he swore, and 'twas in vain
> Thus to deny the issue of my brain.
> Choked with his flattery, I no answer make,
> But, silent, leave him to his dear mistake,
> Which he by this had spread o'er the whole town,
> And me with an officious lie undone.
> Of a well-meaning fool I'm most afraid,
> Who sillily repeats what was well said.

The 'dear mistake' is one that has persisted to this day, and one that Rochester, then enjoying a growing reputation at court as a poet, could only wryly stand by and watch, as his name was attached to countless inferior works passed around his circle. The number of contemporary manuscripts with entirely spurious poems that have 'Earl of Rochester' emblazoned on them, like a guilty secret, testify to this.

As Timon's narrative continues, the parallels with Rochester's life become even clearer. His friends Sedley, Buckhurst and Savile are all absent from the dinner, but 'Halfwit and Huff, Kickum and Dingboy', typical representatives of knavish idiocy, are all present. For the hapless Timon, 'no means nor hopes appear of a retreat', and the appearance of the wife of one of the fops, Sparkish, is the final straw:

> A wife, good gods! A fop, and bullies too!
> For one poor meal, what must I undergo?

The threatened wife duly appears, the incursion of age having 'left her with more desire than power to please', and her conversation is coquettishly focused entirely on love, 'and hardly from that subject would remove'. As ever, remembering the biographical details of Rochester's own life at this point gives extra spice to the poem; when 'my lady' wonders, in relation to Louis XIV's extra-marital successes, 'how heaven could bless / A man that loved two women at one time', the unspoken but implicit comparison is with Rochester's own marriage to Elizabeth and affair with Elizabeth Barry. Their dining companions are a charmless bunch; when Huff is asked whether 'love's flame he never felt', his reply, delivered bluntly, is 'Do you think I'm gelt?'

As usual with Rochester's satires, merely guying the easy targets of predatory women and foolish fops was not enough. It soon transpires that their host lost an estate given for loyal service on Charles's behalf, which was spent 'whoring and drinking, but with good intent'. Here, Rochester subtly ridicules the free-handed way in which many (including himself) benefited from royal largesse, only to find themselves useless at coping with the responsibility. As for 'my lady', she is far from an admirer of Rochester's poetry, which is seen as 'unfit for modest ears', preferring the two Cavalier poets Lucius Cary, 2nd Viscount Falkland, and Sir John Suckling; the joke is that their more modest verse is a far cry from the Bacchanal that is developing at the table.

The second half of the satire is less immediately enjoyable, consisting mostly of the various clueless hurrahs arguing about their preferred poets and dramatists with all the breezy bluster of the truly uninformed literary critic. Here, the author, whether still Rochester or Sedley, shows a fine grasp of the Restoration literary scene, as one of his characters praises Etherege for writing 'airy songs and soft lampoons, the best of any man', and now forgotten figures such as Elkanah Settle, John Crowne (who dedicated his heroic drama *The History of Charles the Eight of France* to Rochester) and Roger Boyle are all discussed. (Amusingly, Dryden's play *The Indian Emperor* is praised by the host, who, presumably in his cups, 'had said nothing in an hour'.) Eventually, the bravoes fall to violent disagreement about the competing merits of literature and the chance of future war—the heat is cooled only by the appearance of 'six fresh bottles'—and Timon flees:

I ran downstairs, and with a vow nevermore
To drink beer-glass and hear the hectors roar.

Unsurprisingly, Rochester did not pursue this unlikely sounding wish. Shortly after his daughter's christening at Adderbury, he returned to court, where the ever-present noise that he had likened to being 'shut up in a drum' continued to vex him. At last, frustrated and angered, he began writing a poem that would take revenge upon everyone. Not just the usual chorus of faithless lovers, imbecilic fops, priapic monarchs or talentless dramatists, but, this time, a far wider panorama of society. He would write a satire that would discuss the great issues of the day, without the sexual or scatological humour that had become his trademark, but with overtones of Montaigne or Hobbes. If people would mock and belittle him, after all, then he would give them intellectual grounds to mock and belittle themselves. More ambitious than anything he had ever written before, the poem would be simultaneously the apotheosis of his literary career and the final time that he ever produced work of this brilliance.

[8]

'A Satire

AGAINST

REASON

and

mankind'

✵

[*1674*]

WHEN HE BEGAN what became his most ambitious work in spring 1674, Rochester called the poem, portentously, 'A Satire against Reason and Mankind'. Though he was still only twenty-seven, his implied aim was as grandiloquent as Milton's *Paradise Lost* had been the previous decade. Not content with mocking humanity, Rochester also intended to take aim at reason, which he calls the *ignis fatuus*, itself a reference to the ninth book of *Paradise Lost* and meaning 'foolish light' or 'will-o'-the-wisp'. Inspired by his loathing of the hypocrites and knaves who surrounded him, as well as by an intellectual curiosity that had seldom been given full rein in his poetry before, Rochester aimed to show his friends (and enemies) that he was a serious and considered thinker, rather than simply a rake about court. Mixing his customary wit and intellectual clarity with anger and passion, Rochester's poem of 221 lines is believed by many to be his greatest and most enduring work. When it circulated around court, it was ascribed to 'a person of honour', a wittily double-edged attribution that became more telling when the satire was read.

As he wrote it, England was in a state of flux. With the country all but bankrupted by the failures of the Anglo-Dutch wars, there were many politically unaffiliated men and women who quietly regretted that the stringent morality of the Commonwealth had been replaced by such profligacy. The joy and optimism of the Restoration had given way to a growing sense that Charles II had no clear idea how he wanted to govern the country. As he and his familiars devoted themselves to a life of sexual and sybaritic abandon, their existence might as well have happened on the moon for all the good that it did for an increasingly weary, impoverished and put-upon populace. The government—the so-called Cabal Ministry of Buckingham and the king's other high councillors—grew increasingly unstable and fell in September 1674, with the result that Buckingham and Charles's old tutor Hobbes's earlier fears that life would become 'solitary, poor, brutish, nasty and short' without the strong presence of a committed sovereign seemed to be on the verge of realization.

The influence of Hobbes on at least the first half of 'A Satire' is impossible to overstate. Pilloried for perceived blasphemy after a 1666 bill that outlawed atheism and profaneness, Hobbes in 1674 was a diminished figure, much revered by continental philosophers but unable to publish anything on human conduct or reason in England. The term 'Hobbist' became less a mark of intellectual respect than a sneering denigration of renegade, atheistic spirits; ironic, perhaps, given that it referred to one who believed in the absolutist rule of a monarch. Anthony à Wood refers to Rochester having become 'a perfect Hobbist' under the influence of the court. Meant as an insult, this comment unintentionally gives an accurate summary of Rochester's philosophical and social views.

Rochester had already written one poem, 'Love and Life', which owed a significant debt to Hobbes. As with all of Hobbes's philosophy, the blend of pragmatic common sense and implied *carpe diem* sensibility—if it is only the present that has any point, take full advantage of it—proved a strong influence on Rochester, whose desire to write a satire on reason as well as mankind stemmed from another passage in *Leviathan* in which Hobbes attempts to explain the curiously sinuous definition of what 'right reason' and 'false reason' are. He claims that:

> reason itself is always right reason, as well as arithmetic is a certain and infallible art; but no one man's reason, nor the reason of any one number of men, makes the certainty; no more than an account is therefore well cast up, because a great many men have unanimously approved it.

In other words, mass consensus cannot be taken seriously as a means of decision-making. Hobbes makes the subsequent point that what he terms 'natural wit' is found principally in two things: 'celerity of imagining', or speed of passing from one thought to another, and 'steady direction to some approved end'.

However, Rochester's aim in writing 'A Satire' was not so much to produce a philosophical treatise as to offer an entertainingly biting commentary on the mores of his time. The loose, conversational tone of the opening sets the scene for Rochester's attack on humanity:

> Were I (who to my cost already am
> One of those strange, prodigious creatures, man)
> A spirit free to choose, for my own share,
> What case of flesh and blood I pleased to wear,
> I'd be a dog, a monkey or a bear,
> Or anything but that vain animal
> Who is so proud of being rational.

In these seven lines, Rochester offers a treasure trove of motifs and themes that recur throughout his work. The metaphysical poetry of Donne and Marvell hangs over the image of the 'case of flesh and blood', with Rochester's own spirit encased in his all too corporeal and weak form. The choice of animals is far from coincidental: the dog was associated with Charles and the court; the monkey was a sly allusion to Rochester's own pet, shown with him in his most famous portrait; and the bear is a likely reference to the tavern of that name, as referenced at the beginning of 'A Ramble in St James's Park'. All this is counterpointed by man, 'that vain animal', and his pride in being 'rational'. The irony practically drips from the page.

The next section of the poem offers a concerted attack on the Hobbesian definition of false reason and the willingness of the weak-willed to be beguiled by what he terms 'pathless and dangerous wandering ways'. Rochester's satiric evocation of reason as a sixth season that will 'contradict the other five' is soon undercut by his sardonic dismissal of it as 'an *ignis fatuus* of the mind' and one that will leave both 'light of nature' and 'sense' behind. His sights are initially set on the philosophical compass of 'error's fenny bogs and thorny breaks', but it is quite clear that all the seeker of reason will find himself in is 'doubt's boundless sea'. Rochester offers a wry comment that books will 'bear him up awhile', while 'bladders of

philosophy' offer a life raft of sorts, but eventually all will fail. The
will-o'-the-wisp offers some fleeting distractions, but eventually
and inevitably 'eternal night' beckons. The final part of this section
offers Rochester at his most nihilistic:

> Then old age and experience, hand in hand,
> Lead him to death, and make him understand,
> After a search so painful, and so long
> That all his life he has been in the wrong.
> Huddled in dirt the reasoning engine lies,
> Who was so proud, so witty and so wise.

Two centuries later, Tennyson would recite the couple of dozen lines
of this part of the poem by heart, rising to rhythmic exaltation on
the final ironic stresses. Its theatrical quality comes from the pes-
simistic worldview expressed by the poet-speaker, here building
to the height of his own rhetoric. Rochester's often overlooked gift
for metaphor and imagery is here shown in full flower, with man,
the 'reasoning engine', merely 'huddled in dirt' after the long and
painful search. There are possible echoes of Milton's 'two-handed
engine' from *Lycidas*, just as the use of the word 'engine' brings
Robert Boyle's writing on chemistry to mind. Of course Milton and
Boyle, brilliant and dangerous though they had been, would themselves end up huddled in dirt in good time, just like every other
thinker and writer of the age.

If Rochester was anything as a writer, he was self-aware, and the
next part of 'A Satire' finds him taking aim at those who lived by
their charm and intelligence. It is virtually inconceivable that the fifteen lines that follow were not written about himself and his friends,
as a kind of living epitaph:

> Pride drew him in, as cheats their bubbles catch,
> And made him venture to be made a wretch.
> His wisdom did his happiness destroy,
> Aiming to know that world he should enjoy.

> And wit was his vain, frivolous pretence
> Of pleasing others at his own expense,
> For wits are treated just like common whores:
> First they're enjoyed, and then kicked out of doors.
> The pleasure past, a threatening doubt remains
> That frights th'enjoyer with succeeding pains.
> Women and men of wit are dangerous tools,
> And ever fatal to admiring fools:
> Pleasure allures, and when the fops escape,
> 'Tis not that they're belov'd, but fortunate,
> And therefore what they fear at heart, they hate.

The tone here has altered from the jauntily conversational first-person voice of the opening into something sterner and more didactic. Rochester might almost be preaching a mountebank sermon, with the quasi-biblical incantations of the lines only undercut by the wit and sharp self-awareness imbued within them. It is certainly the case that Rochester's career at court owed much to his 'pride', but the barely submerged anger in his dismissal of wit as a 'vain, frivolous pretence' shows his disillusion with the way in which he had become as much the king's lapdog or pet monkey as the actual animals, an amusing distraction from the weightier affairs of state. 'Dangerous tools', such as Rochester, were banished from court and only allowed to return when it was felt that sufficient reparation had been made, or when the king needed their presence once more (this looks back to 'Timon', too, with its focus on men of wit being taken up by 'admiring fools'). Some might label this simple cynicism, but for Rochester by this point royal favour had become insufficient reward for having given his life and his health to the service of debauchery. This is alluded to here, first in the reference to 'common whores', and then in the 'succeeding pains', where Rochester's ever-present syphilitic agonies persisted.

A recurring theme throughout Rochester's writing is a hatred of cant and bigotry. This is seen first in the dismissal of the fops as a breed of whom he says 'what they fear at heart, they hate', but then more explicitly in the appearance of 'some formal band and beard', the depiction an allusion to a Restoration Anglican clergyman, who has come to take Rochester to task for what he perceives as his 'degenerate mind'. As the poem briefly turns into a dialogue, Rochester effortlessly slips inside the skin of a pedantic, querulous figure, adding another persona to the many others that he had adopted, both in poetry and in life. The 'band and beard' could have been based on Gilbert Burnet, who had arrived at court in 1674 and had received some preferment from Charles, becoming a royal chaplain. However, Rochester's generally amicable relationship with Burnet, who would become an important figure later in his life, suggests that he had no especial grievance towards him, and it is more likely that Rochester based the character on his old theological sparring partner Isaac Barrow.

> Then, by your favour, anything that's writ
> Against this gibing, jingling knack called wit
> Likes me abundantly; but you take care
> Upon this point, not to be too severe.
> Perhaps my muse were fitter for this part,
> For I profess I can be very smart
> On wit, which I abhor with all my heart.
> I long to lash it in some sharp essay,
> But your grand indiscretion bids me stay,
> And turns my tide of ink another way.

The self-appointed essayists and moralists who criticized the wits of court (as Burnet subsequently did) were seldom blessed with the literary talent of Rochester and his circle, and so the band and beard's impotent growling of his wish that 'my muse were fitter for this part' and his unconscious proclamation that 'I can be very smart / On wit' are clearly added for comic effect. All the same, this moral man has set his sights on Rochester's 'grand indiscretion', and once again Rochester adopts a persona to criticize himself, to dizzyingly kaleidoscopic effect:

What rage ferments in your degenerate mind,
To make you rail at reason and mankind?
Blest, glorious man! To whom alone kind heaven
An everlasting soul has freely given,
Whom his great Maker took such care to make
That from himself he did the image take
And this fair frame in shining reason dressed
To dignify his nature above beast;
Reason, by whose aspiring influence
We take a flight beyond material sense,
Dive into mysteries, then soaring pierce
The flaming limits of the universe,
Search heaven and hell, find out what's acted there,
And give the world true grounds of hope and fear.

Rochester here once again returns to his old tutor Francis Giffard's biblical edicts to mock the clichéd religious terminology that this section of the poem is littered with. 'Kind heaven', 'everlasting soul' and 'great Maker' are all the stuff of leaden scriptural language, used here purely in an attempt to mock the clergyman using them by showing his lack of imagination as he eulogizes 'Blest, glorious man'. By this point in the poem, it is quite clear that man, whether Rochester or his fellows, is anything but.

As the band and beard finishes, Rochester, returning to his own first-person avatar, takes up his statements as a means of ridiculing him explicitly, rather than implicitly. Describing him belittlingly as 'mighty man', Rochester first mocks the clergyman's derivative arguments, even listing the obscure sources that his clichéd views are taken from. He then goes on to say that it is this 'reason' he has the greatest cause to despise, 'that makes a mite/ Think he's the image of the infinite'. Rochester wore his contempt for organized religion proudly, at least at this point in his life, and similar ridicule is extended both to the 'short life, void of all rest' that all endure—again, the echo of Hobbesian language—and to the organized representative of God, or, as he puts it, 'this busy, puzzling stirrer-up of doubt / That frames deep mysteries, then finds 'em out'. The implicit reference is to God moving in mysterious ways: if the ways are so lacking in mystery that they can be found out, then the 'infinite' is all too unimpressive.

Further satire follows of the 'frantic crowds of thinking fools' who populate 'reverend bedlams, colleges and schools'. If Rochester is to be believed, then the philosophical and intellectual thought of the age was essentially 'nonsense and impossibilities', ministered to by 'modern cloistered coxcombs'. However, to say that contemporary intellectual life in England was as poor as Rochester makes out was disingenuous. In 1674 figures of the magnitude of Milton (who died in November that year), Robert Boyle and Thomas Browne were all renowned for their work in a variety of fields, much of which was groundbreaking in its intellectual breadth. Hobbes, although a prophet without honour in England, was still alive and highly regarded by many. The likes of Isaac Newton and John Locke were quietly establishing their own reputations, and the greatest architect of the day, Christopher Wren, had been knighted the previous year in recognition of his rebuilding of London after the Great Fire. Likewise, looking beyond England, Rochester is likely to have encountered the philosophy of Descartes and the astronomy of Galileo while on his grand tour the previous decade, all of which represented rather more than the 'nonsense and impossibilities' he mocks. The key philosophical argument of the day, which he refers to twice in the poem, was whether the universe was really infinite or bounded by its own 'flaming limits'; to have proved the former trod perilously close to disputing the existence of heaven and hell. It was not a time of wilful ignorance.

Nevertheless, it remained a time of superstition and doubt. Boyle's enormous success within the field of natural philosophy was balanced by his unwavering belief in alchemy, as well as other eccentric views such as his claim that all humanity was inevitably descended from Adam and Eve (in his will, he left instructions that a series of lectures be funded in his name promoting Christianity and attacking 'notorious infidels', ranging from Muslims and Jews to atheists and deists; no mention of inter-Christian disagreement was to be allowed). The famous ceremony of 'touching the king's evil' was one widely adhered to by many—including Rochester a couple of years previously—despite little visible sign of success. Witchcraft was still believed to be prevalent. Catholics were rumoured to be in thrall to diabolical practices. The less said about medical care in many cases, the better.

With such uncertainties thus in place, the *carpe diem* spirit displayed by many seemed the best way of dealing with a mercurial and ever-shifting world. Rochester acknowledges this in 'A Satire' when he echoes Hobbes's own distinctions between 'right' and 'wrong' reason:

> Our sphere of action is life's happiness,
> And he who thinks beyond, thinks like an ass.
> Thus, whilst against false reasoning I inveigh,
> I own right reason, which I would obey:
> That reason which distinguishes by sense
> And gives us rules of good and ill from thence,
> That bounds desires with a reforming will
> To keep 'em more in vigour, not to kill.

Again, this references *Leviathan*, specifically the statement:

whatsoever is the object of any man's appetite or desire, that is it, which for his part he calleth good: and the object of his hate and aversion, evil... for these words of good, evil and contemptible, are ever used with relation to the person that useth them: there being nothing simply and absolutely so.

The remarkable shifts in tone and voice across the first half of the poem show Rochester at his most technically accomplished, retaining the substance of the argument that he wishes to make and keeping his attack on hypocrisy and 'false reasoning' current. As a topical satire, it could hardly be improved upon. Rochester, once again adopting his poetic libertine persona, makes a further argument to show why 'his' reason is a better one than that of his interrogator:

> Your reason hinders, mine helps to enjoy,
> Renewing appetites yours would destroy.
> My reason is my friend, yours is a cheat;
> Hunger calls out, my reason bids me eat;
> Perversely, yours your appetite does mock:
> This asks for food, that answers 'What's o'clock?'
> This plain distinction, sir, your doubt secures:
> 'Tis not right reason I despise, but yours.

There is little about Rochester's poetic persona here that is penitent or humble—instead, he boasts about 'renewing appetites yours would destroy'—but the devil-may-care spirit conveyed is nonetheless a more likeable and sympathetic one that that of the 'formal band and beard'. When the poem first appeared at court, and possibly beyond, in late 1674, its readers might not have ended the first section of 'A Satire' wholly convinced that Rochester had managed to offer the definitive refutation of 'wrong reason' and a pure explanation of 'right reason', but his argument is conveyed with such attractive verve that most would have been carried along with his wit and energy. The poetry, once again, reflects the man.

With a shift in emphasis from philosophical musing to social criticism comes the second part of the satire, 'Of Mankind'. It is heralded by Rochester, announcing:

> Thus I think reason righted, but for man,
> I'll ne'er recant; defend him if you can.
> For all his pride and his philosophy,
> 'Tis evident beasts are, in their degree,
> As wise at least, and better far than he.

Rochester here returns to the paradox that he, or whoever was responsible for the satire 'Tunbridge Wells', stated at its end:

> Thrice happy beasts are, who, because they be
> Of reason void, are so of foppery.
> Faith, I was so ashamed that with remorse,
> I used the insolence to mount my horse;
> For he, doing only things fit for his nature,
> Did seem to be by much the wiser creature.

While John Stuart Mill would famously state nearly two centuries later that 'It is better to be a human being dissatisfied than a pig satisfied... if the pig [is] of a different opinion, it is because [it] only knows [its] side of the question', Rochester, himself no stranger to swinish pleasures, took the argument that man's 'pride and his philosophy' failed to conceal his innately beast-like nature. Thus, he provides a mocking comparison between an idealized hunting hound, Jowler, and a prominent Whig of the time, Sir Thomas Meres, claiming that Jowler's ability to find and kill hares was a more useful one than Meres's ability to act as a chairman on committees. As with Milton, Rochester looks back to a prelapsarian world, although his poetry is less concerned with the absence of original sin than it is with the surfeit of tiresome meetings.

The jokes conceal a more serious point. With coruscating irony, Rochester asks whether human or animal principles are 'most generous' and 'just', finally rising to rhetorical splendour by inviting his reader to make his own judgement:

> Be judge yourself, I'll bring it to the test:
> Which is the basest creature, man or beast?
> Birds feed on birds, beasts on each other prey,
> But savage man alone does man betray.
> Pressed by necessity, they kill for food;
> Man undoes man to do himself no good.

Betrayal was something much on Rochester's mind at this time. He considered himself, and the country, betrayed by Charles's unwillingness to adopt the high moral standard of kingship, just as he felt snared by the foolishness and foppery of the court. He had been betrayed by everyone from the low tarts who had given him syphilis to the great men of Whitehall such as Mulgrave, who blackened his name at the slightest provocation, all the while feigning amity and fellowship. No wonder that he wrote 'But man, with smiles, embraces, friendship, praise / Inhumanly his fellow's life betrays', thinking of the double-dealing that he was privy to. Yet he was far from perfect himself, a man who had deceived his wife and children both in his love affairs and in his extended absences from home in the flesh-pots and taverns of London. Money and the desire for recognition led him to return to the deafening clamour of the world of court, as well as royal command on occasion, and if the devil did indeed enter him at Brentford, then it was the price he paid for supping with him so regularly.

Perhaps the best way to look at 'A Satire' is as a symphonic poem. The humour and mild self-deprecation of the first movement has now given way to a far angrier and more tumultuous sense of half-controlled fury, where Rochester lashes out at everyone he can think of, the cruelty of their actions devastatingly taking place 'not through necessity, but wantonness'. It is possible that he sat down to write the poem with this escalating sense of misanthropic discontent as part of his literary scheme, but it is as likely that he became seduced by his own argument, rising to yet grander heights of disdain as he progressed. The crowning irony is that he wrote the poem while he was relatively happy; had he written it when he was in a worse state, it might have been an unreadable screed of bitterness and pain.

Rochester was in roughly equal parts bold, reckless and pragmatic. Even if there was some justification in his being pilloried as a coward by Mulgrave for exercising a rare sense of self-preservation in refusing to duel with him, his actions throughout his life—whether his abduction of Elizabeth, his military service against the Dutch, or the boldness of his libels against Charles and the rest of the court—all smacked of either courage or rashness, depending on your perception. However, if his writing in the next part of the satire is an accurate reflection of his feelings at the time, then Rochester was starting to weary of a life lived without restraint or checks. The tone, by turns angry, scornful and resigned, is the perfect counterpoint to the devil-may-care exuberance of many of the earlier poems.

Rochester begins with the memory of the failed Anglo-Dutch war—which was still fresh—offering implicit criticism of Charles and his generals, as well as men in the wider world and, as ever, himself:

> For hunger or love they fight and tear,
> Whilst wretched man is still in arms for fear.
> For fear he arms, and is of arms afraid,
> By fear to fear successively betrayed;
> Base fear, the source whence his best passions came:
> His boasted honour, and his dear-bought fame;
> That lust of power, to which he's such a slave,
> And for the which alone he dares be brave.

At first glance, this appears to be a simple criticism of man's bestial nature, where his only impulses are driven by hunger or 'love', here a euphemism for sex. Yet the repeated references to 'arms', closely juxtaposed with 'fear', indicate that it is the military world that Rochester is satirizing, with the betrayal he refers to both by and of the ordinary man. Those fighting in the Anglo-Dutch wars were, for him, less lions led by lambs and more hapless sheep being led to the slaughter by their similarly ovine masters. This is made explicit by his sardonic dismissal of 'boasted honour' and 'dear-bought fame', before he takes a wider aim at 'that lust of power'. Rochester was mindful of the fact that his own 'honour and fame' owed no small part to his successful military service, and this rejection of his prizes and accolades as nothing more than baubles shows his disillusionment with the world of *dulce et decorum est*.

Of course, it was not just war that showed man at his most ineffectual. Rochester, apparently satisfied with his denunciation of patriotism as a hollow sham, proceeds to look at the venal, self-satisfied nature of what mankind represents on the wider scale. It is an impressively clear-sighted cry of anger, albeit one lacking in the wit of earlier:

> For which he takes such pains to be thought wise,
> And screws his actions in a forced disguise,
> Leading a tedious life in misery
> Under laborious, mean hypocrisy.
> Look to the bottom of his vast design,
> Wherein man's wisdom, power and glory join:
> The good he acts, the ill he does endure,
> 'Tis all from fear, to make himself secure.
> Merely for safety, after fame we thirst,
> For all men would be cowards if they durst.

It is hard to think of any of his court contemporaries producing such a simultaneously nihilistic and intellectually sophisticated attack on their world. Although he had often before been caustic and dismissive in his poetry, nothing comes close to the way in which, in this poem, he gazes on the entire Whitehall society that he is part of and finds nothing to praise or extol, seeing merely a gaggle of frightened hypocrites acting roles that they are ill-equipped to fill in their 'forced disguise'. Perhaps his banishment from court and subsequent recall had made him bolder, but it had also made him contemptuous of the world he had returned to. Rochester, himself less a phoney actor than a chameleonic performer, could tell an unconvincing line reading or intonation when he heard one.

He ends the main body of the poem by comparing the cowardice that permeates mankind with the essential dishonesty that goes hand in hand with it, describing all men as knaves and using a cynical examination of human nature to justify the comparison: 'if you think it fair / Amongst known cheats to play upon the square / You'll be undone.' As ever, Rochester writes with an eye on the fluidity of truth and integrity. As he says:

> Nor can weak truth your reputation save:
> The knaves will all agree to call you knave.
> Wronged shall he live, insulted o'er, oppressed,
> Who dares be less a villain than the rest.

By this stage, Rochester has written nearly 170 lines of closely argued, occasionally self-contradictory, but brilliant and witty satire on the intellectual and social life of the world he inhabited. As an act of revenge on those he detested, it could scarcely be more devastating, provided of course that the targets of his criticism were not too stupid to miss the point. Apparently hurrying to end the poem, for the first time a note of impatience enters into the satire, as he resumes the dialogue with the clergyman and offers a summary of his arguments:

> Thus, sir, you see what human nature craves:
> Most men are cowards, all men should be knaves.
> The difference lies, as far as I can see,
> Not in the thing itself, but the degree,
> And all the subject matter of debate
> Is only: Who's a knave of the first rate?

The reason why the initial ending feels cheap and rushed is because the language itself lacks the serpentine elegance and rhetorical grandeur that Rochester has revelled in up to this point; it is as if the poet has chosen to reiterate the point made at the beginning that, however seductive his rejection of reason and mankind, he is still one of 'those strange, prodigious creatures, man' and liable to write below par. Nonetheless, even if its tidy encapsulation of Rochester's sprawling and fascinating satire verges on the glib, the final question it asks offers an amusingly double-edged proposition; the reader's only answer, surely, can be to see none other than Rochester himself as the first-rate knave.

Between summer and autumn 1674 the poem was written, widely copied and distributed around court as it stood. Despite its length, it was much read and was of particular interest to the clergy, given the satiric depiction of the 'band and beard'. It was famous enough to be referred to by the clergyman Edward Stillingfleet, in a court sermon preached before Charles on 24 February 1675. Stillingfleet, a quick-witted and intelligent man who would eventually become Dean of St Paul's in 1678, rejected Rochester's arguments and said: 'it is a pity [Rochester and others] had not their wish, to have been beasts rather than men… that they might have been less capable of doing mischief among mankind.' Possibly as a result, Rochester felt it necessary to respond, and so added a coda or 'Addition' of about fifty lines, probably between 1675 and 1676, in which he attempts to redress the balance with continued satiric barbs and scorn. He also altered line 74, changing 'Sibbs' soliloquies' to 'Stillingfleet's replies' and so allowing him specifically to attack his antagonist.

Continuing to criticize 'the pretending part of the proud world', Rochester mocks society for being 'swollen with selfish vanity' and reliant on 'fellow slaves' who try and lord it over one another with 'false freedoms, holy cheats and formal lies'. However, he now concedes the possibility that there might be someone at court who is upstanding and uncorrupted:

> But if in Court so just a man there be
> (In Court a just man, yet unknown to me)
> Who does his needful flattery direct,
> Not to oppress and ruin, but protect
> (Since flattery, which way so ever laid,
> Is still a tax on that unhappy trade);
> If so upright a statesman you can find,
> Whose passions bend to his unbiased mind,
> Who does his arts and policies apply
> To raise his country, not his family,
> Nor, whilst his pride owned avarice withstands,
> Receives close bribes through friends' corrupted hands.

Looking at Rochester's circle of intimates, there is nobody who fits this description. The likes of Buckingham, Savile and Rochester himself were all far from being 'upright' and 'unbiased', after all, and none of them were 'just men'. This is itself a further allusion to Hobbes, who wrote that 'a just man... taketh all the care that he can, that his actions may be all just'. However, it is telling that here, for the first time, Rochester explicitly sets the action at Whitehall, concentrating on a milieu that he knew and understood intimately. It is here that it is accepted that flattery must always be 'needful', rather than offered indiscriminately, and that his 'unbiased mind' will use this flattery for national, rather than personal, gain. The last 'decent' man at court, Clarendon, was not immune to feathering his own nest, thereby attracting a degree of opprobrium on which his enemies thrived.

This fantastical figure, then, seems slightly less likely to have existed in court than an eighteen-year-old virgin. Rochester then turns his attention to the clergy. Mindful of the criticism that the poem received from Stillingfleet, and perhaps stung, he launches a bravura sally of abuse at the corrupted men of God in general, and Stillingfleet in particular:

> Is there a churchman who on God relies;
> Whose life, his faith and doctrine justifies?
> Not one blown up with vain prelatic pride,
> Who, for reproof of sins, does man deride;
> Whose envious heart makes preaching a pretence,
> With his obstreperous, saucy eloquence,
> To chide at kings, and rail at men of sense;
> None of that sensual tribe whose talents lie
> In avarice, pride, sloth and gluttony
> Who hunt good livings, but abhor good lives.

The criticism continues as Rochester castigates the imagined clergy-man for adultery, dominating council business, inefficiency and affectation. However, the point has already been made about the 'sensual tribe' whose fleshly wants dominate their spiritual inclinations. The references to Stillingfleet are most explicit when he refers to his 'vain prelatic pride'. His apparent derision of Rochester is ascribed, typically, to a mixture of envy and a desire to show off his oratorical skills, thereby making preaching nothing more than a 'pretence', with the primary aim that of point-scoring. Hence Rochester's allusion to a sermon preached in front of the king being nothing more than 'chiding', and his knowing self-description as a man of sense.

The poem concludes with a final description of the fantastical figure that Rochester imagines being a sincere man of God rather than merely worldly. The 'meek, humble man of honest sense' that Rochester praises is one who 'preaching peace, does practice continence', leads a 'pious life', and believes the 'mysterious truths, which no man can conceive'. If there is a barely concealed scepticism about this figure, it is thrown open by Rochester's typically dramatic and ironic statement:

> If upon earth there dwell such God-like men,
> I'll here recant my paradox to them,
> Adore those shrines of virtue, homage pay,
> And, with the rabble world, their laws obey.

Rochester's view of 'God-like men' is, necessarily, an insincere one, strengthened by his mocking description of them as 'shrines of virtue'. For him, the world in which he lived was essentially rotten, with even the best of men compromised and dedicated to little more than self-interest. His fantastical creations of a good statesman and a faithful clergyman remain safely fictional. 'A Satire', in its extended form, remains a coruscating attack on Rochester's world, but also on the nature of intellectual and social achievement, reducing it to nothing more than puffed-up vanity and grubby cheating. The final couplet accepts all this, wearily, leaving the reader with a devastating belittlement of what 'reason' and 'mankind' can ever aspire to:

> If such there be, yet grant me this at least:
> Man differs more from man, than man from beast.

'Something of the

ANGEL

YET

UNDEFACED

in him'

✤

[1675–1676]

FOR A YEAR that would prove catastrophic for Rochester, 1675 began well enough. On 4 January Charles approved a request to erect a home for him, paid for out of royal funds, in the shape of 'a small building in his Majesty's privy garden at Whitehall between the Lord Keeper's Lodgings and the Lodgings his Lordship now possesses'. This was a clear sign of favour, as the cost of such an erection was far from cheap at around £200, indicating Rochester's continued place at the heart of the court that he claimed to despise so openly. This paradox—the more he cavilled against the court, the greater his standing became—amused him. In a letter, he claimed that 'they are at present pulling down some part of my lodging', indicating that his gratitude, such as it was, was limited.

The following week, on 12 January, Rochester attended the first performance of William Wycherley's *The Country Wife* at Drury Lane. The play was outrageous, even by the standards of the day, revolving around a committed rake, Horner, who feigns impotence in order to facilitate access to the ladies of 'quality' and innocent, untutored girls from the country, including the titular wife, Margery. Examples of its unfettered smut include a lengthy scene where 'china' becomes a sexual innuendo, and the immortal line 'Wife! He is coming into you the back way!' Even the title contains an obvious pun.

Despite his involvement with the theatre, whether as a spectator, an occasional collaborator or mentor of Elizabeth Barry, there were few contemporary writers who Rochester considered particularly talented, other than Etherege and Wycherley, both of whom were his friends. Although later in 1675 he paid lip service to Thomas Shadwell's abilities in 'An Allusion to Horace', claiming that his 'unfinished works do yet impart / Great proofs of force of nature', he also made a further dig at the writer, claiming that they had 'none of art'. The insult stung, and Shadwell began work on a play based on the Don Juan legend, *The Libertine*, which had a central character,

Don John, who exhibited a familiar joie de vivre and unrestrained Bacchanalian impulse.

Rochester's own impulses in early 1675 were mainly being channelled into his love affair with Elizabeth Barry, which engaged him in a way that none of his more casual dalliances had ever managed. He wrote her numerous letters that strike a balance between the ardently passionate and the knowingly arch. (One even ends *in medias res*, as Rochester is distracted by a Porlockian type: 'a damned impertinent fool bolted in that hinders me from ending my letter.') He might say 'you are stark mad, and therefore the fitter for me to love' and declare 'so much wit and beauty as you have should think of nothing less than doing miracles', but this is immediately put into context by the statement that 'there cannot be a greater [miracle] than to continue to love me'.

Sometimes it is hard to remember that, beneath Rochester's intellectual brilliance and social derring-do, he was subject to the same whims and caprices that everyone else was, and when he calls himself 'the wildest and most fantastical odd man alive', his characteristic exaggeration and theatricality do not obscure the depth and sincerity of his feelings for Elizabeth Barry. He writes 'I must ever call the day I saw you last, since all time between that and the next visit is no part of my life, or at least like a long fit of the falling sickness wherein I am dead to all joy and happiness', and in so doing he strips away the artifice of his poetry and his other personae in favour of something more revealing and heartfelt. This is, at last, the real Rochester.

Or so it might appear. His declarations of love could also be the rote pronouncements of someone who is on uncertain ground, perhaps for the first time, and is taking refuge in clichés as a result. Elizabeth Barry was far from conventionally beautiful, making his statement 'you are the most afflicting fair creature in the world' a double-edged one; and it is extraordinary that a writer of Rochester's linguistic gifts could not come up with something more original than 'I do you justice in loving you so as woman was never loved before'.

However, it is churlish to assume that Rochester was engaging in an affair with Elizabeth Barry as an intellectual challenge, or out of boredom. Certainly, he had unlimited opportunities to fritter himself away in carnal dalliance with others, whether with the women of quality at court or the whores in the cheap brothels and taverns he frequented, but specific details in his correspondence with her make it appear as if her presence in his life by this point had become the most important one, as he claims to 'love [her] above all the world, whatever becomes of the King, Court or mankind and all their impertinent business'.

It was this 'impertinent business' that saw him appointed Master, Surveyor and Keeper of Charles's hawks on 24 January, another badge of honour to add to the other titles that he had acquired by this point, which included the prestigious positions of Ranger and Keeper of Woodstock Park and his role as Gentleman of the Bedchamber, as well as his commission in Prince Rupert's horse guards. Another word for these might be bribes: Charles needed Rochester's help as a trusted member of his entourage to pass such bills as his Disaffected Persons Bill of May 1675, which would prevent 'the Dangers which may arise from persons disaffected with the government'. In other words, Charles, feeling his power steadily weakening, sought to increase his status as an absolute monarch by having the authority to imprison anyone who stood against him, and was willing to hand out bribes to his favourites in order to be able to rely on their support. Savile and Buckingham opposed the bill on principle, disliking the idea of a ruler who could lock up anyone in the country on a whim, but Rochester bided his time, for the moment at least.

While political intrigues dominated London, country life at Adderbury was more sedate. In the midst of his affair with Elizabeth Barry, Rochester returned there and wrote to his wife, who, tiring of her dealings with Anne Wilmot, was lingering at her family house in Enmore. Rochester was, for once, alone, noting: 'I find none but the housekeeper, the butler and rats, who squeak mightily and are all in good health.' His casual reference to the sparsity of the staff, including a couple of 'gentle and penitent' maids, indicates that Rochester's financial affairs were far from healthy, and certainly not ample enough to support a thriving household. The casual, matter-of-fact way in which he writes to Elizabeth about domestic matters—including a dig at his mother's continuing poor temper ('were my mother pleased, all were pleased, which God be pleased to grant')—stands in amusing contrast to the passionate entreaties and effusions that he poured out in his letters to Elizabeth Barry.

One of these letters, apologizing for breaking an appointment, claims 'the Devil has laid a block in my way'. It soon proved to be more accurate than Rochester had perhaps intended. Although he had only recently turned twenty-eight, he was starting to become one of the senior figures of the Ballers, along with Savile and Buckingham. Other young aristocrats and their associates were coming to court, such as the ridiculous and foul-smelling Will Fanshaw, 'a meagre person of small attainments and unpleasant habits', who married into the low-level aristocracy and was thus tolerated on the peripheries of Whitehall; and the young writer Francis Fane, with whom Rochester collaborated on various anonymous lampoons attacking and ridiculing Mulgrave, which, as usual, were distributed around court in manuscript. Lampooning was a commonly accepted means of attacking one's enemies, with the cover of anonymity used to produce invective that ranged from the brilliantly penetrating to the merely obscene. Rochester himself had been lampooned since his arrival at court—if it is assumed that 'Regime de Vivre' is about him, rather than by him (see page 71), it anticipates a great deal of the satire that would later be directed at him. A lampoon was not necessarily intended as a grave insult—certainly 'Regime de Vivre' is affectionate, after a fashion—and many welcomed the fact that they had a sufficiently high profile to merit satire.

When they were not mocking others at court, Rochester and Fane worked on drama together. Fane's first play, *Love in the Dark*, was not up to the standards of, for example, Wycherley's brilliance, but a Rochester-penned epilogue gave it some kudos nonetheless, and the two worked on a revision of *Valentinian*. Rochester became a mentor to many young playwrights and was generous with both his time

I. ABOVE John Wilmot, 2nd Earl of Rochester, in a portrait after Sir Peter Lely. Rochester, the 'wicked lord', lived exuberantly and died at thirty-three, having—according to Dr Johnson—'blazed out his youth and health in lavish voluptuousness'.

2. ABOVE Charles Stuart flees Cromwell's forces following the royalist defeat at Worcester, September 1651. The figure in the distance, riding as a decoy in the guise of a huntsman, is Henry Wilmot, future 1st Earl of Rochester and father of John Wilmot.

3. BELOW Wadham College, Oxford, c.1675. John Wilmot took up his place here in January 1660, at the age of just twelve.

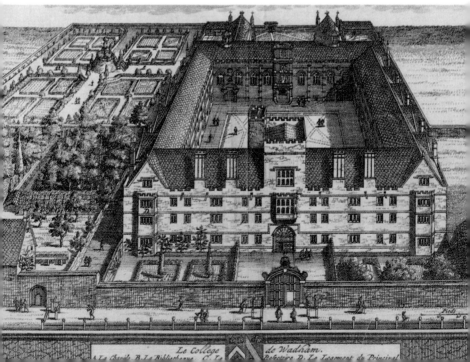

Le College   de Wadham.

4. ABOVE LEFT
Anne St John, by the
Dutch-born court artist
Sir Peter Lely (1618–80).
Rochester's mother
combined piety with a
staunch sense of duty to
her family. Woe betide
anyone who aroused her
enmity.

5. ABOVE RIGHT
Elizabeth Malet,
Rochester's long-
suffering wife, by Sir
Peter Lely. Despite
Rochester's attempt to
wed her by force (1665),
their eventual marriage
(1667) would be a lasting
and productive union.

6. BELOW A Dutch
raid on English ships in
the River Medway, 1667,
by Pieter Cornelisz van
Soest (fl.1640–67). The
large ship to the right of
centre is
HMS *Royal Charles*, which
has just been captured
by the Dutch.

7. ABOVE *The Crimson Bedchamber*, by Sir John Baptist Medina (1659–1710), a portrait group of gentlemen with musical instruments, traditionally said to depict the so-called 'CABAL' ministry of Charles II's closest advisors (1668–*c.*74). The group includes George Villiers, 2nd Duke of Buckingham (centre), Rochester's mentor at court.

10. LEFT Charles II, portrayed by John Michael Wright (1617–94). The man whom Rochester would mock as 'the easiest King and best-bred man alive' had an uneven relationship with his protégé, veering between amused tolerance and anger.

11. BELOW Nell Gwyn, by Sir Peter Lely. 'Pretty, witty Nell', an actress and sometime prostitute, was Charles's favourite mistress. She was on good terms with Rochester, who interceded nobly on her behalf for her inheritance.

8. OPPOSITE LEFT
Charles Wilmot, Rochester's only son, as depicted by a follower of Lely. Named after his godfather the king, Charles was a sickly boy who suffered from illness—possibly congenital syphilis—throughout his short life, and died the year after his father.

9. OPPOSITE RIGHT
Elizabeth and Malet Wilmot, by Sir Peter Lely. Rochester's two youngest daughters were both advantageously married off to local aristocrats by their grandmother, who took care that no trace of their father's notoriety would endure past his death.

12. RIGHT The title page of
George Etherege's comedy *The Man
of Mode or Sir Fopling Flutter* (first
performed in 1676). Rochester's
friend Etherege depicted him as
the rake Dorimant, of whom it is
said 'I know he is the devil, but
he has something of the angel yet
undefaced in him.'

13. BELOW A banquet at the court
of Charles II, in an engraving by
Peter Philippe (*c*.1640–after 1700).
Royal banquets were raucous and
drunken affairs. When Rochester
chose to enliven one such occasion
by destroying Charles's prized
sundial, he found himself banished
from court.

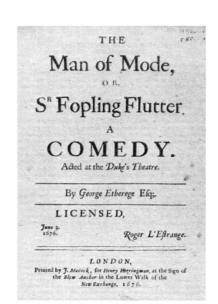

THE

Man of Mode,

OR,

Sᴿ Fopling Flutter.

A

COMEDY.

Acted at the *Duke's Theatre*.

By *George Etherege* Esq;

LICENSED,

June 3.
1676.   *Roger L'Estrange.*

LONDON,

Printed by *J. Macock*, for *Henry Herringman*, at the Sign of
the *Blew Anchor* in the Lower Walk of the
New Exchange, 1 6 7 6.

14. ABOVE Elizabeth Barry, in a portrait by Sir Godfrey Kneller (1646–1723). Barry was the greatest actress of her day, originating many famous roles. She and Rochester, who was both besotted by and jealous of her, conducted a passionate five-year love affair that resulted in the birth of a daughter.

15. LEFT Gilbert Burnet, by John Riley (1646–91). The ambitious and worldly clergyman was responsible for propagating the (possibly fictitious) tale of Rochester's final deathbed repentance, which made his name and career.

16. ABOVE *The Death of Rochester,*
by Alfred Thomas Derby (1821–73).
The posthumous rehabilitation of
Rochester as a repentant sinner
saved reached its nadir with this
treasurable piece of Victorian
kitsch, complete with shafts of
heavenly light.

17. RIGHT Johnny Depp as
Rochester and Rosamund Pike
as his wife Elizabeth Wilmot in
The Libertine (2004). Despite a
committed performance from
Depp, Laurence Dunmore's film
of Rochester's life proved to be
a muddled and disappointing
experience. The enjoyment, alas,
was all too imperfect.

and liberal attitudes. Thomas Otway, who was also besotted with the 'deceitful muse' Elizabeth Barry, was the mere 'scum of a playhouse', but Rochester was magnanimous enough in romantic victory to intercede on Otway's behalf with Charles in order to obtain funds for his plays—though he still describes him as 'puzzling Otway' in 'An Allusion to Horace' (some texts have this as 'blushing' or 'puffing', making a more explicit dig at his apparent lack of talent).

If it is accepted that Rochester was not the sole author of *Sodom*, then no complete play can be ascribed to him, something of a surprise for a man so immersed in the traditions and language of the theatre. There does exist, however, a tiny fragment of the beginning of a comedy in Rochester's hand, probably written in the late 1660s, featuring the character of Mr Dainty. Dainty, a quintessential fop, is introduced 'in his nightgown, singing', although what he is singing—'*J'ai l'amour dans le coeur et la rage dans les os*', roughly translated 'I have love in the heart and fury in the bones'—makes him an unusual protagonist, with unexplained hints of anger and disquiet that are subsequently undeveloped.

Dainty bewails, in a parody of an aubade (sunrise song), that he has been asleep for 'seven dull hours... for naturally I hate to be so long absent from myself'. Traditional Restoration tropes of permissiveness are nodded at: 'methinks not to sleep til the sun rise is an odd effect... and makes the night tedious without a woman.' Dainty refuses to read books, as they speak of 'other men's affairs'. He arrogantly states: 'I am resolved to write some love-passages of my life... I divert myself by reading my own story, which will be pleasant enough.'

There then follows some mediocre back-and-forth with a servant boy (a character who will reappear in Rochester's poem 'To the Postboy'), and some half-hearted introduction of other characters and hints at a plot that involves Dainty fighting with his young charge Squabb over matrimonial ties to the (presumably wealthy) Sir Lionel's daughters, even while Dainty is bedevilled by his would-be lover Mrs Manners. The fragment ends, dangling, just before the promised introduction of Squabb. While Rochester did not continue the play, its very existence is still of some interest insofar as it suggests that his dramatic experience stretched only so far as writing about the world he inhabited. Dainty is not Rochester, but he is a character firmly of the court and his milieu.

Meanwhile, one of the other crucial characters in Rochester's life, Charles, was continuing to lose his grip. The Disaffected Persons Bill was rejected by the Lords in early June 1675, and in order to avoid a war with France, Charles agreed to a secret deal with Louis XIV whereby, in exchange for continued bribes of £100,000 a year, he would ensure ongoing neutrality in the event of any European wars, thereby leaving Louis' continued hunger for power unchecked. He even offered to dissolve Parliament if they stood in the way of this. Even though this was not public knowledge, Charles's lackadaisical attitude towards kingship was far from admired. Rochester's sentiments about the 'scandalous and poor' monarch were now less an exceptional piece of scurrility and more a generally held belief. The king might have tried to endear himself to the wits about court by getting drunk with them at lavish dinners, but even while they took his hospitality, they still refused to respect him.

And then Rochester's run of good fortune came to an abrupt halt.

The twenty-fifth of June 1675 was a warm early summer's day in London. The evening had certainly seen rare sport amongst the merry gang, who had dined with Charles at court earlier that evening and were now embarrassingly drunk. The rakes and bravoes, including Sackville, Buckhurst and others,* headed into the Privy Garden at Whitehall, where they came across a new piece of ostentation by Charles. He was a keen collector of astronomical items, and the crown jewel in his collection was a large, ornate sundial set with a complex design of glass spheres, on which portraits of the royal family were engraved. It had been constructed a few years earlier by Reverend Francis Hall, professor of mathematics at Liège University, and was rumoured to be the most expensive and

---

* Although not Savile, fortunately for him.

elaborate instrument of its kind in western Europe. It was commonly regarded as the king's pride and joy, and took up a prominent position in the garden. A sensible or moderate man admired it from a distance, and then steered well clear. Rochester had no intention of doing any such thing.

To the horror of his friends, he drew his sword and threw himself at the sundial, apparently taking exception to its phallic shape. According to one source, he was heard to yell: 'What! Do you stand here to fuck time?' (Another, more restrained account had him say: 'Kings and kingdoms will tumble down, and so shall you.') He then attacked the elaborate structure, madly slashing away at it. Emboldened by alcohol and the adrenaline of transgression, his work was soon finished. The priceless object lay in ruins over the garden. Returning to their drink-sodden senses, the terrified bravoes ran away from the now roused watch, in desperate hope that they would not be found out. Most avoided detection; Rochester, the ringleader, did not.

When Charles discovered the destruction of his beloved toy, he became apoplectic with rage and left court immediately to attempt to calm himself, much to the consternation of his hangers-on, who had no idea of his whereabouts for ten days. It turned out, rather prosaically, that the king was on a short cruise aboard the royal yacht. But the damage was done. Rochester fled from court immediately, knowing that disgrace would follow him. While he had been banished before, and allowed to return before, Charles's anger this time was unprecedented. When what must have been an almighty hangover had abated, Rochester guessed he had finally overstepped the mark and lost Charles's favour forever. At the time, he was twenty-eight. He had five years left to live. Or, to look at it another way, five years left in which to die.

What his wife and children made of his forced rustication can only be surmised, especially as it seemed inevitable that he would be stripped of his titles and pensions. He was more a burden than a respected husband and father. He also found himself in debt; one letter, dated 2 July, records a payment of the not inconsiderable sum of £152, which was an added difficulty.

At the same time, Rochester found himself deprived of the company of Elizabeth Barry at the apex of his passion for her. He knew he could not rely on her faithfulness or constancy and wrote her a letter in his exile that swings giddily between the wheedling and the suspicious. He describes how 'you may know you are not a moment out of my thoughts' and continues to call himself 'your creature and servant', and demands that 'happiness of all kinds' be absent from his life. Nonetheless, remembering she had suffered the previous advances of such court hangers-on as Otway, he ends his epistle by writing: 'both in love and jealousy, pray mankind be far from you.' It would be several months before he saw her again, during which time she would appear in the leading role of Draxilla in Otway's play *Alcibiades* at the Dorset Garden Theatre. Otway, relishing his former mentor's discomfort and the chance to gain intimacy with Elizabeth Barry once more, referred to the incident of the smashing of the sundial in his prologue:

> The Bacchanals all hot and drunk with wine
> He led to the almighty thunderer's shrine,
> And there his image seated on a throne
> They violently took, and tumbled down.

How the king, or Rochester, received this cheeky dig is not recorded.

A poem that Rochester probably wrote while lingering at home at this time is 'The Disabled Debauchee', which is dated 1675 on the existing manuscript copy. In its parody of the form of the heroic stanza, it looks back to Dryden and other far more earnest poets, but the sentiments it expresses are altogether closer to home as Rochester, still only twenty-eight but with more experience of the seamier side of life than others thrice his age had accumulated, reflects on what has gone before. It begins by using a metaphor of military conflict to denote bawdier adventures:

As some brave admiral, in former war
Deprived of force, but pressed with courage still,
Two rival fleets appearing from afar,
Crawls to the top of an adjacent hill.

From whence, with thoughts full of concern, he views
The wise and daring conduct of the fight,
Whilst each bold action to his mind renews
His present glory and his past delight.

This is Rochester at his wittiest, with an intellectual conceit worthy of Donne, yet also with a delightfully innuendo-laden sensibility. On an initial reading, the allusions to 'deprived of force', 'two rival fleets' and 'the wise and daring conduct of the fight' can be taken straight, perhaps with the half-submerged memory of his own gallant conduct in the Second Anglo-Dutch War. However, this is wry satire, rather than celebration, and it soon becomes clear that his sensibility is an entirely different one.

An excellent argument for claiming that Rochester had qualities far beyond the centuries-honoured tag of 'smutty poet' is the fine balance that he achieves here between witty conceit and wryly elegiac self-knowledge. When he writes 'When my days of impotence approach', he refers to both sexual and creative stagnation, with Rochester perhaps reflecting on the way in which other, lesser talents such as Dryden and even Buckingham appeared to thrive, as he reluctantly lingered in Adderbury in 'lazy temperance'. This is one of the first times that he acknowledges poetically that his illnesses were caused by his own agency, namely by 'pox and wine's unlucky chance', but his uneasy half-loathing, half-loving relationship with the 'pleasing billows of debauch' is expressed in his longing recollection of 'fleets of glasses' and 'volleys of wit'. The verse ends with a moment of pure reflected *carpe diem* spirit: 'Past joys have more than paid what I endure.'

As the poem continues, it becomes an account of the corruption of youth mixed with boastfulness. Rochester calls to mind his

Oxford tutor Robert Whitehall as the poet thinks of himself taking a virginal youth and 'the ghost of my departed vice' and thoroughly corrupting him, by telling him of his exploits when he was 'strong and able to bear arms'.

Rochester revels in the details of a rampantly lewd life. From the mock-heroic account of 'handsome ills', which consist mainly of scraps with prostitutes, pimps and night watchmen rather than gallant battles against great warriors, to a lasciviously evoked allusion to bisexuality and a ménage à trois—'the best kiss was the deciding lot / Whether the boy fucked you, or I the boy'—'The Disabled Debauchee' represents Rochester at his most theatrically unashamed, as he ironically adopts the persona of a mentor, advanced in both years and moral decrepitude:

> Thus, statesman-like, I'll saucily impose,
> And, safe in action, valiantly advise;
> Sheltered in impotence, urge you to blows;
> And now, being good for nothing else, be wise.

Whether Rochester was ever wise is debatable, but the sly wit and poetic intelligence of 'The Disabled Debauchee' make it one of his most enjoyable and accessible pieces.

Meanwhile, Savile had some more bad news for the exiled Rochester. It was rumoured at court, by Mulgrave or one of his other enemies, that Rochester had libelled Charles's mistress Louise, Duchess of Portsmouth. Perhaps out of some otherwise submerged sense of self-preservation, or simply because he had no animosity against her, the duchess was so far one of the few great ladies at court whom Rochester had *not* libelled; even the allusions to her in 'A Satire on Charles II' are almost flattering, with her description as 'the most dear of all his dears' affectionate compared to the vitriol directed towards Charles. However, as Rochester had noted so accurately in 'A Satire against Reason and Mankind', the court was a place full of backbiting and intrigue, and one of the easiest ways to come into royal favour was by supplanting a man who was currently in the depths of ignominy.

Accordingly, a letter that Rochester wrote to Savile in August 1675 indicates his horror at the 'more than ordinary indignation' that was felt against him. Perhaps hoping that the letter would be distributed more widely, he first attempts to solicit sympathy by claiming that he is 'bruised and bed-rid' after a fall from his horse, before openly refuting the allegations against him. As usual, this is done in a theatrical and rhetorically ostentatious fashion: 'What ill star reigns over me, that I'm still marked out for ingratitude, and only used barbarously by those I am obliged to?' The cynical might mutter that the reign of the ill star, present in some capacity ever since the coming of the comet that heralded Rochester's arrival at court in December 1664, was mightily reinforced by his outlandish behaviour. He also knew that his recent actions had put him beyond the pale, so there is an arch side to his self-confessed disbelief. Nonetheless, the letter's balance of outrage and surprise has a different tenor to the witty resignation of his other correspondence with Savile. That it was meant for public, even royal, consumption can be seen from his indignant insistence that his supposed libel was 'a false, idle story' and that 'I have no more offended her in thought, word or deed'—another use of religious language to sanctify a statement—'or uttered the least thought to her contempt or prejudice, than I have plotted treason, concealed arms, trained regiments for a rebellion'.

It is conceivable that the references to arms and training regiments for rebellion are a desperate attempt to remind interested parties of Henry Wilmot's similar actions, and hence the bond between the two families, just as they indicate the comparatively petty nature of the supposed offence. Throughout the letter, he seeks to portray himself as honest and wronged. While he claims that 'if there be upon earth a man of common honesty who will justify a tittle of her accusation, I am contended never to see her', he skilfully creates the possibility that his nemeses at court are far from possessed of this common honesty.

His reference to Louise as 'more an angel than I find her a woman' is clearly designed to be fed back to her as flattery, but there is an edge of panic in Rochester's refutations. While, at the time of writing, Charles was apparently unaware of the feud—'for her generous resolution of not hurting me to the King, I thank her'—Rochester knew that it was inevitable that gossip of this sort would reach royal ears eventually, noting worriedly: 'I do not know how to assure myself the Duchess will spare me to the King.' Even Savile, who was in royal favour to the extent of having accompanied Charles on his trip on the yacht the previous month, had to be treated with the kid gloves of diplomacy. Rochester, hoping for reassurance, writes that he is unafraid of this incident damaging their friendship, and claims: 'I dare swear you don't think I have dealt so indiscreetly in my service as to doubt me in the friendship I profess to you.'

At last, Rochester's tone changes from atypical bluster and fear into something more measured. Asking that he be given a fair hearing by Louise upon his return to court, as even a footman might expect, he puts the blame for the libel on 'a less worthy creature', and seeing that his reputation runs the risk of lying in tatters, attempts to defend it: 'I would not be run down by a company of rogues, and this looks like an endeavour towards it.' Rochester, a man who had made many enemies on his ascent to the top, was now frightened that, on his descent, those he had trodden on contemptuously would make the small effort required to give him a kicking in return. This explains his almost childish desire to be reassured of his standing with others, begging Savile to 'send me word how I am with other folks' and hoping that the Lord Treasurer and, more fancifully, Charles might be prepared to take his side in the matter.

If Rochester's fear seems out of character, it should perhaps be viewed as another exercise in realpolitik. Unable to defend himself in person, he had to use the willing Savile as a proxy to keep what remained of his name intact. Failure would spell disaster and ruin, both for him and for his family.

A second letter, sent soon afterwards, strikes a less panicky and more reflective note. Abandoned by many of his fair-weather acquaintances, Rochester writes to the steadfast Savile that 'if it were the sign of an honest man to be happy in his friends, sure

I were marked out for the worst of men, since no-one e'er lost so many as I have done, or knew how to make so few'. The Louise business continued to trouble him, although fear-induced flattery has given way to defiance, as he claims: 'this may be a warning to you that remain in the mistake of being kind to me, never to expect a grateful return, since I am so utterly ignorant how to make it.' He considered himself ill used by Louise, given that the only crime he was guilty of was one of 'cunning', but his resentment at the 'cunninger' world of the court, with her in it, was at its height. He draws a distinction between his heartless enemies—'those whom I have obliged may use me with ingratitude and not afflict me much'—and the would-be Judases he saw himself surrounded by, whom he curses heartily. Paranoia and poetic exaggeration were familiar bedfellows for Rochester.

Some of the few friends he had left, apart from Savile, included Fleetwood Shepherd, a well-known court wit who added a postscript to Savile's earlier letter and receives thanks for being a man of 'fluent style and coherent thought', and the wealthy politician Henry Guy, a confidant of Charles; it was through him that Rochester hoped to return to royal favour. However, the earl has no illusions about the severity of his situation: 'I shall scarce think of coming til you call me, as not having many prevalent motives to draw me to the Court, if it be so that my master has no need of my service, nor my friends of my company.' The fat, jovial Savile was a true foul-weather friend, a debt graciously acknowledged by Rochester in another letter, when he thanks him for his forbearance in 'the trouble I have given you in this affair' and hints at his gratitude to Savile for distributing bribes from his own pocket, or 'growing poorer' on his behalf. For Rochester, he was 'the only man of England that keeps wit with... wisdom'.

Others were less sanguine. Charles, far from forgiving Rochester, decided to continue his humiliation. On 29 October Rochester received a letter from Sir Joseph Williamson, the Secretary of State, informing him that, after his death, the Rangership of Woodstock Park would not pass to his heirs, but would instead revert to his uncle, Sir Walter St John, to be held in trust for a distant relative of his, Edward, Earl of Lichfield. This was a severe blow indeed, showing how far out of favour he had fallen. On one of his few, low-key visits to London during this time, Rochester sent a petition to Charles, begging him to change his mind, but to no avail. He was given a couple of token payments, amounting to around £1,000, as an acknowledgement of some of the money that he had not been paid for his various roles, but after late November 1675 he was effectively debarred from the royal purse. As he lingered in Adderbury late that year, everything seemed lost. Rochester was poor both in pocket and in health. He made no obvious signs of contrition for his behaviour in the Privy Garden, apparently considering Charles fair game for insults, but the accusation that he had libelled the blameless Louise hung heavy on him. The only small consolation during this time was that he had a third daughter, Malet, born to him in December. The unusual christening was a reference to his long-suffering wife, whose maiden name the girl took.

The only poem of any significance that he wrote at this time was a stinging attack on Dryden, in 'An Allusion to Horace'. Dryden had looked for a new patron in Rochester's absence and was taken up by Mulgrave, who ensured that his new play, *Aureng-Zebe*, was performed in front of Charles in November. While he remained Poet Laureate, it never hurt to have another wealthy friend at court. By this time there was little love lost between Dryden and Rochester; Dryden and his play *The Indian Emperor* had been openly mocked in 'Timon', and, a few years before, *The Conquest of Granada* had been similarly ridiculed in *Sodom*, for which Dryden believed Rochester responsible. Nonetheless, Dryden's affiliation to Mulgrave appeared to be a calculated snub, and Rochester responded in kind with an opening sally of considered abuse:

> Well, sir, 'tis granted I said Dryden's rhymes
> Were stolen, unequal, nay dull many times.
> What foolish patron is there found of his
> So blindly partial to deny me this?

Rochester goes on to allow that Dryden's plays contain 'wit and learning' but are full of 'heavy mass' and therefore tedious and wordy. After a tour of ridicule of the contemporary writers of the day (a few friends such as Etherege, 'a sheer original', and Wycherley conspicuously excused), he returns to further castigation of the hapless Poet Laureate:

> Dryden in vain tried this nice way of wit,
> For he to be a tearing blade thought fit.
> But when he would be sharp, he still was blunt:
> To frisk his frolic fancy, he'd cry 'Cunt!'
> Would give the ladies a dry bawdy bob,
> And thus he got the name of Poet Squab.

Byron, in the opening of his epic *Don Juan*, would attack his own Poet Laureate enemy Robert Southey in exactly the same way over a century later, gaily claiming that Southey was 'quite a dry bob, Bob'. In both cases, the allusion is to impotence, specifically orgasm without emission, and Rochester gives the added mockery of describing the short, round Dryden as a 'squab'. Dryden (like Southey) exhibited a mannered pomposity that endeared him to royalty, even as Rochester's (like Byron's) more outrageous libertine writing and personae made him too shocking a figure to be a tame writer. It is impossible to imagine Rochester as Poet Laureate, even if he had not been a courtier. In the case of Dryden, his failed attempt to be 'a tearing blade' mirrors the 'reverend band and beard' of 'A Satire against Reason and Mankind', with his own impotent wish to be sufficiently witty to attack wit itself in a 'sharp essay'. However, Dryden, a man who was apt to make ill-considered exclamations such as inviting assembled guests to group sodomy, would always be blunt, both in speech and in attitude. Rochester criticizes him for further 'gross faults his choice pen does commit' and ridicules his 'loose, slattern muse', claiming that his major works 'were things perhaps composed in half an hour'. Rochester even offers some valuable literary criticism to Dryden, and to others, including himself:

To write what may securely stand the test
Of being well read over, thrice at least
Compare each phrase, examine every line,
Weigh every word, and every thought refine.
Scorn all applause the vile rout can bestow,
And be content to please the few who know.

Nonetheless, Rochester retained an amused fascination with the ridiculousness of Dryden. In a letter to Savile written early the next year, Rochester says of Dryden, with whom he was said to be 'out of favour' after the appearance of 'An Allusion to Horace': 'I have ever admired [him] for the disproportion of him and his attributes.' He goes on, with knowing absurdity, to compare the Poet Laureate to 'a hog that could fiddle, or a singing owl', and says, disingenuously, 'I cannot but be fond' of him.

Rochester was far from finished with his quarrels, though, picking a fight with the poet, wit and courtier Carr Scrope, a former friend of Buckingham's who had become an ally of Mulgrave's. Scrope was described witheringly, in 'An Allusion to Horace', as 'the purblind knight / Who squints more in his judgement than his sight / Picks silly faults, and censures what I write'. For some men in the depths of disfavour, creating new enemies might have been seen as unwise, but from this time forth, whether out of boredom, mental illness brought on by the effects of syphilis or a desire to shock, Rochester seemed intent on causing as much havoc as he could. The world had rejected him, his reasoning went; therefore, he would reject everything that others held sacred.

While enduring a long and tedious winter sojourn in Adderbury, the earl received news of his own death on 29 February 1676. It is probable that this was a scurrilous rumour started by his enemies, but his continued absence from court could also have led to such a story being circulated. Of course, had he actually been declared dead, it would instantly have invalidated his Rangership of Woodstock Park and the accompanying stipend, so he wrote to Savile, and by extension to the court, to inform him that accounts of his demise were greatly exaggerated, sardonically noting: 'it was no small joy to me that those tidings prove untrue... my passion for living is so increased that I omit no care of myself, which, before, I never thought life worth the trouble of taking.' There is a dig at Charles— 'the King, who knows me to be a very ill-natured man, will not think it an easy matter for me to die now I live chiefly out of spite'—and Rochester, though careful to ask after Savile and his other intimates' health, notes the paucity of those friends.

That the rumours of Rochester's death were taken seriously can be seen by a letter written to him by the Treasury Secretary Robert Howard. Dated 7 April, it offers some solidarity with the beleaguered poet: 'though this town is apt enough to like an ill entertainment better than a good one, yet I cannot believe them so stupid as to be insensible [to] what they should have lost by your death.' Howard, who professed himself 'so well pleased with your health', was a better politician than he was a doctor in his blithe dismissal of Rochester's illnesses, which included everything from temporary blindness and joint pain to urinating blood, the hallmarks of tertiary syphilis and gonorrhoea. Alluding to how Rochester's physician had acted like 'an angry impeacher' against his way of life, Howard offered him some heavy-handed statements of jocular support, but any sense that not all had turned against him was undeniably welcome.

One of his few other remaining allies was George Etherege, the wit and playwright. Etherege had come to public attention in 1664 with the farce *The Comical Revenge, or, Love in a Tub*, and moved in the same circles as Rochester and his cronies. Known as 'gentle George' on account of his pleasant and charming temperament, he had not written a play since 1668, when he produced *She Would If She Could*. Spending the years from 1668 till 1671 in Constantinople as secretary to the English ambassador Dennis Harvey had given him a keen eye for observation, which he put to good use in his next and most famous work, *The Man of Mode*, which had its first performance at the Duke's Theatre on 2 March 1676.

While the play's subtitle, *Sir Fopling Flutter*, refers to its outrageous fop character—who was based on the 'man of fashion' of the day, Beau Hewit—the main character is in fact Dorimant, an affectionate portrait of Etherege's friend Rochester. Dorimant is a dashing, devil-may-care seducer, of whom 'a thousand horrid stories have been told', but whose wit and intelligence mark him out as an attractive and charismatic protagonist. The most famous description of Dorimant comes when his former mistress Mrs Loveit (the names of the characters are, as ever in Restoration comedy, far from subtle) says of him: 'I know he is a devil, but he has something of the angel yet undefaced in him, which makes him so charming and agreeable that I must love him be he never so wicked.' In the same scene, Etherege even tips a nod to Rochester's 'A Satire against Reason and Mankind', when Loveit's servant Pert announces: 'Your knowing of Mr. Dorimant, in my mind, should rather make you hate all mankind.'

The play ends happily, with Dorimant pledging fidelity to the witty Harriet: 'The first time I saw you, you left me with the pangs of love upon me, and this day my soul has quite given up her liberty.' Etherege's concern to maintain good relations at court is clear in his having the play's prologue and epilogue written, respectively, by Scrope and Dryden, simultaneously flattering their vanity and allowing Rochester to be amused by his proxy's juxtaposition with two of his enemies.

While Dorimant was strutting glamorously upon the stage, applauded by the multitude, Rochester continued to cool his heels in the country, bored. He wrote to Savile complaining about 'the tediousness of doing nothing', and cynically dismisses the world as a place 'still so insupportably the same that 'twere vain to hope there were any alterations'. His fear and anger at his dismissal from court had given way to resignation, although he notes wryly that 'Livy and sickness' have given him a hitherto unsuspected interest in politics. His contempt for Charles was unabated; continuing the themes of his satire, he writes: 'Kings and princes are only as incomprehensible as what they pretend to represent, but apparently as frail as those they govern.' Rochester wrote in Lent—'a season of tribulation'—and dropped vague hints about giving up drinking and wenching upon his eventual return to town, but there seemed no imminent prospect of this, especially as a subsequent letter requests a visit to Woodstock by Savile and Buckingham in order to amuse him.

This or another similar visit duly took place, and debauched antics occurred. Rochester recalls in a later letter how a naked romp around Rosamund's Well in Woodstock Park saw 'two large fat nudities', presumably Buckingham and Savile, disporting themselves around 'the poor violated nymph', who was the unfortunate spectator of 'the strange decay of manly parts'. It is worth remembering that, while the urban legends of Rochester's public debauchery soon became incredible after his death, there was often some basis in fact. There may be some exaggeration in the retelling when Rochester writes to Savile: 'prick, 'tis confessed, you showed but little of, but for arse and buttocks (a filthier ostentation, God wot!) you exposed more of that nastiness in your two folio volumes than we all together in our six quartos.' Nonetheless, it shows that Rochester's Woodstock sojourn was not entirely uneventful.

At last Savile's subtle but persistent interjections with Charles, emphasizing (and probably exaggerating) his friend's contrition, went in Rochester's favour, and he returned to court in May 1676. The reason for Rochester's return was not sentimentality: Charles needed his vote in the Lords, and his earlier remarks to Savile that he was now interested in politics saw him brought back as a useful servant to a man he despised. It was a changed world. His former tormentor, Louise, was now out of favour with Charles, having had a miscarriage in March, and would be packed off to Bath in June. The Italian temptress Hortense Mancini, Duchess of Mazarin, had arrived in England in December 1675 disguised as a boy, having fled her mad husband Mazarin, and swiftly captured Charles's interest. Ironically enough, the king had proposed to her while in exile in 1659, but had been rejected on the grounds that he lacked prospects. Her masculine attire acting as a signal of her rumoured bisexuality,

Mancini's arrival was greeted with horror by most of the country, and she was given the sobriquet 'the great whore'. Sermons were preached against her, and her Catholicism held up as another sign of Charles's lack of morals. Rochester wrote a poem imagining a dialogue between Nell Gwyn and Louise, which, although typically bawdy, was not without some sympathy for the exiled duchess:

NELL: When to the King I bid good morrow
          With tongue in mouth, and hand on tarse,
          Portsmouth may rend her cunt for sorrow,
          And Mazarin may kiss mine arse.
PORTSMOUTH: When England's monarch's on my belly,
          With prick in cunt, though double crammed,
          Fart of mine arse for small whore Nelly,
          And great whore Mazarin be damned.

Rochester, meanwhile, continued to be worried about Elizabeth Barry's constancy. A melodramatic letter that he sent to her shortly before his return to London questions whether 'there be yet alive within you the least memory of me', and talks of how 'your favours are to me the greatest bliss this world… can bestow'. However, he knows the ways of actresses in London and makes allusion to her suspected infidelity: 'when you give another leave to serve you more than I… it will not be in your power to reward that more deserving man with half so much happiness as you have thrown away upon my worthless self.'

As with many witty men, Rochester was better at dealing with these matters in the abstract than in reality. Returning to court, he had his first meeting with Charles in nearly a year, at which he received the hugely displeasing news that Elizabeth Barry had indeed been unfaithful to him. Informing Rochester of his mistress's infidelity might seem petty behaviour for a monarch, but Charles, who had been informed of the situation by Nell Gwyn, saw it as evening the score for the damage done the previous year. Rochester sent her a letter in equal parts dismayed and panicked, asking for an appointment at 10 a.m. that day and saying: 'the affair is unhappy, and to me on many scores but on none more than that it has disturbed the heaven of thought I was in.' It was an indication both of his love for her and of his naïvety that Rochester expected her to be faithful; he was disabused in the most violent way.

However, the matter was settled and their affair resumed as before, albeit now with a greater amount of jealousy and grumbling on Rochester's part. Letters of his to Elizabeth Barry around this time eschew poetic conceits and expressions of undying love in favour of suspicion. 'I know by woeful experience what comes of dealing with knaves', he claims, and upon being proved correct in his suspicions that her neighbour was acting as a bawd on another's behalf, declares: 'May no man share the blessings I enjoy without my curses.' He ends one letter asking that she 'may remove my fears and make me as happy as I am faithful', a piece of classic Rochesterian disingenuousness. Despite his avowed intent to restrain himself in matters vaginal and vinicultural, he soon returned with his friends to his old haunts of the taverns and brothels.

Rochester was received back at court both with disdain and with admiration. A fellow Groom of the Bedchamber, Henry Bulkeley, wrote to him, 'I don't wonder you fall into such persecutions as your last, since you live in an age when fools are your most powerful enemies.' Bulkeley, equally weary of court life, describes how 'a committee of those able statesmen assemble daily to talk of nothing but fighting and fucking at Locketts [a famous inn], and will never be reconciled to men who speak sense and reason'. Perhaps Rochester smiled wryly at the last allusion. Bulkeley was fond of duels and frequently imprisoned as a result, but there was no doubting his courage, nor his respect for the infamous rake-poet.

If it seemed, briefly, that things had taken a turn for the better, Rochester was soon involved in an affair that would plunge him into even deeper opprobrium. He headed to the fashionable races at Epsom on 17 June, nearly a year after the incident in the Privy Garden, with Etherege, another rake named George Bridges and a young soldier, Billy Downs. They soon abandoned the turf in favour of the bottle. Late that night, all were drunk. Coming upon some passing fiddlers, the group demanded that they play for them, and, when this request was reasonably refused, they showed their displeasure by abusing the unfortunate musicians.

Hearing this commotion, a nearby barber came over and, about to be abused in his turn, diverted attention by suggesting a visit to the house of the fairest woman in Epsom. This seemed like a fine plan, so the revellers agreed, only to be shown by the savvy barber to the house of the local constable. Hearing a raucous disturbance outside his door, the constable demanded to know what the men wanted, only to be peremptorily informed that they needed a whore. He, not being able to satisfy their request, refused to let them in, but four strong, inebriated men were not to be trifled with, so they broke down his door and set about him, injuring him badly. Eventually, the unfortunate constable escaped and called the local watch, who duly appeared fully armed.

Etherege, the most sober of the group, was able to calm the watch down with a 'submissive oration', and they departed. Had the matter ended there, all would have been well. However, Rochester, disappointed that the evening would end without further sport, drew his sword upon the constable, who then shouted 'Murder!' Downs, attempting to calm the situation, made to restrain Rochester, only for his actions to be misinterpreted by the returning watch. Downs was struck on the head with a staff and then had a pike thrust into his side. Panicking, Rochester and the others fled, abandoning the unfortunate Downs to his fate; he died of his wounds a few days later. Aghast, his fellow revellers returned to London and the consequences of their sport.

While, technically, it was the watchmen who were responsible for Downs's death, few were in any doubt that the affair was Rochester's fault. At best, his actions were atypically cowardly—even his friend and supporter Marvell described how he 'abjectly hid himself'— and, at worst, he had single-handedly justified every slur and slander that had been placed upon him (by way of contrast, no such blame attached itself to Etherege or Bridges, who were never indicted for any crime). It was rumoured that Rochester would be tried for murder, and so, once again, he left court, this time voluntarily. Charles would not in any case have been a sympathetic ally to a crime of violence and cowardice. This time, to avoid the law, it was said that Rochester had left for France, but in fact he returned to the country, full of self-loathing, which he expressed in one of his most cuttingly autobiographical poems.

If most of Rochester's writing is clear-sighted about his frailties and failures, it is often leavened by wit or a distancing conceit. In the case of one of his darkest works, 'To the Postboy', there is no such palliative. Instead, he writes a poem that stands out as a scream of self-laceration, rather than attacking the society in which he lived. It could accurately be termed 'A Satire: On Myself', were satire not too gentle a term for the vituperative sentiments expressed.

The poem takes the form of a dialogue between Rochester and a young letter-bearer, although this description implies a greater amount of exchange than the mainly one-sided work contains:

ROCHESTER: Son of a whore, God damn you, can you tell
    A peerless peer the readiest way to hell;
    I've outswilled Bacchus, sworn of my own make
    Oaths would fright Furies, and make Pluto quake;
    I've swived more whores more ways than Sodom's walls
    E'er knew, or the College of Rome's Cardinals.
    Witness heroic scars—look here, ne'er go! –
    Sear cloths and ulcers from the top to toe.
    Frighted at my own mischiefs, I have fled
    And bravely left my life's defender dead;
    Broke houses to break chastity, and dyed
    That floor with murder which my lust denied.
    Pox on't, why do I speak of these poor things?
    I've blasphemed God, and libelled Kings.
    The readiest way to Hell, Boy, quick, ne'er stir!

POSTBOY: The readiest way, my Lord's by Rochester.

Admitting his cowardice and complicity in Downs's death, Rochester condemns himself for his failings, implying that his selfishness has finally resulted in an event of tragic consequence. After writing it, he disappeared from view. Had any of his friends read the poem— which did not appear until the twentieth century, when it was published by the Rochester scholar John Hayward—they might have assumed that it was a theatrical parting shot from a man destined to die by his own hand.

He did not. Instead, his love of ostentation and disguise lent itself to his most bizarre persona yet.

[10]

'THIS FAMOUS

pathologist

Doctor

BENDO'

❖

[1676–1677]

TOWER STREET was one of the most prosperous parts of London in June 1676. Predominantly inhabited by the emerging middle class of the day, it was home to aspirant tradesmen of the higher kind, as well as to a range of itinerant chancers. These included everyone from alchemists to confidence tricksters, all of whom hoped to make a few shillings from gullible passers-by before the law got wise to their unseemly antics. It was a place where people could adopt new identities if they were on the run from their creditors or family, with only the ever-present shadow of the Tower of London in the background to remind them of the punishment for their transgressions.

Into this milieu arrived a gorgeously attired figure, 'the noble doctor, Alexander Bendo'. Dr Bendo was said to have arrived straight from Italy and was dressed in the rich clothes of his native homeland, including an enormous green gown, exotic multi-coloured furs, a substantial and noble beard, diamonds and jewels aplenty, and a great gold chain hung around his neck, a gift from the king of Cyprus for curing his daughter Princess Aloephangina. Being an Italian—and a papist to boot—he spoke no English, but instead communicated with his servants and familiars by means of a complicated series of hand gestures, all the while muttering to himself in a strange and unfamiliar tongue.

His arrival, even in ever-shifting Tower Street, caused quite a sensation. He lodged at a local goldsmith's house, next to The Black Swan tavern, and soon set about declaring his presence. Town-criers and hawkers were sent out into the streets to announce the coming to town of the good Dr Bendo and to dispense handbills he had written, in which he announced his many accomplishments and patients cured. The bill itself was altogether more literate and well versed in the English language than might have been expected of an Italian. It begins by praising 'the famous metropolis of England' and 'its worthy inhabitants', but bemoans the fact that the city has become inundated with 'a numerous company of such, whose arrogant confidence, backing their ignorance, has enabled them to impose upon the people either premeditated cheats, or… the palpable, dull and empty mistakes of their self-deluded imaginations'.

Bendo, a man of brilliance and integrity, instead offered something quite different from this 'bastard race of quacks', who were mired in 'a repute of mere mists, imaginations, errors and deceits'. He was all too aware that he was in a world 'where virtue is so frequently exactly counterfeited and hypocrisy so generally taken notice of', and that his own name might be regarded with suspicion. He assured Londoners that 'if I had intended any such foul play myself, I should [not] have given you so fair warning by my severe observations upon others', and cites a parable of the coward and the valiant man: 'the valiant man holds up his head, looks confidently round him, wears a sword, courts a lord's wife and owns it, so does the coward; one only point of honour excepted, and that's courage… makes the distinction.'

Bendo, being Italian and therefore given to floral verbosity, illustrated this with many other examples designed to show his wisdom and integrity. Only the hard-hearted could have read his bill and doubted his straightforward, manly honour. Then, he came to the crux of the matter. Bendo offered cures for scurvy, joint pain, bad teeth, poor skin, leg aches, obesity, consumption, kidney stones and other painful illnesses, all of which he would deal with in 'great secrecy'. Bendo, a man of great moral stature, was keen that his bill should be wholesome and family-oriented, and made sure that no word 'bears any unclean sound', unlike others he had seen, 'as bawdy as Aretine's dialogues, which no man that walks warily before God can approve of'. His kindness and dedication extended to ensuring that 'the reproachful mistakes of barren wombs' might be cured by him as well, a matter of immense delicacy and caution.

Bendo was understandably coy about where he had obtained his medical knowledge, instead saying that his 'secrets' came from the best part of fifteen years' wandering in France and Italy, and in the latter 'women of forty bear the same countenance [as] those of fifteen'. Finally, he ended his bill with a ringing statement explaining why it should benefit him to bring about these cures:

> Should Galen himself look out of his grave, and tell me these were baubles, below the profession of a physician, I would boldly answer him, that I take more glory in preserving God's image, upon one good face, than I should do in patching up all the decayed corpses in the world.

Dr Bendo, this scrupulous figure of honour and trust, announced that he would be 'at home' at his lodgings from 3 until 8 p.m. each day, and commended himself to the good people of London. Only the most suspicious would read this bill, with its protestations of medical skill, mixed with a little continental wisdom, and fail to run straight to Tower Street to be waited upon by the good doctor. Or, to give him his more accurate name, the disgraced John Wilmot, 2nd Earl of Rochester.

Rochester's interest in play-acting and disguise reached its zenith with the creation of Bendo. Run out of court and fearing prosecution for his involvement in Billy Downs's death, he decided that the best option he had was to disappear for a couple of months. Fleeing to the continent was too expensive an option for him to consider, so laying low in the city at the epicentre of his world appeared the best solution. Whitehall had little authority in the half-ruined streets, with which he was all too familiar through his visits to the brothels there.

However, he had no wish merely to hide in the house of one of his friends, and so concocted an elaborate scheme, aided by his most trusted servant, the aptly named Thomas Alcock. Alcock had had some education, being able to read and write, as can be seen by his 1687 account of these adventures, *The Famous Pathologist, or, The Noble Mountebank*. Most body servants—those entrusted with their masters' clothing and shaving—would have been able to read, at least, but fewer were entirely literate. Rochester and Alcock proved a well-matched pair.

Rochester decided to adopt the guise and manner of a physician, whose sudden appearance in town could be explained away by his being Italian. There were other, less showy means of evading the law and court displeasure, but once the initial idea had occurred to him, Rochester took great pleasure in elaborating on it in an ostentatious and public fashion. In this spirit, he created an apparently sincere but actually satirical document, 'Alexander Bendo's Bill', which simultaneously offers a pitch-perfect parody of the countless other mountebanks and charlatans who set themselves up to offer miraculous cures to the gullible and unwary, while mocking the society that allowed them to prosper.

In the bill he attacks the great men of court, just as he had done throughout his satires:

> the politician... finding how the people are taken with specious
> miraculous impossibilities plays the same game, protests, declares,
> promises... things which he's sure can ne'er be brought about; the
> people believe, are deluded and pleased.

He also takes time to mock religion, describing 'the expectation of a future good, which shall never befall them', and ends by describing the political climber as nothing more than 'a mountebank in state affairs'. Had one of those men, a Scrope or a Mulgrave, read Bendo's bill, they might have been alerted to the presence of Rochester in their midst, still engaged in mocking society's ills. But the Italian— what was his name again?—was just another mountebank, no different to scores of others. It is hugely doubtful that anyone at court would have read his bill, or cared if they had.

Rochester was far from the only person trying his hand at this fraud. A contemporary account, entitled *The Character of a Quack-Doctor*, describes exactly what the average mountebank's strategy consisted of:

> First, he prevails with some associate porters and tripe-women to
> call him Doctor... [He] deals as a private mountebank, and makes
> every blind alehouse he comes in his stage, where he tells a thousand
> lies of his miraculous cures, and has his landlady at his elbow to

vouch them: he bribes all the nurses he can meet with, and keeps
a dozen midwives in pension to proclaim his skill at gossipings, he
endears the chambermaid by a private dose, to bring him in with
her mistress; the new married citizen's wife… comes to him for the
reputed ability of his back, not his brains, and the suburb gamers
admire him for toping a pot so sociably.

Rochester could certainly tope a pot sociably with the best of them,
but his intention was a more elaborate one. It took some effort and
expense, as Alcock put it, to 'tacitly and satirically [expose] that
ignorant sort of people, the mock astrologers, mountebanks, quack
salvers, empericks and their insensible admirers', but he was more
than equal to the charade. Bill prepared and distributed, he hired a
few casual labourers (the 'associate porters' who were easily bribed
for a few pennies), sat back and awaited custom.

London was intrigued, so it was not long in coming. It was given
out that Bendo could offer anything from 'paint, powder, ointments'
to 'opiates, tinctures and chemical preparations of all sorts'. These
drugs were in fact made out of a mixture of 'ashes, soot, lime, chalk,
old wall, soap, and indeed anything that came to hand' while the
two men were walking the streets, and coloured accordingly. Alcock
vividly describes the goings-on in the 'laboratory' (in fact a small
room in the goldsmith's house), which was full of 'real mirth and
continual hearty laughs':

Some stirring an old boiling kettle, of soot and urine, tinged with
a little asafoetida and all the nasty ingredients that would render
the smell more unsavoury; others tending the fires, some luting the
retorts, others pounding bricks, and scraping powders from them.

The assembled company were attired 'like the old witches from
Macbeth', and Rochester oversaw the whole charade, weighing and
packaging the medicines, while dressed in a tatty old gown like the
one that his old tutor Robert Whitehall had given him to abet his
sneaking into the taverns of Oxford. Bendo's nonsense was soon a
success. His prices deliberately undercut the local apothecaries and
drugsters, who swore and damned him, but he was much beloved

by the poor, who described him as 'a conscionable good doctor' and prayed for his continued success.

Nor were his abilities purely medical. The multi-faceted doctor could deal with predictions, omens and interpretations of dreams. On occasion his work required him to see his female clients naked, a state of affairs that undoubtedly delighted Rochester, but he was sufficiently into his masquerade to adopt another elaborate scheme to keep Bendo's name respectable. His prospective patient would therefore make an appointment to be attended by Mrs Bendo, a grave, matronly woman of sober appearance, who would caress her visitors in a purely respectable fashion. Sometimes, if the caresses went well, Dr Bendo offered his strictly professional cure for infertility; Burnet notes that his technique was 'not without success', suggesting that Rochester's bastards littered London society for years, possibly generations, afterwards.

It is difficult to think of many other significant literary figures who would drag up to achieve their sexual ambitions. But the iconoclastic spirit of Rochester's life is hard to compare to that of other poets, or indeed of other men. Rebounding from the horrors of Epsom, he found a practical expression of his contempt for society in all its forms with the ridiculous creation of Bendo, who could happily have stepped onto the stage of the Theatre Royal, Drury Lane unchanged and acted in his own Restoration comedy: in Alcock's words, *The Famous Psychologist, or, The Noble Mountebank*.

At last, Bendo came to an end. Rochester began to tire of his charade after a couple of months, deciding that there was greater entertainment to be had in his own guise at court, especially as there was no danger of criminal proceedings against him (after all, nobody of quality had died in the Epsom affray). While he never talked publicly about his adventures, he spoke to some of his friends about the Bendo masquerade,* and was still sufficiently mindful of it to discuss it with Burnet towards the end of his life. Besides, he was missed at court. Charles's anger with him had passed, as usual, and

---

* It was, for instance, sufficiently well known for Savile to allude to 'your chemical knowledge' in a letter of 15 August.

word was sent to him (probably by Savile) that his presence would not be unwelcome any more. So he returned to Whitehall, after what Alcock knowingly described as 'the quickest voyage from France that ever man did', and was received with renewed royal favour. He was seen dancing at a ball the night after his return, as if nothing had happened in between.

As for Dr Bendo, he vanished into thin air, with no explanation for his sudden disappearance. Alcock wryly noted that the rumour went around that Bendo, his wife and their entire ménage were an enchanted crew, raised and now dispersed by necromancy. This story was swallowed whole by many of their disappointed, or embarrassed, patients, who saw witchcraft as the only logical explanation for the rapid departure of the noble Italian. His name was whispered incredulously for years afterwards around Tower Street and beyond, by his 'patients', creditors and observers, but it was not until Alcock, in a letter to Rochester's daughter Anne over a decade later, told the whole story that the connection between Rochester and Bendo was made public. The tale, then as now, was an outrageous one.

There are many reasons why Rochester became Bendo. He needed to lie low for a few weeks, the masquerade offered him some easy entertainment (and access to women), and it tied in with his interest in play-acting and disguise. Yet there is something biting and angry about the satire of Bendo's bill, which, given that the last thing Rochester had written was 'To the Postboy', also has about it a sense of Rochester degrading himself. He was by now very ill, the early signs of tertiary syphilis beginning to show, and the entire episode has to be seen as one of the last hurrahs of a man who knew that his end was not far away. Bendo represented an attack on society, but it also represented Rochester attacking himself.

The peerless peer was back in favour at court, his masquerade undetected, but his troubles with both Elizabeths continued. A letter from his wife, probably sent while Rochester was going about as Bendo, implied that she had not heard from him in a considerable time, suggesting that she was as much in the dark about his adventures as everyone else. She writes, piteously, that 'the uncertainty of [not hearing from you] very much afflicts me; whether this odd kind of proceeding be to try my patience or obedience, I cannot guess, but I will never fail of either when my duty to you require them'. Wondering whether he was staying in Bath, she provides some inadvertent humour when she says: 'I am confident you will find so much business as will not allow you to come into the country.' The letter ends poignantly, though, when she talks of their children and 'the long hopes I have lived in of seeing you'.

Much business had indeed been done over the previous couple of months, and Rochester, freed of the shackles of Bendo, prepared to resume his own business with Elizabeth Barry. Letters he wrote in early summer 1676 hint at the Bendo affair, but being easily intercepted, they are not explicit. In one he writes: 'I will not tell you my endeavours nor excuse my breach of promise… but I hope to give you a better account shortly.' In another, presumably a reply to a vexed missive from her, he claims: 'That I do not see you is not that I would not… but for these reasons you [shall] know hereafter.' These letters were probably written towards the end of his time impersonating Bendo. However, he was attempting to make amends, and in his statement that 'I can give you no account of your business as yet, but of my own part', he hints at his attempts to obtain for her a role in a play.

This part was probably Leonora in Aphra Behn's play *Abdelazer*, which was staged at the Dorset Garden Theatre in July. Behn was a fascinatingly quixotic character, even by the libertine standards of the day. One of the first women to earn her living as a writer, she had lived a chequered life, having aroused controversy first for her Catholic upbringing, then for her service to the crown as a spy in the Second Anglo-Dutch War, in which she had adopted the code name 'Astrea'. After some time in a debtors' prison—perhaps because she had not been sufficiently recompensed for her work, a typical piece of royal thoughtlessness and ingratitude—she began an independent career, achieving some success with her early Restoration comedies *The Forced Marriage* and *The Amorous Prince*.

The nature of Rochester and Behn's relationship has always aroused controversy. Each had a licentious reputation: Behn, a very merry widow, had been the mistress of John Hoyle, a bisexual lawyer with republican sympathies, and Rochester was, well, Rochester. No letters between the two survive, but their literary interests had a great deal in common. Her poem 'The Disappointment', in particular, owes much to Rochester's own style, so much so that it was often thought to have been by him and was attributed as such in the first collection of his poetry. While it treads very similar territory to 'The Imperfect Enjoyment', the key difference is that it looks at an interrupted sexual encounter from the perspective of the woman's, rather than the man's, desire. The unapologetic treatment of longed-for sexual gratification was considered acceptable from a poet such as Rochester, but the forthright expression of female sexuality was a step too far, even in this supposedly libertine age.

It is amusing to speculate that Rochester and Behn tried and failed to have a sexual encounter, which both then wrote about from their separate perspectives. No evidence for this supposition survives, however, and it seems likely that Rochester's interest in helping Behn was dictated by friendship rather than erotic desire. Behn was eight years Rochester's senior, a considerable age gap at that time. He assisted her with her writing, for which Behn praised him in a poem that she wrote after his death, and provided her with an introduction to the hard-drinking, hard-cursing life of court. She, meanwhile, paid him homage both direct and indirect, most notably in her 1677 play *The Rover*, which features a swaggering, witty rake-hero whose success with women is matched by his naval prowess. It was almost obligatory for a Restoration comedy of this time to feature a Rochester-libertine character—this was more a reflection of the writers' affection for their friend than a sign of intellectual poverty—and, making the debt explicit, her protagonist is named 'Wilmore'. Building on her previous stage success, Elizabeth Barry once again acted in a Behn play, appearing as Wilmore's cross-dressing love, Hellena.

However, even while Elizabeth Barry found success in *Abdelazer*, her entanglement with Rochester was increasingly trying. Rochester's letters appear to offer constant contrition for his behaviour, presumably because he kept expressing his drunken jealousy at her suspected infidelities whenever he saw her. In one, he pleads: 'if I love anything in the world like you... may I ever be as unlucky and as hateful as when I saw you last'; in another, he juggles a playful mock-penitential style ('Receive my confession and let the promise of my future zeal and devotion obtain my pardon for last night's blasphemy against you') with what appears to be sincere embarrassment at his actions: 'til I have mended my manners, I am ashamed to look you in the face.' A previously unpublished letter from around this time sees Rochester describe himself as 'the idlest man alive' and apologize for 'a proof of that ill quality of sin' that Elizabeth Barry has been privy to; he claims that 'something fell out that ought not to have hindered me seeing you last night, but it did' and begs forgiveness and a chance to see her.

Rochester's mercurial dealings with Elizabeth Barry were inevitably coloured by his growing belief that his protégée was no longer in love with him. His letters make grand protestations of his own undying affections and fidelity—conveniently, he appears to forget the existence of his wife and children—but are constantly underpinned by statements such as 'endeavour to give me some undeniable proofs that you love me' and 'for your sake use not that power... so unmercifully as you did last time'. Whether a loving drunkard or a drunken lover, he remained incapable of sobriety or restraint, which explains why Elizabeth Barry wanted to keep her distance.

Eventually, in August 1676, Rochester returned home to Adderbury for the first time in several months. Anticipating trouble, he sent his wife a letter in which he alluded to his spending money from her Somerset estates—as her husband, he had the right of access to these—and tried to mollify her by saying, 'I intend to give you the trouble of a visit, 'tis all I have to beg your pardon for at present.' As before, it is likely that the coming of the prodigal father was greeted with weary resignation, rather than unfettered joy.

Bored with his rustication, Rochester was more interested in the court gossip, which he received in abundance from Savile in a letter dated 15 August 1676. Savile, apologizing for his epistolary interruption of Rochester's domestic bliss, remarks that London 'is full as foolish, full as wise, full as formal and full as impertinent as you left it'. Recounting a list of deaths and romantic entanglements (one including their Epsom partner in crime, George Bridges), Savile strikes a world-weary note, claiming that 'were I not too old and much too fat for poetry, surely all this stuff should inspire me'. He was bound for Paris on court business; in a letter to Savile from Oxford the following month, Rochester expresses a desire to head to Europe on a reprise of his grand tour, 'for the improvement of my parts'. Knowingly flirtatious, he writes: 'if the temptation of seeing you be added to the desires I have already, the sin is so sweet that I am resolved to embrace it.'

Sin aside, Rochester was tired and worn out, as was his poetic muse. Compared to the previous few years, which had seen the composition of around fifty poems, encompassing everything from satires on the state of mankind to bawdy squibs about impotency, his writing was now far less prolific and, when it came, was more likely to be devoted to attacking his enemies than adding anything substantial to the world of literature. A small exception is his lyric poem 'A Song of a Young Lady to her Ancient Lover'. Perhaps influenced by his romantic difficulties with Elizabeth Barry, compounded by infidelity and impotence, Rochester adopts a female perspective to examine his woes:

> Ancient person, for whom I
> All the flattering youth defy,
> Long be it ere thou grow old,
> Aching, shaking, crazy, cold;
> But still continue as thou art,
> Ancient person of my heart.

The poem is a curious but affecting mix of the self-lacerating and the self-pitying. It can be taken as implicit commentary on Elizabeth

Barry's life, amidst the 'flattering youth' who would wish to importune her, with Rochester viewing himself as little more than 'aching, shaking, crazy, cold'. At the age of twenty-nine, he was hardly ancient or old, but his exhausting, pell-mell existence had undeniably left him worn out. The second verse soon moves into wish-fulfilment. The young lady will bestow 'brooding kisses' on 'withered lips' and will 'thy youthful heat restore… and a second spring recall'. As she swears fidelity—'Nor from thee will ever part / Ancient person of my heart'—the reader might be forgiven for finding this unlikely. Rochester's attentions soon turn to his 'dead cinder':

> Thy nobler part, which but to name
> In our sex would be counted shame,
> By age's frozen grasp possessed,
> From his ice shall be released,
> And soothed by my reviving hand,
> In former warmth and vigour stand.
> All a lover's wish can reach
> For thy joy my love shall teach,
> And for thy pleasure shall improve
> All that art can add to love.

It is a telling insight into Rochester at his most insecure and troubled, worried about matters sexual and romantic, but still able to imbue navel-gazing narcissism with humour (there is a touch of the mock prudery of Bendo in the refusal to name 'thy nobler part' because of the 'shame' involved in so doing) and, by the final couplet, with a touch of unadorned romanticism:

> Yet still I love thee without art,
> Ancient person of my heart.

These sentiments were at odds with how the affair between Rochester and Elizabeth Barry was progressing. In a letter sent from Adderbury on 7 October 1676—presumably by this stage Rochester no longer cared whether his wife learnt of the affair or not, as she eventually would do—he adopts a new tone, a clipped, diffident rebuttal of an angry missive from her. He shrugs off her 'uncharitable censure' and, in response to some criticism that she has heard from 'wretches', notes that they are 'so little valuable that you will easily forget their malice'. He indicates that he will be returning to London in two days' time, with the intention of resuming their affair.

Rochester's life in London, especially without Savile and with only a partial resumption of royal favour, was increasingly empty. With the Rangership of Woodstock Park no longer due to go to his son after his death, tensions between him and Charles remained. The latter offered him no further sinecures, and even his existing allowances were seldom paid. He resumed the usual round of drinking and wenching in his old haunts of the city, but carnal pleasure failed to satisfy him. In a rare letter to his wife, he writes: 'my head has been perpetually turned round, but I do not find it makes me giddy; this is all the wit you shall expect in my first letter.' Relations with Elizabeth Barry, affected by suspicions and distrust on both sides, were far from cordial. Her 'wretches' were still impugning his name, and despite Rochester's pleas that he was still 'thoroughly your humble servant', there was clearly deep distrust on her part. When he writes 'Madam, I found you in a chiding humour today, and so I left you', there is obvious irritation, only partially masked by the black wit of the following sentence, when he expresses a desire not to see her before the next day, 'til when neither you nor any you can employ shall know whether I am under or above ground'.

As a partial result of this boredom, his hitherto neglected legitimate children preyed upon his mind. His eldest daughter, Anne, was now eight, and it would only be a few years before she was a marriageable prospect, just as his son Charles, although only five, had to be educated and instructed how to be a gentleman. Thomas Alcock, his accomplice in the Bendo saga, became tutor to both Anne and Charles as he was both trustworthy and literate.

Alcock's arrival at Adderbury from London was accompanied by a letter that Rochester intended for Charles. One of only a couple of letters to his son that survive, it is both poignant and revealing. Soliciting his son's gratitude for the arrival of his tutor, Rochester requests that he be 'obedient and diligent', saying 'you are now grown big enough to be a man if you can be wise enough'. He was told to 'serve god, learn your book and observe the instructions of your parents first, and next your tutor, to whom I have entirely resigned you for this seven year'. This differed from Rochester's own education at Burford Grammar School, which began when he was about nine and ended when he was admitted to Oxford at twelve. Clearly Rochester believed his son would be better instructed by a tutor with wide experience of the world than in one of the local schools. He notes that it is this education that will make him 'happy or unhappy forever', and praises his son by saying, 'I have so good an opinion of you yet I am glad to think you will never deceive me, dear child.' He counsels learning, obedience and diligence, and ends by saying 'that you may be [good] are my constant prayers'. The mention of religion and prayer, although clearly designed to instruct his son, is a world away from the mockery of scripture that can be seen in his letters to his wife and Savile.

When he was not urging virtue on the young, Rochester's court life proceeded as before. He associated with Buckingham a great deal, drinking and scheming; Buckingham, who by now stood in open dissent to Charles, was attempting to become leader of the newly formed Country party, which was a non-partisan coalition of Tories and Whigs, and aimed to reduce or remove all sources of organized power, whether it be royal or Parliamentary. Buckingham tried to seduce Rochester into participation, and Rochester, whose political interest was growing stronger at this point, gave tacit support to his scheme—a dangerous act for one whose reputation was still marred by his actions of the past few years. When not amusing himself by writing scurrilous satirical verse that mocked his enemies Dryden and Shadwell, Rochester, accompanied by Buckingham, Savile and others, attended the opening of Wycherley's *The Plain Dealer* in December 1676. The play proved predictably scandalous, with its hints of lesbianism and cross-dressing, and delighted Rochester and his circle, for whom controversy and upset were an excellent counterpoint to an evening at the theatre.

The year 1677 began with further machinations, both political and poetic. On 15 February Parliament reconvened, with Rochester present. Representing the House of Lords as its speaker, Buckingham seized the initiative, citing a statute that Parliament, which had been dissolved for the previous fifteen months, was ineligible to be in session. This was a bold move, but a foolhardy one; few were willing to stand in open opposition to Charles, and so he, along with a small number of supporters including Anthony Ashley Cooper, Earl of Shaftesbury, found himself committed to the Tower on 16 February for gross insubordination. Their confinement was a purely punitive one, where visitors were refused and they were kept under close guard at all times. Nevertheless the quick-thinking Shaftesbury managed to obtain permission to have his own cook during his imprisonment, on the grounds that he might be poisoned by his enemies, who included Charles's enforcer, Thomas Osborne, Earl of Danby.

The disproportionate severity of the sentence indicated, first, that Charles was vexed and frightened by the open challenge to his regal authority, and second, that Buckingham was fully out of favour. It was a considerable decline from his previous position as chief minister, in its own way a reversal of fortune as substantial as Clarendon's had been in the previous decade. Rochester, however, remained loyal to his old mentor, and began intriguing, along with Buckhurst, to secure his release from the Tower. To do so, he turned to an unlikely source of support, the courtesan and actress Nell Gwyn.

'Poor, laborious Nelly' had been, by this time, supplanted in Charles's bed, but not in his affections. Though she continued to appear on the stage, she enjoyed a lifestyle that most of the actresses of the time could only imagine, with a substantial townhouse in Pall Mall, of which she had been granted the freehold by Act of Parliament in 1676, and a country estate, Burford House in Windsor, as well as sundry gifts of cash and clothing. Tellingly, she was never to be ennobled or granted a title; the idea of bestowing such a bauble on a mere *actor* was unthinkable until Henry Irving received a knighthood in 1895. Charles might have loved her, but socially she remained the lowest of his mistresses. She remained close to Charles, offering him 'breakfasts and concerts'—and, presumably, a good deal more besides.

It was due to Buckingham's agency in 1667 that Charles and Nell had begun their love affair, and because of this well-remembered kindness Rochester enlisted her as an ally in his quest. She responded cautiously at first to his overtures; not only was Rochester's reputation as a rake and blackguard well known by this point, but persistent rumours of his turbulent relationship with Elizabeth Barry were heard all over the playhouses. Their increasingly fraught dealings might well have turned many fellow actors and actresses against him.

Rochester's behaviour over these months, however, proved entirely atypical, being sober, well judged and selfless. For once, he behaved like an honest politician—the sort of character he had hoped for in 'A Satire against Reason and Mankind', 'who does his needful flattery direct / Not to oppress and ruin, but protect'. He was a constant presence on committees and in public offices, speaking in the House of Lords and gaining some approval by doing so. If his desire was to indicate to Charles that he had, at the age of nearly thirty, finally achieved what was expected of him, it worked.

However, the suspicious Nell was a harder nut to crack. Eventually, Rochester hit upon the simple but brilliant idea of supporting her claim for various lands in Ireland, which she had been granted by Charles and wished to retain in order to provide an income for herself and her children, but which were being disputed in the Irish Claims Court. In a letter dated 22 April 1677 to Arthur Capel, Earl of Essex and Lord Lieutenant of Ireland, Rochester suavely alludes to both royal favour and his own influence in the matter. Beneath the shower of clichéd flattery ('there is nowhere to be found a better friend or worthier patron'), the implication is clear: I am a man of stature, in good standing with the king, and this matter had better be sorted, quickly. It was: by June the tide was turning in her favour, and by November the land was hers, earning her a not inconsiderable income of £800 a year, or around £65,000 in today's money.

In return for this assistance, Rochester solicited Nell to help by bringing her kind influence to bear on Charles. It was a delicate matter; Charles was famously indulgent to his favourites, but, as with Rochester's destruction of the sundial two years before, his favour could swiftly be withdrawn after an insult or attack. A petition that Buckingham sent Rochester from the Tower in April 1677 begs him to 'lose no time in making use of the King's good nature and kindness to me', knowing that the longer he was incarcerated, the more likely 'certain well natured persons' with no love for Buckingham would ensure that his stay in the Tower was a permanent one.

Eventually, the combination of Nell's sexual charms and Rochester's enhanced political standing saw Buckingham released from the Tower in July 1677, initially for a month's parole and then permanently. A grateful letter from Buckingham to Rochester was sent shortly afterwards, enclosing a gift of 'two of the civillest carps' and praising him for his kindness; he claims that 'I have not contaminated my body with any person below my quality since I saw you', and adds: 'I am now very busy drinking your Lordship's health.' Buckingham, like Rochester, was adept at flattery, and in a letter dating from August protests: 'I assure you as long as I live you shall find me heartily and entirely your servant.'

Almost incredibly, Buckingham believed that he might yet resume royal favour and win the position of Lord Steward. While conniving for this role with the Cabinet Council, he stayed at Rochester's lodgings in Whitehall, living in debauchery and womanizing—'the usual life', as Marvell sardonically called it. Buckingham's enemies treated this open flouting of his pardon with horror—they persuaded Charles that a man with so little contrition had no place at court, and accordingly he was unsuccessful in his endeavour. With nothing left for him in Whitehall, he was 'advised' to leave court for his estate in Berkshire, Cliveden, where he intrigued from afar and hoped for a return to royal favour and influence.

If obtaining Buckingham's release was a rare high point for Rochester, the rest of his life was less happy. Rochester impregnated Elizabeth Barry in March or April 1677, but they continued to distrust one another. Rochester's letters are alternately wheedling or simply dismissive, and that she doubted his fidelity as much as he did hers is obvious, and probably deserved. A typical letter of his begins, with a combination of weariness and indignancy: 'My visit yesterday was intended to tell you I had not dined in company of women... if your anger continue, show yourself at the play that I may look upon you and go mad.' A greater formality also crept in; another, previously unpublished, letter is signed 'Your humble servant, Rochester' and states: 'do me the favour to let me speak with you as soon as you please, it concerns yourself a little, and therefore very much.'

He also carried on his rivalries and fights with various other members of court. Chief amongst these was the ridiculous Sir Carr Scrope. A short, angry and affected man who fancied himself a wit and man about town, Rochester had already mocked him as the 'purblind knight', and wrote a vicious parody of one of his love songs to Cary Frazier, a famous beauty of the court. His hatred stemmed in part from his belief that Scrope was making advances towards Elizabeth Barry. Scrope's original begins, in classically dull 'literary' style:

> I cannot change as others do,
> Though you unjustly scorn,
> Since that poor swain that sighs for you
> For you alone was born.

It continues in similarly plodding and verbose manner. Rochester's altogether sparkier parody takes aim at both Scrope and Frazier:

> I swive as well as others do;
> I'm young, not yet deformed,
> My tender heart, sincere and true,
> Deserves not to be scorned.

> Why Phyllis, then, why will you strive
> With forty lovers more?'
> 'Can I', said she, 'with nature strive?
> Alas I am, alas I am a whore!'

A tit-for-tat war of words soon began between the two, albeit one that was unequal from the start. Scrope's heavy-handed description of Rochester as 'the top fiddler of the town' in his 'In Defence of Satire', complete with mockery of his 'buffoon conceits' and his cowardice at Epsom, was soon answered by the unparalleled vitriol of 'On the Supposed Author of a Late Poem in Defence of Satyr'. Rochester was seldom driven to anger by his enemies, but the allusion to Downs's death and his own complicity in it was a step too far. The resulting blast of hatred was quite sensational. Scrope is mocked for his 'unmeaning brain', for being 'a lump deformed and shapeless', 'the most ungraceful wight', possessed of a 'grisly face', nothing more than an 'ugly *beau garçon*', and, in the best metaphor in the poem:

> Where, dreadfully, love's scarecrow thou art placed
> To frighten the tender flock that long to taste,
> While every coming maid, when you appear,
> Starts back for shame, and straight turns chaste for fear.

He is roundly abused as 'half witty, and half mad, and scarce half brave', 'half honest, which is very much a knave', and 'entirely... an ass'. The wit of earlier satires is here drowned beneath personal opprobrium and what feels like a recklessly unchecked outpouring of fury.

Rochester was moved to such anger in part by an unfortunate incident that occurred in early June 1677, when he was dining at a tavern in Pall Mall and a cook there, a Monsieur Du Puis, was stabbed by an unpleasant character named Floyd. Although Rochester had nothing to do with the affray, the rumour soon went about that he was responsible, and his reputation was low enough after the Epsom affair for many to believe it. When Rochester had been at the pinnacle of royal favour, Scrope would not have dared criticize him in these terms. Now, he was fair game. Scrope responded to the attack in a dismissive and contemptuous fashion, mocking Rochester as nothing more than a 'poor feeble scribbler', who is described by the world in 'bad terms' and behaves like a 'vexed toad', full of 'pox and malice'. The most cutting line comes at the end, when Scrope attacks Rochester both personally and poetically: 'Thy pen is full as harmless as thy sword.'

Rochester, by now goaded into intemperance, produced a final and definitive burlesque on Scrope, entitled 'On Poet Ninny'. Taking a popular contemporary figure of mockery from Shadwell's 1668 play *The Sullen Lovers*, it soon becomes clear that Rochester's pen was anything but harmless, as he sneers that Scrope cannot 'ev'n offend, but with thy face', and mocks him as 'so wretched and so base', composed of 'harmless malice and of hopeless love'. Further abuse follows. The unfortunate Scrope is a 'nauseous creature' of equal parts 'pride and ugliness', and a 'conceited ninny and a fop'. Once again, Rochester refers to Scrope's unsightly appearance:

> Thou art below being laughed at; out of spite,
> Men gaze upon thee as a hideous sight,
> And cry 'There goes the melancholy knight!'
> There are some modish fools we daily see,
> Modest and dull: why, they are wits to thee!

He ends with a cruelly effective parting shot that alludes to Scrope's lack of popularity at court:

> The worst that I could write would be no more
> Than what thy very friends have said before.

It stung, and it is telling that no further replies from Scrope exist. Nonetheless, Rochester knew that the final couplet had a self-referential quality to it. His own friends were few and far between.

There was still the ever-loyal Savile, as well as Buckingham and a few other reliable cronies and drinking companions (including his former tutor Robert Whitehall, who in 1677 sent Rochester one of the twelve copies of his collection of biblical verses, the *Hexastichon hieron*, as a gift for his son Charles, possibly with a view to being allowed to guide Rochester *fils* in the same way that he had mentored Rochester *père*). These few aside, his fair-weather acquaintances had long since tired of him. His response to this was to behave ever more outrageously, perhaps on the grounds of diminished responsibility occasioned by his illness, or maybe because he simply thought he had nothing left to lose.

There is a story that was recounted later by George Etherege of Rochester's behaviour around this time. It best conveys the remarkable gulf that had opened by now between the cynical worldliness of Rochester's antics and his almost childlike yearning for a better world. Present but submerged throughout his life, it came to the fore towards the end, and would be skilfully and mercilessly exploited by Burnet and others. Etherege's story bears retelling in full:

> Often on some frolic, when as a mountebank or merchant, or as companion to the King, he seemed to be borne on the wings of enjoyment, his face would cloud over: and once at a debauch, when all his wit, his spirit, his abundant grace were more intoxicating than the wine, and he seemed himself to be Pan or the young Bacchus, he clasped my arm till the fingers wounded me and whispered passionately into my ear: 'It isn't there: it isn't there.'

The search for 'it' would take up the remainder of Rochester's life.

'*Past joys*

HAVE MORE THAN

PAID

what

I ENDURE'

✤

[*1677–1678*]

THE LATEST KNOWN surviving portrait that exists of Rochester was painted in mid-1677 by Peter Lely, court painter to the great and wicked alike. Lely was an old man by that time, but he was still sufficiently in vogue to have painted an official portrait of Charles in 1675, looking an apt combination of debauched and stately. His depiction of Rochester makes an interesting contrast with that executed by an unknown artist, whether Huysmans, Wissing or another, the decade before (see page 106). Whereas the young Rochester is represented almost coquettishly, with the humorous touches of the monkey and the laurel wreath, the older Rochester gazes out of the frame with more than a little ennui. Attired, as before, in the now ironic heroic garb of a breastplate and in flowing robes, the expression on his face is of barely restrained contempt for the world that he was living in. The monkey is notably absent.

Lely, always a flattering diplomat at the canvas, concealed any tell-tale sign that his subject was suffering from the advanced stages of tertiary syphilis, such as the chancres that by now adorned his body, but even the painter's art could not obscure the fact that the delicate balance of Rochester's health was finally tipping over into irrecoverable illness. His face is thin and drawn, with what were his voluptuously full lips now looking pursed and suspicious. The syphilis that Rochester was suffering from had been affecting his body for at least the last decade. Whether it was first contracted at Oxford, on his tour of Europe or in the early days of the Ballers at court, he was now paying the price for those heady days. The illness had progressed beyond the unsightly but curable stages of primary and secondary syphilis, which included skin rashes, warts, fever and hair loss. Now, Rochester suffered an abundance of indignities and torments, and knew from association with other sufferers what the outcome of the disease was likely to be: dementia, followed by the collapse of the nervous system and heart failure. The last few years of his life were destined not to be happy ones.

In August 1677, conscious that his health was failing, Rochester returned to Woodstock. In his absence, his enemies plotted to ruin what remained of his reputation. A panicked letter from Buckingham to Rochester on 11 August suggests that the likes of Mulgrave, ironically referred to as 'my noble friends at court', are attempting to 'lie most abominably of your Lordship and me', by ascribing a traitorous libel to Rochester. Buckingham adds that he, Lord Dorset and Fleetwood Shepherd would head to Woodstock to discuss the matter. It is doubtful whether Rochester cared a great deal, but he replied promptly, presumably cheerily and reassuringly, to invite him. As Buckingham's swift response, on 19 August, states: 'your kind letter has given me more satisfaction than I am able to express.' In the end, it was only Buckingham who headed to Woodstock in late October 1677, the others thinking better of associating with Rochester at this time.

Buckingham and Rochester both shared something of a penchant for al fresco nudity, and during the couple of days that Buckingham stayed, the two men bathed in the river and then ran through a nearby field to dry themselves. They were observed by some locals, and the story soon exaggerated itself into an account of gross debauchery—something that was wryly denied by Rochester. His health remained poor and was not helped by such adventures, although he was able to make a joke of it; in a letter to his wife, he notes: 'my pains are pretty well over, and my rheumatism begins to turn to an honest gout, my pissing of blood Doctor Wetherley says is nothing.' Even his near-blindness—'my eyes are almost out'—was said to be curable, as long as he ate meat and drank a medicinal cordial. The touch of Alexander Bendo's tinctures in the latter amused Rochester, even as he literally pissed his lifeblood away.

He had no illusions about the seriousness of his condition, whatever he said to Elizabeth. In an increasingly rare letter to Elizabeth Barry, who was about to give birth to his child, he claimed 'this is the first service my hand has done me since my being a cripple', and, writing painfully, he expressed his love for her: 'I assure you that you are very dear to me, and as long as I live, I will be kind to you.' He also wrote to a concerned Savile, who asked for clarification of 'the scurvy report of your being very ill' and who, poignantly, begged for Rochester's return to town because without him it was 'so dull'. In a letter that exhibits all the wit and mock-religiosity that characterize his exchanges with Savile, Rochester calls himself 'almost blind, utterly lame and scarce within the reasonable hopes of ever seeing London again', but he is still not 'entirely mortified and dead'. He even, with knowing outrageousness, alludes to sodomy at the end of the letter, which he dispatched care of the handsome young French musician James Paisible, who had been entertaining him, and describes himself as '*un bougre lasse*', or 'a tired bugger'. He could scarcely have risen to any sexual activity in his weakened condition, but the allusion was a signal to Savile that, maimed though he was, the fight had not yet left him.

Savile visited Rochester at Woodstock in late October, and found him somewhat recovered, if indeed he had not been exaggerating his account of his disposition for dramatic and comic effect; he wonders in a subsequent letter how 'a man both lame and blind could be so merry'. A laundry list of court gossip and news follows, including that the jovial oaf Tom Killigrew is a recent widower and 'laments his condition that fortune has made it possible for him to play the fool again' and that the odorous court hanger-on and clown Will Fanshaw has had a daughter. He also alludes to how the court poets have been shocked by a libel allegedly composed by Rochester at Woodstock (which had materialized at the fashionable coffee-house, Will's, no doubt placed there by one of Rochester's enemies in town). He ends the letter by begging for Rochester's return, 'though upon crutches'.

This 'libel' could have taken many guises. It might have been one of Rochester's intemperate late satires upon Carr Scrope, finally coming into public consciousness. It could just as easily have been Scrope's own 'In Defence of Satire', wrongly ascribed to Rochester, or any one of the dozens of poor imitations of his work. Or, indeed, it could have been a brilliant but now lost poem, fleetingly seeing general readership. In any case, Rochester, ignorant of its content, responded to Savile by asking for a copy and declared himself jubilant about any insult paid to 'that most unwitty generation' of court scribblers.

Rochester allowed Buckingham and Savile to visit him on his sick bed, but he kept his wife at arm's length. He was ashamed of his sickness and appearance, but also, in his hard-living way, he, like his father, found the presence of a wife to be an irritation, and took pains to avoid her while he led his simulacrum of a bachelor existence. That this caused her much misery can be seen by her letters, one of which only came to light in 2006. She writes how she does not expect to see him in the country, or even in London, 'for I believe from my heart it is not the inconvenience of a winter journey that hinders you from giving me oftener the happiness of your company, but merely the disagreeableness of mine'. That Elizabeth was depressed at Rochester's continued absence seems clear; in another letter, she begs him to come to Adderbury, 'though I cannot flatter myself so much as to expect it', and says that she will be 'not a little rejoiced' if he sends for her to come to Woodstock. She signs herself 'your faithful humble wife', displaying a humility and pathos that might have moved another man.

Not Rochester, whose conviction that death was imminent led him, in his reply to Elizabeth on 20 November 1677, to describe himself as happier that he had 'the torments of the stone upon me' than 'the unspeakable one of being an eyewitness to your uneasiness'. That she would be a 'much respected widow' when rid of him offered him a sense of release; he alludes to an 'affliction' that has beset him for the past three years, which could have been either his affair with Elizabeth Barry or the development of syphilis, or both. Love and disease were equal in Rochester's mind; both transmitted by sex, both tearing through the mind and both resulting in nothing but unhappiness and loss.

Perhaps the thought of imminent death, and its attendant release from pain, perversely cheered him. There were those in town openly hoping for his end, although more charitable souls were keen to hear of his recovery. In another November letter to Savile, he had recovered something of his old joie de vivre, calling himself 'the grievance of all prudent persons' and 'the scorn of ugly ladies (which are very near all)'. Away from the ugly and beautiful alike, he had time to think about Elizabeth Barry, then nearing the end of her pregnancy. He sent her maids to attend her in her confinement, but received no news from her about the birth of their child. Eventually, he learnt from Savile, rather than Elizabeth Barry, that she had given birth to a daughter, who was also christened Elizabeth. Despite her successes on the stage, Barry still wanted for money; Savile alluded to 'a friend and protectress' of hers, implying that Rochester had been ungenerous both in funds and in presence towards one who had, after all, loved him and borne his daughter. Rochester's response was to write to her, expressing his delight that both she and her child were delivered safely, and sending her 'trifles', presumably some sweetmeats or jewellery. Money, despite Savile's hints, was not forthcoming, indicating either callous disregard or, at best, a thoughtless lack of real interest in his illegitimate daughter and her mother. His ever-present penury does not excuse his refusal even to visit them, although perhaps his ill health made it impossible. Nonetheless, if he had been well enough to caper around Woodstock naked two months before, it seems strange that he was unable to pay at least a brief visit to his once beloved mistress.

Others were similarly frustrated by the lack of Rochester's company. He wrote to his young nephew Edward Lee on 23 December, now heir apparent to Woodstock Park, to cancel a planned Christmas visit, claiming that 'the change of the weather makes it a dangerous journey for a man in no better health than I am'. In an effort to provide for his own family, Rochester tactfully describes himself as a kind uncle and a faithful servant, attempting to head off the criticism that Lee had heard about him by saying 'the character you have of me from others may give you some reason to consider this no farther than good nature obliges you'; he then ridicules the idea by saying: 'if I am ever so happy to live where my inclinations to you may show themselves, be assured you shall not want very good proofs.' His good nature was not shown by a Christmas visit to his family;

instead, he sent his wife (still lingering in Adderbury) a lamb, and purchased his mother a ham and a doe. Feeling better, he planned a trip to London, to reacquaint himself with the 'rakehells' and to see his new child for the first time. As ever, it was an eventful visit.

The year 1678 saw Rochester reach the end of his long affair with Elizabeth Barry. Their daughter's birth, far from bringing about a rapprochement, led to what Rochester described as a 'torment of repentance' on her part, and in an unusually anguished and troubled letter that he wrote to her soon after returning to town, he expresses his hurt at how he found 'you repent the kindness you showed me, and undervalue the humble service I had for you'. Lacking Elizabeth Barry's voice in these exchanges, any interpretation of her side has to be imagined. She had just given birth, probably after a long and painful labour, to a child by a man who was widely rumoured to be evil beyond belief and who had been largely absent from her life for the previous six months. This man, who was said to have other mistresses as well as a wife, was riddled with syphilis, with which he had almost certainly infected both her and her child, and offered no financial support, preferring to palm her off with a box of petty gifts. It is easy to imagine her frustration and misery.

Rochester's own feelings are more complex. That he made use of Elizabeth Barry for his own enjoyment is true, but it is equally likely that he was in love with her, helping her burgeoning theatrical career out of pure altruism and relishing his involvement with one who matched him for wit and irreverence—as, of course, his wife had in the early days of their courtship and marriage. When he writes that their love 'is equally unjust and cruel to us both, and ought therefore to die', it is not mere posturing, but imbued with a genuine sense of imminent loss. His subsequent letters to her alternate wildly and intemperately between self-loathing, self-pity, fury and a desire to correct falsehoods—or, as he describes it at the beginning of one such epistle, written immoderately at 3 a.m., 'anger, spleen, revenge and shame'. One moment, he is writing 'give me leave to pity myself, which is more than ever you will do for me'; the next he is claiming that he values her too much to be capable of neglect.

By this stage, Rochester was too ill to behave with restraint and decorum; then again, he had seldom behaved with restraint and decorum before. In March 1678 he collapsed while in London, probably on account of the weakness of his syphilis-ridden body, and once again it was rumoured that his death was imminent. He was seriously ill for about a month, and it is telling that no letters of his survive from this period, or indeed until June. Too weak and fragile at first to return to the country, he lay on his potential deathbed in his Whitehall lodgings, occasionally attended by clergymen praying for his immortal soul—something that he took no active part in.

His friends gave what support they could. There is no record of Charles offering any assistance, moral or financial; either he was too busy arranging secret treaties with Louis XIV, or he had no interest in bothering himself over his sometime supporter. Instead, Rochester was visited by the likes of Will Fanshaw and Jack Verney, son of his mother's friend Ralph Verney, who reported in a letter of 25 April to his father that Rochester 'has been very ill and very penitent, but is now bettering'. Others, like Savile and Rochester's young protégé, the poet and dramatist Francis Fane, were themselves indisposed with various illnesses, but managed to write either consoling letters, or, in Fane's case, a Horatian ode, 'To the Earl of Rochester, upon the report of his sickness in town'.

Rochester, believing himself at death's door, made certain gestures in the direction of moral improvement, hence the presence of clergymen and Verney's comment that he was 'very penitent'. This drew the attention of various ambitious ministers, not least the Chaplain of the Rolls, Gilbert Burnet, who was also a friend of Savile's father George. Through him Burnet became aware of Rochester and heard the mutterings from the gutter, although he only became a pivotal figure in the earl's life the following year. He later wrote that this illness 'brought him so near death when I first knew him, when his spirits were so low and spent, that... he did not think to live an hour'. Yet, by May, Rochester had recovered sufficiently to endure the sixteen- or seventeen-hour journey from London to Adderbury, presumably in as much comfort as the cramped environment of a four-horse carriage would allow, where he convalesced at his family home.

It is here that he wrote, or at least completed, one of his last major poems, 'Upon Nothing'. Differing greatly in both form and tone to his earlier, long satirical works, it is particularly noteworthy because at least one draft, currently residing in the National Archives in Kew, has corrections and amendments in Rochester's mother's handwriting. This might either indicate a posthumous edit, or, more interestingly, suggest a literary collaboration between mother and son. However, Anne's sensibilities were so different to Rochester's that it is most likely that her role was as maternal amanuensis, rather than inspired poet.

Whether she was aware that 'nothing' was contemporary slang for vagina is unclear, but the religious overtones within the work stem from a source other than Rochester's jokey appropriations of scriptural language to amuse his friends and lovers. The poem addresses the philosophical and theological issue of the world being created out of a void, wherefore 'nothing' is the source of all things. The poem begins in quasi-Miltonic style:

> Nothing, thou elder brother even to shade,
> Who had'st a being, ere the world was made,
> And well fixed, art alone of ending not afraid.
>
> Ere Time and Place were, Time and Place were not
> When primitive Nothing Something had begot
> Then all proceeded from the great united – What?

The word that springs to mind reading this is 'portentous'. The first half of the poem feels atypical of Rochester's work, eschewing humour or social commentary in favour of grandiose allusions to Genesis and musings on original sin. It might be the work of another writer (potentially Buckingham, who is credited with the first six verses in the copy-text) were it not for the later return of emphasis to traditional Rochesterian tropes:

> Yet this of thee the wise may truly say:
> Thou from the virtuous nothing dost delay,
> And to be part of thee the wicked wisely pray.
>
> Great Negative! How vainly would the wise
> Enquire, define, distinguish, teach, devise
> Didst thou not stand to paint their vain philosophies!

Thus Rochester returns to his favourite poetic idea: a righteous attack on both vanity and puffed-up pride. This manifests itself in social satire against both kingship—'That sacred monarchs should in council sit / With persons highly thought at best for nothing fit'; and court—'While weighty something modestly abstains / From princes' coffers and from statesmen's brains'. The concept of 'nothing', now less a religious one than its secular equivalent, 'dwells with fools in grave disguise' of an ecclesiastical nature, consisting of 'lawn sleeves and furs and gowns, when they like thee look wise'. As in 'A Satire against Reason and Mankind', the appearance of godliness to these is far more important than its sincere expression. The final two verses, comprising a list of wittily xenophobic and social abuse, represent a complete volte-face from the language of the beginning, as Rochester details how 'nothing' has become commonplace for many:

> French truth, Dutch prowess, British policy,
> Hibernian learning, Scotch civility,
> Spaniards' dispatch, Danes' wit are mainly seen in thee;
>
> The great man's gratitude to his best friend,
> Kings' promises, whores' vows—towards thee they bend,
> Flow swiftly into thee, and in thee ever end.

Only Rochester could end a poem of this nature with the witty jokes of a Restoration stage character.

On 2 June 1678, this 'great man' had cause to be grateful to his own best friend. He received a reassuring missive from Savile, who alluded to the 'scurvy alarums' he had heard of Rochester's health, but mentioned his relief at having heard that he was on 'the improving hand': 'if there be a man living gladder than myself, I am much mistaken.'

Savile was also suffering. He took a rueful enjoyment in letting Rochester know about his own illnesses—'the return of my venereal pains have thrown me back to dry mutton and diet drink'—and about a disagreement that he had had with John Maitland, Earl of Lauderdale, whom Savile had opposed in the Commons over the question of military action against France. A letter to Lauderdale sent in May 1678 gives a good account of how Charles behaved with those, such as Savile and Rochester, whom he believed stood against him:

> The King, upon the first sight of [Savile] fell into such a passion, that his face and lips became as pale (almost) as death, his cheeks and arms trembled, and then he said to Saville, 'You villain, how dare you have the impudence to come into my presence, when you are guilty of such baseness as you have shown this day? I do now and from henceforth discharge you from my service, commanding you never to come any more into my presence, nor to any place where I shall happen to be.'

Such outbreaks of royal petulance, even amongst his favourites, were considered sufficiently usual for Savile not even to bother mentioning it to Rochester, but instead to bemoan that the cancelled war against France would disappoint 'the fine gentlemen' and 'this noble army'. It is likely that Rochester read his friend's pro-military sentiments, smiled thinly and considered how false an idea *dulce et decorum est pro patria mori* was to him—a man who had served with conspicuous honour a decade before and now seemed fated to die in a far more ignoble fashion.

The one thing that Rochester was always keen to receive from court was gossip, the more scurrilous and sordid the better, and a lengthy update was soon provided by Savile. At times, the laundry list of baseness provided by 'a friend in town' verges on the comic. The unfortunate Fanshaw was suffering from syphilis-induced arthritis, with his mouth standing 'quite awry', and Savile mocks him as 'the only creature upon earth poorer and pockier than myself'. The existence of another—Rochester—was tactfully omitted. He writes of nobles scheming to prove the illegitimacy of others and of great ladies indulging in machinations to seat their relatives in positions of high state, the whole thing watched over by the ageing and increasingly unimpressive Charles, sardonically called 'Charlemagne' by Savile.

Savile asked for Rochester's help, but the enfeebled earl was taking his leave from court occupations. He replied gracefully, noting his continued illness in a flattering fashion by saying: 'Any kind of correspondence with such a friend as you is very agreeable, and therefore you will easily believe I am very ill when I lose the opportunity of writing to you.' Comparing himself unfavourably to a contemporary Polonius-like figure, a Master of Requests called Thomas Povey, who 'hinders further compliment', Rochester, still far from well, strikes an elegiac note in his letter, perhaps unironically inviting comparisons with 'The Disabled Debauchee', when he writes at the end: 'you may judge whether I was a good pimp or no… but some thought otherwise and so, truly, I have renounced business; let abler men try it.'

Rochester refers to Savile's own afflictions as a 'glorious disgrace', and the tenor of much of his letter is atypically serious. Clearly conscious that he might be near death, he produces a list of sensible, unhistrionic advice on how to deal with Charles, directed towards 'your friend' Nell Gwyn but also implicitly towards Savile. Rochester would have benefited from it himself, had he deigned to follow it. As an example of an aristocrat's thoughts on how to deal with the day-to-day business of keeping the king happy, it is fascinatingly unadorned:

> Take your measures just contrary to your rivals; live in peace with all the world and easily with the King; never be so ill-natured to stir up his anger against others, but let him forget the use of a passion

which is never to do you good; cherish his love wherever it inclines, and be assured you can't commit greater folly than pretending to be jealous: but on the contrary, with hand, body, head, heart and all the faculties you have, contribute to his pleasure all you can and comply with his desires throughout; and for new intrigues, so you be at one end 'tis no matter which; make sport when you can, at other times help it.

The impression that Rochester consciously gives of Charles, even while appearing to flatter him, is that of a petulant, spoilt child, one easily bored and likely to be dangerous when out of sorts. This explains Charles's inconsistent attitude towards bad behaviour at court, enjoying the outrageousness of it unless he himself was affected by it, and forgiving everything except personal insults almost immediately. Ridiculous though he appeared at times, he was still the divinely ordained monarch of England (albeit after some earthly interjection), and the most significant figure at court, as Rochester, Buckingham and Savile all knew. The allusion to Nell contributing to his pleasure with 'hand, body, head, heart and all the faculties' is a likely reference to 'A Satire on Charles II' and its description of 'poor, laborious Nelly / whilst she employs hands, fingers, mouth and thighs / Ere she can raise the member she enjoys'.

Savile appreciated such a piece of arch, bawdy buried treasure. Even at his most sincere, Rochester was incapable of solemnity. In his reply of 15 June 1678, Savile flatters Rochester by referring to the 'good news' of the length of his letter, comparing his rustication to 'this wicked place of temptation'. Like Rochester, Savile was wearying of court life. Older than Rochester at thirty-six and considerably heavier, he lacked his younger friend's former energy and dedication to all things debauched. Thinking himself out of favour with Charles and describing himself as 'of late so battered in politics', he saw his role as MP for Newark as scant compensation for his fall from grace. He knew that he should quit the stage—'if there be a man alive who ought to retire from business and have no more civil plots, it is myself'—but a combination of greed and his loathing of his nemesis Lauderdale kept him in place a while longer.

The corpulent, good-natured and jolly Savile had a Falstaffian quality to him, one that Rochester recognized in a reply to him shortly afterwards, in which he begins with an allusion to the 'merry fat gentleman's' comment in *Henry IV, Part 2*, that 'if sack and sugar be a sin, God help the wicked'. Rochester was ill, but his gentle teasing of his friend continued. He writes, wryly, 'I confess that upon several occasions you have put me in mind of this fat person', but attempts to cheer him by saying 'all your inconveniences... draw very near their end'. Rochester himself hints that he is coming to terms with the fact that his own inconveniences are drawing to a close: 'I'm taking pains not to die without knowing how to live on when I have brought it about.' He mocks human affairs as 'nonsensical', comparing them unfavourably with his pet monkey (an echo of 'A Satire against Reason and Mankind', as well as an allusion to the famous portrait of him), but the first glimmer of a greater interest in religion and the afterlife can perhaps be gleaned from this fleeting allusion. With time on his hands and the 'improving' presence of his mother, Rochester spent his days reading both scripture and the writings of such contemporary philosophers as Locke and Hobbes. He did this out of both curiosity and fear.

A decidedly corporeal complaint that Savile and Rochester shared was syphilis, or 'the French disease'. Its prevalence in society had spread across the classes, and its rise, occasioned by casual sex with sufferers, led to the grim joke 'one night with Venus, a lifetime with mercury'. It was so widespread by the mid-1670s that both physicians and, in graver cases, surgeons had to be enlisted in the quest to find cures; the national obsession with the disease was such that doctors were frequently attended by hypochondriacs, who were not satisfied until they had been diagnosed with syphilis and treated accordingly. A contemporary physician, Richard Wiseman, published a book in 1676 entitled *Several Surgical Treatises*, in which he took a robust attitude towards his patients, describing how other inferior doctors 'ruined both their bodies and their purses' and how his methods were the right ones. These involved a stringent course of mercury steam baths, colloquially known as 'the sweats', which were thought at least to arrest the disease's progress.

Rochester had been suffering from it for at least the previous decade, but Savile was a comparatively recent victim. A letter to Rochester of 25 June 1678 ends in uncharacteristically vicious style when he states 'women are bitches whom God confound'. The explanation soon came in a subsequent letter, dated 2 July, from a 'sweat shop' in Leather Lane in Hatton Garden. He described it as 'a neat privacy', where he would reach 'the last act of a tedious course of physic which has entertained me ever since December last'. The disease was agonizingly painful. Summoning up what remained of his Falstaffian wit, Savile writes: '[had I chosen] whether I would have undergone what I suffered, or have turned Turk, notwithstanding all my zeal for the true Protestant faith, I doubt my whole stock of religion had run a great hazard.'

The only minor consolation—and that a doubtful one—was that there was no particular stigma attached to visiting the sweat shop. Savile reports that he was joined by Jane Roberts, court lady-in-waiting and sometime mistress to both Rochester and Charles, who was in the final throes of suffering. He claims that 'what she has endured would make a damned soul fall a-laughing at his lesser pains', and that the agonies she experienced 'were so far beyond description and belief' that the usually garrulous Savile felt it wiser to draw a veil over them. Light relief, of a sort, came when they were joined by the ever-unfortunate Will Fanshaw, who pretended that his own syphilis was scurvy in order to keep his wife ignorant of his extra-marital predilections; Savile sardonically describes him as 'a filthier leper than ever was cured in the gospel'.

After the usual round-up of gossip and tittle-tattle, Savile finishes his letter by describing his present home 'as remote from noble court notions as either Oxford or Banbury'. The idea of the horrific environs of Leather Lane as some kind of enchanted kingdom amused Rochester, who wrote back: 'were I as idle as ever ... I should write a small romance.' It was typical of his wit and invention that, even in the midst of severe illness—'a damned relapse brought by a fever, the stone and some ten diseases more'—he sought some new way of entertaining his friend in distress. He characterizes the fat, ailing Savile as a knight-errant, speaking 'the most passionate fine things' to the rather distressed damsel Jane Roberts. Yet almost before he has begun his conceit, Rochester abandons it, writing half-apologetically, half-pathetically: 'it is a miraculous thing when a man half in the grave cannot leave off playing the fool and the buffoon.'

The end seemed imminent for Rochester. He was under no illusions about the appalling state of his health, and sarcastically adapted an old drinking song of John Fletcher's: 'But he who lives not wise and sober / Falls with the leaf still in October.' Another blow came when Savile, recovered both in health and in royal favour, departed for France to take up a diplomatic post in Paris. He entreated Rochester to accompany him, claiming, probably rightly, that the warmer climate of France would suit him better than another cold and grim English winter. Yet both funds and poor health would prevent Rochester from leaving Adderbury until much later in the year.

As it so happened, staying out of London was the wisest move that an ailing Rochester could have made, as a bizarre and remarkable series of events was about to unfold that would turn the established order in England upside down.

12

'NOR CAN

weak truth

YOUR

reputation

SAVE'

✳

[1678–1679]

SOME VERY STRANGE men came to prominence in the Restoration, but few were stranger than Titus Oates. Born in 1649, he had an undistinguished childhood, being a snot-nosed brat with few friends and unfounded delusions of grandeur. The only thing remarkable about him was his unremitting unpleasantness. Physically repulsive and charmless, he was given to swearing in what was said to be a 'harsh and loud' voice. Expelled from Merchant Taylors' School by the master, William Smith, for cheating him of his tuition fees, Oates vowed vengeance on Smith, just as he would later swear undying hatred of his former tutors at Gonville and Caius College, Cambridge, where he was sent down for the once-in-a-lifetime combination of idiocy, buggery and his 'canting, fanatical manner'. Lucky not to be imprisoned, he failed to take advantage of his good fortune. Conning his way into a vicar's position in Kent in 1673, he duly accused the local schoolmaster of sodomy, hoping to obtain his post once this unfortunate had been imprisoned.

Oates, a prolific and ardent homosexual himself, was fond of using accusations of this kind to malign his enemies and improve his standing in society. Unfortunately, as these were always false, and hypocritical to boot, they were normally seen through. After his lies were exposed, he was forced in 1675 to flee on the ship *Adventure*, taking a position as a naval chaplain en route to Tangier. It was an unhappy journey, ending with Oates, by now a drunkard, being sacked for homosexual practices on ship, but it gave him the germ of an idea. What, wondered Oates, if I first infiltrated the Catholic establishment, and then alerted the world to the existence of a so-called 'Popish Plot' to kill Charles and overthrow the monarchy, thereby elevating me to the top echelons of society?

As often happens with bizarre and borderline insane plans, it worked superbly at first. Oates was received into the Catholic Church in 1677, under the assumed name of Samson Lucy. Around this time he fell in with a similarly mad co-conspirator, Israel Tonge, a puritanical fanatic who was convinced that the Jesuits were on the verge of invading England. After the two bonded by writing anti-Catholic pamphlets—something normally incompatible with attending a seminary to be a priest in the church, as 'Samson' was—Oates, by now armed with a fraudulent doctorate from the University of Salamanca, managed to convince Tonge that there was a Jesuit plan well in play to assassinate both Charles and his brother James, as part of a Catholic conspiracy stretching across Europe. The two men constructed an indictment of forty-three articles against the Jesuits. This they then passed to an acquaintance, Christopher Kirkby, who on 13 August 1678 buttonholed Charles while he was taking a walk in St James's Park.

Charles was often approached by cranks and conspiracy theorists, and so initially took little notice. However, when it was mentioned that it involved a direct threat to his life, he was concerned enough to elicit an investigation by his first minister, the Earl of Danby. The greatest irony was that Charles was himself highly sympathetic to the Catholic faith, albeit in private, so the existence of such a conspiracy struck him as ridiculous in the extreme. In due course, the trail led back to Oates, who began to provide forged letters implicating various figures in the plot. As luck would have it, one of those fingered, the Duchess of York's secretary Edward Coleman, had long been suspected of harbouring anti-establishment views, being a Catholic keen to see the re-establishment of the Roman Church in Britain. Oates appeared before the Privy Council in late 1678 and was questioned at length about his sources and the involvement of various figures. He lied, wildly, inventing evidence and implicating Catholics or suspected Catholics almost at random. However, there was just enough corroborative proof for his falsehoods to be taken at face value, even in spite of his habit of contradicting himself almost immediately. The mysterious murder of Sir Edmund Berry Godfrey, a staunch Protestant and leading MP, on 12 October 1678 helped whip up a tide of anti-Catholic feeling, as his death was immediately blamed on papists, and acknowledged or rumoured Catholics were duly banished from a twenty-mile radius around London. Given that, in a country with a population of around six million, Catholics made up no more than one per cent of the total, this was overkill. By this time, Oates was sufficiently in favour to be given lodgings at Whitehall, a monthly pension of £40, and, more importantly, the right to have his ridiculous statements heard in public, and believed. Titus Oates, cheat, liar, apostate and sodomite, was about to become the most influential man in England.

Initially, Rochester's involvement in all this was tangential. He was probably unaware of Oates's first accusations, which concerned Jesuit priests and the likes of Coleman. However, as with all hysterical conflagrations, the flames of suspicion soon spread beyond the usual suspects, and Oates accused five leading Catholic lords of treason, namely Arundel, Bellasyse, Petre, Powis and Stafford. Charles refused to believe these accusations, but he was powerless to act against the groundswell of public opinion, which was cynically whipped up by the Earl of Shaftesbury. Shaftesbury, no friend of Charles since his imprisonment in the Tower of London the previous year for supporting Buckingham, saw Oates's lies as a means of repressing royal power, as well as of implicating the Catholic gentry, and the lords concerned were duly imprisoned in the Tower on 25 October 1678. No aristocratic Catholics could rely on their high standing to save them from public humiliation, and possibly worse. Unfortunately, these included Rochester's wife Elizabeth.

Elizabeth had converted to Catholicism a decade before, at Rochester's behest, shortly after their marriage. The priest who converted her was a known Jesuit, Father Thomson, whom Rochester had been introduced to by his former servant Stephen College. Rochester did not undergo a similar conversion, his own religious beliefs being more questionable, but given the strong Catholic presence at court—James, Duke of York, was a keen supporter of the faith who would formally convert in 1668, albeit secretly, and Charles's wife Catherine of Braganza was loathed by many for her Catholicism, which she made no effort to hide or recant—it was politically expedient to be seen to be on the right side, and one's sympathies could be expressed more than adequately by being married to a Catholic.

There were other expressions of anti-Catholic feeling in the years following, such as the 1673 Test Act which punished Catholics alongside Nonconformists by refusing to let anyone who believed in transubstantiation hold public office,* but nothing came close to the severity and fervour with which the Popish Plot dominated public opinion. Rochester, aware that both he and Elizabeth would be accused of fantastical crimes if attention turned to them, returned to London alone in early November 1678, only to find himself in the midst of a witch-hunt that was growing in size and scope by the day. There were those in Adderbury, such as his disgruntled former servant College, who would happily claim that the wicked Lord Rochester was a Catholic sympathizer. In the ghastly serendipity of the time, College became a drinking companion of Rochester's former steward Stephen Dugdale, who united with Oates in November 1678 to begin making accusations against Catholic aristocrats. What these accusations were barely mattered, although once again Catholics were said to be responsible for the Great Fire in 1666. In the febrile and paranoid atmosphere of the time, just to be labelled 'different' was enough to ensure suspicion, a trial and even execution if found guilty.

Whether or not Rochester knew of College and Dugdale's acquaintance, he was all too aware that murmurings and mutterings were flying around, and decided to put himself at the centre of the storm. He could rely on Buckingham's support in interceding with Shaftesbury, who was rapidly becoming a hugely prominent figure in national opinion, but he knew that patronage and the help of friends were not enough. Despite his weakened state and continued illness, he attended the House of Lords on several occasions in November and December 1678. During this time, he took part in a debate on the trustworthiness of Titus Oates (if he spoke, his opinion of Oates,

---

* The irony of this being passed with royal assent only became fully clear after Charles's death.

a man of legendary hypocrisy and repulsiveness, can easily be surmised); and on 4 December he publicly swore, along with the other lords, an oath of loyalty to Charles and to the Protestant faith. They were acting out of fear as much as patriotism; the previous day had seen the five 'popish lords' found guilty of high treason, and none wanted to join them in the Tower.

By this time, Charles knew that Oates was a charlatan and a liar, and had developed a significant personal animosity towards him, as Oates, along with another of his equally crooked partners in crime William Bedloe, had accused Queen Catherine of plotting to murder Charles. A step too far even for Oates, who was by now increasingly drunk on power and wine, it resulted in Charles, who suspected the guiding hand of Shaftesbury in the accusation, sending for the blundering bugger. At a private audience with the king on 24 November, and with the Privy Council the next day, Oates was cross-examined over the details of how the queen was privy to a Catholic conspiracy against her husband. His lies were easily exposed by their inconsistencies, and he was confined to his lodgings and his papers seized.

Under any normal circumstances, Oates would have been put on trial and hanged for his perjury and lies, and the whole disagreeable business would have spluttered to an anticlimactic end. Unfortunately, Edward Coleman had by now been tried (with Oates as chief witness), found guilty of sedition, and duly executed on 3 December. The result of this was that Oates, although known privately to be a dangerous fantasist, was pardoned and allowed to act as a key witness in several subsequent trials. This may seem incredible, but—as with the Salem witch trials just over a decade later—a carefully choreographed hysteria whipped up by a few cynical parties had turned into a smorgasbord of far-fetched stories. A second gunpowder plot was suspected, fuelled by stories of digging near the House of Commons. A French invasion of Dorset was said to be imminent. Catholics were in league with the devil. And so it went on.

While all this spiralled ever further out of control, Rochester, whose ostentatious proof of his Protestantism had kept his name safe for the moment, left London and returned to the country for further recuperation. The religious hysteria had both frightened and repulsed him, and it was around late 1678 that he began to correspond with the deist Charles Blount, whom he had met on his last visit to court. Blount was another 'perfect Hobbist' who, for Rochester, stood out from the 'frantic crowds of thinking fools' that dominated the age less on account of his intellectual brilliance than the fortunate coinciding of his interest in man's immortal soul with Rochester's increasing belief that his own death was imminent. Born in 1654, he had been brought up in great comfort by his free-thinking libertine father Henry, eschewing the conventional school and university-based education of the day and instead being allowed to express sacrilegious and challenging ideas of the sort that normally resulted in, at best, censure, and at worst incarceration. Ironically, he had written a defence of Dryden's *The Conquest of Granada*, 'Mr Dryden Vindicated', in 1673, the existence of which probably amused his new correspondent.

Blount's letters to Rochester, while often a turgid hotch-potch of contradictory ideas loosely cribbed from the likes of Hobbes and Milton, at least indicate that Rochester, while busily occupied with trying to keep his family's name from being besmirched, was still engaged with the philosophical ideas of the day. His first letter to Rochester dates from December 1678, and refers to 'your Lordship's candour', which 'gave me the freedom of venting my own thoughts'. No doubt Rochester, no longer interested in hiding his opinions, gave voice to apparently heretical thoughts that excited and stimulated Blount.

An area where the two men agreed was in the 'wickedness of men's natures', and also in the metaphysical belief that there was a divide between the flawed, doomed corporeal body and the transcendent soul. However, at the end of 1678, Blount published a book entitled *Anima mundi, or, An Historical Relation of the Opinions of the Ancients concerning Man's Soul after This Life, according to Unenlightened Nature*, which promptly attracted mass disapproval. Either by design or through intellectual incompetence, Blount appears to argue for the immortality of the soul, but does so in such an ambiguous and half-hearted way that the book becomes an ironic refutation of what it appears to be claiming. This led to much controversy, at a time when arguments over religion could reach fever pitch, and the book was publicly burnt in early 1679.

Blount's politics were those of the Whigs. Like Buckingham and, to some extent, Rochester, he stood against the establishment, and joined the Green Ribbon Club, an organization that reflected the loathing of Catholicism widely disseminated by the Popish Plot and the suspicion that the royal court harboured too many papist sympathizers. At this time, the so-called 'Exclusion Crisis' had begun, triggered by the belief that the Duke of York's accession to the throne after Charles's death—potentially hastened in the event of a plot to assassinate him—would result in England becoming a Catholic country once more. Shaftesbury and others tried to bring about an Act of Exclusion that would have removed James from the line of succession—something that Blount, a card-carrying believer in Oates's fantasies, doubtless supported.

Rochester did not. He loathed the excesses and emptiness of kingship, but faced with the prospect of either continued royal patronage and support—albeit in a reduced form from previous years—or a cut-price solution where one of Charles's various bastard children was 'legitimized' through a compromise of some kind,* he took the attitude 'better the devil you know' and continued to support Charles. In this, ironically, Buckingham joined him. Although he remained a committed Whig, Buckingham similarly disapproved of the court skulduggery, and thus sowed the seeds of his eventual quasi-reconciliation with Charles by refusing to offer his influence and support to the Act. Bereft of the universal acclaim of court worthies that it needed, the Act accordingly failed.

Rochester returned to court in early 1679 to find that the clamour of

---

* It was, for instance, seriously proposed by the Exclusionists, led by Shaftesbury, to put about the story that Charles's early mistress, Lucy Walter, had been married to him, and thereby to legitimize the Duke of Monmouth.

the Popish Plot showed few signs of abating. Although he continued to be weak and prone to fits of illness, a combination of a diet composed mainly of pure milk—commonly believed by physicians to be a cure for weakness and anaemia—and the intellectual and social excitements of town gave him a purpose and strength that he had lacked while idling in the country. While he had few illusions that he was likely to recover fully, the torpor of the previous year had given way to a need for drastic action.

One of these areas was in finally severing relations with Elizabeth Barry. Although their love affair had been over since the birth of their daughter Elizabeth in late 1677, the final straw came when Rochester, aided by one of his servants, removed the child from Barry's keeping in March 1679 while she was appearing at the Dorset Garden Theatre, and had her taken to live with his other sons and daughters. What Elizabeth Wilmot felt when presented, as a fait accompli, with the task of raising her husband's illegitimate daughter—by an actress, to boot—can only be guessed at, but her resignation to most aspects of her husband's life probably meant that the arrival of the infant was less of a surprise than it might have been to most other long-suffering wives.

Elizabeth Barry was distraught at the seizure of her daughter. The final surviving letter that Rochester sent her, soon after the abduction, is a businesslike affair. 'I am far from delighting in the grief I have given you by taking away the child', he claims, admitting the 'ill nature' of his actions, but he lays the blame at her door, announcing that it was she 'who made it so absolutely necessary for me to do so'.

Why, exactly? Rochester was jealous of her inconstancy and reputation for loose living, but then he was hardly guiltless himself. To claim that the child would be brought up in a happier and more stable environment amongst its half-siblings than as the daughter of an actress was a more effective argument, save that the child's father was impecunious and severely ill. What little money the family had was provided by the child's stepmother and grandmother. It is most likely that he acted out of pique, choosing to end an all-consuming passion in the coldest and most decisive way he could. He offers a couple of platitudes, claiming that the child will be brought up so well that 'you need not apprehend any neglect from those I employ' and that she will eventually be restored to Elizabeth Barry 'a finer girl than ever', but he ends in a curiously half-patronizing, half-sympathetic register: 'you would do well to think of the advice I gave you, for how little show soever my prudence makes in my own affairs, in yours it will prove very successful if you please to follow it.'

No record exists of any further encounters between the two, or of the eventual return of the child Elizabeth to her mother, whose reputation was besmirched both by her association with Rochester and by her subsequent affairs with such notables of the theatrical world as Etherege and Buckhurst. However, Rochester may have seen her at least once more, in February 1680, when she played the lead role in Otway's domestic tragedy *The Orphan* at Dorset Garden. The play, a baroque fantasia of unrequited love, was written by Otway with his own passions for Elizabeth Barry in mind, and Rochester, had he watched his former protégé's work, might have been moved. Certainly, the rest of the audience were: a contemporary account reports how Barry 'forced tears from the eyes of her auditory, especially those who have any sense of pity for the distressed'. Some described her as little more than a whore, but Rochester's behaviour towards her also attracted sympathy, and it is telling that her career truly achieved greatness after she and Rochester parted. Acting until 1710 and commonly regarded as the finest female lead of the Restoration age and beyond, she never married nor had any further children, and died in 1713 at the age of fifty-five.

Away from personal involvements, Rochester became embroiled in a motion to impeach Charles's first minister Danby for high treason. Danby had made too many enemies, especially the all-powerful Shaftesbury, and was now arraigned for his involvement with Louis XIV in supplying money to Charles in exchange for an undertaking not to invade France. It was irrelevant that he had been acting on Charles's instructions rather than on his own behalf; he was judged and found wanting, despite Parliament being dissolved throughout January 1679, and it was little surprise when his inevitable deposition by Titus Oates, the snot-nosed face of doom, came on 22 March.

Danby was not alone in his fate. On 9 April, a day after his impeachment, four of the five Catholic lords (Bellasyse was too ill to attend) were sent to the Tower to await their trial for high treason. That this extraordinary state of affairs was not regarded as unusual was symptomatic of a country in chaos. Nobody trusted anyone, with neighbours deposing neighbours on the slightest pretext and anti-Catholicism practised as fervently as any religion. Rochester was born into a country obsessed with seeking out witches and burning them; three decades later, all that the social and intellectual advances of the Restoration had achieved was to advance from burning women suspected of witchcraft to beheading men suspected of Catholic sympathies.

Rochester kept as low a profile as he could. He was often at the House of Lords, but few letters from him survive, possibly because he thought it was politic not to adopt any potentially contrary opinions or viewpoints. A couple of brief, cryptic missives to his wife are the only indication of his state of mind at this point. He offers the view that lingering in the country would be 'best for me'; he wishes that he had been in London 'a month ago than at this time' and expresses a desire to return to her 'when I am in any tolerable health'. In another, he is slightly more explicit. He gives a wry description of the hysteria that he faces on every side: 'London grows very tiresome... things are now reduced to that extremity on all sides that a man does not turn his back for fear of being hanged.' He is typically witty about this—'an ill accident to be avoided by all prudent persons'—but the danger for anyone who was seen as a dissident was real enough. Unusually, Rochester found himself muzzled by his own fear of the situation he was in. The great satirical poem that he could have written about this strange, horrific and hilarious dispute between heaven and earth was never put to paper.

Word soon spread abroad about the strange situation in England. Savile, still in Paris, wrote to Rochester on 6 April 1679, presumably ignorant of what was going on, as the letter consists of little more than tittle-tattle and a further request that Rochester visit Paris and stay as Savile's guest. A later letter, dating from 20 June, indicates that Savile is now aware of the debacle, as he talks of 'the great changes that have happened in England since I left it'. By now, Parliament had been dissolved so that the proposed Exclusion Bill that would have put forward the illegitimate Duke of Monmouth as heir apparent could not be passed, Danby was in the Tower, and public hysteria was growing, whipped up by the increasingly powerful and influential Shaftesbury.

However, Savile was more upset by his friend's neglect. He alludes to his not having heard from Rochester, despite having sent him some gifts—'I have now been four months forgot by your lordship'—and is hurt by this, judging by his comment:

> [I have shown] a most particular kindness and service for you... I may reasonably presume that either you are not well, or I am not well with you; either of these... would afflict me extremely.

On a cheerier note, Savile wishes Rochester some of the 'good wine I daily drink', and notes that French beer and tobacco are of a deeply inferior quality.

Rochester had not meant to ignore his Falstaffian friend, but the continual tumult at court, as well as his poor health, meant that writing to his friends was a more arduous process than usual. He had begun to write to Savile on 30 May 1679, ascribing his failure to reply to 'neither pride or neglect... but idleness on one side, and not knowing what to say on the other'—the latter statement presumably a coded reference to contemporary events rather than an uncharacteristically tongue-tied admission on Rochester's part.

The letter took him nearly a month to complete, only being sent to Savile on 25 June 1679; he acknowledges the reason in his early claim that 'changes in this place are so frequent that Fanshaw himself can no longer give an account why this was done today, or what will ensue tomorrow'. Briefly outlining the mercurial political situation, Rochester strikes an atypically grave and socially committed note, one that he self-mockingly acknowledges is 'a taste of my serious abilities and to let you know I have a great goggle-eye to business'. He praises Savile for his 'high Protestancy in Paris', in which Savile had acted as a protector of the country's remaining Protestants, interceding with the French court to ensure that they were treated decently (for which he was accordingly soon appointed England's French ambassador). Then, moved by Savile's letter of 20 June, Rochester declares, 'I thank God there is yet a Harry Savile in England', before announcing his intention of drinking Savile's health with Sir William Coventry (Savile's great-uncle) 'til Shiloh come, or you from France'. Shiloh, a term loosely used for the Messiah, indicates that Rochester's religious contemplations remained ever present, perhaps all the more so in a time of such uncertainty.

Rochester, feeling paranoid and exhausted, left London in late June 1679, and headed to Woodstock. He spent some time with Coventry, a local resident at nearby Minster Lovell, a clear-headed and generous man who tried to calm him. Rochester, however, still oozed spleen, as can be seen by one of his last poetic works. Dating from around this time, it is an attack on his nemesis Mulgrave, indicating that, regardless of his health and the national situation, Rochester was unable to let a perceived slight rest. Entitled 'My Lord All-Pride', it positively reeks of vituperation against Mulgrave, as if Rochester, knowing he has less time to live than he would have liked, wants to settle a final score against his most significant enemy.

The poem appears to respond to some unknown lampoon or satire of Mulgrave's from earlier in 1679. Mulgrave, who by this point had become a significant public figure and rejoiced in such titles as Governor of Hull and Lord Lieutenant of the East Riding of Yorkshire, continued to be an implacable foe of Rochester's. It is likely that it was he who spread rumours of Rochester's death a few years before, and his close association with Dryden offered a calculated snub, on the part of both men, to Rochester's poetic and social standing; the implication was that they were the modern, successful figures, Rochester a ruined has-been.

As with 'A Ramble in St James's Park' and his satire on Charles, personal loathing colours the poem's sentiments. From the opening salvo, it is clear that Rochester has scores to settle:

> Bursting with pride, the loathed impostume swells;
> Prick him, he sheds his venom straight, and smells.

The weak couplet aside, the reference to venom makes the nature of Rochester's anger explicit, and a grudge permeates the poem. Belittling Mulgrave as nothing more than 'so lewd a scribbler', who 'writes with as much force to nature as he fights', Rochester sneers at the 'baffled fop', 'hardened in shame', who is not only mocked by schoolboys but capable of no original thought of his own; instead, he is forced to rake 'among the excrements of others' wit / To make a stinking meal of what they shit', in a clear allusion to his involvement with Dryden.

As usual, vivid description is key to the pungent physicality of the poem. Mulgrave is ridiculed for his 'red nose, splay foot' and—in a phrase first used in his June letter to Savile—'google eye', to say nothing of his 'stinking breath'. In a touch that will bring a smile to anyone who has misspent too much time by the seaside, Rochester even compares Mulgrave to Punchinello, the ancestor of Mr Punch; only the most even-handedly humourless might compare the spat between the two men to a Punch and Judy fight, although the inevitable arrival of the Devil would have rather different consequences for Rochester. Mulgrave's military prowess is similarly mocked as 'vile success', which has done nothing more than turn him 'like Harlequin to jest'. Rochester refers to the sighting of an elephant at Smithfield's Bartholomew Fair in early September 1679, turning this piece of bestial trivia into an attack on Mulgrave's hulking physical appearance and sneering that 'all his brother monsters flourish there'.

Eventually, wearied by his own vitriol, Rochester writes some valedictory final lines that might apply to himself as much as to Mulgrave:

Go where he will, he never finds a friend;
Shame and derision all his steps attend.
Alike abroad, at home, i'th camp and court,
This Knight of the Burning Pestle makes us sport.

The final allusion to Francis Beaumont's burlesque drama satirizing heroism is an explicit reference to Mulgrave's red nose and the 'vile success' of his supposed military triumphs. Yet, if there was anyone for whom 'shame and derision' was a constant presence in their life, it was Rochester, who, weak and weary of existence, was aware that his own sport was drawing to a close.

Rochester did not return to London until early October 1679. The summer months had been eventful, not least because Charles had been very ill after catching a severe chill on 21 August while in Windsor; his death would have led to mutterings of a plot against his life, possibly masterminded by the French, which would then have led to insurrection or foreign war—or perhaps even both. Had Charles died and Shaftesbury made a bid for yet greater power, his public standing was such that he could have succeeded. Stranded in Paris, Savile writes of Charles's potential death that 'the very thought of it frightens me out of my wits', and adds that, were Charles to die, then chaos would ensue. Thankfully for those who were not convinced by the veracity of the Popish Plot, he soon recovered. He was sufficiently aware of the public hysteria to redress a perceived pro-Catholic bias at court by sending the Duke of York to Belgium in September 1679 and by publicly stripping Monmouth of his title of commander-in-chief of the army.

Rochester spent much of the summer removed from this excitement in Woodstock, where his subsequent correspondence makes it appear likely that, with Elizabeth Barry absent from the picture, he forged a closer relationship with his family than he had had in years, if ever. Rochester was still desperately ill, but he was sufficiently in remission to seek a measure of grace, obtained by both the social acceptance of his family and a newly kindled spiritual interest.

A letter that he wrote to his wife shortly after his return to town adopts an apparently warm and penitent tone, strikingly different from the blasé and glib epistles he had sent her before. Claiming that '''tis not an easy thing to be entirely happy', he goes on to praise her for her enduring kindness and compassion towards him. Perhaps because of her, and his mother's, influence, he begins to display a sense of penitence: 'I myself have a sense of what the methods of my life seem so utterly to contradict.'

He was by no means po-faced about this, noting wryly that 'I must not be too wise about my own follies, or else this letter had been a book dedicated to you and published to the world', but he warmly expresses a desire to head to Adderbury after the Newmarket races and asks that 'in the meantime think of anything you would have me do, and I shall thank you for the occasion of pleasing you'. He even sent the letter care of a servant, Mr Morgan, whom he was rusticating 'because he plays the rogue here in town so extremely that he is not to be endured'. The sentiment reads as if it is tongue in cheek—Rochester was not known for showing contempt towards his servants—but it might also be a self-conscious acknowledgement of his weariness at the way of life he has led for so long. This is echoed in a reply to a letter from his son Charles, in which he takes pleasure in playing the good father, chastising his son for writing 'seldom' and instructing him in obedience to his grandmother and teachers, which will make him 'happy here and forever'; in particular, he should 'avoid idleness [and] scorn lying', in which case 'god will bless you, for which I pray'.

The heartwarming sentiments of the letters were not entirely true. Rochester was not a reformed soul, especially when he returned to London. He had taken a young Frenchman as his valet, Jean-Baptiste de Belle Fasse. The man's surname may not have been the one he was christened with, as it was a pun on *belles fesses*, or 'beautiful buttocks', and given what he subsequently wrote to Savile, it is likely that Rochester, having sworn off the whores of London, instead enjoyed the sexual favours of this good-looking Catholic. At a time when to be accused either of sodomy or of Catholic sympathy would have resulted in death, Rochester's actions were reckless in the extreme, and on 1 November 1679 he sent his valet to France, out of harm's way. He dispatched him to Savile in Paris, along with a cryptic and serpentine letter in which he attempts to explain Belle Fasse's arrival and the goings-on in London while still taking care to cover himself in the event of the letter's discovery. It shows another side of Rochester, that of the double-dealer and intelligence gatherer.

He begins by apologizing for the 'great strait' that he finds himself in, and drops Savile the written equivalent of a wink at the style of writing he is about to attempt: 'you may have forgot the familiar one we used heretofore.' Thereafter, everything he writes has an ironic twist or multi-faceted meaning. His description of London as a place 'in such a settled happiness and such merry security' is so obviously a lie that it comes as little surprise that Rochester immediately undercuts it by referring to 'the misfortunes of malicious mistaken fools', presumably an allusion to Titus Oates, and giving an ironic dig at 'the policies of the times... which expose new rarities of that kind every day'.

He then gets down to business, in what becomes his most explicit reference anywhere in his letters to his bisexuality. He calls his news 'Gyaris et carcere digna', a quotation from Juvenal's first satire which literally means 'fit for prison or chains'; Juvenal was satirizing a corrupt and fanatical country, so the allusion is far from coincidental. Rochester calls the less than literate Belle Fasse 'this pretty fool the bearer', but inserts heavy innuendo into the letter about how his 'qualities will recommend him more' and how, if Savile was to meet him, 'the happy consequence would be singing'.

'Singing', as used here, is as blatant a double entendre for sex as 'china' was in Wycherley's The Country Wife, and Rochester reinforces this by his statement that 'your excellence might have a share not unworthy the greatest ambassadors nor to be despised even by a cardinal-legate'. Savile, the implication runs, will be rewarded for his discretion with some forbidden pleasure. Rochester, continuing to pimp his valet, gloats that 'the greatest and gravest of this Court of both sexes have tasted his beauties', and, throwing caution to the wind, claims that 'Rome gains upon us here in this point mainly'—a shameless allusion to Catholic buggery, which was believed to be widespread and had been encountered by Rochester on his grand tour. He then mocks the Popish Plot by claiming that 'there is no part of the Plot carried with so much vigour and secrecy as this'—namely, Belle Fasse's induction into the decadently sexual world at court. One has to pity the unfortunate young man, cynically tossed from pillar to post as if he were nothing more than a human version of the leather dildoes so popular with men and women of 'quality'.

Belle Fasse duly pimped, Rochester then uses a complex and, in places, near-indecipherable series of codes to describe the contemporary political situation to Savile, all too aware that to be more explicit risked more than simply his own skin. Nonetheless, his attempts at discretion are relatively easy to unravel with some understanding of the time in which he was writing, possibly suggesting that some masochistic part of Rochester wanted to be discovered and punished—the same part, perhaps, that had once given rise at dinner to the scandalous lampoon about Charles. A typical example of this is how, to denote Monmouth's illegal return from his banishment, Rochester refers to 'Mr S—'s apology for making songs on the Duke of M—, with his oration-consolatory on my Lady D—'s death'—allusions which are near-incomprehensible now but would have been quite clear to Savile. He refers elsewhere to the ongoing series of persecutions of the Catholic lords in the Popish Plot and alludes to the debate about the Exclusion Act. Conscious that he is corresponding with a high-ranking ambassador as well as his friend, Rochester offers Savile the option of refusing to hear any more information: 'I durst not send [more details] to you without leave, not knowing what consequence it might draw upon your circumstances and character.' He indicates, nevertheless, his willingness to be an assiduous passer of secrets, claiming that in 'a correspondence of that kind… I dare presume to think myself capable'.

Sex aside, the letter's assertion of privileged information was presumably of use to Savile, as Rochester wrote again on 21 November

1679 in more explicit terms, referring to how 'the lousiness of affairs in this place is such… 'tis not fit to entertain a private gentleman', before going on to ridicule those who were de facto in charge of the country as 'spies, beggars and rebels'. As if in unconscious fulfilment of 'A Satire against Reason and Mankind', Rochester writes that 'busy fools and cautious knaves' are on the rise, and openly so, 'hypocrisy being the only vice in decay amongst us'. It was the crowning irony of his life that, after being pilloried for being the wickedest man in London, Rochester found himself outdone in a society where 'few men here dissemble their being rascals and no woman disowns being a whore'.

There were still occasional efforts to maintain the national sanity, but they were short-lived. The increasingly deluded and power-hungry Oates had been arrested on 19 November 1679 on an accusation of assault brought by his former servants, but such was his influence and standing that he was soon acquitted of what was described in outraged terms as 'the horrible and abominable crime of sodomy'. The sinless sodomite was soon intent on revenge. Rochester notes, drily: 'Mr Oates was tried two days ago for buggery and cleared… the next day he brought his action to the King's Bench against his accuser… for the honour of the Protestant cause.' The men who accused him, John Lane and Thomas Knox, might have acted out of loathing for their employer, or out of a genuine disgust at his actions, but their mistake was attempting to change the course of the inexorable tide. Oates, regardless of his guilt or innocence, was the living embodiment of the Popish Plot. Should he topple, then many others would fall along with him.

Moving from national to personal concerns, Rochester mentions that he is enclosing 'a libel in which my own share is not the least', which had also antagonized Charles. This libel was contained within a poem, 'An Essay upon Satire', that was written by Mulgrave, still smarting from his humiliation in Rochester's 'My Lord All-Pride'. Rochester also believed that Dryden was either partially or wholly responsible for it. Obviously indebted to 'A Satire against Reason and Mankind', the opening of which it half-apes, half-parodies, it feels oddly disconnected from the time of composition, concentrating on attacking court figures rather than addressing the Popish Plot. Perhaps this stemmed from an earlier poem, but it also indicated that Dryden and Mulgrave saw themselves as being above the common concerns of everyday people.

Most of the work consists of attacks against their perceived enemies, either implicitly (Charles is described as 'sauntering', perhaps a dig at the merry monarch's apparent insouciance in the face of national emergency) or explicitly, in the case of Rochester, who is attacked at length towards the close of the poem. It is not hard to see why he was furious at his denigration. Beginning with the writer claiming 'Rochester I despise for want of wit', the satire pokes ridicule at an apparently enfeebled figure, rather than at a man thought worthy of consideration as an equal, or even as the diabolic rakehell of repute. The first dozen or so lines, especially, bear reprinting:

> Though thought to have a tail and cloven feet;
> For while he mischief means to all mankind,
> Himself alone the ill effects does find:
> And so like witches justly suffer shame,
> Whose harmless malice is so much the same.
> False are his words, affected is his wit;
> So often he does aim, so seldom hit;
> To every face he cringes while he speaks,
> But when the back is turn'd, the head he breaks:
> Mean in each action, lewd in every limb,
> Manners themselves are mischievous in him:
> A proof that chance alone makes every creature,
> A very Killigrew without good nature.

The 'ill effects' referred to in the poem are probably Rochester's advanced illnesses, but might also be a dig at his reduced social standing, a statement supported by his 'harmless malice'. Rochester is accused of many of the failings that he levelled against his own

enemies throughout his writing—sycophancy, backstabbing, hypocrisy and, worst of all, a lack of wit. Ironically, if Mulgrave was
involved in the satire, it is considerably better and more cutting
than the banalities of his earlier writing, indicating the presence of a
more experienced co-writer, such as Dryden. It is not hard to imagine
Rochester being driven to fury by this, but the next lines become
even more cutting and dismissive:

> For, there's the folly that's still mix'd with fear,
> Cowards more blows than any hero bear;
> Of fighting sparks some may their pleasures say,
> But 'tis a bolder thing to run away:
> The world may well forgive him all his ill,
> For every fault does prove his penance still:
> Falsely he falls into some dangerous noose,
> And then as meanly labours to get loose;
> A life so infamous is better quitting,
> Spent in base injury and low submitting.

This again refers to the affray at Epsom and Billy Downs's death,
with its allusions to cowardice and running away, but it also hints at
the original source of the friction between Rochester and Mulgrave
ten years before—namely, the aborted duel that Mulgrave had
demanded because of a perceived libel by Rochester. Finally, as if
to rub salt in the wound, his literary achievements are comprehen-
sively mocked:

> I'd like to have left out his poetry;
> Forgot by all almost as well as me.
> Sometimes he has some humour, never wit,
> And if it rarely, very rarely, hit,
>
> 'Tis under so much nasty rubbish laid,
> To find it out's the cinderwoman's trade;
> Who for the wretched remnants of a fire,
> Must toil all day in ashes and in mire.

So lewdly dull his idle works appear,
The wretched texts deserve no comments here;
Where one poor thought sometimes, left all alone,
For a whole page of dullness must atone.

Dryden and Mulgrave here unwittingly provide the first existing example of literary criticism of Rochester's writing. Calling
it forgettable, soporific, full of unpleasantness and lewdness, and,
finally, dull, they prefigure what countless others were to say over
the next three centuries. By this stage, with a couple of exceptions,
Rochester had written his canon of poetry, so there is no way of discounting this as a reference to his earlier, unformed work. Did they
have a point?

Dryden and Mulgrave's comments can be taken at face value.
Rochester's writing can sometimes be called 'nasty rubbish', though
it is usually intentionally so, and some of this material is occasionally 'lewdly dull'. Much of a poem such as 'Signior Dildo', whether
or not Rochester was its sole author, feels devoid of genuine wit,
preferring bawdy scatological humour instead. Likewise, there are
moments in his poetry that are redolent of a young man whose desire
to reach for greatness overwhelms his grasp; even 'A Satire against
Reason and Mankind', his most significant and lasting achievement,
and one that Mulgrave and Dryden reference throughout their own
satire, struggles with its own structure of paradox upon paradox.
Elsewhere, there are jokes that do not work; obscure ideas inad-
equately explained; duff rhymes, lines, verses and even entire poems
that many readers will find less than compelling—not to mention
an unashamed use of four-letter words that means that Rochester's
poetry is never going to be found on the standard school syllabus. At
least not officially.

Set against this, Rochester's greatest poems, humorous or serious,
offer something entirely different from the run-of-the-mill, would-
be metaphysical writing that was prevalent at the time. At his best,
Rochester was responsible for some of the wittiest, most bitingly
satirical and scatologically sexual poetry ever written, in which,

even today, some of the more extreme sexual material is both funny and shocking. Balancing high classical art and social allusion with low tavern humour and hilariously vitriolic attacks on his enemies, he stands poles apart from his contemporaries, with his work offering a thrillingly theatrical range of personae, all commenting on the vagaries of the time in which he lived. It would be overstating the case to regard him as significant a lyric poet as a Marvell or a Donne; however, he did epitomize the age in which he lived in all its conflicted, squalid glory. Therefore, Dryden and Mulgrave's final sneer—'learn to write well, or not to write at all'—might have been noted by a more temperate Rochester, rejected, and batted back at them with all the anger, charm and wit that he was capable of.

Unfortunately, this did not happen. Rochester's response, 'An Epistolary Essay from MG to OB upon their Mutual Poems', can be viewed either as a satirical account of Mulgrave, the MG of the title, writing to his fellow poet Dryden, or OB;* or alternatively as a late example of Rochesterian autobiography. The arguments in favour of the first viewpoint are that MG is mocked and made to look ridiculous throughout. Claiming early on that 'I'd be content t'have written *The British Prince*'—a notoriously dreadful verse epic by Edward Howard—MG is shown to be variously pedestrian ('I'm none of those who think themselves inspired'); arrogant ('I, who am of sprightly vigour full'); and hilariously misguided ('Thus I resolve of my own poetry / That 'tis the best, and that's a fame for me'). MG might appear to cast off something 'so foolish and so false as common fame', but he has a distinctly coquettish stance towards that coy mistress. The ending of the poem has an amusingly ironic charge:

> These things considered make me, in despite
> Of idle rumour, keep at home and write.

Rochester in late 1679 would have been best served by taking his own advice, even if the words are put into the mouth of a pompous idiot.

* The 'OB' perhaps stands for 'Old Bays'—an allusion to the laurel wreaths with which the young Rochester once crowned his monkey as it tore up poetry.

It was Dryden whom Rochester thought mainly responsible for 'An Essay upon Satire', albeit in association with his patron Mulgrave, as Rochester mentions in his letter of 21 November to Savile. While Rochester delivers no explicit invective against Dryden in the letter, his name was soon associated in town gossip with an ugly and cowardly act of revenge.

On 18 December Dryden was walking home to his lodgings in Long Acre, Holborn, through Rose Lane in Covent Garden, after an evening spent at Will's coffee-house in nearby Bow Street, the informal club of the various city wits. He had been visiting the coffee-house for around fifteen years, and enjoyed the opportunity to converse there with the likes of Etherege and Wycherley. However, his night was soon to be ruined as he was set upon by three anonymous men, armed with cudgels, and beaten senseless before they fled into the night, disturbed by the arrival of others. Even by the often casually violent standards of the time, this was a brutal attack.

Dryden was severely injured, so much so that it was initially thought his life might be in danger (in his later years he often complained of lingering pains, dating from the assault). As he had not been robbed, despite being well dressed and a figure of note, speculation soon led to the suspicion that the attack had been conducted by hired thugs acting on behalf of an anonymous patron. Upon his recovery, Dryden offered a £50 reward in the *Gazette* newspaper for information, but nobody ever came forward. Who injured him, and why, remains one of the mysteries of the age. However, it is Rochester's name that has often been linked to the attack, both at the time and subsequently, on the grounds that a man with as low a reputation as he had was capable of anything.

That Rochester loathed Dryden by this point is certain. The relationship between the two men, never entirely easy, had long since disintegrated, turning to distrust and contempt. Rochester was never given to the excessive personal violence of, say, the Earl of Pembroke—the unhinged brother-in-law of Louise de Kérouaille, who was probably responsible for the unsolved murder of Sir Edmund Berry Godfrey. Nevertheless, he was certainly capable of rash and hasty actions, as the destruction of Charles's sundial and the fatal affray at Epsom demonstrated. He had threatened Dryden with cudgelling in the past, and now might have followed through on his boasts. It would have been a step too far for Rochester himself—still a peer of the realm, and ill to boot—to have attacked Dryden, but it can easily be imagined that in a moment of vitriol he had hired some anonymous thugs and, knowing Dryden's likely movements, told them to lay in wait for him on a dark alley. The resulting punishment would have been swift, violent and highly satisfactory to a bruised poetic ego.

The major problem with this theory is that Rochester, much weakened and in a poor state of health by this time, is unlikely to have had the energy to conduct a clandestine operation that would have involved hiring efficient batterers. The discretion of Dryden's assailants, even when a large sum was on offer for a confession, indicates that the men who performed the beating had a greater reason to remain silent than mere money. The trail therefore leads to far higher places than Rochester, namely to Louise de Kérouaille, Duchess of Portsmouth.

She, along with Charles, had been insulted in 'An Essay upon Satire', and while the king might have been blasé in the extreme about another rain of vitriol being poured upon his periwig, Louise was unlikely to have taken the insult so calmly. As Rochester had found a few years previously, she was an implacable enemy, and doubtless reacted angrily to being described as 'false, foolish, old, ill-natured and ill-bred'. If she had suspected Mulgrave of the insult, then his status as an aristocrat placed him above normal recriminations. Dryden, however, was a mere poet, and so could be assaulted with impunity—and by royal bodyguards. These men were strong, discreet and probably happy to perform an act of revenge on behalf of their wronged king and his mistress.

A likely solution, then, is that Rochester rejoiced at Dryden's comeuppance, but had not taken any active part in arranging it himself. Instead, this cowardly act of violence against a physically harmless writer was justified by some of the highest in the land as a means of maintaining the status quo. It is impossible to say whether Charles knew of the planned assault or condoned it if he did; the final irony, of course, is that Dryden was and remained Poet Laureate, which he was unlikely to have done if he had offended the king. It seems an act of severe literary criticism, in the case of one's court poet, to tacitly support having him brutally beaten, and Charles, for all his wild outbreaks of temper, was not a man who typically engaged in underhand pursuits and skulduggery of this kind. Yet, during the wild abandon of the Popish Plot, many otherwise sane people found themselves acting out of character.

Describing Rochester at this point—in the final stages of tertiary syphilis—as sane would be mistaken. He was confused, vulnerable and desperate to provide a substantial legacy beyond the libels and tittle-tattle that were invariably associated with his name. To help him do this, he needed someone more substantial in philosophical matters than Blount; someone who could be even more of a confidant than Savile; and, finally, a substitute father figure who might be a source of comfort at the end of his days.

The cost would be higher than he could ever have imagined.

'SOME FORMAL

band & beard

takes me

TO TASK'

❋

[1679–1680]

WHEN ROCHESTER first encountered the clergyman Gilbert Burnet, neither had any inkling it would become a life-changing friendship for both men. They possibly first met in 1673, when Burnet travelled to London for a short visit in order to obtain a licence to publish a book and, being in favour with Charles at the time, was subsequently made a royal chaplain. However, the wheel of fortune soon turned, and Burnet was exiled from his native Scotland in 1674 after falling out with the influential John Maitland, Duke of Lauderdale, over what the jealous duke saw as Burnet's overstated influence at court.

Estranged from Charles because of Lauderdale's innuendo and unable to return to Scotland because he faced likely imprisonment, Burnet spent the following years quietly establishing himself as a theological and philosophical man of substance. An excellent orator, charismatic and full of his own self-importance, Burnet was never short of admirers, who helped him to obtain such sinecures as Chaplain of the Rolls Chapel. He never wanted for money or influence. Evelyn calls him 'a person of extraordinary parts', and he made a great impression on all those he encountered.

What the legendarily dissipated Rochester and Burnet might have made of one another in the mid-1670s can only be imagined. Burnet was only four years older than Rochester, but for the most part the two men were poles apart. Burnet was a man of conservative theological instincts who was canny in his choice of friends and supporters, and whose stern upbringing at the hands of his father, a puritanical Scottish lawyer, had instilled within him a vigorous belief in right and wrong. Rochester was in most respects the opposite; his mother may have been equally stern, but she had failed to impose any great moral understanding upon him. If they did meet in 1673, it was not an important encounter. It is just possible that Burnet was guyed within 'A Satire against Reason and Mankind', but much more likely

, that the figure Rochester had in mind was his greater nemesis Isaac Barrow.

While Rochester's health declined, Burnet researched and wrote the first book of his *History of the Reformation of the Church of England*. The first volume was published in early 1679 and dealt with the age of Henry VIII, with enough coded allusions to the present day to appeal to those critical of the increasing chaos in Restoration England. Thus, the chaos of the Inquisition, with witches, wizards and sodomites being condemned to the ever-burning fires of hell, was a subtle reference to the similar turmoil of the Popish Plot, just as the moral and spiritual failures of Henry VIII's court could be compared to the lax standards of Charles's.

Rochester read the book, something of a cause célèbre on its release, and was impressed, even recommending it to Charles, whose response was allegedly that Burnet would be better off keeping his mouth shut while the king lived—or he would suffer the consequences. (Burnet noted that he had 'very strange impressions' of Charles as a result.) This endeared Burnet to Rochester, as did his compassionate counselling of Rochester's former mistress, the unfortunate Jane Roberts, who spent the last part of the year dying of syphilis in hideous agony. Word spread to Rochester that Roberts, with whom he had had 'an ill concern', had been treated by Burnet 'neither with a slack indulgence nor an affrighting severity', but with unjudgemental and robust Christian charity. Intrigued and grateful, Rochester suggested a meeting with Burnet in October 1679 via a mutual acquaintance, possibly George Savile, Marquess of Halifax and elder brother to Henry. The invitation was duly accepted, and they began a series of weekly conversations about religion and morality that lasted for the next six months.

Rochester had always been a polarizing figure. Those who liked him, such as Savile, Etherege and Aphra Behn, were unswervingly loyal to him, even after his death. His enemies, such as Scrope, Mulgrave and latterly Dryden, expressed little other than censure and contempt. What he had lacked was a figure of the middle ground: someone detached from the narrow, hysterical world of court with whom he could talk on an equal level and discuss his spiritual interests and ideas. This was what Burnet provided. Rochester saw in him something of the uncorrupted prelate of 'A Satire against Reason and Mankind'—'a meek, humble man of honest sense', who led a pious and godly life.

Nonetheless, their first meeting was a tempestuous one. According to Burnet's subsequent account of their conversations, *The Life and Death of John, Earl of Rochester*—a somewhat self-promoting work, first published as a book in 1680 by the leading printer Richard Chiswel and intended as a didactic account of sin—Rochester opened their discussions by airily saying that he would use Burnet in a more free and open manner than he had done with other clergymen, speaking candidly, straightforwardly and without prejudice. He also offered Burnet the tempting possibility that he might be willing to change his mind about religion; by doing this, he presented himself as potentially a great prize for the would-be reformer—a soul within reach of penitence and salvation. All the same, Burnet 'saw into the depths of Satan' in Rochester, and he knew that the devil had the power to assume a pleasing shape. If he failed in his task, humiliation and the end of a growing reputation as a leading theologian would follow. Work had to be done.

Burnet's presence in Rochester's life smacked of genuine reforming zeal, but it also reflected a cynical realization that a successful and high-profile conversion would cement the clergyman's place within English national life forever. Although he was by no means unsuccessful, he was ambitious and had his eye on a lucrative and influential bishopric. In this game of political chess, Rochester was as much a pawn to be taken as he was a source of interest, albeit a rather more independent-minded and turbulent pawn than Burnet was used to.

Rochester offered Burnet what he termed 'a full view' of his life and career up until that point, from which Burnet quotes frustratingly brief and redacted extracts, especially when other people are involved. Some of it—the account of his naval service at Bergen, for instance, and his friend Montagu's premonition of his death there—feels entirely of a piece with his poetic and epistolary concerns of the period, not to mention his intimations of his own mortality. However, there are already hints of Burnet's own editorializing and subjective recollection, something acknowledged when he states: 'I am not so sure… of all said by him to me.' This is understandable; his aim was to celebrate his own achievement, rather than present an objective account of Rochester's life and, in particular, the concerns of his last months.

Burnet refers to Rochester's drinking as something that made him 'extravagantly pleasant' and led him 'deeper and deeper in intemperance', and builds up to the shocking revelation that 'he told me for five years together he was continually drunk… not all the while under the visible effect of it, but his blood was so inflamed that he was not in all that time cool enough to be perfectly master of himself'. The sly note of knowing exaggeration ever present in Rochester's letters is here dropped for the moral outrage of a man for whom five years spent drunk was among the greatest of sins. This is mirrored in his description of Rochester's love of disguise and theatricality being put to the service of mere 'mean amours' or 'diversion', a reductive way of describing his intense engagement with illusion and personae.

Nonetheless, the picture Burnet presents of Rochester is accurate enough in its specific details to feel coherent, especially in his musings on death. Burnet notes that Rochester said to him, when he was ill shortly before they met: 'he did not think to live an hour… his reason and judgement were so clear and strong… that he was fully persuaded that death was not the spending and dissolution of the soul, but only the separation of it from matter.' Rochester apparently admitted to a feeling of 'great remorse for his past life', which was meat and drink to Burnet, but this was soon qualified as being merely 'general and dark horrors' rather than 'any convictions of sinning against God'. Any conversion would not be easily won; an ill Rochester had complied reluctantly with his friends sending in men of God to minister to him, but 'he had no great mind to it', and only joined in their prayers in the most perfunctory fashion.

So their conversations continued, while the hysteria of the Popish Plot played out in the background. Rochester's health was still shaky, and he relapsed into fits, but he seemed better than he had done for some time, revived by the intellectual excitement of charged debate and the opportunity to cause some mischief. He was engaged, physically and intellectually, by the substantial Burnet, whose significant charisma and physical presence charmed many others (Dryden wrote a poem-cum-love letter, with all the passion of a schoolboy crush, calling him 'a portly prince and goodly to the sight', before sighingly comparing him to Homer's Jupiter).

Whether or not the reports of their discussions are accurate, they offer a compelling insight into post-Restoration ideas of morality and religion. Burnet presents himself as a liberal theologian, and Rochester as a sceptic and humanist. The tenor of Burnet's account of their conversations is less antagonistic than might have been the case at the time, with Burnet skilfully synthesizing their differing viewpoints to emphasize the areas of agreement between them. Both concurred that scrupulous observance of doctrine was less important than living a decent life amongst one's fellow men, with Burnet appearing to define 'religion' as no less a social entity than a divine one. Neither disputed the existence of God, with Rochester claiming that he had never known 'an entire atheist, who fully believed that there was no God'.

Entering into the spirit of intellectual glasnost, Rochester describes his former immorality as stemming from carnal desires, with Burnet claiming 'he had made himself a beast, and had brought pain and sickness on his body'. This stands in apparent contrast to Rochester's other statements that he believes in 'the gratification of natural appetites', especially 'the free use of wine and women', as long as nobody is hurt by such sensual indulgence. However, this is where the two differ. Burnet, using the themes of Rochester's own poetry against him, argues that mere sensual indulgence should remain subservient to human wisdom, which in turn leads to 'higher and more lasting pleasure'. It is a new spin on conventionally Puritan ideas; Burnet does not reject the body's natural appetites out of hand, but instead claims that they must be subjugated to 'a law within [Man] himself'. Rochester is unenthused; he describes this as 'enthusiasm or canting', and claims not to understand such an idea. Touché.

Throughout Burnet's report of their conversations, he skilfully presents Rochester as intelligent, witty and engaged, but also curiously naïve and easily persuaded of the folly of his arguments. Burnet claims to have 'reason and experience' on his side throughout, in contrast to Rochester's passion and heat; over and over again, his theme is that religion and its application in everyday life are as concrete and easily proved as the existence of a favourite tavern or a beloved playhouse. Rochester, under his tutelage, acknowledges that there is a 'supreme being', whether nature or God, and that 'the soul did not dissolve' after death. Nonetheless, he remains an iconoclast, rejecting the concept of heaven and hell as mere 'rewards or punishments', and claiming that religious worship is nothing more than the self-serving 'inventions of priests'.

Burnet's rebuttals of Rochester's arguments acknowledge his contempt for priests, whom Rochester compares to the 'mountebanks who corrupt physic' (perhaps like Dr Bendo), and for the scriptures, which Rochester criticizes for their 'strange stories' and 'seeming contradictions, chiefly about the order of time'. Like many a rationalist since, Rochester had an unarguable point, and one that Burnet was unable to rebut in any satisfactory manner. Instead, he is reduced to talking weakly of 'evidence' and reading scripture as an allegorical exercise in spirituality rather than as literal truth. Rochester, unconvinced, notes that 'all this might be fancy' and calls it 'the showing of [a] trick', which Burnet castigates him for, calling it an 'ill use of his wit'.

In Burnet's account of their conversations, Rochester frequently appears more enlightened and open-minded than his sparring partner. He ridicules the way in which conventional Christian teaching is loaded against women, 'except one in the way of marriage', and its failure to allow them 'the remedy of divorce' (perhaps he was considering how Elizabeth could have taken such a remedy against him at the height of his profligacy). Burnet, on the other hand, refers to women simply as man's property. Rochester's loathing of corrupt clergymen, meanwhile, is expressed simply but beautifully in his statement: 'Why must a man tell me I cannot be saved, unless I believe things against my reason, and then I must pay him for telling me of them?'

It is unlikely that any money changed hands between Rochester and Burnet for their conversations—Burnet's greater reward would lie elsewhere and Rochester was impecunious, as ever. Nevertheless, the theme of salvation is never far from their thoughts, whether expressed as a 'high reward', in Burnet's words, or, from Rochester's perspective, in the 'difficult terms' (presumably those ecclesiastically imposed) of arriving at such a point. On and on their arguments run, sometimes with the two reaching agreement about what Burnet terms the 'mistakes and calumnies' that have beset religious observance, but more often coming to a stalemate.

Thus it is a surprise to find, at the end of Burnet's account of their conversations, that Rochester appears to be, if not entirely converted, then mostly convinced by what Burnet has said. He is said to wish to 'change the whole method of his life; to become strictly just and true, to be chaste and temperate, and to forbear swearing and irreligious discourse, to worship and pray to his maker'. While refusing to call himself a truly religious man—he has yet to arrive 'at a full persuasion of Christianity'—Rochester announces that he will 'never employ his wit to run [religion] down, or to corrupt others'. Burnet concludes their debates by admonishing Rochester to clear himself of the 'distempers, which vice brought on' and the 'flights of wit, that do feed atheism and irreligion'.

If their conversations, which ended in March 1680, really did conclude in the way that Burnet describes, he might have considered his efforts well spent. A penitent, chastened Rochester, if not the full convert that he had hoped for, was a significant success—something that would do no harm whatsoever to his reputation. Whether Rochester knew that Burnet planned to publish an account of their conversations or not cannot be known, but it is likely that, if Burnet did mention it, Rochester would have given him his blessing with a certain wry approval. Besides, Rochester seemed to be in remission from the worst of his illness; there would be every chance, it appeared, for the two to have further discussions and for this particular prodigal to be returned to the fold once more.

Burnet was mistaken in two regards. First, Rochester was far closer to death than either of them guessed. And second, far from convincing Rochester of the glories of heaven and the immortality of the soul, he had only served to make him even more sceptical.

While Rochester met with Burnet, he continued to correspond with Charles Blount, with whom he discussed the topics that he was speaking to Burnet about. While Burnet offered a theological orthodoxy that was by turns reassuring, frustrating and doggedly old-fashioned, Blount rejected 'the harangues of the parsons [and the] sophistry of the schoolmen' in favour of a philosophical perspective that stretched back to Pliny and Philostratus. He expressed theologically dangerous sentiments carefully, allowing Rochester to consider the image of a 'humdrum deity chewing his own nature, a droning God sit hugging of himself' even as he made a great show of contradicting it.

Had Blount been writing to a man who was convinced by the substance of Burnet's arguments, then he would have been wasting his time, or worse. However, one of his letters to Rochester dates from 7 February 1680—towards the end of the latter's Burnetian conversations—and responds to a poem that he had been sent. Blount describes it as 'your most incomparable version of that passage of Seneca's', which, even allowing for his typically florid exaggeration, was accurate. Rochester's last poem, 'A Translation from Seneca's *Troades*', takes its inspiration from the second act of *Troades*, but is entirely original in the despairing, weary language and sentiments contained within it. It is possible that the poem does not date from early 1680 but instead was written years before. Certainly, the intellectual vitality and bleak wit that are displayed throughout are at odds with Rochester's ill health at the time, although it is likely that the cut and thrust of his conversations with Burnet had temporarily rejuvenated him. What matters most is that he was sufficiently engaged with Blount to send him the poem as his own contribution to their discussion, indicating that, whether it was newly minted or an older piece, he was excited by the matters they were discussing and saw this poem as a relevant statement of his thoughts.

Not that he was especially optimistic—on the basis of this evidence—about the undiscovered country that awaited him:

> After death nothing is, and nothing, death:
> The utmost limit of a gasp of breath.
> Let the ambitious zealot lay aside
> His hopes of heaven, whose faith is but his pride;
> Let slavish souls lay by their fear,
> Nor be concerned which way nor where
> After this life they shall be hurled.
> Dead, we become the lumber of the world,
> And to that mass of matter shall be swept
> Where things destroyed with things unborn are kept.
> Devouring time swallows us whole;
> Impartial death confounds body and soul.
> For Hell and the foul fiend that rules
>
> God's everlasting fiery jails
> (Devised by rogues, dreaded by fools),
> With his grim, grisly dog that keeps the door,
> Are senseless stories, idle tales,
> Dreams, whimseys and no more.

Lacking the passion and vituperation of his earlier satires, even those of the previous year against Dryden and Mulgrave, it has an elegiac, haunted quality that suggests that Rochester knew that the end of his life was near. It rejects the comparative optimism of earlier metaphysical writing, such as Donne's tenth Holy Sonnet, 'Death be not proud', in favour of a bleaker set of conclusions; perhaps thinking of Hamlet's musings on fate as much as Seneca, Rochester rejects the 'senseless stories' of hellfire and damnation in favour of endless emptiness, with 'impartial death' failing to make any distinction between anyone whose time has come.

If 'A Translation' was written in late 1679 or early 1680, it is conceivable that 'the ambitious zealot... whose faith is but his pride' refers to Gilbert Burnet, either directly or unconsciously, although the continued presence of Burnet in Rochester's life even after their formal conversations had finished indicates that a degree of amity existed between the two men. Of course, Rochester seldom let personal friendship get in the way of a telling phrase or a good joke.

In any case, the poem impressed Blount a great deal, which led to that verbose deist delivering his most telling judgement on Rochester's philosophy. He praised Rochester's 'divine and immortal mind', and grandly declared that 'the hand that wrote it may become lumber, but sure the spirit that dictated it can never be so'. Unwittingly, Blount was delivering the counter-argument to Mulgrave's rejection of Rochester's writing. Rochester's hand, and the rest of his body, would inevitably become lumber, and he would never write another poem. His questioning spirit would live on.

Occasional bursts of animation aside, Rochester remained unwell. A letter from his mother's agent, old John Cary, to Rochester's de facto guardian, the politician Ralph Verney, dated 4 January 1680, states that 'my Lord Rochester's health has been, and is like to be very troublesome'. Nonetheless, either from ignorance of the extremity of his illness or from bravado, he continued to make sporadic appearances at court when he was in London, painfully dragging himself to the House of Lords to involve himself in intrigues and government business. One especially ill-conceived piece of activity involved his support of a young aristocrat and fellow Gentleman of the Bed Chamber, James Douglas, Earl of Arran. The hot-headed Scot wanted to woo a young lady of fortune, Miss Pawlet, but she was promised to the far more suitable (and much older) Edward Conway, and this match, which was coordinated by the Speaker of the Commons, Sir Edward Seymour, was given royal approval.

Arran, who had been led to believe by Pawlet's family (rather than the bride-to-be) that he was the preferred match, was incensed, and Rochester, who was bored and nostalgic for his own days of frustrated wooing, took his part. When Arran insulted Seymour on 9 March by spitting at him in the House of Commons, Seymour took the opportunity of defusing a politically awkward row by challenging Rochester to a duel on the pretext that Arran's rash actions had been on his instruction. Seymour knew that Rochester was in poor health, and so when the latter agreed to fight the duel on horseback because of a supposed 'weakness in his limbs', both men knew that it was mere foreplay to the inevitable cancellation of the duel; this duly came about when Charles commanded both parties not to take part, shortly before issuing a proclamation that duels were to be abandoned between all persons of quality. Therefore, honour was satisfied for everyone save the unfortunate Arran, who had a warrant issued for his arrest and fled to Scotland to lie low. He never did marry Miss Pawlet; instead, after inheriting his father's title of Duke of Hamilton, he continued to lead a violent and hot-headed existence. He would eventually die in 1712 in a duel over a disputed inheritance, although not before killing his opponent Charles Mohun (Charles's proclamation, it appears, did not survive his reign).

Rochester was in good enough favour with Charles to be one of the party who headed to the Newmarket races in late March 1680, although their stay there was brought to a premature end on 31 March, when fresh rumours of an Irish plot against Charles's life led to their swift return to town. The Popish Plot, in all its fantastical details, continued to poison every part of English life. Rochester, however, was confronted with some more banal, though equally distressing, news. Rather than returning to London with the rest of the court, he headed to Enmore to visit his wife's estates. En route, he lodged for a few days at the small town of Bishop's Stortford in Hertfordshire, where he was made aware, by Savile, of a blackmail attempt that had been lodged by a 'Mr P'.

Who the mysterious Mr P was, and what he was blackmailing Rochester about, can only be surmised. Rochester's reputation was such that he was unlikely to have been alarmed by an accusation of anything other than involvement in the Popish Plot, or, conceivably, of sodomy, itself closely connected with 'Catholic practices'. It is possible that 'Mr P' is an (intentional?) misprint for 'Mr B', and that this is an allusion to Jean-Baptiste de Belle Fasse of beautiful buttocks fame, Rochester's valet-cum-sexual plaything, whom Savile had had the pleasure of encountering when he was sent to Paris. In his reply, Rochester is shocked, remarking on 'the indirectness of Mr P's proceeding' and commenting that 'misery makes all men less or more dishonest'. He is 'not surprised to see villainy industrious for bread', especially as he lives 'in a place where it is often so *de gaieté de coeur*'—for the fun of it, the use of French perhaps a reference both to Savile's Parisian sojourn and (if Belle Fasse was the culprit) to the blackmailer's nationality.

Like Wilde two centuries later, Rochester's attitude towards potential exposure was a mixture of bluster and arrogance. He knew that the witch-hunts that were tearing the country apart were looking for any excuse to pounce on anyone displaying signs of popish behaviour, and sodomy with a Frenchman and presumed Catholic would have seen him immediately arrested and incarcerated in the Tower. If his concern for his own safety was negligible, he was aware that his behaviour, and his wife's Catholicism, plunged his whole family into danger. Nonetheless, his letter to Savile alternates between thanking him for the 'kindness and care' that he had shown in alerting him to the blackmail attempt and for his continued friendship, and bravado: 'I give him leave to prove what he can against me.'

It is the last surviving letter that Rochester sent Savile. He does not refer to his health, either because he thought that he was better, or because he considered that more important matters were at hand. The two men did not meet again before Rochester's death, and thus a great friendship died as well. Savile was a tirelessly loyal and devoted figure in Rochester's life, and it is fitting that in the last letter that we have by Rochester he calls himself Savile's 'faithful, obliged, humble servant', thereby emphasizing the debt that he owed to his true friend.

Rochester attempted to shrug off the blackmail threat, but he was frightened and depressed by the sense of the end approaching, with respect to both his reputation and his health. A fragment of a letter that he wrote to his wife around this time talks of 'so great a disproportion between our desires and what has been ordained to content them', and—perhaps thinking of Belle Fasse's treachery—he suggests that 'were [a] man's soul placed in a body fit for it, he were a dog, that count anything a benefit obtained with flattery, fear and service'. He pleads with Elizabeth not to mislay his letter—'it is not fit for everybody to find'—and, typically, ends with a remark about drinking: 'your wine was bought last week, but neglected to be sent.' Perhaps Rochester took solace in it himself.

For the next month, an uneasy sense of calm existed. Rochester's illness appeared to have abated enough for him to travel between Woodstock and Adderbury, albeit probably with the help of his servants, and he thought, rashly, that he was in a state of improved health. This led him to undertake another visit to Enmore to see his wife in mid-May, in blazing heat. The exertion of the swift ride proved to be his undoing, as he inflamed an ulcer in his bladder, causing him agonizing pain and discomfort. Suffering hideously, he had to be brought back to Woodstock by coach, along treacherous, bumpy roads, arriving at the lodge on 20 May 1680.

When he returned to Woodstock, he must have known that his drama had reached its final act. There would be no more fortunate remissions, no more drinking, wenching and mischief-making. Instead, Rochester was going to die. Yet, even as he prepared to accept the inevitable, racked with pain, new twists and turns would illuminate his final days. He had never lived a conventional life, and it was fitting that the circumstances of his death would be equally unusual and theatrical.

'A MAN
·half·
IN THE
grave'

✤

[May–July 1680]

ON 1 APRIL 1680 Rochester turned thirty-three. It was a significant number: Christ died at thirty-three, and the Muslim cleric Al-Ghazali claimed that the inhabitants of heaven would remain 'youths of thirty-three years of age'. Whether Rochester was still entertained by these coincidences and moments of serendipity while he was lying, a month later, in Woodstock Lodge on what would become his deathbed—an elaborate and Gothic construction of Elizabethan origin made of carved black oak—can only be guessed at.

When Rochester returned from his abortive trip to Somerset, his death looked imminent. His stomach ulcer had ruptured, leading to 'vast quantities of purulent matter in his urine'. As he oozed pus, the pain was agonizing. His mother, Elizabeth and his children were sent for, and arrived at Woodstock along with the family doctor Alexander Radcliffe, who confirmed the seriousness of Rochester's condition. Word soon spread to court that Rochester was on his deathbed, and Charles, disturbed by reports of his erstwhile protégé's suffering, dispatched his own physician, Thomas Short, who could do little other than prescribe asses' milk, which was believed to help with the body's inflammation.

A letter that his mother's agent John Cary sent to his guardian Ralph Verney on 1 June 1680 gives a bleak account of his health. Cary states that 'I much fear my Lord Rochester hath not long to live', and talks of his weakness and illness. He is more optimistic about his spiritual condition; he writes how 'he is grown to be the most altered person, the most devout and pious person as I generally ever knew, and certainly would make a most worthy brave man, if it would please God to spare his life'.

Thus Cary was the first to articulate what would be one of the most commonly accepted stories about Rochester—namely that, in the face of death, he repented of all his sins and his former wickedness, accepted God, and became a credit to his family in his final days. This became central to Rochester's reputation as a penitent and was repeated for centuries as fact; indeed, many believe it to be the case today.

It is a stirring, dramatically satisfying story, with a pleasing circularity to it, and it is not hard to see why it has been so beloved by everyone from clerics to critics. There is only one problem: the evidence that it occurred stems entirely from a few interested parties, all of whom had their own reasons to put about the tale of Rochester's final conversion.

Rochester's mother's chaplain, Robert Parsons, arrived to visit Rochester on 26 May 1680, preparing to administer the last rites. Parsons was the same age as Rochester and had studied at Oxford at the same time, where the two became friends. Rochester arranged for Parsons to receive the lucrative academic post of esquire bedel, a junior ceremonial officer responsible for conferring degrees, in 1670, and he introduced him to his mother when he became curate at Adderbury shortly after his ordination in 1671. Thus Parsons came as much in the guise of a comrade-in-arms as in that of a man of God.

Rochester was enfeebled, but his brain was still active, whirling between exhaustion and terror. When Parsons arrived, he greeted him with joy and relief, but told him that, meditating upon his conversations with Burnet, he had become disenchanted with God and religion, vowing, in Parsons' account, 'to run them down with all the argument and spite in the world'. Parsons goes on to say that 'like the great convert St Paul, he found it hard to kick against the pricks'; the unfortunate choice of word in the allusion seems fitting when used of Rochester. Parsons' account tells how Rochester developed an 'extraordinary respect' for his status as a clergyman, and how he talked animatedly about his former unworthiness and his new-found love of God. Parsons puts this down to 'divine grace' having entered into his soul after his earlier scepticism. The more cynical might doubt the likelihood of a desperately ill man communicating in as lucid a manner as this. At best panicking and desperate, and at worst insensible, Rochester was not the most reliable of communicants.

It is certain that, by this time, Rochester had a far greater interest in religion and God than he had shown before, partly as a result of his conversations with Burnet, and partly out of a desperate fear that was creeping up on him along with his death, as can be seen by his referring to mortality throughout his writings. He was also compos mentis enough to beg Elizabeth, successfully, to abandon the Catholic faith that she had been practising for the past decade and to return to what Cary describes as 'her first love, the Protestant religion'. This was heralded as a sign of Rochester's keen identification with his spiritual side, and it might have been. It is altogether more likely, however, that, knowing his end was imminent, he wanted to be sure that his wife would be safe from the worst of the Popish Plot. Being the widow of a man as notorious as he would inevitably arouse suspicion, especially as she did not enjoy the royal favour that her husband did, and abandoning a faith that she had only ever adopted for the sake of expedience was the logical course. As before, spiritual needs took second place to earthly ones.

Rochester's illness worsened throughout early June. In addition to his ulcerated bladder, he was suffering sporadically from fever and sweating profusely, and was unable to eat hot food. His death was thought to be at hand, so much so that Burnet, rueful that he had failed to be present for a spectacular deathbed conversion, wrote to Halifax on 5 June that 'he must be dead by this time', and, with a tinge of envy at his own absence, notes that 'he has expressed great remorse for his past ill life... [he] dies a serious penitent and professes himself a Christian'.

Burnet had heard this from, of all people, Rochester's clown-like and malodorous acquaintance Fanshaw, himself recovering from a syphilitic attack, whose gullibility in such matters was impressively advanced. Fanshaw decided to head to Woodstock, possibly from a wish to be at his friend's bedside, but equally possibly because he hoped for some remembrance in the will. He arrived, preceded no doubt by his foul body odour, on 8 June, intending to stay a week or so, in order to attend the funeral and the reading of the will.

Fanshaw was surprised to find, on his arrival, that Rochester was weakened but not dead, and that he was heard praying. Corroborating this with Dr Radcliffe, he headed to see his erst-while drinking and whoring companion, and was dumbfounded to hear Rochester, in some pain, deliver what sounded like a set speech about how their former lewdness and profanity had now been super-seded by 'a judge and a future state', and to exhort Fanshaw into a better way of life. This was reported by Radcliffe, many years after the fact, so it has the ring of truth about it, coming as it does from a disinterested party (Anne Wilmot's version is rather more colour-ful). Rochester is even reported by Dr Radcliffe to have said: 'I am not mad, but speak the words of truth and soberness.' A trembling Fanshaw, believing that his friend was diabolically possessed, fled Woodstock for London. When he returned to town, he had a simple answer for those who were anxiously enquiring about Rochester's health and state of mind: 'mad'.

Thus a dichotomy had developed. In Woodstock, there were several people gathered who had a vested interest in Rochester's return to God, if not to health. In the wider world, his fate was met with sad shrugs and sighs. Charles's doctor Short soon returned to court, con-vinced that he could not help the dying earl any more; also, as a known member of the decadent Whitehall set, his continuing pres-ence did not meet with the approval of Rochester's mother who, for the first time since her son's childhood, was playing a substan-tial part in what little remained of his life. She dismissed Short as a 'popish physician' and mocked his opinions as half-heard murmur-ings obtained by eavesdropping at keyholes.

Anne Wilmot had spent most of her life disappointed. Her first husband, Sir Francis Henry Lee, had had his life cut short early by smallpox, while her second husband, Henry Wilmot, had been a rois-tering heavy-drinking hearty, more notable for his absences from his wife's side than his presence there. Her elder children by Lee, Francis and Henry, had long since died, and now it seemed that Rochester was about to meet the same fate. A less stoic woman might have been forgiven for abandoning hope and God and giving in to a selfish instinct to mourn and wail. Anne, however, was indefatigably tough. Whether it was keeping her family's estates together in the midst of Commonwealth rule or, as now, dealing ruthlessly with those she considered surplus to requirements, she rose to every occasion with gusto and determination.

The letters that she wrote to her sister-in-law, Joanna St John, while Rochester lay on his deathbed are undeniably affecting to read, as she charts the decline of her 'poor son' in his final illness. Yet, from the first sentence of her first epistle—'It has pleased God to lay his afflictive hand upon my poor son in visiting him with a sore sickness'—it is clear that her aim is as much didactic as maternal. The difference between the language that she uses, which is suffused with references to God, Christ and heaven, and the casualness of her son's is startling in its contrast. What it does show is that Anne Wilmot was very far from being a disinterested party in her son's apparent penitence and conversion.

The account Fanshaw gave in town of Rochester's condition had at least one positive consequence, as he was able to tell all and sundry that the earl was clinging onto life. He might even have exaggerated his possible recovery; Burnet notes in a letter to Halifax of 12 June, possibly on the basis of what he had heard from Fanshaw, that Rochester 'is in a probable way of recovering, for it is thought that all ulcerous matter is cast out'. Burnet also claims that 'all the town is full of his great penitence', but, with a hint of sour grapes at his not being involved, notes: 'I hope [this] flows from a better principle than the height of his fancy'. Burnet believed that Rochester, even at the height of his previous illness, retained 'the free use of his reason... plain reason, stripped of fancy and conceit', but he knew that he was in a far worse state now.

A weakened Rochester continued to drink asses' milk (which Cary was attempting to procure from Ralph Verney), but it was felt by many that he had turned the corner and was over the worst. He was capable at least of shakily signing a previously unpublished letter to the Earl of Arran on 8 June, probably written by his mother, in which, apparently, he repents of his 'wretched life' and asserts that 'when I remove from here, I hope it shall be to heaven, where I will stay for you, and pray for you'.

Sometimes, he was 'disordered in the head', murmuring incoherently but without any malice, and at other times he was heard to pray. His mother was anxious that this was not simply mocked as 'the words of a madman', as she had heard muttered, but 'such as come from a better spirit than the mind of mere man'. Anne was not deaf to the rumours that she and Parsons were brainwashing Rochester, but dismissed these as nothing more than the jealous utterings of the wicked and diabolic of the world. She put it about that Rochester wished to cast off his old acquaintances, claiming that he said: 'Let me see none of them, and I would to God I had never conversed with some of them.' This may have been true of the likes of Fanshaw, but it beggars belief that he would have refused to receive Savile, had his jovial friend made a final pilgrimage to Woodstock. In fact, Savile did briefly return from Paris in July 1680, but it seems that he did not have an opportunity to head to Rochester's bedside, something that would later cause him significant regret. Anne was on firmer ground with a report that Charles drank his health at court, which Rochester was said to treat with contempt. Knowing the strained, and ultimately unresolved, relationship between the two, this at least rings true.

Some were less unhappy about Rochester's illness. A satirical lampoon did the rounds of court, entitled 'Rochester's Farewell'. Believed by some to have been by Rochester himself, it is a crude parody of his work, and whether it was put into circulation to damage what remained of his literary reputation or out of a sincere, if misguided, belief that it was by him, it succeeded in making him seem ridiculous and untalented. It is easy to sympathize with Anne when maternal concern breaks through and she exclaims: 'there never was so great a malice performed as to entitle my poor son to a lampoon at this time, when, for aught they know, he lies upon his deathbed.'

As a response, a 'Remonstrance' soon appeared, dated 19 June and purporting to be the final declaration of Rochester's penitence and abandonment of the wickedness of the world. It was written by Anne and signed in an unsteady hand by Rochester, who might or might not have had a clear idea what lay within the document. Comparing it with Anne's letters and Parsons' sermons is an interesting exercise. Its tone is formal, measured and a million miles away from anything that Rochester himself ever wrote in his poetry or letters; it talks of how 'I detest and abhor the whole course of my wicked life' and praises 'the pure and excellent religion of my ever blessed redeemer, through whose m rits alone, I one of the greatest of sinners, do yet hope for mercy and forgiveness'.

It does not take the world's most thoroughgoing cynic to suspect this to be the work of Anne and Parsons in collaboration, rather than the genuine expression of a desperately ill man's repentance. To completely dismiss Rochester's near-fanatical interest in religion at the end of his life would be a step too far; certainly, a combination of fear and sustained indoctrination by those around him played their part in directing his thoughts towards God and the afterlife. Yet the lucid, public tone of the 'Remonstrance' seems designed both to head off rumours of Rochester's mental incapacity and to promote the idea of his return to God. That it could have had the opposite effect seems not to have occurred to anyone at Woodstock.

Rochester's mind was now beginning to wander in alarmingly public directions. When he was having semi-lucid moments, he would summon to his bedroom virtually anyone on the estate, ranging from the increasingly alarmed John Cary to the domestic servants. Parsons reports that he delivered long, hysterical rants in which he would declare that he was 'the vilest wretch and dog that the sun shined upon, or that the earth bore', and that he wished he had been 'a starving leper crawling in a ditch'. Parsons would later put a providential spin on these statements, claiming that they were the work of a man in extremis coming back to God; read without the religious context imposed upon them, they instead seem to bear the stamp of an ill man who was so utterly out of control that he was threatening to blow apart the entire strategy of a sane return to faith.

There was only one person of sufficient public reputation whose presence would ensure that Rochester's penitence was not seen as the act of a noble mind overthrown, but summoning that person seemed a tacit admission that preparing Rochester's immortal soul for death was beyond their capability. This was none other than Gilbert Burnet, who was unhappily kicking his heels in London. His motives for coming were mixed; while he was driven by a compassionate desire to visit his erstwhile friend and comfort him in his time of distress, he also wished to enhance his own public standing by a high-profile involvement in the deathbed conversion of the century. Burnet had form in this regard: a contemporary pamphlet described him as 'the rough Scot, so remarkable for the sick', and his enemies said of him that his desire to be present at the death of sinners was akin to the enthusiasm of the fox-hunter at the kill.

Burnet would probably have headed to Woodstock long before, had it not been for his fear of royal disapproval. After the death of Jane Roberts, he had written a letter to Charles in which he had indiscreetly put some of the blame for her death at the royal door, which resulted in a mixture of fury and horror from the king, who was all too aware that Burnet now knew where the metaphorical bodies were buried. Knowing that Charles would be highly suspicious of his motives in attending Rochester at his deathbed, he saw it as unnecessarily provocative to attend another former royal intimate who was dying in painful and horrific circumstances; he later wrote that Charles 'fancied that [Rochester] had told me many things, of which I might make an ill use'—an elegant sideways swipe at his unloved monarch.

In the end, a letter, purportedly from Rochester, was sent to Burnet. Dated 25 June, it bears his signature, but the rest is in another hand, either Elizabeth's or Parsons'. As with the 'Remonstrance', the language used is that of the penitent sinner, begging for grace. It begins 'my spirits and body decay so equally together', and then goes on to flatter Burnet, whom Rochester claims to esteem above all other churchmen (whom, in an abrupt volte-face from their earlier conversations, he now claims to 'value ... above all men in the world'); he then begs that, 'if God be yet pleased to spare me longer in this world', Burnet should come to Woodstock to converse further with Rochester. The letter skilfully plays on Burnet's fame-seeking as well as his Christian charity, implicitly offering him the chance to spread the news of Rochester's penitence as he (purportedly) expresses his hope that 'the world may see how much I abhor what I so long loved, and how much I glory in repentance in God's service'.

Burnet was touched by the letter, writing to Halifax on 3 July that 'I have had one of the best letters from the Earl of Rochester that ever I had from any person', and claiming that 'he has a sedate and sincere repentance and a firm belief of the Christian religion deeply formed in his mind'. Yet self-interest stayed his hand, despite his reporting that Rochester 'has little hopes of life', and he remained in London. Nonetheless, he took care to promote himself as the agent of Rochester's conversion; the letter was soon distributed across London in the form of a broadside sheet, as well as appearing in Burnet's subsequent book about Rochester's end.

Meanwhile, Anne continued to write to anyone who might be of some help in her predicament. A letter of 26 June, to Joanna St John, takes care to pour scorn on what was becoming the accepted belief at court, namely that Rochester was dying insane. She claims that Fanshaw's statements of Rochester's madness are baseless; she allows that 'for a night and part of a day for want of rest his head was a little disordered', but insists that this took place 'long since Mr Fanshaw saw him', and describes Fanshaw as both a 'wretch' and 'an ungrateful man to such a friend'. The underlying impression given by her letter is an immense sorrow at her 'poor weak son' and his condition, which was now commonly acknowledged to be hopeless, but also a desperate desire to promote his conversion as sincere, rather than stage-managed.

Rochester, meanwhile, spent his few lucid moments talking to his wife and children, who were brought to their sick father's bedside to hear him offer what paternal edicts he could summon. Rochester knew that his son Charles, in particular, was a sickly boy whose unfortunate inheritance was his father's venereal disease in a form of syphilis that resulted in weakness and lethargy in one so young and undeserving. He told his son not to be a wit, but instead to grow into 'an honest and a religious man, which could only be the support and blessing of his family'. To his other children, he extended the hope that they would grow up in honest and pious ways.

As before, his genuine love of his family sat uneasily with the knowledge that their name would forever be associated with his. Those of his actions at this time that can be ascribed to his own decision rather than to his mother's influence—his desire that Elizabeth abandon her Catholic faith, for instance, or what was reported as his 'tender concern' for his servants—fit with Rochester's essential kindness and his often overlooked care and compassion for others. The grander religious and penitential claims that were being made in his name, meanwhile, carried substantially less weight in terms of simple human decency. It took considerably greater moral strength to explain one's imminent death to one's small children than it did to sign letter after letter decrying oneself as a wicked sinner.

Enlisting the help of others continued. A letter was sent to Thomas Pierce, President of Magdalen College, Oxford, in July, of which no original copy survives, making it impossible to know who the author was (it was, of course, said to be by Rochester). Pierce, an outspoken critic of Catholicism and religious unorthodoxy, was a valuable ally in promoting Rochester's conversion beyond the cloisters of Oxford, and the suspiciously articulate letter that he received has the feel of a solicitation to authority. It begins, somewhat disingenuously, with 'Rochester' claiming that 'my indisposition renders my intellectuals almost as feeble as my person', before talking unfavourably of his 'humble and afflicted mind' and his regret at his 'lewd courses' and 'profane and unhallowed abominations', and going on to list a series of biblical quotations apposite to his situation. The letter reads like the work of a man (or woman) who was intimately familiar with the scriptures and was minded enough to wish his (or her) repentance to be made public. Whether or not it was by Rochester himself, the statement that 'if God shall be pleased to spare me a little longer here, I am unalterably resolved to become a new man' feels sadly ironic; very few had any expectation that Rochester would indeed be 'spared'.

The letter, whoever it was by, had its desired effect, and Pierce visited Rochester in Woodstock. He joined a distinguished list of visitors who included John Fell, Bishop of Oxford, who later wrote letters comparing Rochester's sufferings to those of Job. Fell was a strict disciplinarian, of whom the famous lines 'I do not love thee, Dr Fell / The reason why I cannot tell' would be coined, and his stern presence was presumably one of the less pleasant ones at Rochester's bedside. Burnet later referred to his 'decent plainness', perhaps a euphemism for straight-talking.

Mockingly, Rochester's health appeared to recover slightly at the beginning of July, or at least to stabilize. He had been beset by violent fits and lapses into incoherence in the previous weeks, but the worst of the fever that he had suffered seemed to be behind him. A letter of his mother's indicates that he was no longer dying violently, but instead wasting away, spending most of his days sleeping and talking little when he was awake. An anecdote concerning the continued untrustworthiness of Fanshaw, in which Rochester purportedly said that he would not have returned to his previous life amongst the likes of him for all the world, feels like a spurious addition, consistent with Anne's other letters.

All the while, Burnet found himself torn between his inclinations, selfless and otherwise, and his fear of royal disapproval. Eventually, he decided that it was his Christian duty to visit Rochester, and on 17 July he wrote to Halifax to say: 'I am to go next week... [Rochester] is a little better, but not so that there seems great hopes of his recovery.' He arrived in Woodstock on 20 July, where Rochester was about to reach his own drama's last scene.

As ever in Rochester's life, tragedy was inexorably mixed with comedy. Belle Fasse, restored to Rochester's service after his sojourn in France (perhaps indicating that he was not, after all, the 'Mr P' who had attempted to blackmail him, or that he had been forgiven), did not have a firm grasp of English, and failed to realize who Burnet was, sending him to the servants' hall as if he were a lowly domestic. The image of a downgraded Burnet, pomp rapidly deflated (and by a *Frenchman*, of all people), is a deliciously comic one, even more so when considered amidst the suffering and sorrow that were taking place elsewhere in the house at the time.

Eventually, once it was realized who he was, Burnet was admitted into Rochester's presence on 21 July. It was a less momentous encounter than their previous meetings in 1679; Rochester, who had been dosed with opiates, was barely conscious and hardly able to realize who was in the room with him. However, when he was made aware of Burnet's presence, he reacted with some happiness, or, in Burnet's typically modest account, with 'the tenderest expressions concerning my kindness in coming so far to see such a one'. Burnet admits that he was 'so low, that he could not hold up discourse long at once', but claims that, in between his relapses into lethargy, Rochester was calm and had no fear of death. This was because of his supposed deathbed conversion; Burnet, over-egging the pudding, claims that not only did Rochester speak of this 'as a thing now grown up in him to a settled and calm serenity', but also that he asked the penitent for further details of 'the circumstances and progress of his repentance'.

Even judged by the other claims that Burnet made after Rochester's death, this was playing to the gallery—or, if you will, preaching to the converted. Burnet's account of his final conversations with Rochester contains one striking and fascinating detail, which may or may not be invention. He claims that Rochester informed him that Parsons had read him the fifty-third chapter of the Book of Isaiah, which he had taken to heart. The chapter contains several details that have intense symbolic resonance for Burnet's account of Rochester, as it deals with 'the Man of Sorrows', often believed to be Christ. Whether or not this was intentional on Burnet's part, it certainly adds a further sense of grandiosity to Rochester's final days. The key passage comes in verses 4 to 6:

> Surely he hath borne our griefs, and carried our sorrows: yet we did esteem him stricken, smitten of God, and afflicted. But he was wounded for our transgressions, he was bruised for our iniquities: the

chastisement of our peace was upon him; and with his stripes we are healed. All we like sheep have gone astray; we have turned every one to his own way; and the Lord hath laid on him the iniquity of us all.

What Burnet appears to be claiming verged on sacrilege, but was theologically brilliant nonetheless; he suggests that Rochester was simultaneously the sheep that had gone astray and the servant who had suffered so that others would learn from his mistakes. Effectively, then, Rochester was painted as the sacrificial lamb, but, unlike Christ, a far from guiltless one. It is impossible to know whether Parsons had read the passage to Rochester and it had made some impression, but Burnet was canny enough to realize that, whether Parsons had introduced him to it or whether Rochester had already known it, it would be his own association with the text that would be the one that people remembered.

Rochester was sometimes conscious and relatively lucid for a few moments at a time. Burnet notes Elizabeth's return to Protestantism and observes that Rochester had been 'not a little instrumental in procuring it', going on to say that it was 'one of the joyfullest things that befell him in his sickness'. While Rochester might have seen it in practical, rather than spiritual, terms, his actions were still a blessing, from an evangelical perspective, for Burnet and all other Protestant clergy, who, thanks to the hysteria engendered by the Popish Plot and anti-Catholic feeling, were in a state of ascendancy. If a sinner such as Rochester could not only convert himself, they reasoned, but persuade his wife to do so (even ignoring the fact that she had only become a Catholic for political reasons), it was a marvellous propaganda coup for the church.

Discounting Burnet's account of Rochester's last days as mere fantasy, however, is impossible. He describes how Rochester called his children into Burnet's presence and said: 'See how good God has been to me, in giving me so many blessings, and I have carried myself to him like an ungracious and unthankful dog'; this rings true in spirit, if not in the letter of what was reported, given his sincere love of his young offspring. Likewise, when Rochester, even in the supposed calm of his repentance, is said to lose his temper with a servant and call him a 'damned fellow', Burnet notes his relapse into 'an ill habit grown so much upon him ... I mean swearing'. Perhaps this man was the unfortunate Belle Fasse, in which case his irritation was all too understandable, and the detail offers a human touch amidst the grander eschatological wrangling.

Burnet was with Rochester for four days. Others, such as Anne, Elizabeth and the children, were anxiously watching him for any signs of recovery or even stability, but it became sadly obvious that the final hours of his life had arrived. His last torments were unpleasant in the extreme: as before, pus seeped out of his body along with his urine, and—never a hearty or plump man—he had wasted away to the point where he was horrifyingly thin and listless. His mind no longer engaged, he murmured faintly about how he would live his life when he was better, but all present knew that this was mere illusion.

Satisfied that his work was done and preparing to leave on 24 July, Burnet claims that Rochester desired him to linger a while longer, although it was believed that he was stable enough to live for a few weeks. This, given the severity of the symptoms Burnet describes, seems unlikely. Eventually, Burnet left without ceremony, either because, as he claimed, 'it was like to have given [Rochester] some trouble' to have had a formal leave-taking, or because this worldly man was repulsed and upset by the misery and human pain of the scene at which he was present.

Rochester's only reported comments after Burnet's departure (reported by Burnet, naturally) were: 'Has my friend left me? Then I shall die shortly.' Whether this 'friend' was Burnet, Savile, Christ or someone else can only be conjectured, but in any case, Rochester's words proved to be prophetic. He spent 25 July in silence, occasionally murmuring what might have been prayers but could equally have been incoherent ramblings. Finally, the end came, at two o'clock in the morning.

What did Rochester think about as he prepared for death? Probably he thought about his wife and mother—the one doubtless frightened and distraught at the prospect of what would happen to her after his death, the other preparing to mourn the death of yet another male in her family. It is likely that distant memories of his life's debauchery and carousing shot dimly across his consciousness, like fantastical images of someone else's history. Perhaps it was a lighter recollection he contemplated, such as that of friendship or love, or darker ones, such as the scandals and outrages in which he had found himself involved.

He could have thought of friends, of enemies, of parents, of children. He could have thought of kings, of prostitutes, of courtiers, of actors, of syphilis-racked beggars on the street, of clergymen growing fat on patronage and riches. He could have thought of poetry, of plays, of satires, of lampoons. He could have thought of the greatest heights of excess, and the lowest depths of suffering. He could have thought about God, and prayer. He could have thought about emptiness, and fear. He could have thought about any of the million things that made up his short life. He could have thought about how his name would be regarded in the years, even centuries, to follow. He could even have thought, just before the flickering light of his consciousness was extinguished for the final time, whether he would be remembered after he was gone, and he might have pictured some future biographer trying to reconstruct the final few minutes of his life in imaginative terms.

He could have thought of all these things, and many more. But the time for thought was past. Rochester died, and his eventful life finally came to an end. Yet one door opened just as another closed. As Blount had noted earlier that year, 'the hand that wrote [the poem] may become lumber, but sure the spirit that dictated it can never be so'. Rochester's wasted, ruined body was now nothing more than lumber. But the animating spirit within it, freed from its fleshly cage, would live on in the most surprising and bizarre ways.

'*HUDDLED*
in dirt
THE
reasoning engine
LIES'

*

[1680–1685]

IN 'A SATIRE against Reason and Mankind', Rochester mocks the 'vain animal', man, who only realizes on the point of death that, 'after a search so painful and so long', he has been entirely wrong to search after reason, and miserably accepts his end. This leads to one of Rochester's most powerful metaphors:

Huddled in dirt the reasoning engine lies,
Who was so proud, so witty, and so wise.

Rochester, the proud, witty and (sometimes) wise 'reasoning engine', himself lay dead. But there was no time for poetic simile. As his corpse lay on its deathbed, preparations had to be made, both legal and spiritual, to safeguard what the influential triumvirate of Anne Wilmot, Parsons and Burnet wished his legacy to be.

On 27 July 1680, the day after he died, Rochester's will was read in the presence of his wife, his mother, John Cary and a couple of servants. Unlike most of the documents that bore his name, it was uncontroversial. His daughters Anne, Elizabeth and Malet were all left a legacy of £4,000 apiece, to be paid to Anne, the eldest, when she turned eighteen, and to the others when they became sixteen. Mindful of money still owing, he gave orders that his 'debts upon bond, book debts or otherwise whereunto I have subscribed my name' be paid either from his estate or from arrears of £5,000 that he was owed 'upon several grants or patents out of his Majesty's Court of the Exchequer'. Even in death, he still made a final dig at Charles and his penny-pinching. Other beneficiaries included his valet Belle Fasse, who was given Rochester's fine clothes and linen, his household servants, who were given a year's wages and a mourning suit, and, intriguingly, his love child 'Elizabeth Clark', who was to receive an annuity of £40 a year. Thus he provided for his loved ones, his illegitimate daughter and the semi-anonymous men and women who had been dependent on their capricious master for their keep for many years. His final act was typically generous and thoughtful, rather than rash and flamboyant, even if his love child by Elizabeth Barry did receive rather less than her half-siblings.

The two main executors of his will were 'my dear mother and my dear wife', who were appointed joint guardians of the sickly Charles Wilmot. This arrangement was dependent on good relations continuing between Elizabeth and Anne—something of a trial for both parties—and should Elizabeth remarry or otherwise offend, Anne was to take over the running of the estate. The omnipresent Parsons was awarded the parsonage of Charlinch in Somerset after its incumbent's death or retirement—which, as it was regarded as part of his wife's estate at Enmore, became Rochester's to award by default—and his funeral expenses were to be paid out of what remained of the estate.

After the will was read, Anne Wilmot began to take stock of the state of Woodstock Lodge. As Rochester was no longer able to pass it on to his son or other family, it was now the property of Edward, Earl of Lichfield, who would soon arrive to take possession of the house. Anne, aided by Parsons and her brother Walter St John, set about the Augean task of cleansing the walls of the various 'obscene and filthy' pictures that Rochester had purchased, and once again making a house of dissipation and decadence a right and proper place for a respectable member of society to inhabit. No individual record survives of what was destroyed, but no doubt a wide variety of interesting, rare and beautiful works were sacrificed on the altar of self-serving moral reform. It would not do, after all, for a penitent to be associated with the vulgar trappings of such a past life. According to Parsons' funeral sermon, the destruction of these items had been one of Rochester's dying wishes; whether or not this was true, it is hard to imagine Anne being anything less than zealous in her activities.

However, the wanton destruction of Rochester's ornaments pales into insignificance when compared with his mother's wider project—namely, the complete destruction of her son's written work. Had she paused for thought, or been a more broad-minded woman, she might have considered his work to be more than 'profane and lewd writings', as it was later described; and far from 'being only fit to promote vice and immorality', she might have seen it in fact as a deeply moral condemnation of the hypocrisy and selfishness that defined the age. Her aim was to destroy everything that her son wrote, and her reasoning was that, while his name might remain infamous in the years after his death, soon his reputation as a penitent and a deathbed convert would overshadow what had occurred in his life.

The extent of what Anne destroyed is impossible to know. That Rochester's correspondence contains so many frustrating gaps is doubtless due to his mother's zealous efforts at censorship, with notable absentees including everyone from Charles to Robert Whitehall. It was later suggested by Horace Walpole that Anne had also destroyed Rochester's epistolary memoirs, 'a history of the intrigues at the court of Charles II', consisting of several volumes of letters to Savile. While the remaining letters between Rochester and Savile do an excellent job of outlining both men's witty, discursive view of court and country life, the absence of any reference to literature or poetry is keenly felt, and it can only be surmised how revelatory and eye-opening the burnt letters, diaries and other Rochesteriana might have been. The surviving letters remained in the possession of their recipients, or were otherwise spared Anne's ravages: an oversight on her part, but a fortunate one. A friend of Walpole's, Richard Bentley, suggested that Anne's just reward for her efforts was to spend eternity 'burning in heaven'. Many might agree.

After the house had been cleansed of all base and unnatural elements, it was time for Rochester to be buried, which took place at Spelsbury in Oxfordshire, not far from Woodstock. His remains were interred in the same tomb as his father Henry's, allowing an intimacy in death that had never existed between the two in life. The service took place a fortnight after his death on 9 August 1680, an unusually long time, especially given the condition of Rochester's body when he died. However, this was not because of neglect or carelessness on the part of his executors; instead, the delay was caused by the need for Parsons to write a sermon that was one of the first public proclamations of Rochester's deathbed conversion. Parsons had neither the intellectual drive and conviction of Burnet, nor the fierce family loyalty of Anne, so his task was an onerous one. He had to preach a sermon that simultaneously praised Rochester as a penitent convert, decried the excesses of his life and could be disseminated subsequently as the record of Rochester's last days.

Aided by Anne, who later paid for the sermon to be printed and distributed, Parsons produced his defining public speech. By no means a naturally charismatic man (he claimed in the preface to the published version to be 'unfit... to appear in public, especially upon such a nice and great subject'), he was aware that his responsibility was to legitimize the story of Rochester's end in the most solemn and binding fashion he could. The stolid Parsons took as his text the famous verse from Luke: 'I say unto you, that likewise joy shall be in heaven over one sinner that repenteth, more than over ninety and nine just persons that need no repentance.' He could scarcely have picked a more appropriate verse to fulfil his task.

The eventual sermon that he preached was workmanlike and capable rather than inspired (Burnet would have done a far more impressive and oratorically remarkable job, but would have been open to greater accusations of using the occasion for his own ends). Parsons characterized himself as 'a sad spectator, and a secret mourner for [Rochester's] sins', and took his evangelical task of telling the world about Rochester's conversion as stemming directly from 'his own express and dying commands'. Parsons was self-aware enough to describe this as requiring 'a wit equal to that with which he lived', but excused his plainness by likening himself, disingenuously, to an impartial historian and claiming that 'the proper habit of repentance is not fine linen... but sack-cloth and ashes... the effects it works... are not any raptures of wit and fancy, but the most humble prostrations both of soul and spirit'.

The Rochester that emerges from Parsons' funeral oration is a man from a great and distinguished family, who could have been a leading light of his age but had the misfortune to be born in the wrong time. Charles, whose standing was so low that he could be openly criticized as having no understanding of the service or value of honour, is implicitly described as one of the many 'miserable comforters' who led Rochester into sin and degradation. Parsons' description of Rochester as one who grew debauched under others' influence is half-true, as is his praise of his remarkable wit and intelligence. The most perceptive passage comes when Parsons, having described Rochester as 'the greatest of sinners', tries to explain why this was the case:

> His sins were like his parts (for from them corrupted they sprang), all of them high and extraordinary. He seemed to affect something singular and paradoxical in his impieties, as well as in his writings, above the reach and thought of other men... for this was the heightening and amazing circumstance of his sins, that he was so diligent and industrious to recommend and propagate them.

More conventional pieties about repentance, virtue and the true path follow, but Parsons inadvertently expresses Rochester's remarkable appeal to his friends, lovers and those who have admired him ever since. Rochester was, in death as well as in life, 'high and extraordinary', and there is little about him that was not 'singular and paradoxical', even by the remarkable standards of the age in which he lived. Parsons described his intellectual bravura as impiety and sin, but many chose, instead, to regard it as something to be celebrated and endlessly disseminated—even, perhaps, in the context of a funeral sermon.

Yet close psychological study was not what was required. Parsons' lengthy and exhaustive (and probably exhausting) oration offers some interesting biographical details, along with a number of likely exaggerations and wild excursions into fantasy, such as the unconvincing descriptions of the dying Rochester's final speeches of repentance and his statement that, had he lived, Rochester would surely have been a great religious poet. Nonetheless, it fulfilled its dual purpose of acting as a fitting encomium to a great man and spreading to a wider audience the 'official' account of what took place in Rochester's final days. Never mind that none of Rochester's actual friends or court acquaintances were present at the funeral, or that the truth of what was said was doubtful; Rochester the death-bed penitent was now the dominant image in the public mind. While no record survives of Charles's reaction to Rochester's death, his own deathbed conversion may have been at least in part prompted by his sometime favourite's reported actions.

When Parsons' sermon was printed in Oxford in 1680 by the book-sellers Richard Davis and Thomas Bowman, it proved to be a wildly popular bestseller, skilfully combining an improving moral message with hints of salaciousness. Funeral sermons for the notable were often published, but normally sold no more than a couple of hundred copies; Rochester's funeral sermon, which was distributed through-out the country by Davis and Bowman, sold thousands, making it hugely lucrative. It went through no fewer than twenty-four editions in the course of the following century, and became one of the stand-ard texts of repentance and forgiveness. Parsons was rewarded with an array of benefices and honours, being appointed to a canonship in Glamorgan in 1681 and a rectorate in Buckinghamshire in 1682. For his complicity, he was well rewarded by society and, indirectly, by a satisfied Anne Wilmot, who wished that this would be the final word on her son's turbulent life and legacy. Unfortunately for her, it was not to be.

If Rochester's death was greeted by those immediately around him as a sad and pitiable occasion that should nevertheless be used as an enlightening moral message, his friends and fellow poets were less equivocal. Amidst the general woe and grief that the brightest star of their generation had been extinguished, at least seven poets wrote elegies to Rochester, including Aphra Behn, Anne 'Nan' Wharton and his most talented disciple, John Oldham. They vary in literary merit, but all contain sincerity and affection that belies the later fiction that Rochester died unmourned and unloved by his contemporaries. Some lines of Behn's are typical in their mixture of poetic artifice and genuine regret, as well as their acute awareness of

Rochester's genius as a satirist and commentator on the age:

> His name's a genius that would wit dispense,
> And give the theme a soul, the words a sense.
> But all fine thought that ravished when it spoke,
> With the soft youth eternal leave has took;
> Uncommon wit that did the soul o'ercome,
> Is buried all in Strephon's worshipp'd tomb;
> Satyr has lost its art, its sting is gone,
> The fop and cully now may be undone;
> The dear instructing rage is now allay'd,
> And no sharp pen dares tell 'em how they've stray'd.

The most popular elegy, meanwhile, was Anne Wharton's, which was much praised by contemporary poets such as Robert Waller and Robert Wolseley. Wharton, the 21-year-old niece of Rochester (and rumoured to be a lover), wrote a less artful but more heart-felt account of her uncle's death, which eschews ornate verbiage in favour of what feels like genuine sentiment. The opening is typical:

> Deep waters silent roll; so grief like mine
> Tears never can relieve, nor words define.
> Stop then, stop your vain source, weak springs of grief,
> Let tears flow from their eyes whom tears relieve.
> They from their hearts show the light trouble there,
> Could my heart weep, its sorrows 'twould declare:
> Weep drops of blood, my heart, thou'st lost thy pride,
> The cause of all thy hopes and fears, thy guide!

Wharton writes in a style that, deliberately or not, brings popular hymns of the age to mind, most notably Samuel Crossman's 'My Song Is Love Unknown'. Written under the pseudonym 'Urania', a meta-physical allusion to the muse of astronomy, the confidence and style of the elegy hints at what might been a promising writing career, which was cut short by her untimely death in 1685, when she was attended by Robert Parsons. An occasional correspondent of Gilbert Burnet, she was castigated by him for her supposed bad temper and unchristian attitudes; unlike her uncle, there was to be no yielding, real or imagined, to 'the yoke of God' that Burnet proposed.

Anne Wilmot might have thought that she had done her Christian duty by destroying Rochester's writings, but her efforts were doomed to be in vain. His poems had circulated too widely, and were too well known, for a simple act of book-burning to expunge his memory from the national consciousness. As Anthony à Wood noted: 'no sooner was [Rochester's] breath out of his body, but some person or persons, who had made a collection of his poetry in manuscript, did, merely for lucre's sake... publish them under this title, *Poems on Several Occasions*.' Claiming to be from Antwerp, the book was actually published in October 1680 by an anonymous hack London publisher, and was surreptitiously purchased by many of the great and the good of the day, including Pepys, who kept it locked in a drawer, on the grounds that, 'written before [Rochester's] penitence', it was composed 'in a style I thought unfit to mix with my other books'. Unwittingly, he was the first recorded progenitor of what would be a centuries-long attitude to Rochester: public dismissal, private fascination.

The book itself was a poor representation of Rochester's poetry, being an amalgamation of sixty-one half-remembered jottings, erotica and pornography by other hands, and works floating around by others that were lazily ascribed to the notorious late earl. Those who knew him were outraged, and placed an advertisement in the *London Gazette* of 22 November 1680, decrying the 'libel of lewd scandalous poems lately printed, under the name of the Earl of Rochester' and offering a substantial reward of £5 for information on who the printer and publisher of the book were. It is not recorded whether the attempted discovery was successful. Unfortunately, this confused little volume has the distinction of constituting the first edition of Rochester's collected poems, and warrants a certain grubby footnote in publishing history as a result.

A more lasting testimony to Rochester's memory came in

September 1681, when Nathaniel Lee's play *The Princess Of Cleve* was first performed at the Dorset Garden Theatre. The work itself, an adaptation of a popular French melodramatic novel, was less notable than the eulogy paid to the character Count Rosidore, another stand-in for Rochester. Rosidore is memorably described by the character Count Nemours:

> [he possessed]the spirit of wit... [he] had such an art in gilding his failures, that it was hard not to love his faults: he never spoke a witty thing twice... his imperfections were catching, and his genius was so luxuriant, that he was forced to tame it... how awkward, how insipid, how poor and how wretchedly dull is the imitation of those that have all the affectation of his verse and none of his wit.

There is also an allusion made to his translation of Seneca's *Troades* ('I saw the mighty thing a nothing made / Huddled with worms'), implying that the audience by then was just as familiar with Rochester's last, despairing work as it was with the stories of his deathbed conversion.

Another testament, of sorts, was the publication of Burnet's *Some Passages in the Life and Death of John Earl Rochester* in 1680. A more measured and intellectually satisfying work than Parsons' sermon, it shares the same intent—namely, offering an unapologetically Christian perspective on Rochester's life and death. It is self-serving in the extreme, acting as much as a spur to Burnet's career and reputation as Parsons' pamphlet was to his; in the same year he was awarded the prestigious doctorship of divinity at Oxford, and in 1682 he published the acclaimed second volume of his *History of the Reformation of the Church of England.*

Burnet's open contempt for Charles was expressed by a 'Sermon' at the end of his book that castigates his court for its immorality and vice, but he was less interested in the patronage of the Stuarts than he was in the Anglo-Dutch duo of William and Mary. Seldom a man who picked the wrong side in these matters, Burnet was made William's chaplain in 1688, and was eventually rewarded for his intriguing and his zealotry with the prestigious appointment as Bishop of Salisbury at Easter 1689. In his final book, *A History of My*

Own Time, published posthumously in 1753, he still praises Rochester, saying 'his wit had in it a peculiar brightness', and refers to Bendo, indicating some knowledge of the affair that he had received from his conversations with him, his strained relationship with Charles and his 'great immoralities'. His final comment on his sometime friend, sparring partner and conversion project was to say, of Rochester on his deathbed: 'I do verily believe… he was then so entirely changed that, if he had recovered, he would have made good all his resolutions.' Whether this was wishful thinking, the boastings of an egotist or sincere belief, it sums up Burnet's attitude to Rochester perfectly; he understood the letter of the man, but little of the spirit.

After Rochester's death, the light passed out of Elizabeth Wilmot's world. Still only thirty years old, she was worn out, first by the loss of her husband in the most stressful circumstances imaginable, and secondly by the continued worry and stress of the ongoing Popish Plot. Despite her reconversion to Protestantism, which she took care to advertise by constantly speaking against the 'perversion' of papism, she found little comfort or sympathy from those around her, least of all Anne Wilmot, whose distrust and suspicion of her daughter-in-law was now compounded by her ability to manage the estate in its entirety, should she so wish. It is impossible not to feel enormous sympathy for Elizabeth, a witty young woman whose natural gaiety and joie de vivre were slowly and painfully worn down over the course of her short and increasingly unhappy life. Even her own property at Enmore had been ravaged by her husband's profligacy, leaving her with virtually nothing.

On 27 July 1681, close to the anniversary of Rochester's death, she finally succumbed to what was described as 'an apoplexy', and died suddenly, leaving behind four young orphans. She was buried at Spelsbury, next to her husband and father-in-law. This was not to be the last sorrow visited upon the Wilmot dynasty that year; her son Charles, always sickly and delicate, was never to be given the chance, as the next Earl of Rochester, to live up to his father's instruction that he be 'happy or unhappy forever', as he died on 12 November

1681. His death led to the end of the Wilmot dynasty. The title 'Earl of Rochester' was later resurrected for Laurence Hyde, a staunch supporter of Charles II, perhaps as a tribute to the former holder of the title, or simply as a piece of revisionism. Ironically, Hyde was the son of the Earl of Clarendon, whose rivalry with Buckingham and his supporters, including Rochester, had led to his downfall and exile. And thus the whirligig of time brings in his revenges.

Rochester's daughters led more successful lives. Anne Wilmot, realizing that her family's reputation could only partially be maintained by carefully massaged accounts of deathbed conversions, set about marrying off her grand-daughters to various high-born worthies. The eldest, Anne, who had inherited her father's good looks and was described as possessing 'a tall handsome body', married a wealthy country gentleman, Henry Baynton, in 1685, a match that met with her grandmother's approval. An occasional poet whose spirited attitude reminded others that she was every bit her father's daughter, it is thanks to her that we have Rochester's servant Thomas Alcock's invaluable account of the Alexander Bendo saga, as it was at her request that he wrote it down. Rochester's similarly pulchritudinous second daughter, Elizabeth, married Edward Montagu, 3rd Earl of Sandwich, whose father had been one of her mother's unsuccessful suitors, in 1689. Finally, the youngest, Malet, was married off to the son of one of her father's friends, John Vaughan, Viscount Lisburne, in 1692.

As for Rochester's mother, Anne Wilmot lived to the extraordinarily old age of eighty-two. After seeing all her grand-daughters gainfully married, she left Ditchley for the final time in 1692 and headed to Soho in London, where she lived in the parish of St Anne's. She eventually died in 1696, little guessing that the place where she had made her last home would become notorious centuries later as a home of vice, alcoholic debauchery and sexual freedom—qualities that her son valued a great deal more than she ever did.

As Rochester's family mourned and arranged their affairs, national matters continued. Light relief, of sorts, was offered by the Popish

Plot reaching its final, ridiculous climax. Calamitously for the plot-ters, Chief Justice William Scroggs openly doubted the basis on which the entire plot was supposed to exist, and acquitted the royal physician Sir George Wakeman on a fabricated charge of attempting to poison the king. This was a severe blow to Titus Oates's cred-ibility, and the schemer was soon undone, even as he attempted to denounce Charles (with more accuracy than he realized) and the Duke of York as Catholic sympathizers and papist stooges. The next few years would see Oates lose all standing at court, as well as his pensions and his grand state rooms, and following his arrest for per-jury in 1684, he would eventually be convicted of that offence in 1685. Satisfyingly, his punishment consisted of imprisonment, his (dubi-ously acquired) priestly attire being stripped from him and, best of all, his enduring the humiliation of being pelted in the pillory in Palace Yard, Westminster, before being whipped through the streets from Aldgate to Newgate. It was reported that the unfortunate Oates reacted to this 'with hideous bellowings', and that he suffered 'thou-sands of stripes'. His own fortunes underwent some peculiar ups and downs over the coming years, including an extremely unlikely mar-riage, eventually ending with his unlamented death in poverty and obscurity in 1705.

The year 1685 proved a watershed for many of those who had been prominent in Rochester's life. In addition to his daughter Anne's marriage and his niece Anne Wharton's death, it saw Robert Whitehall, Rochester's unlikely mentor and former tutor, raise his final pint pot in Oxford in July. Rochester's former protégé and romantic rival Thomas Otway had already died in dire poverty in April, reputedly choking on a piece of bread that he had begged from a passing stranger. And, most importantly, the year marked the death of Charles II.

By the beginning of 1685, Charles, middle-aged at fifty-four but physically run-down, was a shadow of the dashing young man who had fled across England with Henry Wilmot thirty-five years before. His reign, which had started so glamorously and excitingly with the Restoration, had descended into a bitter and sordid mixture of grubby sexual intrigues (and resulting illnesses) with wildly unsuitable mistresses, ill-considered foreign adventures, shameless profligacy and his own idleness. He might have been the greatest king who ever ruled England—a constant reminder of why the comparative intellectual poverty and social barbarity of the Commonwealth should never have existed, let alone stood any chance of being repeated. Instead, Rochester's caustic dismissal of him as a 'merry monarch, scandalous and poor' seems all too fitting.

And yet it is hard to dislike Charles. Partly this is because of the lasting good that he did in his reign, such as the promotion of the theatre, of great architects such as Wren and Hawksmoor, and of free-thinkers and philosophers such as Hobbes and Locke. His treatment of Rochester was capricious and, in instances such as depriving his family of Woodstock Lodge, petty, but he also showed remarkable forbearance and tolerance in indulging his surrogate son's far from inconsiderable bad behaviour. Many monarchs would have stripped him of all his titles and allowances forever, but, under Charles, Rochester was able to thrive. It seems unlikely that he would have risen to similar fame, or infamy, in the reign of a non-entity like James II, or even under Charles I. Rochester needed the chaos, dirt and occasional gleaming beauty of the Restoration court to be the poet and social commentator that he became. Without them, he would have been little more than a second Robert Whitehall.

The final reason to have at least a grudging affection for Charles was his considerable personal charm. After suffering a sudden apoplectic fit on 2 February 1685, he died four days later. Although the speed of his demise led some to suspect poisoning, it is more likely to have been caused by a mixture of kidney dysfunction, due to the excessive eating and drinking in which he had indulged, and lingering venereal disease. His final act of any significance was to be received into the Catholic Church, possibly prompted by his brother James, but two remarks he made on his deathbed sum up his character even more clearly than his conversion. Speaking of his mistresses, he asked James to 'be well to Portsmouth [Louise de Kérouaille], and let not poor Nelly starve'. While James had no love for Louise, who eventually returned to France, he granted Nell Gwyn a pension of £1,500 and paid her debts. And, as Charles prepared to meet his own end, he looked around at the royal physicians, the hangers-on, and all those who had some interest in his life or death, and summoned up his final vestige of wit. 'You must pardon me, gentlemen,' he croaked just before midday on 6 February 1685, 'for being so long a-dying.'

His funeral took place the following week, ironically enough on Valentine's Day. It was a low-key, inglorious event, without glamour or expense, so much so that Burnet noted in his later *History of My Own Time* that 'the expense of it was not equal to what an ordinary nobleman's funeral will rise to'. If a symbolic point was being made by those who buried Charles, it was clear what it was. The Restoration, in all its conflicted, strange and hideous glory, was at an end, and would never be repeated.

16

'ALL MY
Past Life
IS MINE
no more'

❖

[*1685–*]

IN THE YEARS after Rochester's death, the mourning of his friends and family began to give way to the appearance of a new emotion. Neither regret nor scorn, it could be categorized as the gradual emergence of a legend. It was aided by the disappearance of everything attached to Rochester. First, his friends, wife and king slipped away one after another, taking with them all their memories of the private man, as opposed to the public rakehell. Buckingham, in and out of favour with James Stuart, died in 1687, as did Savile, who moved smoothly from a debauched youth into a respectable middle age as Commissioner of the Admiralty and Vice-Chamberlain to James, inconveniently interrupted by terminal poor health. Then, in a series of unfortunate events, virtually everywhere that Rochester had lived ceased to exist. His homes in Adderbury and Ditchley were demolished by their new owners, the Earls of Lichfield, with only the rear wall of the main block of Adderbury still remaining today. Woodstock Lodge was trampled beneath the vast behemoth that would eventually become Vanbrugh's Blenheim Palace. It still survives today but in much reduced and altered form, standing, as if ashamed, by the latter's Combe Gate. Even his home in Whitehall would soon become lumber, destroyed by a fire in 1691. It was as if a deity, whether spurned or accepted, was taking care to erase any vestige of Rochester's life in the hope that he might be forgotten.

While his aged mother hoped for this, save the memory of his deathbed 'repentance', it was not to be. Before very long, Rochester's life and death became a folk tale, whispered in taverns in Woodstock, Whitehall and elsewhere. Just as his poems were conflated with others in pirated editions made up from manuscript copies of dubious origin that were then passed off as authentic, so local legends and apocryphal stories were cited as fact, despite there being little or no evidence for their veracity. It was said, for instance, that when he had been loitering in Adderbury, he had relieved his boredom by dressing up as an itinerant tinker, who had then destroyed the various pots and pans of his would-be clients. This anecdote, although probably embroidered and exaggerated, has at least the ring of truth; Rochester, always fond of disguise and role-playing, relished the chance to play new parts.

There were, of course, stories that played on the darker side of his reputation. The most disturbing, and bizarre, of these was an account that began to circulate towards the end of the seventeenth century, shortly after the death of Buckingham in 1687. It was said that Rochester and Buckingham, during one of their many expulsions from court, amused themselves by renting a disused country inn, where they pretended to be tavern-keepers in an attempt to get the local gentry drunk while they seduced their wives. If there is a possibility that something like this occurred, as a quasi-reprise of Bendo, the tale's doubtfulness increases with the subsequent detail that there was, somewhat inevitably in this sort of tale, an old miser with a beautiful young wife, and Rochester was said, with Buckingham's connivance, to have distracted the miser in the tavern while he seduced the wife in her home, robbing the husband in the process. One of the few details that rings even slightly true is that he was said to have donned female attire for such a seduction; memories of the virtuous Mrs Bendo are never far away. After this, the usual misanthropy that accompanies such prurient cautionary tales becomes clear. Rochester allegedly abandoned the now ruined wife after she had been seduced by Buckingham, encouraging her to become a prostitute, 'the only trade for which you are now suited'. The husband, upon learning of his wife's ruin and the loss of his fortune, hanged himself in grief. Rochester and Buckingham, far from being moved by this, apparently found it hilarious, and regaled many a dinner table with this boisterous anecdote.

Were this story true, in whole or in part, then it would be difficult to think well of Rochester. The times when he behaved conspicuously badly in his life—such as his near-abandonment of his wife and children, his cowardice at Epsom and the arrogant destruction of Charles's sundial—are hard to defend, but his actions stemmed from carelessness, drunkenness or panic, rather than from calculated malice. If one believes the Bendo episode to have been bad behaviour, then it stemmed less from a desire to hurt than from his fascination with theatricality and the creation of a deliberately satiric persona, designed to mock the society he inhabited. Similarly, it is unlikely that two figures of the public reputation of Buckingham and Rochester had the time, patience and interest to go to the trouble of styling themselves as innkeepers for some casual seduction and theft. While the story has a certain fictitious interest, its occasional inclusion in biographies of Rochester as fact is a depressing testament to widespread credulity when it comes to his notorious reputation.

However, in the decades after Rochester's death, most of the comments on his reputation were at least partially accurate, and tended to be flattering. Anthony à Wood's 1692 description of him as 'a person of most rare parts', with 'delightfully adventurous and frolicsome' enthusiasms, is typical, as is his moralizing comment that 'the affections of the dissolute... heightened his spirits (enflamed by wine) into one almost uninterrupted fit of wantonness and intemperance'. Wood also notes that Rochester's supposed deathbed conversion had been big business ever since his death, commenting that a pamphlet had been published entitled *The Two Noble Converts; or The Earl of Marlborough and the Earl of Rochester: Their Dying Requests to the Atheists and Debauchees of the Age*, but that 'this was feigned and merely written by a scribbler to get a little money'. There was a good deal of residual warmth for Rochester; Aubrey approvingly cites Marvell's comment that Rochester was 'the best English satirist and had the right vein' and laments, ''Twas pity death took him off so soon.' An anonymous 1695 squib nailed his enduring popularity:

> Let this describe the nation's character
> One man reads Milton, forty, Rochester.

This adulation continued into the first half of the eighteenth century, aided by Anthony Hamilton's ghostwritten memoirs of Philibert, Comte de Gramont. Gramont was a French nobleman who had been at the Restoration court at various times in the 1670s, and Hamilton, his brother-in-law, wrote a highly embellished account of the life and times of Charles and his courtiers, including Rochester. *Memoirs of the Comte de Gramont*, first published in England in 1714, flatters most of the characters depicted in it, showing the age as an enlightened (and Enlightened) one, with Charles as a wise and regal king. While its publication was partly designed to embarrass the new Hanoverian king, George I, by praising the Stuart dynasty that he had supplanted, it was a huge popular success, and the stories within it were quickly accepted as fact, despite the length of time that had elapsed between the events described and the composition of the book.

Rochester's presence in the book is comparatively benign, although his poetry is all but ignored. Instead, he is presented as an arch (in both senses) seducer; he is described as 'the man in England who has least honour and most wit', one whose ready determination to bed as many women as possible leads him into amusing scrapes with the queen's maid of honour, Goditha Price, and her rival for Rochester's affections, a Miss Hobart. The book, replete with much hammy dialogue and tongue-in-cheek authorial moralizing, is an entertaining enough read as a work of fiction revolving around real people—a kind of Restoration comedy redux—but the flowery tone and somewhat clichéd presentation of Rochester mean that this can be safely disregarded as fantasy. Again, some biographers have decided that Gramont and Hamilton's work is a valuable source of otherwise unknown material about Rochester and regurgitated it without qualm. A more discerning reader might hesitate to swallow it so blithely.

The literary aristocracy of the time varied in its appreciation of Rochester's work, ever mindful of the life that it stemmed from. Daniel Defoe was an admirer, comparing him to Virgil, Horace and Milton, and openly wished that the genius of satire and wit that Rochester and some of his contemporaries possessed were alive in the Augustan age. Pope, however, was always ambivalent about Rochester. On the one hand, unwilling to acknowledge him as a fellow satirist and decrier of society, he publicly described him as nothing more than 'a holiday writer', a gentlemen amateur rather than a poet, and, taking a moral line, called him 'of a very bad turn of mind, as well as debauched'. Set against this, he compares him favourably with the likes of John Oldham, saying that he has 'much more delicacy' and (a double-edged compliment, this) 'more knowledge of mankind'. His private views were more nuanced. His poem 'On Silence' is a clear homage to 'Upon Nothing', and his late poem 'Imitations of Horace' alludes to Rochester, indicating that the latter's poetry grew on him throughout his life.

Rochester's popularity continued until at least the middle of the eighteenth century. He is referred to in passing in Fielding's *Tom Jones*, albeit in an obscene context,* and the titular character of the same author's *Shamela* is supposed to be reading his poems, and is therefore referred to as a 'damned, impudent, stinking, cursed, confounded Jade'. Rochester would have been delighted to have heard such trenchant and informed literary criticism. However, his fame (or infamy) stemmed as much from his life as from his verse.

Rochester's work was taken more seriously in Enlightenment France. In the late 1720s Voltaire alluded to his reputation as nothing more than that of 'the man of pleasure', but writes 'with regard to myself, I would willingly describe in him the man of genius, the great poet'. He even compares 'A Satire against Reason and Mankind' favourably with the original by Boileau, praising its 'licentious impetuosity and fire'. A later judgement was more balanced. Voltaire praises him for the extremity of everything from his ideas to his dissipation; but he also alludes to his dilettantism, saying that he was 'attracted to nothing unless it was extraordinary, which he very soon got tired of', and commented that, although he was 'wiser and more eloquent than any other young man of his period', he never gave 'himself the trouble of going into anything

* Fielding refers to 'the rude answer that Rochester once gave a man, who had seen many things'. This is an allusion to the poem 'To all curious critics and admirers of metre', which lists various worldly wonders and ends with the words: 'If you have seen all this—then kiss mine arse.' Ironically, the poem is almost certainly not by Rochester.

deeply'. This is more accurate, and fair, than most English criticism of Rochester. Over and over again, his poems begin brilliantly, with a first third, or first half, of thrilling wit and invention, only to be followed by a gradual decline as the initial impetus of writing seems visibly to wane. In his best work, the momentum lasts throughout, but Voltaire's point is infinitely more useful than yet another lazy description of Rochester as 'a smutty poet'.

Unfortunately, laziness and moralizing went hand in hand in Britain for the mid-eighteenth century's literary critics and writers. As Rochester's poetry was difficult to get hold of even in an expurgated and muddled form, most judgements were made on his reputation. David Hume sneered in 1757 that 'the very name of Rochester is offensive to modern ears', and while he praises 'such energy of style and such poignancy of satire', he makes the damning comparison that the ancient satirists 'no more resemble the licence of Rochester than the nakedness of an Indian does that of a common prostitute'. The following year Horace Walpole claimed that the poems contained 'more obscenity than wit', and openly denounces Marvell's view that Rochester was a satirical master, saying 'indelicacy does not spoil flattery more than it does satire'.

Even when the poetry did appear, it was in a compromised version. A typical example is a 1761 forgery, which came with a tortuously convoluted preface explaining how the poems were given by Rochester on his deathbed to a manservant:

> [He] was commanded to have them destroyed, but… disobeyed his master's wishes, and dying many years after, left the manuscripts to his daughter. She, believing herself to be in possession of her father's will, visited a young advocate who told her what the papers were, and knowing her to be poor, received them instead of a fee.

This was, of course, an obvious lie, but gives a telling depiction of how Rochester was regarded then. Still, the preface was accurate enough, extolling the work to those who had 'youth, fire, wit and discernment', as well as hoping it might not be 'distasteful to those cool readers who have lived 'til pleasure lost its relish'.

One reader who had perhaps lost relish in pleasure by the late eighteenth century was Samuel Johnson, whose verdict on Rochester in his 1779 biographical work *Lives of the English Poets* would be one of the major sources for subsequent criticism of him, in both senses. Johnson offers a potted account of his life, with undue emphasis placed on his cowardice and wickedness; it contains this treasurable paragraph:

> Thus, in a course of drunken gaiety, and gross sensuality, with intervals of study perhaps yet more criminal, with an avowed contempt of all decency and order, and a resolute denial of every religious obligation, he lived worthless and useless, and blazed out his youth and his health in lavish voluptuousness.

Johnson wrote his book in an enormous hurry, which meant that his comments on his subjects tended to be black and white, rather than nuanced. He has a few words of praise for Rochester's poetry—it 'still retains some splendour beyond that which genius has bestowed'—and singles out 'Upon Nothing' as his strongest work. Yet he also criticizes his poems for being 'commonly short, such as one fit of resolution would produce' and having 'no particular character... [they] are commonly smooth and easy, but have little nature, and little sentiment'. He ends by bemoaning 'a life spent in ostentatious contempt of regularity', and, in what was to become a common refrain, asks rhetorically what Rochester might have been capable of had he lived. That what Rochester did achieve was far ahead of most of his contemporaries (and successors) was not something that occurred to Johnson, whose moral view of him as an idle debauchee overshadows everything else. The deathbed conversion is mentioned in passing, and Burnet's account of it commended for its piety.

The first half of the nineteenth century continued this trend. Rochester's coruscating social satires and bawdy lyrics were miles away from the concerns of the Romantic poets, and so he was dismissed as, variously, 'a melancholy proof of the final effects of genius perverted and talents misapplied' (Charles Cooke, 1800); one upon whom 'the mark of the beast is set visibly on [his] forehead' (Thomas

·Moore, 1806); and a man who 'displayed considerable talent without producing any one poem of distinguished merit' (Robert Chambers, 1836). As a man and as a poet, he is found wanting, with some writers even openly questioning why his name had remained in discussion for the past century, hinting that it might have been kinder to allow him to descend into obscurity.

There are two noticeable exceptions to this, one explicit and one implicit. William Hazlitt, never afraid to offer an iconoclastic view, praised Rochester in an 1818 lecture, saying: 'Rochester's poetry is the poetry of wit combined with the love of pleasure, of thought with licentiousness.' Unlike many others, he does not dismiss him as merely a holiday or part-time poet, claiming that 'his extravagant heedless levity has a sort of passionate enthusiasm in it; his contempt for everything that others respect almost amounts to sublimity'. Like Johnson, he praises 'Upon Nothing', but also says, with just a touch of hyperbole, that 'his epigrams were the bitterest, the least laboured and the truest that were ever written'. This appreciation was something that he was consistent about; in his 1824 book *Select British Poets*, he praises Rochester's wit for being 'keen and caustic', and makes the telling comment that 'his verses cut and sparkle like diamonds'. A diamond is a dazzling decorative object, but is famously hard as well; the comparison was an apt one.

However, there was one figure who would be compared with Rochester, both favourably and otherwise, from the moment that, as he put it, 'I awoke one morning and found myself famous'. This was George Gordon Byron—Lord Byron—a man who was, as his sometime paramour Lady Caroline Lamb described him, 'mad, bad and dangerous to know'. The similarities between the two, in terms of both their lives and their poetry, are striking. Both inherited titles while still children after the premature deaths of their hard-drinking fathers, and both subsequently had difficult relationships with their mothers. Both went on to scandalize society with their sexual libertinism and bitingly satirical verse. Both were repeatedly unfaithful to their wives, and were believed to enjoy sex with men and women. Both were constantly in debt thanks to their financial profligacy. Both were notorious figures who nevertheless represented the complexities and contradictions of their time in miniature, and both died young, Rochester at thiry-three and Byron at thirty-six, with their memoirs posthumously destroyed for fear of the scandal contained within.

Of course, there are also crucial differences. Byron travelled throughout Europe, eventually dying in Greece in 1824. After his grand tour, Rochester only made it as far as France later in his life, and then infrequently. Byron appalled society by allegedly having an incestuous affair with his half-sister Augusta Leigh, which led him to leave England; Rochester's most notable extra-marital sexual dalliance was with Elizabeth Barry, although rumours persisted that he had had an incestuous affair with Anne Wharton, his niece. Rochester's circle was that of the court and its aristocratic milieu; Byron, although lumped by posterity into the exclusive gang of the Romantic poets, had few wishes to befriend Georgian royalty, instead preferring the company of fellow devil-may-care adventurers. Perhaps in this he was not so very different from his precursor, after all.

The two also differed in their poetry. While both wrote in an accessible, conversational register that makes their work immediately appealing, Rochester tended to concentrate on shorter, more pointed satires and lyrics, with none of his poems stretching to more than a couple of hundred lines. Byron, meanwhile, thrived on length and discursiveness. His greatest work, *Don Juan*, runs to 16,000 lines, and remained unfinished even then. It offers lines worthy of Rochester, especially in the opening Dedication, with its dismissal of his nemesis Southey building to a fine piece of ribaldry:

> You, Bob, are rather insolent, you know,
> At being disappointed in your wish
> To supersede all warblers here below,
> And be the only blackbird in the dish.
> And then you overstrain yourself, or so,
> And tumble downward like the flying fish
> Gasping on deck, because you soar too high,
> Bob, and fall for lack of moisture quite a dry Bob.

A Byron and Rochester aficionado might therefore reasonably expect there to be some confluence between the two, some letter of Byron's in which he praises his spiritual forefather, some poem dedicated to 'the great John, Earl of R'. Unfortunately, no such document exists. The Romantic poets are suspiciously quiet about Rochester; Coleridge never mentions him, and Byron's allusions to him are limited, and give little impression other than a vague lack of interest. He certainly knew of his work, but—perhaps fearing that the similarities were too great and might be used against him by his many enemies—chose not to comment on it in any great detail. Thus a promising literary association is mostly rejected.

There is, however, one small and delicious piece of serendipity. Arguably Byron's most famous lyric is 'She walks in beauty', composed in 1814 and inspired by his cousin by marriage, encountered one night at a ball. The name of this cousin was none other than Anne Wilmot, the wife of Sir Robert Wilmot, a politician and colonial administrator. Whether or not he was a descendant of Rochester, in this tiny but pleasing way the fortunes of the Byrons and Wilmots are forever tied together.

As the Victorian era hove into view, Rochester's reputation began to be viewed differently once more. In an age of muscular Christianity and institutionalized sentimentality, his purported conversion became the most noteworthy thing about him. A typical example of this was a religious tract, published anonymously in 1840, from the British Tract Society, *The Conversion of the Earl of Rochester*, which took Burnet's account as its basis and then shamelessly embroidered it, as it criticized Rochester's 'wicked practice, the lies he invented and the revengeful spirit in which he indulged'. It builds to the final insult that Rochester was nothing less than the English Voltaire, a statement that it is hard to imagine Rochester not being flattered by, especially given Voltaire's rare and prescient appreciation of his work.

Even art followed this trend for lionizing Rochester the penitent. The minor painter Alfred Thomas Derby produced a memorably ghastly painting around 1850. Entitled either *The Death of Rochester*

or *A Last Request of the Earl of Rochester*, it depicts a pallid Rochester
on his deathbed in the arms of Elizabeth Wilmot, being ministered to by a clergyman, presumably Burnet but equally possibly
Parsons. What lifts the picture from mere mundanity into the gleeful
realms of kitsch is the heavenly light shining from the window onto
Rochester, presumably to take his penitent soul up to heaven. The
only things lacking are a stirring rendition of the Hallelujah Chorus
and the text of Luke 15: 11–32—the Parable of the Prodigal Son—plas-
tered underneath.

Thankfully, there were still those who remembered Rochester as
a poet rather than a subject for tracts. Tennyson was especially fond
of 'A Satire against Reason and Mankind' and could quote lines 12
to 28 by heart, with 'almost terrible force', according to one biographer. These lines were also much loved by the famous Master of
Balliol, Benjamin Jowett. There is also some acknowledgement that
the poet and the man might be separated. Edmund Gosse, the scholar
and critic, wrote in an introduction to a selection of his poems in an
anthology that 'by a strange and melancholy paradox the finest lyri-
cal poet of the Restoration was also its worst-natured man'. Gosse
describes him (unfairly) as 'shifting and treacherous as a friend', but
also capable of 'tenderness and quiet domestic humour' in his letters
to Elizabeth and of 'sweetness and purity of feeling' in his lyrics.

Gosse, like many early editors of Rochester, was hamstrung by
both the uncertain attribution of many of the poems, and also what
he termed the 'Parnasse Satyrique', into which Stygian pit of immorality 'a modern reader can scarcely venture to dip'. It also says something of how low Rochester's reputation had fallen that Gosse, a man
who had some good to say of him, described him as 'a petulant and
ferocious rake'. With friends like this ... Nonetheless, he makes the
case for comparing Rochester to both Dryden and Donne, and makes
a rather beguiling comparison between Rochester's poetic muse
and 'a beautiful child which has wantonly rolled itself in the mud'.
Unfortunately, this was about as flattering as many Victorian judgements on Rochester got; many openly wondered why his poetry was
not burned as mere obscenity.

It was not until the 1920s that any serious critical interest in Rochester's poetry, rather than his life, would emerge. This was for two reasons. The first is that Rochester's anti-establishment sensibilities were a better fit in a world where the Modernist writings of such figures as T. S. Eliot (who described him as 'courtly and polished' and, like Gosse, compared him favourably to Donne), Ezra Pound and James Joyce frequently flirted with carnality, as well as implicitly and explicitly celebrating seventeenth-century literature. The second is that, after the cataclysmic slaughter of the First World War, a cynical and disillusioned air came over those who had survived, and they looked for writers as totems who could offer something other than the bluff imperial certainties of the Victorian age. Rochester as a deathbed penitent was of no interest to them, any more than his sexual escapades were. Instead, they responded to him as someone who had been lied to by those around him, and had rejected these lies in favour of striving for a more complex, more difficult but infinitely more rewarding truth.

The 1920s saw such editors as Eliot's friend John Hayward and Johannes Prinz attempt to produce editions of Rochester's poetry with biographical introductions, but they were stymied both by the absence of any consensus on what the Rochesterian canon consisted of, and by the stringent obscenity laws of the time. When Graham Greene wrote his biography, *Lord Rochester's Monkey*, in the early 1930s, he was forced to use the bowdlerized versions of the poetry in existence, in which the last line of 'Upon his drinking in a bowl', for instance, becomes the mealy-mouthed 'And then to love again', rather than the pungent 'And then to cunt again'. If this was intended as a sop to frightened editors, it did not work. Greene, then regarded as a minor novelist, was unable to convince his publisher that they needed a life of Rochester, and so the book gathered dust before being published in 1974, unaltered since its first conception.

As a reader would expect, given Greene's lifelong fascination with unconventional anti-heroes and others who had wandered from the proper path, he had an enormous interest in Rochester's singular career. Although the book is next to useless as a serious biography, as a consequence of the unreliability of the sources Greene was using, it frequently offers fascinating parallels with Greene's own novels: compare, for instance, Rochester as an adulterous husband to Henry Scobie in *The Heart of the Matter*, or his propensity for social disorder to that of Pinkie in *Brighton Rock*. Greene also has a typically trenchant view of the deathbed conversion, writing that if Rochester was touched by the hand of God, 'it did not touch him through the rational arguments of a cleric. If God appeared at the end, it was the sudden secret appearance of a thief.'

There were other major Rochester scholars throughout the twentieth century, whose exploration of his writing helped to lift his reputation from the mire into which it had sunk in the years before. Even as late as the 1930s, however, he was still regarded with contempt by F. R. Leavis, who described him with a treasurable—even Rochesterian—double entendre: 'Rochester is not a great poet of any kind; yet he certainly had uncommon natural endowments.' Special mention must go to David M. Vieth, whose unexpurgated edition of Rochester's poetry in 1968 was the first such; and to Vivian de Sola Pinto, who knew whereof he wrote, having been an expert witness for the defence in the *Lady Chatterley* trial in 1960. Pinto's 1962 biography of Rochester, *Enthusiast in Wit*, talks despairingly in its introduction of how Rochester 'has been even more unfortunate than the metaphysical poets' when it comes to his infamy, and bemoans how 'his reputation was at the mercy of three sections of the English public, the Puritans, the Bacchanalians and the Gossips'. Pinto writes at the end of his introduction 'the time is now ripe for a revaluation of Rochester'. Half a century on, it still is.

After Rochester's death, many expected a rash of books and plays featuring him as a character. It is something of a surprise that, over the past three-and-a-quarter centuries, there has been comparatively little in the way of dramatic representation of a man whose every public action spoke of theatricality and performance. After the works that depicted him in his lifetime and shortly afterwards, most famously Etherege's *The Man of Mode*, there was a conspicuous dramatic silence throughout most of the eighteenth century; proof, perhaps, that Rochester was too large and complex a figure for playwrights to deal with.

In the nineteenth century, the first time that his avatar took to the stage was in 1829, when a French drama, *Rochester*, written by Benjamin Antier and Théodore Nézel, appeared in Paris. The French always were receptive to Rochester as a man, if not as a poet, as can be seen by his presentation by the Comte de Gramont as one of England's most notable figures, and Voltaire's praise of him. The work itself was of negligible merit, drawing heavily on the Don Juan myth and representing Rochester as an archetypal rake and libertine. However, Verdi saw the play and was impressed enough by the characterization of its anti-hero to plan his first opera, entitled *Rocester*, in 1835. Unfortunately he decided to change the setting from Restoration England to medieval Italy, and the work became the now forgotten *Oberto*, which received its premiere in 1839.

A more notable appearance, of sorts, came in Charlotte Brontë's 1847 novel *Jane Eyre*, where the brooding and tormented Byronic hero bears the name Mr Rochester. Although this could be mere coincidence, Brontë had read and refers to the work of Samuel Johnson, including *The Lives of the English Poets*, and it is conceivable that she was also familiar with William Henry Ainsworth's 1841 Restoration potboiler *Old St Paul's*, in which Rochester, as usual characterized as a cunning lecher, appears in disguise—as, of course, Brontë's Rochester does. However, attempting to draw parallels between her characterization of a passionate but ultimately noble and penitent figure and Johnson's depiction of a man consumed by 'lavish voluptuousness' seems a doomed endeavour.

The twentieth century saw surprisingly few fictional appearances of Rochester, and when he was depicted, it tended to be in 'popular literature' as a stock rogue-seducer who was reformed by the love of a good woman at the end, as in Barbara Cartland's 1979 bodice-ripper *A Serpent of Satan*. Anyone who has ever trudged their way through a book in Cartland's oeuvre will know what to expect: a virginal heroine, a wicked lord, coyness in the final bedroom scene, and much

breathily delivered dialogue along the lines of 'I must be dream-
ing... I did not even dare to pray that you would love me'. Even
as critics of the stature of Germaine Greer, Harold Love and Keith
Walker produced valuable work about him, it seemed as if novelists,
playwrights and film-makers were cowed by Rochester or—worse—
unaware of him.

This changed in 1994, when Stephen Jeffreys' play *The Libertine*
was staged at the Royal Court Theatre, in a production directed by
the then artistic director Max Stafford-Clark. The play begins with
Rochester addressing the audience, making the bold claim 'You will
not like me' and announcing 'What I require of you is not your affection but your attention'. A more familiar note is soon struck, when
he declares: 'Ladies. An announcement. I am up for it. All the time.'
Generously, he soon extends this offer to the gentlemen in the audience as well.

The play has its moments of high comedy and pathos, but, in
its original form, it often feels like *Carry On Up The Restoration*, with
Jeffreys taking the relationship between Rochester and Elizabeth
Barry, and his training her in the ways of naturalistic acting, as
the central focus of the play, before ending with Rochester's death.
Arguably a more interesting dynamic, between Rochester and
Charles, was later explored in a 2004 play by Craig Baxter, *The
Ministry of Pleasure*, which was produced at a London fringe theatre
to mild critical interest.

However, *The Libertine* enjoyed an American production in 1996 by
the acclaimed Steppenwolf theatre company, with John Malkovich
playing Rochester. Anyone who has seen his superbly reptilian
Valmont in the film *Dangerous Liaisons* will know that Malkovich
has an unparalleled ability to combine charm and menace, so he was
perfectly cast, and the text was substantially revised. Malkovich
was sufficiently fond of the play to buy the rights and to produce a
film version, which eventually appeared in cinemas in 2005, after a
lengthy and convoluted production process.

Despite the casting of Hollywood A-list star Johnny Depp as
Rochester (Malkovich, gracefully accepting he was too old at fifty

to play a man who died at thirty-three, took the role of Charles II instead), Samantha Morton as Elizabeth Barry and an excellent range of British character actors including Rosamund Pike (as Elizabeth), Tom Hollander (Etherege), Francesca Annis (Anne Wilmot) and Jack Davenport, the film is unsatisfying. Part of this is because a low budget and a decision to film exteriors in murk-o-vision combine to make the Restoration world a dingy, repellent place. Which may of course have been the point, but it makes it an unpleasant environment to spend time in.

Depp channels his recent success as Captain Jack Sparrow in the first *Pirates of the Caribbean* film into his performance, conveying something of Rochester's charm and charisma but little of his decency, capacity for intellectual brilliance or emotional turmoil—although, to be fair, these facets are undeveloped in the script, adapted by Jeffreys from his play. Instead, there is undue emphasis on Rochester's alcoholism, as there is in Jeremy Lamb's 1993 biography *So Idle A Rogue*. There are small pleasures, such as a typically forthright score by Michael Nyman and some farcical moments of knockabout comedy, but the far from dissimilar Restoration drama *Stage Beauty* about the cross-dressing actor Ned Kynaston, with Billy Crudup and Claire Danes, made many of the same points in a more enjoyable manner when it was released in 2004.

The film also offers, deliberately or not, one of the more egregious blunders in recent historical cinema. Towards the end, a syphilis-racked Rochester, anachronistic false nose tentatively in place, drags himself into the House of Lords to deliver a rousing speech in support of the succession of Charles's brother, James, despite his being a Catholic. An addition to the original play, it works well as a symbol of Rochester's redemption, showing a talent for public speaking and a compassionate attitude towards Catholicism, and makes for a stirring climax. Unfortunately this speech was delivered not by John Wilmot, but by the subsequent Earl of Rochester, Laurence Hyde, whose sister had originally been married to James. It is one thing for Rochester's poetry to be misattributed, but for aspects of his life to be similarly mixed up seems even more unfortunate.

In addition to Nyman, who set 'Signior Dildo' to music in the film, other contemporary composers have been inspired by Rochester's life and writing. The Dutch composer Hans Kox wrote a chamber opera in 2003, *Rochester's Second Bottle*, which takes its title from a letter of Rochester's to Savile praising the wit and wisdom that the second bottle gives drinkers. Meanwhile, the much-lauded James MacMillan was inspired by the so-called 'monkey portrait' in the National Portrait Gallery to write a work in 1990, *... as others see us...*, which takes Rochester and others, including Byron, T. S. Eliot and Henry VIII, and offers 'sound paintings' of each. As MacMillan puts it, speaking of the Rochester segment: 'the two musics influence each other, and after passing through the rhythms of the French overture (popular in the court at this time), the Poet becomes Monkey and Monkey becomes Poet.' Rochester and his monkey remain inextricably entwined.

And so, at the start of the twenty-first century, Rochester still occupies a stealthily underground position in popular understanding. Beloved by musicians, writers and artists—that most Rochesterian of rock stars, Nick Cave, namechecks him, 'riddled with the pox', in his 2004 record 'There She Goes My Beautiful World'—his work seems to look sardonically on at society and reject it, even today. In an era which reflects many of the hypocrisies and dual standards that Rochester loathed, his poetry has never been more relevant, nor his willingness to subvert the dull orthodoxies of conformity in favour of an iconoclastic expression of self. Everyone has their own interpretation of who Rochester was, whether it is the angel undefaced, the devil incarnate or something in between, and that is how it should be. As Rochester himself wrote, musing on fate, fortune and love:

> All my past life is mine no more;
> The flying hours are gone,
> Like transitory dreams given o'er
> Whose images are kept in store
> By memory alone.

Whatever is to come is not:
How can it then be mine?
The present moment's all my lot,
And that, as fast as it is got,
Phyllis, is wholly thine.

Bibliography

❖

THERE HAVE BEEN many editions of Rochester's poetry published over the centuries. Some—ancient and modern—are of limited use, thanks to their credulous inclusion of far too many dubiously and occasionally outright absurdly attributed poems. However, it is very hard to go wrong with either of the two major modern editions, *John Wilmot, Earl of Rochester—The Poems and* Lucina's Rape—ed. Keith Walker and Nicholas Fisher (Wiley-Blackwell 2010) or *The Works of John Wilmot, Earl of Rochester,* ed. Harold Love (Oxford 1999), both of which offer as comprehensive a canon as can be imagined. The most famous twentieth-century edition, and the one of most use to a casual reader, is *The Complete Poems of John Wilmot, Earl of Rochester,* ed. David M. Vieth (Yale 1968), which made several controversial decisions—ordering the poetry by perceived chrono-thematic order; modernizing the text; excluding many poems that were thought to be canonical—but is nonetheless well worth reading. All three collections were used extensively in the preparation of this book.

The letters have been edited carefully and perceptively by Jeremy Treglown, and his sadly out-of-print edition (*Rochester's Letters,* Blackwell 1980) is the near-definitive one, only omitting those letters that have been discovered since its publication, and which have been resurrected and discussed here. I live in hope that some of Rochester's correspondence will one day rematerialize; it goes without saying that I would be grateful to hear from any readers with further information on this.

In terms of previous biographies, Rochester has suffered from the attentions of those who have sought to bend his life and work to their own purposes, leading to some dissatisfying and patchy books, especially in the past couple of decades. The best-known is Graham Greene's *Lord Rochester's Monkey* (Bodley Head 1974), but the most useful and perceptive that I encountered in my research is James William Johnson's *A Profane Wit* (University of Rochester Press

2004), which, while aiming at a more specialized academic market than I have done, offers a variety of insights into both Rochester's life and his family milieu, as well as a fresh and thought-provoking look at the poetry. Other earlier biographical studies that proved of help included Vivian de Sola Pinto's *Enthusiast in Wit* (Routledge 1962) and the very first of all, Gilbert Burnet's 1680 *Some Remarkable Passages in the Life and Death of the Right Honourable John, Earl of Rochester*, which, for all Burnet's inevitable bias, is at least written by someone with first-hand knowledge of Rochester, and is invaluable as a result.

Although this is not primarily a critical work, it would be wrong to omit many of the volumes that have offered helpful perspectives on the poetry and, often, the life. Some of the best include *That Second Bottle*, ed. Nicholas Fisher (Manchester University Press 2001), a compilation of thought-provoking and provocative essays; *The Spirit of Wit*, ed. Jeremy Treglown (Blackwell 1982); *Rochester: The Poems In Context*, ed. Marianne Thormählen (Cambridge 1993); and *Rochester and Court Poetry*, David M. Vieth & Dustin Griffin (UCLA 1988), invaluable as a means of placing Rochester in his time and age. Vieth's book *Attribution in Restoration Poetry* (Yale 1963) which, despite the title, mainly focuses on Rochester, is a fascinating companion to his edition of the poetry and helps clarify many of his attributive decisions. An excellent source of much contemporary—and subsequent—comment on Rochester is *Rochester: The Debt To Pleasure*, ed. John Adlard (Fyfield 1974), which draws on sources both familiar and unexpected to give a kaleidoscopic view of how the Earl was regarded by all sectors of society.

In terms of more specific chapter-by-chapter further reading, the following all proved invaluable, many throughout the book. Titles are organized here according to their first appearance.

⚜ CHAPTER 1

FRASER, Antonia, *King Charles II* (Weidenfeld & Nicholson 1979)

HIBBERT, Christopher, *Charles I* (Weidenfeld & Nicholson 1968)

LOCKYER, Roger (ed.), *Clarendon's History of the Great Rebellion* (Oxford University Press 1967)

OLLARD, Richard, *The Escape of Charles II* (Hodder & Stoughton 1966)

PLOWDEN, Alison, *In A Free Republic: Life In Cromwell's England* (Sutton 2006)

SMITH, Geoffrey, *The Cavaliers In Exile* (Palgrave 2003)

⚜ CHAPTER 2

BARKER, Nancy Nichols, *Brother To The Sun King* (Johns Hopkins 1989)

EVANS, G. R., *The University of Oxford, A New History* (IB Taurus 2010)

GARDINER, Robert (ed.), *The Registers of Wadham College Oxford, 1613–1719* (1889)

MALLET, Charles Edward, *A History of the University of Oxford* (Methuen 1924)

WELLS, J., *Wadham College* (F. E. Robinson 1898)

WRIGHT, Thomas, *Circulation* (Chatto & Windus 2012)

⚜ CHAPTER 3

BÉDOYÈRE, Guy de la (ed.), *The Diary of John Evelyn* (Headstart 1994)

DOLMAN, Brett, *Beauty, Sex And Power* (Scala/HRP 2012)

KEAY, Anna, *The Magnificent Monarch* (Continuum 2008)

KEEBLE, N. H., *The Restoration* (Blackwell 2002)

LATHAM, Robert (ed.) *The Diary of Samuel Pepys* (Penguin 2003)

MILLER, John, *Charles II* (Weidenfeld & Nicholson 1991)

PICARD, Liza, *Restoration London* (Weidenfeld & Nicholson 1997)

UGLOW, Jenny, *A Gambling Man* (Faber 2009)

WILSON, Derek, *All The King's Women* (Hutchinson 2003)

❧ CHAPTER 4

CHARLTON, John (ed.), *The Tower of London* (HMSO 1978)

RAWSON, Claude, *Satire and Sentiment 1660–1830* (Cambridge University Press 1994)

❧ CHAPTER 5

HOPKINS, Graham, *Constant Delights* (Robson 2002)

HUME, Robert D. and Love, Harold (eds), *Plays, Poems and Miscellaneous Writings Associated with George Villiers, Second Duke of Buckingham* (Oxford University Press 2007)

HUTTON, Ronald, *Charles the Second* (Clarendon Press 1989)

LINNANE, Fergus, *The Lives Of The English Rakes* (Portrait 2006)

WILSON, John Harold, *A Rake And His Times: George Villiers, 2nd Duke of Buckingham* (Frederick Muller 1954)

❧ CHAPTER 6

FEATHER, John, *A History of British Publishing* (Croom Helm 1988)

WYCHERLEY, William, *The Country Wife And Other Plays*, ed. Dixon, Peter (Oxford University Press 2008)

❧ CHAPTER 7

PINTO, Vivian de Sola, *Restoration Carnival* (Folio Society, 1954)

❧ CHAPTER 9

MARGOLIOUTH, H. M. (ed.), *The Poems and Letters of Andrew Marvell* (Oxford University Press 1971)

❧ CHAPTER 10

ALCOCK, Thomas,
*The Famous Pathologist,
or, The Noble Mountebank,*
ed. Pinto, Vivian de
Sola (University of
Nottingham 1961)
KATRITZKY, M. A., *Women,
Medicine and Theatre, 1500–
1750: Literary mountebanks
and performing quacks*
(Ashgate 2007)
TODD, Janet, *The Secret Life
of Aphra Behn* (André
Deutsch 1996)

❧ CHAPTER 11

CLARKE, T. E. S. &
Foxcroft, H. C., *A Life of
Gilbert Burnet* (Cambridge
University Press 1907)

❧ CHAPTER 12

KENYON, John, *The Popish
Plot* (Heinemann, 1972)
LANE, Jane *Titus Oates*
(Andrew Dakers 1949)

MARSHALL, Alan,
*The Strange Death of Edmund
Godfrey* (Sutton 1999)
WINN, James Anderson,
John Dryden And His World
(Yale University Press
1987)

❧ CHAPTER 16

ELIOT, T. S., *The varieties
of metaphysical poetry*, ed.
Schuchard, Ronald
(Faber 1993)
FARLEY-HILLS, David
(ed.), *Rochester: The Critical
Heritage* (Routledge &
Kegan Paul 1972)
HAMILTON, Anthony,
*Memoirs of the Comte de
Gramont* (Routledge 1930)
NORMAN, Charles,
Rake Rochester (Crown
Publishers 1954)

Acknowledgements

✤

IF WRITING A BOOK of this nature is like running a marathon, then thanking those who have been invaluable in its construction and editing is more akin to the post-run pint. First amongst equals in the tavern of gratitude is my inspirational agent, Georgina Capel, whose enthusiasm for the project has been a constant buoy in its genesis, and the champagne will be on me next time. Drinks shall also be bought in abundance for all at Head of Zeus, especially Tom Webber, whose sympathetic and perceptive editing helped raise the text several substantive notches, my excellent copy-editor Ben Dupré, and Richard Milbank, whose intelligent and compassionate shepherding of the project is matched only by his indulgence towards those who, like me, occasionally take a glass of wine at lunchtime. It is, I like to think, what Rochester would have wanted.

A sober nod must be given to the many institutions and libraries and research institutes used in this project, a few of the most helpful of which have been the Bodleian, the British Library, Nottingham University, Wadham College, the Heinz Archive at the National Portrait Gallery, and, for a late-in-the-game discovery of some invaluable and previously unpublished letters, the Scottish National Records office. The London Library has been my base for the book's creation, and a more comfortable and accommodating place to work is hard to imagine. I would also like to thank the Society of Authors for awarding me their Elizabeth Longford grant for historical biography, and I hope that the finished book repays their faith in the subject. My thanks also to Faber and Faber and Tom Stoppard for the use of the quotation from *Arcadia*, and to Pan Macmillan and Colin Dexter for their permission to cite the 'fake Rochester' poem from *Death is Now My Neighbour*.

A toast will then be offered to the many people who generously offered help, advice and encouragement along the way, including Lucy

Worsley, Jeremy Treglown, Marianne Thormählen, Will Gompertz, Rowley Leigh, Donald Eastwood, Chris Lochery, Simon Renshaw, James Carter, Sarah Davidson, Sean Herdman-Low, Caru Sanders and, in particular, Nick Fisher, whose enthusiasm for all things relating to John Wilmot led to a couple of hugely enjoyable meetings and a much appreciated read of the first draft, to say nothing of many perceptive comments on points of detail. Large measures will be bought for James Douglass, Emrys Jones, Joseph Wilkins and James Dunn for many useful and enthralling conversations about their perspectives on seventeenth-century life and poetry, as well as my university tutors Anna Beer, Julian Thompson and Mark Atherton, all of whom in their various ways sent me down this particular path, for which they can be praised or blamed accordingly.

A glass will also be raised to absent friends, namely my father Andrew Larman, who bought me my first collection of Rochester's verse and fatefully piqued my interest, and Sebastian Horsley, whose Rochesterian wit and flamboyance were only matched by a kindness and generosity that I believe his spiritual forebear would have appreciated. Then a further glass will be had with the far from absent Sophie Gregory, who has been an invaluable sounding board and source of debate for most of the questions and ideas raised in this book over the past decade. 'Much wine had passed, with grave discourse...'

Finally, as the evening winds down, I must offer three particularly heartfelt expressions of thanks before last orders. My grandparents Barbara and Raymond Stephenson have been a source of invaluable support and assistance to me for more time than I can remember, and I am delighted that I can repay their faith in me with the appearance of this volume. No less gratitude is extended to Dan Jones who, in the unorthodox surroundings of a transatlantic plane journey, convinced me that my thoughts about Rochester and his milieu could be marshalled into a book of this nature, and his insightful and often trenchant subsequent conversations with me have been both inspirational and enjoyable, and have shaped the narrative in more ways than I can give him credit for. However, it is to my fiancée Nancy

Alsop that the last word must go (as ever). She has been an invaluable and sympathetic companion throughout the writing and editing process, and it is little exaggeration to say that without her warm and insightful guidance, suggestions and enthusiasm, the book and I would both be much poorer.

Picture credits

✤

1 · John Wilmot,
2nd Earl of Rochester.
The De Morgan Centre, London/
The Bridgeman Art Library

2 · Charles Stuart with
Henry Wilmot.
Hulton Archive/Getty Images

3 · Wadham College, Oxford.
Mary Evans Picture Library

4 · Anne St John.
Cobbe Collection, Hatchlands Park/
United Agents LLP

5 · Elizabeth Malet.
Topfoto

6 · A Dutch raid on English ships
in the Medway.
Topfoto

7 · *The Crimson Bedchamber.*
Private Collection/De Agostini Picture
Library/The Bridgeman Art Library

8 · Charles Wilmot.
Lydiard House & Park, Swindon

9 · Elizabeth and Malet Wilmot.
Topfoto

10 · King Charles II.
The Art Archive/DeA Picture Library

11 · Nell Gwyn.
The Art Archive/Army and Navy Club/
Eileen Tweedy

12 · Title page of *The Man of Mode*.
Wikimedia Commons

13 · A banquet at
the court of Charles II.
The Art Archive

14 · Elizabeth Barry.
Topfoto

15 · Gilbert Burnet.
National Portrait Gallery

16 · The Death of Rochester.
Private Collection/Christie's Images/
The Bridgeman Art Library

17 · Still from *The Libertine*.
Isle of Man Film Ltd/
ODYSSEY/KOBAL

ENDPAPERS
Panoramic view of London *c.*1670,
looking from Southwark
towards St Paul's Cathedral,
by Wenceslaus Hollar
(1607–77).
Guildhall Library & Art Gallery/
Heritage Images/Getty Images

Index

❖

C

'An Allusion to Horace' 23, 140,
201, 205, 214–15, 216; ascribing
Sodom to debate 149–51, 162, 205,
214; assessment of 289–90;
Chloris songs 127–9, 135;
coarsening of verse 127;
collaboration with Fane on *Love in
the Dark* 204; critical interest in
twentieth century 358–9;
criticism of by Johnson 353;
decline in output 237; 'The
Disabled Debauchee' xv–xvi, 72,
174, 208–10, 261; 'The Discovery'
97, 98; Dryden and Mulgrave's
criticism of 288–9; 'An Epistolary
Essay from MG to OB upon their
Mutual Poems' 290; 'Fair Chloris
in a pigsty lay' 128; 'The Fall' 115;
first poem attributed to 36–7;
forgery of (1761) 352; gift for
metaphor and imagery 184; 'Give
me leave to rail at you' 97–8;
greatest love lyric 114; growing
reputation at court as a poet 175;
hatred of cant and bigotry in
works of 185; 'The Imperfect
Enjoyment' 129, 135–7, 143, 145,
235; 'Impia blasphemi' 37;
influence of Hobbes 182; 'Love
and Life' 182; masculine frailty
and sexual frustration as central
feature of 135–6; monkey as key
motif in later work 107; 'My Lord
All-Pride' 280–2, 286; 'On Poet
Ninny' 246; 'On the Supposed
Author of a Late Poem in Defence
of Satyr' 245; as playwright
205–6; Pope's view of 350–1;
posthumous view of 351–4, 357,
359; publishing of *Poems on Several
Occasions* after death 338; qualities
209; 'A Ramble in St James's Park'

23, 140–5, 172–3; 'A Satire against
Reason and Mankind' 32, 43, 107,
173, 177, 181–98, 210, 242, 289,
297–8, 299, 331, 351, 357; 'A Satire
on Charles II' 163–5, 166, 210, 262;
and 'Signior Dildo' 162–3, 289;
'A Song of a Young Lady to her
Ancient Lover' 237–8; and
'Timon' 172, 174–7, 185, 214; 'To
Her Sacred Majesty, the Queen
Mother' 37–8; 'To the Postboy'
205, 223–4; 'A Translation from
Seneca's *Troades*' 304–6;
treatment of love in 100–1; and
'Tunbridge Wells' 172–4, 190;
''Twas a dispute twixt heaven
and earth' 96–7; 'Upon his
drinking a bowl' 161; 'Upon
Nothing' 258–9, 351, 353, 354; view
of by Hazlitt 354; view of in
Enlightenment France 351–2;
Voltaire's view of 351–2; 'While
on those lovely looks I gaze' 100–1
Rochester (play) 360
'Rochester's Farewell' 318
Rome: visiting of by Rochester
during Grand Tour 45
Royal Charles (ship) 92, 108, 164
Royal Society 30
Royalists 1, 4, 6, 8, 10, 11, 13, 18–21,
24, 30, 51–2
Rump Parliament 11, 28, 31, 53
Rupert, Prince 6, 60, 91, 92
Russell, Ken ix

S

Sackville, Charles *see* Buckhurst,
Lord Charles
St John, Joanna 317, 321
St John, Sir John 6

A note on the types

❧

THE TEXT TYPE is
11 on 14pt Van Dijck,
a digital recutting of
a metal face first issued
by Monotype in 1935
and based on types
thought to be designed
in the second half of
the seventeenth century
by Dutch punch cutter
Christoffel Van Dijck
(1606–69).

THE DISPLAY TYPES
are from a collection
known as 'the Fell Types',
after Dr John Fell (1625–86),
Bishop of Oxford and
Dean of Christ Church,
who acquired them
at great personal expense
from the best European founders
of the time, Garamond, Granjon,
and Van Dijck among them,
also commissioning his
'personal type-founder',
Peter de Walpergen, to cut
larger sizes at Oxford.
The types were subsequently
bequeathed by Fell to
Oxford University Press,
over which he had exerted
a profound influence
during his lifetime, and are
held there to this day.

———

The digital re-creation
employed in this book
is by Igino Marini
iginomarini.com